Victoria by the Grace of God

D1116195

The Royal Office of

Master of
the Horse

M. M. REESE

Threshold Books Limited

General Editor: Barbara Cooper

Editorial Assistants: Kate Robertson, Marabel Hadfield

Designer: Jonathan Gill-Skelton

Text research: Kate Robertson, Margery MacLaren,
Colin MacLaren, Gwen Cherrell, Marian Kekwick

Picture research: Margery MacLaren, Enid Moore

© Threshold Books Limited 1976

Text set in Monophoto Garamond 11 on 12pt by
Keyspools Limited, Golborne, Lancs

Printed and bound in England by Lund Humphries,
The Country Press, Bradford, Yorkshire

All rights reserved.
No part of this publication may be reproduced, stored in a
retrieval system, or transmitted, in any form or by any
means, electronic, mechanical, photocopying, recording or
otherwise, without prior permission of the publishers:

Threshold Books Limited
200 Buckingham Palace Road
London SW1

ISBN 0901 36690 0

*Half-title illustration: Letter Patent appointing the
8th Duke of Beaufort as Master of the Horse to
Queen Victoria in 1858*

*Frontispiece: The 10th Duke of Beaufort, Master of the Horse
to King Edward VIII, King George VI and Queen Elizabeth II,
at the Royal Mews on the morning of Trooping the Colour, 1975*

Contents

Acknowledgements

The author and publisher wish to thank Her Majesty the Queen for graciously permitting them to use the Royal Archives and to reproduce pictures from the Royal Collection. They also gratefully acknowledge the generous help and encouragement of His Grace the Duke of Beaufort, Master of the Horse. They are indebted to Sir Robin Mackworth-Young, Royal Librarian, Miss Jane Langton, Registrar, and Miss Elizabeth Cuthbert, Assistant Registrar, at Windsor, for their advice and for so assiduously checking the manuscript; to Sir John Miller, the Crown Equerry; Sir Oliver Millar, Surveyor of the Queen's Pictures; Major W. S. Phelps, Superintendent, Captain R. E. Fletcher, Comptroller of Stores, Mr J. M. Carlisle, Chief Clerk, and Mr P. G. Goodman, Office-Keeper, at the Royal Mews; Mr Lawrence James of Sedbergh School; J. P. Brooke-Little Esquire, Richmond Herald, and his assistant Miss Mary Rose Rogers at the College of Arms; Mr and Mrs Sanders Watney; and Mrs Frame Hastings. Invaluable help in the production of the book was also given by the Countess of Sutherland, the Earl of Westmorland, the Lady Aldington, the Lady Sherfield, the Hon. Mrs Alexander Ramsay of Mar; Mr I. Cresswell of the Norfolk and Norwich Archaeological Society; the Director of the Verulamium Museum at St Alban's, the Keeper of the Department of Archaeology at the National Museum of Wales, the Director of the Scottish National Portrait Gallery; Mr Peter Twite of the Jockey Club; Miss Grace Holmes, Assistant Archivist at St George's Chapel, Windsor; Mr A. B. Bartlett, Archivist at Beaulieu Manor; Miss S. Wimbush at the National Portrait Gallery; Mr F. Thompson, Assistant Secretary to the Society of Antiquaries of London; Mrs D. Bolton, Private Secretary to the Earl of Pembroke; Mrs S. Wileman, Secretary to the Earl of Jersey; Lionel Stopford Sackville Esq; the Leicestershire Archaeological and Historical Society; and the Archivists of Cumbria, Hampshire, Hereford and Worcester, Norfolk, Suffolk, Warwickshire, the West Riding and the North Riding of Yorkshire, who helped in the tracing of early Masters of the Horse.

Author's Note   Unless otherwise shown in the text, the main sources of material are: for the mediaeval period, the Calendar of Patent Rolls; for the 16th and 17th centuries, the Calendar of State Papers; from 1900 onwards, the records of the Royal Mews. Books which have been a useful source of information are: W. J. Thoms *The Book of the Court* (1838); J. P. Hore *History of the Royal Buckhounds* (1892); Lord Ribblesdale *The Queen's Hounds* (1897); L. M. Larson *The King's Household before the Norman Conquest* (1904); C. M. Prior *The Royal Studs of the Sixteenth and Seventeenth Centuries* (1935); S. B. Chrimes *Introduction to the Administrative History of Mediaeval England* (1959); A. R. Myers *The Household of Edward IV* (1959); J. M. Beattie *The English Court in the Reign of George I* (1967); S. Anglo *The Great Tournament Roll of Westminster* (1968); J. G. Russell *The Field of Cloth of Gold* (1969).

I wish to record my special obligation to the publisher, Barbara Cooper, whose idea it was to produce this book and who inspired and directed it at every stage. I am also deeply grateful to all those responsible for the research of text and illustrations.

M. M. Reese 1976

List of Illustrations

Introduction

The Master of the Horse is the third great officer of the Royal Household, ranking immediately below the Lord Steward and the Lord Chamberlain; and by virtue of these high offices all three, being peers, have precedence over other peers of the same rank.

Today the Master is the senior personal attendant to the Sovereign on all state occasions when horses are used. These occasions are of course much less frequent than in the days before the motor-car, but for such events as coronations, royal weddings, the opening of Parliament or Trooping the Colour, the pageantry of former times is seen once again, with the state coaches drawn by the superb grey and bay horses, the coachmen and postilions in scarlet, and the royal entourage in the uniform traditional to their rank. Through the Crown Equerry, who is head of the Royal Mews Department, the Master is responsible for the perfection of the horses and carriages. By tradition he is on horseback for coronations, royal funerals and Trooping the Colour. Nowadays the Metropolitan Police provide him with a horse trained to be accustomed to crowds. His place in carriage processions depends upon the nature of the ceremony: at Royal Ascot he usually rides in the Queen's carriage; on other occasions he is in the carriage that immediately follows the Queen and the Royal Family.

Until the eighteenth century the Sovereign rode on horseback at his coronation, the Master following him with 'the led Horse of State', and as a result of this it is now his privilege to ride in the coach with a sovereign who comes to the throne without a consort. The Earl of Albemarle rode in the coach with Queen Victoria at her coronation; and if after all King Edward VIII had gone unmarried to his crowning, the Duke of Beaufort would have been with him in the leading carriage.

In ceremonial processions the Master wears a uniform designed for the office by King Edward VII, who had high sartorial notions and was very particular that public figures should be dressed suitably to their dignity. (Deeply affronted by a prime minister who came to an evening party wearing trousers instead of knee-breeches, he remarked: 'I suppose that you have come in the suite of the American ambassador.') The Master's uniform is a red tunic slashed with gold, with gold epaulettes; white breeches and gloves; long black riding-boots with gold spurs; and a cocked hat with white plumes. On his chest is the star of the Order of the Garter.

In former times the Master's responsibilities covered a much wider field than they do today. According to an eighteenth-century document

> to him is committed the charge of ordering and disposing all matters relating to the King's stables, races [studs], breed of horses, as he had anciently of all the Posts in England. He hath the power of commanding all the equerries, and all the other officers and tradesmen employed in the King's stables; to all of which he gives, by his warrant to

3. Two of the greys which drew the royal landau for the Silver Wedding celebrations in 1972: 'Beaufort', bred by the Master of the Horse, and 'Frobisher', an Oldenburg.

the avenor [his chief administrative officer] the oath of allegiance, etc., for the true and faithful discharge of their duty. He has the charge of the revenues appointed for the service and maintenance of the King's horses, for the expenses of the stables, for coaches, litters, sumpter horses, etc. He has also the privilege, which no other servant of the Crown hath, of making use of any horses, pages or footmen belonging to the King's stables; so that his coaches, horses and attendants are the King's, and have the King's arms and liveries. At any solemn cavalcade he has the honour to ride next behind the King, and leads a led Horse of State.

Though this great officer hath no rank assigned to him by the Act of Precedency in the time of Henry VIII, yet by virtue of his office he precedes other great officers at court.

The Present State of England (1742)

Over the centuries the Master of the Horse has been, under various titles, the keeper of the royal stables when the horse was the only efficient means of transport and communication. He has been in varying degrees responsible for the removal of the king's itinerant household from one residence to another; for the provision of horses for the king at war, the king visiting his possessions in France, the king hunting, jousting or racing; for the maintenance of the royal studs; for the purchase from overseas of foreign horses that would improve the native stock; for the harbingers and purveyors who rode ahead of the court to command lodgings and provisions; for the messengers who conveyed the king's wishes and orders to outlying districts. An officer with this weight of responsibility needed the confidence, if not the personal regard, of the king. His precedence as a great officer of the Household has depended upon this.

The office has not gone unrewarded. In earlier days the Master lived in the Household and had a generous 'diet' of food and service. Later he received a salary in excess of £2,000 and had, at the Crown's expense, carriages and a dozen liveried servants. Always, too, he enjoyed a lavish 'patronage' in the subsidiary employments at his disposal. But during the nineteenth century the office became 'political' and the Master came and went with changes of government; and even today if the Master takes his seat in the Lords, he has to be a 'cross-bencher' and accept a tacit convention that he must not vote against the Government.

A decline in the operational importance of the office began with the gradual passing of Household duties into the public sphere when the Crown surrendered its hereditary revenues for steady increases in the Civil List. But it was accelerated by the advent of the railway, and then the motor-car and the aeroplane, as swifter modes of transport than the horse. There became less and less for the Master and his officers to do, and with the appointment in 1854 of the Crown Equerry as the administrative head of the department, receiving daily instructions from the court, the Master became a ceremonial officer charged with waiting upon the Sovereign on summons issued through the Lord Chamberlain. Where once he had substantial emoluments and perquisites, including the right to take possession of the state coach if he happened to be in office when the monarch died, he now has no salary, no claim to his personal expenses, and no right of residence at court. The rooms reserved at Kensington Palace when the Master comes to London in performance of his duties are by 'grace and favour' of the Queen.

This change in the Master's status followed a further reorganisation during the 1920s, when the Earl of Granard held the office, which formally transferred his executive command of the stables to the Royal Mews Department, now controlled by the Crown Equerry. While the Master retains the duty of personal attendance upon the Sovereign, which has been among his duties since the earliest times, the Royal Mews is the transport office of the Royal Household. It maintains, under the Master's supervision, the horses, carriages and motor-cars used on state occasions. It is responsible, too, for the Royal Family's travel arrangements, whether for a forty minute visit somewhere in London or a three-week visit in Edinburgh, or anywhere else in the country. It works closely with the Queen's Flight of the Royal Air Force and with the Royal Yacht *Britannia*, and always manages to achieve the precise timing which is essential when visits have to be calculated in minutes. The movement of the Court *en masse* is an exercise in logistics which would leave many a senior Services officer in despair, but always the Royal Mews carries out its function as transport department quietly and smoothly, to ensure that the right people with the right luggage are in the correct place at the correct time. The Department's full responsibilities are discussed at some length at the end of this book.

The whole cost of the Royal Mews now falls upon the Civil List, which means that it is financed by the taxpayer. It is distinct in this respect from the Sovereign's private residences, and all the sporting recreations of the Royal Family – polo, shooting, racing, combined training and driving, the stud and other horses kept at Windsor – which are paid from the Queen's private income and are not a public charge. But that part of the Royal Household that is maintained through the Civil List is increasingly under the pressures of inflation, and it has been argued that the ceremonial functions of the Mews merely keep alive an outworn and meaningless tradition, and preserve in the horse a transport animal that has no place in the streets of modern cities. If such contentions prevail, the British people will be turning their backs upon a significant part of their history.

Though political malice adds its leaden contribution to the difficulties of the Royal Mews, the publication at this time of a book on the Master of the Horse is far from being a graveside lament. If anything emerges from the present study, it is that the Master's office has usually been most solid and secure and successful when the incumbent and the Sovereign have shared a personal interest in horses and have been able to ride them. For various historical reasons that will become apparent to the reader, this interest has not always existed. (Within the last hundred years, it is said, one Master had the job because a civil servant approached the wrong man, and he 'always looked like a sack on a horse'.) But the office has always flourished when the right man has held it, and no one has done so with greater distinction than Henry Hugh Arthur Fitzroy Somerset, KG, PC, GCVO, MFH, tenth Duke of Beaufort, who was appointed on 21 July 1936.

This book is published to celebrate his forty years as Master: a period of office lasting longer by almost a decade than that of any of his seventy-four predecessors. Though produced with the generous help of the Royal Library, the Master personally, and the staff at the Royal Mews, it does not pretend to be an 'official' history. In order to compress two thousand years into a manageable form, it has had to be selective. It has also relied upon a certain amount of conjecture. Anyone familiar with the haphazard spelling and terminology of mediaeval scribes will know that they habitually called the same people and institutions by different names and titles. Thus it has been difficult to give a wholly satisfactory account of the 'marshals' and 'keepers' who in earlier times looked after the royal studs and stables in various parts of the country, especially as royal consorts and princes and princesses often had their own Masters in their separate establishments. From the reign of George III the record becomes fuller and more reliable, and the task of selection accordingly more difficult. It may be felt that the later chapters include ephemeral matters of little importance. So indeed they do, but these illustrate the varied activity of what is essentially a working establishment; and today's events very soon become tomorrow's history.

CHAPTER ONE Origins

The Celts, the earliest inhabitants of Britain of whom we have much knowledge, were not horsemen. These tall, fair-haired, blue-eyed people were Indo-Europeans who came originally from the basin of the middle Danube, and their first settlers arrived here some 600 years before Julius Caesar. 'Forests are their cities,' a Roman geographer noted disapprovingly of their primitive settlements, and the Celts lacked the planned initiative of true colonists. In some areas their hill-forts might be protected by dykes and other simple devices, but their usual method was to clear sufficient space in the woodland for the log huts of the tribe, and there they drank and sang and gambled, and dreamed of war and honoured their pagan gods, until the exhaustion of the land, or maybe the appearance of an invading tribe, compelled them to move on to somewhere else.

When Julius Caesar first came to Britain in 55 BC, he found that some of his native opponents were on horseback, but their mounts, about the size of a modern Welsh pony, were too small, and too short in the leg, to be effective in a real military engagement. The Celts' engine of war was a low-slung, two-wheeled chariot drawn by two of these ponies. The clatter of its iron-tyred wheels made it a formidable psychological weapon when it was launched into battle to the sound of the long animal-mouthed trumpets designed to appal the enemy, and the warriors were equally terrifying as they advanced down the poles of the chariot to hurl their stones and javelins. Afterwards they would fight for a while on foot, while the skilled charioteers withdrew for a short distance where they could, at need, pick up the fighting men and convey them to another part of the battle. Caesar estimated that he was confronted by some four thousand of these chariots, and he noted that as mobile infantry they had the effectiveness of an organised cavalry unit.

Although the Celts were skilful in cross-breeding the native stock with Arab horses brought to Britain by Greek and Phoenician traders, methods of war that might be decisive in a tribal cattle-raid were obsolete by Roman standards. Besides, the Celts had no idea of concerted planning. Each tribe fought its own battle, and within the tribe each chieftain sought the individual glory that would bring him to that haven beyond the skies where he would join his gods and other superannuated warriors in endless wine and song. Caesar's first invasion was in the nature of a reconnaissance, to give him the measure of the enemy. When he came again the following year, his preparations were more elaborate. As many as eight Gallic legions were assembled at Boulogne, including slingers, archers and four thousand horse, to attack a country whose interminable mists shrouded the edge of the world. Transport problems compelled more than a third of this force to be left behind, but the invaders had instructions to immobilise the enemy by destroying their horses. Caesar defeated Cassivellaunus, the dreaded king of the Catuvellauni who lived in the area of Buckinghamshire and Berkshire, and since he had the advantage of being

his own war correspondent, he was able to represent this as a major triumph over the Celtic peril. He conveyed to Rome a huddle of prisoners of the second rank: 'a loot of slaves,' Cicero called them, 'and I don't expect any of them to be a scholar or a musician.'

It was nearly a hundred years, in AD 43, before the Romans came again, and in the meantime resistance had been softened by a quiet process of Romanisation by settlers from Gaul. Immigrant Belgic tribes were already habituated to the Roman obedience, and Rome had made treaties to protect client chieftains against unruly neighbours. In AD 43 four legions were brought over under the command of the veteran Aulus Plautius, and this time the conquest was thorough, ruthless and efficient. As soon as it was safe for him to do so, the fat Emperor Claudius came in person to the island, accompanied by his praetorian guard and a detachment of ceremonial elephants. Sporadic local resistance culminated in the revolt in 61–2 of Queen Boudicca of the Iceni, who inhabited Norfolk and Suffolk. Joined by the

4. Roman cavalryman fighting Picts: detail from the 'Bridgeness' distance slab which marked the beginning of the Antonine Wall in Scotland and was dedicated by the 2nd Legion to the Emperor Hadrian. The horse is probably of Caspian origin.

5. *The importance of the horse in early Britain is evident from this gold coin of the Catuvellauni period.*

tribes of Essex, she ravaged St Albans and London, but when she faced the full might of the legions near Towcester, her hordes were helpless against the sophisticated Roman methods. The chariots were entangled in a cunning network of ropes and stakes, and with the collapse of their immediate striking weapon, the rebels broke in flight, only to find their retreat blocked by the wagon-loads of women and children who had come to cheer the expected victory.

The Romans stayed until 410, a period as long as that which separates the first Queen Elizabeth of England from the second. They never reached Ireland or the north of Scotland, and they made no permanent impact on the Scottish Lowlands. Elsewhere they brought the *Pax Romana*: the clearing of forests and the construction of roads and bridges (in a primitive community always the most liberating achievement of an occupying power), laws, institutions, towns, peaceful trading, more comfortable living, the extirpation of the Druids with their loathsome human sacrifices, and eventually an acceptance of Christianity.

A Roman legion of about five thousand men had among its auxiliary troops a limited number of relatively small cavalry squadrons, called *alae* ('wings'). In battle they were employed on the flanks to come in at speed to consolidate the ground won by the infantry and engage in pursuit, and even when the cavalry arm was strengthened by the military reforms of Constantine, it was only of secondary importance as one of several specialised units that supported the main body of the legion. Each legion had in addition about 120 mounted men employed as messengers to carry dispatches between the military posts. The two thousand miles of road built by the Romans were used almost exclusively by government and military traffic. The natives had to keep to the old ridgeways, such as the Icknield Way along the Berkshire and Chiltern escarpment, and in times of emergency a special permit had to be obtained for the use of the government 'posting service', meaning the posts on the road that connected the military and administrative centres. Thus the official who, during the Roman occupation, most nearly corresponded to the marshal or stables officer of later times was the man who was in charge of the small detachments of messengers, directed their business, and saw that they were properly mounted and equipped. Probably this was an *eques*, a young knight being groomed for senatorial rank. But the correspondence is not a strong one, since the Roman organisation had no equivalent of the small princely households from which the Master of the Horse was to emerge.

The Romans left when the legions were needed to defend the heart of an overstretched empire. At Adrianople in 378 the horsemen of the invading Goths destroyed the imperial infantry and for a thousand years established the cavalry as the dominant arm in war, until the armoured knight, now cumbrous and heavily overweighted, was mastered by the bowmen; and later, with the development of gunpowder, fire-power became the crucial factor in all but the limited conditions of guerrilla campaigning.

When the legions left Britain, they took with them the merchants, the lawyers, the revenue officers and all the professionals who had done their stint in distant parts in conscious acknowledgement of an imperial mission. As in our own time, the 'planned withdrawal' of an occupying power left the abandoned territory in rudderless confusion, a prey to new servitudes. The British could only try to strike a bargain with fresh invaders.

By 450 the Germanic immigration had begun. It was not a conquest in the usual sense. North-western Europe was in turmoil after the collapse of Roman power, and when the first settlers sent back the message that 'the land is sweet', wave upon wave of immigrants fled from their imperilled homes and came to Britain to enslave

6. Romano-British bronze bit of the 1st century AD.

the inhabitants or to push them westwards into the hills of Wales. These new settlers continued to arrive until early in the seventh century, and through them Britain came to be known as England. They were mostly Angles, Jutes and Saxons from the Low Countries and northern Germany, and they were little changed from the western tribes whom the Roman historian Tacitus described in his *Germania* in about AD 110. Tacitus praised the vigorous, freedom-loving qualities that he found in each *comitatus* or tribal group, and especially the passionate loyalty that the *comites*, or armed companions, showed to their chieftain. The chief supplied his companions with arms and horses for their battles, and rewarded their valour with gifts of swords, bracelets and other cherished ornaments. In return it was their duty to protect him at all times and guide him by their counsel; and if he fell in battle, it was the ultimate disgrace for any of them to leave the field until he had been avenged. To the advantage of the enemy, this often meant that they all died.

This heroic but improvident spirit was carried into England, and it is important to our story because the *comitatus* was the nucleus of the royal household to which the Master of the Horse still owes his office. It was a long and erratic development, interspersed with bloody fighting as the Saxons crushed the native aristocracy, exterminated Christianity and made relentless war upon one another. It was not until the tenth century, after the earlier ascendancy of Northumbria and then of Mercia, that the country acknowledged the supreme authority of the Cerdinga House of Wessex, and even this reluctant, hard-won unity was only achieved through the common danger brought by the Viking invasions. There is a scarcity of reliable written evidence: the earliest genuine charter dates only from 679, and we have little information about the royal household before 900. But it is possible to assume a general picture of a country dotted with these warrior bands whose territory gradually expanded as they overcame their neighbours; and when expansion created new judicial and administrative responsibilities, the ruler made grants of land to his companions as representatives of his authority. The ruler – the *princeps* of Tacitus – called himself king or prince and ritually claimed descent from his pagan gods and heroes. His companions may be identified across the centuries as *duces*, earls, ealdormen, reeves, gesiths, thegns, huscarls and stallers. Chronicles and charters complicate matters by using these terms interchangeably. They all indicate membership of the military governing class in pre-Conquest England.

A more illuminating kind of evidence comes, as it often does, from myths and poetry. The heroic compulsions of Anglo-Saxon society were the inspiration of *Beowulf*, an epic poem probably written by a Christian monk of the eighth century about legendary events supposed to have happened in Scandinavia two hundred years earlier. The story is traditional folklore which shows the Saxons' awareness of the imminence of their gods, their simple exultation in valiant deeds, and the comradeship by which alone these deeds were made possible. The unknown poet suggests the nature of the primitive royal household when he praises the diversity of gifts to be found among the king and his companions:

One can steer the prow on the dark waves, know the currents, pilot the company over the wild ocean, where bold seamen ply the oars . . . One is a brisk servant in the mead-hall. One is well skilled with horses, wise in the manage of a steed. One is quick at the dice, one is witty at the wine-drinking, a great dispenser of the beer . . . One is skilled with the hawk . . . One has affection because men delight in his mind and speech.

As the heady liquor of fermented honey passed round the little wooden hall, 'loud to the harp the lilt made melody' and the bards sang of the glories of the chieftain and his tribe: long golden hours in which the future became less menacing and – as perhaps in the rugby songs of our own day – the immediate past grew ever richer in achievement.

The Saxon spirit also impregnated the legend of the Celtic hero King Arthur, who in the folk literature of the Welsh Marches was reputed to have slain 960 men in a single charge. When the legend was revived and refashioned by Geoffrey of Monmouth in the twelfth century, he read back into the past the feudal military organisation of his own day: there were no 'knights' in England before the Conquest. But his tales of the Knights of the Round Table had some basis in the close-knit loyalties of the Saxon *comites*, whose valour was celebrated yet again in the *Song of Maldon*, written in 991, many years after the Saxons had begun to settle into more peaceful habits. This uncompleted poem tells of the Vikings' victory over Byrhtnoth, ealdorman of the East Saxons, a veteran 'grey in war'. Knowing that the odds were against them, 'he bade each warrior leave his horse, drive it afar and go forth on foot, and trust to his hands and his good intent'. Afterwards, as he lay dying on the field of battle, he thanked the gods for the joy of earth and knew that his companions would fight to the end over his fallen body. These men vow to make good the promises not lightly given in the mead-hall:

> All desired one of two things, to lose their lives or to avenge the one they loved. 'Remember the words we uttered many a time over the mead when, seated on the benches, heroes in our lord's hall, we made our boast about our hard strife. Now it can be proved which of us is bold.'

An old warrior promises that 'never shall the steadfast men around Stourmere reproach me that I journey lordless home.'

> Thought shall be the braver, heart the keener;
> Mood shall be the more as our strength grows less.

'Mood' survived until Shakespeare's day in this sense of a valiant rage; and on

7 (above). Bodyguard of thegns, or 'comites'. The thegn was a man of noble birth, whose conduct was governed by honour and truth and who at all times was prepared to give his life for the king or royal family. The bodyguard stayed close to the king, moving shoulder to shoulder as in a Roman phalanx, their weapons at the ready.

finding 'our lord all cut down, the hero in the dust', the old man vows that although young in years, 'I will not leave the field, but purpose to lie by my lord's side, by the man I hold so dear.'

This Saxon ideal of a close personal service survived the coming of the hard-headed Normans and to some extent humanised the rigidities of feudal organisation. An American historian has said that the relationship of the rulers and their companions was 'the highest and holiest that the Teutonic mind could imagine. It was the hero's delight in life, his home after death. The scenes of earth were re-enacted in the halls of the Anses, where the brave ones fought and Woden rewarded his followers with gold.' This heroic loyalty developed into an essential sinew of government when the king granted lands to his chosen gesiths – a word meaning companion – in return for certain supervisory and administrative duties. During the seventh century the gesith was superseded by the thegn, 'one who serves', and although historians have tried to explain this change, there was no significant difference of function. The thegns became a hereditary land-owning aristocracy of service, with armed service in the field continuing to be their principal obligation. On their own estates the thegns might have lesser thegns contracted to them on certain conditions of service, and they were responsible for order and justice throughout their territories, which might be scattered over several counties. With the gradual absorption of many petty princedoms into the larger kingdoms, these thegns became very important men, but they were never released from personal dependence upon their lord. On a thegn's death his heir could not inherit until he had surrendered to the lord the pick of the dead man's horses and arms, together with a sum in gold. This was called a heriot, and it implied the notion that all a thegn's possessions were the property of the lord and had only been lent to him by grace and favour.

The responsibilities of an enlarging kingdom required the kings to have a

8. One of the first known illustrations of a Saxon walled town. Horses figure prominently in the attack. This drawing and those in figures 7, 10, 12 and 13, from a 10th-century psalter, illustrate the various day-to-day activities of a Saxon king and his court.

permanent court and nucleus of permanent officials. The court was still a tiny wooden building, not much larger than the hall of the Celts and the early Saxon immigrants. There were partitioned apartments for the lord and his family, and outbuildings for the staff, but distinguished visitors, including the thegns, sat on benches and slept on the floor. In Wessex the thegns were required to spend a third of their time at court: which explains why the senior household offices usually had three incumbents, and why none of them ever became too powerful. The Anglo-Saxon court never had the overbearing *major domus* of the Merovingian Franks. The four principal officers in this court were the disc thegn, the bed thegn, the butler and the horse thegn. The disc thegn, also known as seneschal, *dapifer* or sewer (server), served the dishes at the royal table, and in time he became the steward, the head of the household. The butler, really bottler, supervised the cup-bearers and the royal drink. The bed thegn, later the chamberlain, was in charge of the royal bedchamber, and he became very important because it was there that the king kept his money, his jewels, the royal seal and the state documents. The horse thegn, as his title shows, was responsible for the stables. As early as 730 the chronicler Bede wrote of these household officers as *ministri regis*, men of wisdom and administrative experience who counselled the king and helped him to rule, as well as holding positions of trust and responsibility in their own districts. They would not, therefore, be expected to carry out menial tasks, and they must already have had a small permanent staff at court to perform the routine duties. It would only be on important ceremonial occasions that the disc thegn personally tasted the dishes and laid them before the king, or the bed thegn personally prepared the royal couch, or the horse thegn personally raised the king into the saddle.

Information about the horse thegn is disappointingly scanty. Ine, who ruled in Wessex from about 690 to 726, mentioned among his 'horse vassals' a Celtic 'horsewealh' who was his messenger to the west, one who 'performs the king's errands'. He was an important man because his 'wergild' – the compensation due from the murderer or his kin if he were killed – was fixed by Ine at 200 shillings. As a messenger carrying the royal orders to different parts of the kingdom he may not have been directly connected with the administration of the stables, but the maintenance of a messenger service was one of the most responsible duties of the department. Horse thegns are mentioned in a ninth-century charter of the Mercian king Bertulf, and two are named in Alfred's service in 897, Ecgulf and Wulfric. Wulfric was also 'wealhgerefa', a frontier official on the western boundary of the king's territories. This dual responsibility indicates a particularly valued servant, but we do not know whether it was a common practice to give the horse thegn additional duties or whether in this case the man or the circumstances were exceptional.

Although there is a scarcity of documentary evidence, the status of the horse thegn was growing fast. Initially the Saxons were not great horsemen. The coming of age of a Saxon sheds an interesting light on their limitations in this respect. Saxon youths reached their majority at fifteen but this was to be raised to twenty-one by the Normans when in the eleventh century they introduced larger horses and heavier equipment which Saxon youths were unable to manage. They were foot soldiers who fought with spears, scorning body armour until they discovered from the conquered Britons the uses of a mail shirt. But gradually they learned to fight on horseback, and there was a considerable mounted force in Ecgfirth's expedition against the Picts late in the seventh century. Even the lesser chieftains had a retinue, however small, and some sort of officer, probably quite menial, to look after the horses. As long as there was constant fighting among petty chieftains operating on a

9. Another early picture of armed Saxon horsemen. The native ponies at that time would have been Celtic, crossed with imported stock, no more than 12 hands, with small heads and hooves.

uillain ſ. equam de noiſ ſuo ſ̄ie dwerne.

ſau ʒeþde þa to reꝼeꝺ. Iacob com to ſocboꝛ ʒ ſaꝺcꝼaꝺe dꝺ̄ hyp   hær
ʒe celo metꝛnꝺe dꝺ̄e ſtoƿe naꝼman ſocboꝛ. dꝺt ꝩꝛ ʒetelo abuꝺ ꝺ ſocboꝛ
God ſꝼꝼac to iacobe ʒepað to hū. apiſ ꝼeap to be chel ʒeap ꝺa
ſau ʒ ſaꝺcꝼe þeoꝛod onꝼatꝛe ſtoƿe. dꝺulꝺcne þehe dꝺ þeoꝛod
þa þu ꝼluʒe ꝼꝛau dinne bꝛoðoꝛ. iacob ʒeþoꝛ ꝺa mıꝺ ealꝛe

HIC EXEVNT: CABALLI   DENAVIBVS · ET HIC: MILITES: FEST

small budget, a proper administration, with studs for breeding, was impossible. But the organisation improved with the gradual consolidation into larger kingdoms, and the rulers began to demand taxes or services specifically for the provision and maintenance of their horses. Thus in 875 Ceolwulf II of Mercia sought, as he put it, 'a share of the eternal reward' by freeing the diocese of Worcester from the expense of 'feeding the king's horses and the men who lead them'. The exemption was not entirely gratuitous, since the king was to receive in return six hides of land at Daylesford and an undertaking from the spiritual community to pray for the expiation of his sins. (Cotton MS., Tiber A).

The shock of the Danish invasions ultimately united the English. The new invaders were Norsemen or Vikings from Denmark and the southern half of Norway. They came in their long-boats, each with sixty or seventy men and a dozen horses, raided the off-shore islands and pushed up the creeks and inlets at the mouth of English rivers. The long-boats were fitted with low gunwales to enable the horses to be landed. The treasure of the monasteries, many of which lay by the coasts, was their first objective. In 793 they destroyed Lindisfarne and extinguished the glory of Northumbrian Christianity, the first and noblest of English schisms. Within a few years the Vikings were raiding annually in the spring, commandeering horses from the coastal farms and pushing miles inland to plunder and destroy. In 850 a force ominously tested the climate by wintering on the Isle of Sheppey in the Thames estuary, and fifteen years later 'the great Danish army' arrived in the expectation of conquering a people who seemed incapable of defending themselves. From a tactical retreat in the Athelney marshes Alfred of Wessex came out to save his own kingdom and force the Danes to agree to partition.

Armed horsemen had become vital in the defence of the realm against the Vikings, as is shown by a famous entry in the *Anglo-Saxon Chronicle* which tells how in 866 the English host 'took up their winter quarters in East Anglia, and there they were provided with horses.' Alfred, and no doubt the lesser rulers also, had studs for the maintenance and improvement of the breed, and keepers and grooms to look after them. The increasing value put upon a horse is evident from enactments raising the compensation to be paid if one was killed or maimed or stolen, and in Alfred's laws the theft of a stud horse was as grave a crime as the theft of gold – or incidentally the theft of bees, whose honey was indispensable for sweetening. Athelstan (924–39) made it an offence 'to sell a horse across the seas' lest it deplete the stock, and a regulation in the same reign shows that horses were also being used for the prevention of crime. The Bishop and reeves of London decreed that searches for criminals within the district should not be abandoned 'until every man who has a horse has ridden out once; and he who has no horse is to work for the lord who rides out . . . instead of him, until he comes home, unless justice can be obtained earlier.' (Cotton MS Otho BX I.)

With the country on a war footing, the horse thegn was no longer responsible just for mounting and saddling his master and maintaining a messenger service. He had also to look after the royal studs and supervise the stables as a military organisation, in addition to his traditional duty of personal service in the field. During the tenth century he was coming to be known as the marshal, from the French *maréchal*, an officer at the Frankish court. The name derived from the *mariscalcus*, meaning a farrier, which clearly shows that the office originated in the stables. But another Frankish officer, the constable, was not known in England before the Conquest, or at least not by that name. Although the word is a contraction of *comes stabuli*, companion of the stable, the constable's duties at the Frankish court were primarily military; and when he was introduced into England,

10. Saxon king and his court. The man to the right, counting money for the king, could be the bed-thegn. The horse-thegn could be among the group at bottom left.

11. Panel from the Bayeux Tapestry showing horses being disembarked near Pevensey on 18 September 1066. The marshal ('maréchal') or farrier would have been concerned in the arrangements. The horses, probably a cross of Norman, Spanish and Flemish breeds, were stallions, with uncut manes and long tails. Their front hooves were shod with heavy nails, for use as an extra weapon.

his work was mainly with the army, although he did for a time combine this with supervision of the marshal's duties in the stables. Thus the *comes stabuli* was not a direct forerunner of the Master of the Horse.

Under Alfred's son and three grandsons – the average life-span of his six immediate successors was only 34 years – the eastern half of England was recovered, and Athelstan, eldest of the grandsons, won in 937 a decisive battle at Brunanburh, in Lincolnshire, over a mixed force of frustrated Vikings, Cumbrians and Scots. 'Through God's grace he alone ruled all England which before him many kings had held between them,' says the *Anglo-Saxon Chronicle*. The chronicler's account of the battle has all the pride of traditional English heroism:

> In this year King Athelstan, lord of nobles, dispenser of treasure to men, and his brother also, Prince Edmund, won by the sword's edge undying glory round Brunanburh. [They] clove the shield wall, hewed the linden-wood shields with hammered swords, for it was natural for men of their lineage to defend their land, their treasure and their homes in frequent battles against every foe.

By this victory English monarchy for the first time became of some international

consequence. Athelstan, although apparently himself unmarried, contracted his sisters to foreign princes, and his crowned head was stamped upon his coins. He also, as we know, forbade the export of horses in any circumstances, except as presents to monarchs: which may indicate that the English stock had some reputation on the Continent. The gifts shrewdly made to foreign rulers were reciprocated, and Athelstan was able to improve the native breed through presents of 'running horses', valued for speed and endurance, from Germany and elsewhere. King Edgar (959–75), son of Edmund who fought at Brunanburh, was drawn along the Dee at Chester in a boat rowed by six, or some say eight, submissive princes, and from a rebellious kinglet in Wales he demanded a tribute of three hundred wolf-heads a year. He had been on the throne for fourteen years before, at the age of thirty, the clergy pronounced him mature enough to wear the crown. His coronation at Bath in 973 set a pattern that has been followed ever since. Led into the church by two bishops, he prostrated himself at the altar while the venerable Archbishop Dunstan sang the *Te Deum*. Edgar then swore a solemn oath to deal justly with 'the Church of God and all His Christian people', and the congregation said prayers for 'your servant Edgar whom we have chosen . . . for royal authority

12. Thegns with hounds and hawk. In Anglo-Saxon times, hunting and hawking were an essential part of the education of a young nobleman. Alfred the Great was said to have been an expert huntsman at the age of twelve.

over Saxons and Angles'. After his anointing, the King received the ring and sword as symbols of his office, the crown was placed on his head and the sword and sceptre put into his hands. His acceptance by the great men of the realm was followed by the acclamation of the citizens outside the church: '*Vivat rex, vivat rex in aeternum.*' This ceremony has survived in its essentials for a thousand years; and it is reasonable to suppose that the King's marshal, whoever he may have been, was in personal attendance during the procession just as Masters of the Horse have been at coronations ever since.

The glory did not last. When the Danes returned in 980 they were confronted only by the feckless, treacherous Ethelred the Unready, who lost his throne by

13. The two noblemen here could be horse-thegns. Dressed in simple robes based on the Roman toga, they carry spears with pennons, an early form of standard.

deviousness and empty bluster. In 1016 the Saxon council gave the crown to the Viking Cnut, aged only twenty-two, son of a Polish mother, leader of a war-band, but an adaptable opportunist who on his acceptance of Christianity received the baptismal name of Lambert by which he is never known. Cnut introduced two officers unknown to the Old English society, the huscarl and the staller, and incorporated them into his household. The huscarls were professional soldiers in a way the Saxons had never been: 'wolf-coats they call them, that bear bloody shields in battle, that redden their spear-heads when they come in to fight', carrying two-edged swords inlaid with gold. Like the old Saxon 'hearth guard', they were bound in close relationship with their lord and with each other, and they could be called upon for political advice. But their services were paid in money rather than land or privileges, and they did not drift away into civilian occupations as the gesiths and thegns had done. They might be sent out to collect taxes, but they did this, as they did everything else, as law-enforcers of an occupying power.

For the administrative work of the household Cnut largely relied on the offices he found at the court of Wessex. In fact the rights and duties of the thegn were more closely defined than in the earlier Saxon laws. Cnut's laws reveal the existence of the 'geneat', a free man who owed certain services for his land. On the thegn's estate one of the geneat's duties resembled that of the marshal in the royal household, as he was to 'carry messages far and near whenever he may be ordered' and also 'furnish means of carriage'. (*Rectitudines Singularum Personarum*.) But Cnut brought with him the Norse term 'staller', which may have been given to the head of the household, who was the steward, but more likely indicated the holder of any senior post. By a false etymological inference it was once thought to indicate the chief officer of the stables, but 'staller' has no connection with 'stabler'. No doubt certain stallers performed the marshal's duties, and a marshal might therefore have been called a staller, but that is another matter.

Cnut's death was followed by a dynastic struggle which ended in 1042 with the accession of Edward the Confessor, the only surviving son of Ethelred the Unready. Edward, a pious but ineffectual albino, had spent twenty-five years in exile in Normandy, but although certain French influences appeared at his court – we begin to meet the *écuyer*, the squire of the body who attended a knight – the organisation of the household did not change and the marshal did not acquire the status of the French *maréchal* or the constable. Edward had his huscarls, and during the reign there were eight stallers, usually three of them serving at a time. Some of these survived as individuals into the reign of William the Conqueror and are noted in Domesday Book, but the office itself disappeared at the Conquest. The huscarls disappeared too, fighting their last battle at Hastings, where they were cut to pieces over the body of the fallen Harold. It was the customary suicide of a military élite, and very convenient for the enemy; but the obstinate loyalty of the Saxon *comitatus* would live on in the code of chivalry, and its organisation would form the nucleus of the Norman household.

So far, then, it is possible to conclude that the Master of the Horse originated in the marshals – nearly always more than one, or a chief and his deputies – who supervised the stables at the courts of the Old English kings and their dependent lords. They organised the king's messengers and looked after his horses in peace or war, although it does not appear that they had any specifically military duties other than those required of them in their position as thegns. Probably, too, although there is no certain evidence of it, the marshal had the honour of riding forth with his lord on high ceremonial occasions; and certainly when the court was on the move, as it often was, he was the transport officer responsible for all the arrangements.

14. *Horse's eye-shield of the Romano-British period, 2nd century AD. It is fashioned from bronze and measures some 4 inches in diameter.*

15. *Stirrup-iron from the time of King Edgar, which would be similar to those used by the horsemen in the early drawings. Probably of Danish origin, it is inlaid with copper.*

The Norman Household

The *Curia Regis* of the Norman kings preserved the organisation of the old Saxon household. Three times a year, usually during the great festivals of the Church, the King met his 'great council' of earls, bishops and tenants-in-chief, which corresponded to the Saxon Witan; but the day-to-day work of policy-making and administration was performed by the 'continuous council' of men close to the King, the household officials who accompanied him on his journeys. The court was still located wherever the King happened to be. Although certain departments gradually acquired permanent locations, the great machine of government continued to be peripatetic until well into the thirteenth century.

The structure of the Norman household may be discovered from the *Constitutio Domus Regis*, an interesting document drawn up at the end of the reign of Henry I (1100–35). The division was into the chapel, the hall, the chamber and the outside department, and the rates of pay and allowances show that the marshal, although he had important duties, was still of a relatively humble status. Two reasons may be suggested for this. First, the horse thegn 'arrived late', as it were, compared with other senior members of the household. His duties in the stables were not of the highest importance until the English learned how to use the horse in warfare and their mounted warriors fought the Danes. Secondly, despite his increasing responsibility, his work was performed outside the hall. Although indispensable to the household, his service was then less personal and less intimate to the King than the attendance of the officials within the court. The will of King Eadred of Wessex, who died in 955, makes no mention of the marshal in a lengthy list of household officers. Even if the office were temporarily vacant during a change of personnel, it is still a surprising omission – unless of course it was a clerical oversight of the kind that so frequently occurred in the early documents.

Much the grandest member of the household was the chancellor, who received 5*s*. a day, whether resident or not, together with one simnel (bread of the finest flour), two salt simnels, a sextary of clear wine (the original meaning of claret), a sextary of ordinary wine, one thick wax candle and forty pieces of candle. The stewards, the master butler, the master chamberlain, the treasurer and the constables received the same pay and allowances when absent from court on the King's business, but only 3*s*. 6*d*. a day, and less munificent rations, when resident. (Stewards and constables appear in the plural because at the time these offices were being held in rotation, as often with the thegns of the Saxon court.) Next in gradation came the master dispensers of the bread, the larder and the butlery, at 2*s*. 10*d*. *extra domum* and 2*s*. when resident; and then the master of the writing-office, the clerk of the dispense and the deputy chamberlains, at 2*s*. whether resident or not.

It is only now that we come to 'John the Master Marshal', who is bracketed with

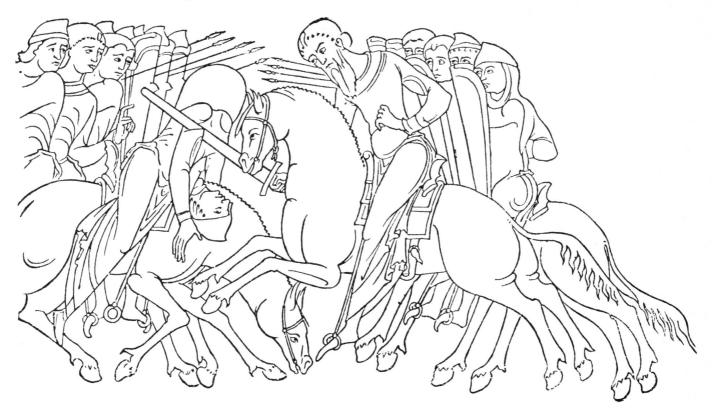

the two deputy constables in receiving 2s., one salt simnel, one sextary of ordinary wine, one wax taper and twenty-four pieces of candle *extra domum*, and 14d., with half a sextary of ordinary wine and 'sufficient candles', in residence. Various subordinate officials and servants follow, with the rate descending gradually to 1d. a day and even to the provision of food without any wages.

The chancellor may have received his title from William I, but his office was not new. In Saxon times, and indeed for long afterwards, the only literate men were the clergy. Thus the King's chaplain was, apart from his spiritual duties, head of the *scriptorium* or writing-office, where the ordained clerks wrote out the King's laws, charters, deeds and communications; and his title of *cancellarius* comes from the Latin word for the lattice screen in the royal lodgings which separated them from the less erudite residents. The chancellor was the custodian of the great seal that was impressed on documents, as a mark of authentication, by monarchs unable to write their name. During the reign of Henry I his deputy, 'Robert of the Seal', had his pay increased from 10d. to 2s. a day, with a corresponding improvement in his allowances. This, together with the chancellor's own pre-eminence in the *Constitutio*, suggests an expansion of secretarial duties which would shortly establish Chancery as a separate office, still dependent on the King but now detached from the household.

To the treasurer this had already happened, in the first important administrative development of the Norman period. The Saxon 'bed thegn', who formerly looked after the king's treasury, had at some time since the conquest lost his financial responsibilities. These had probably become too much for him, and they had passed to the separate court of the Exchequer. The treasurer of the household now looked after household finances only, and the master chamberlain and his deputies, in

16. Mounted soldiers of the late Norman/Angevin period. The drawing is a copy from a 12th-century bible.

17. Aerial view of the New Forest, the only extensive area of royal forest left in England. Established by William I it was for many centuries a hunting preserve, its warrens and chases subject to strict laws.

addition to their duties in the bedchamber, controlled the King's 'privy purse', the funds used for personal and often secret transactions. Within the hall, the steward, the former 'disc thegn', had authority over the larder, the pantry and the kitchen, and the large staff of cooks, bakers, dispensers and serving-men who worked there. Furnishing the royal table was a serious business. On the other hand, the butler, with his staff of cellarmen and cupbearers, was soon to decline in importance and lose his separate functions, partly, it has been suggested, because whereas in Normandy wine-growing was a profitable business, the Normans' efforts to plant vineyards in England met with little success.

The *Constitutio* gives many fascinating insights into the organisation of the royal household. The post of laundress, for instance, was 'in doubt'; but the ewerer, or *aquarius*, who supplied water at table as well as for domestic purposes, was allowed double rations and received a penny a day for drying the King's clothes after a journey, and 4*d.* every time the King had a bath – except when at Christmas, Easter and Pentecost he met his great council, and his ablutions were 'on the house'. It has been necessary to say something of the *Constitutio* for two reasons: first, to indicate an initial stage of the evolution of household offices into permanent offices of state, which will be more fully discussed in the next chapter; and secondly, to show the relative status of the indoor officers and of the constables and marshals who supervised the outdoor department.

The constable, in title a Norman innovation, was at this time superior to the marshal, receiving better pay and allowances, but their respective functions are not

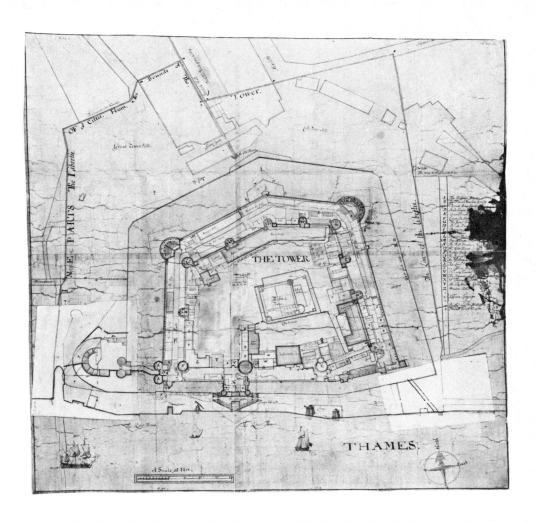

18. Plan of the Tower of London, about 1685, from the collection of the 1st Baron Dartmouth, Master of the Horse to James II. The semi-circular bastion at bottom left is the Lion Tower, site of the royal menagerie from Norman times until the 19th century.

easy to distinguish. They were jointly responsible for the physical order and safety of the household, by guarding the doors, questioning visitors, stopping drunken brawls among the servants or more serious fighting between the retinues of rival lords. They were responsible, too, for overseeing the stables, the kennels, the mews and everything pertaining to the King's journeyings and sport. Thus they controlled and paid a considerable staff of guards, ushers, watchmen, grooms, keepers, huntsmen, farriers and porters. By reason of this financial service they were entitled to attend the Exchequer court, and according to the *Dialogus de Scaccario* (*c.* 1173), the constable was supposed to verify the wages claimed by the King's soldiers and 'of all persons whatsoever, whether they be keepers of hawks or falcons or hunting dogs . . . unless perchance the lord king has previously assigned someone else to this duty'. Mostly this routine accounting was carried out by deputies, the constable and marshal seldom sitting in person in the Exchequer court. In time of war the constable acted as quartermaster-general in charge of the commissariat of the campaign, while the marshal looked after the horses, the baggage-animals and the transport.

It is evident from the *Constitutio* that the outdoor department of the household comprised not only horses but all the hounds, hawks and falcons used in the court's sporting activities; and the chief marshal had responsibility for their feeding and accommodation, and also for the huntsmen, grooms and falconers who trained them. In later times this would still be a responsibility of the Master of the Horse. Even when the buckhounds, otterhounds, harthounds, foxhounds, harriers etc.

33

19. Wood-engraving of the seal of Richard, Constable of Chester, who was standard-bearer of England in 1140. In later times the Master of the Horse was the royal standard-bearer.

20 (opposite). Edward I returning to England from Gascony in August 1274, two weeks before his coronation. From Gascony in the next reign came John Brocas, first Master of the Horse.

21 (overleaf). Grooms and horses, from a 14th-century manuscript in which the text makes it quite clear that horses might be bad-tempered but grooms should be long-suffering. The horses are probably of the type imported into England from Lombardy.

22 (overleaf). King hunting, from an early 14th-century manuscript. The falcon on his wrist was probably a peregrine, which denoted kingship.

had their own masters or keepers, often with their own independent budget, they all came under his general supervision.

The *Constitutio* placed these hunt servants in the fifth and lowest rank of the regular members of the household, although many of them were quite well paid. The horn-blowers had 3*d*. a day; each keeper of the greyhounds 3*d*: 2*d*. for his men and ½*d*. for each greyhound; the keeper of the running hounds 3*d*., with graded sums for his assistants and for the upkeep of the hounds according to their size. 'The huntsmen of the wolf hunt shall have 20*d*. a day for horses and men and dogs, and they are required to maintain 24 running hounds and 8 greyhounds; and they shall have £6 a year wherewith to buy horses, but they themselves say it ought to be £8.' This last entry is of particular interest, since the purchase of horses of all kinds was to become one of the principal concerns of the department.

Within their more specific duties the marshal and his four assistants had a large number of horses under their care, not least the 'sumpters' or packhorses that carried the heavy equipment of all the departments when the court was on the move. Two packhorses, for instance, were provided for the conveyance of the sacred vessels used in worship. The marshals were also responsible for the provision and allocation of billets for resident members and staff and for magnates and foreign envoys visiting the court; and when this caused them to be absent, they received 8*d*. a day, a gallon of ordinary wine and twelve pieces of candle. Again, the marshal was at the hub of the state communications. In his department were the sergeants who acted as the King's messengers, carrying writs, information and instructions to distant parts. Their special fee when travelling on this business was 3*d*. a day: allowances that were recorded in the accounts as *dietae*, 'diet' meaning provision for one day's journey.

Yet another charge upon the marshal, according to the *Constitutio*, was to 'have tallies for the gifts and liveries which have been made from the king's treasury and from his chamber; and it is his duty to have tallies against all the king's officials as evidence for all things.' (A livery was the provision of food and clothing for retainers and servants. It might also include provision for horses: whence its anachronistic survival in 'livery stable'.) As supervisor of the stabling, the marshal was in a position to know who was at court and who was not, and he was required to obtain 'tallies' or receipts for the payments and allowances handed out. This enabled the treasurer and the chamberlain to keep a check on their disbursements and foil those unscrupulous people who might try to claim remuneration for days when they were not present, or travel allowances for days when they had not left the court. It was a useful, if tedious, duty, and household ordinances later in the mediaeval period continue to refer to it.

In addition to all these services in the household, the marshals who served the Norman kings were kept busy in warfare and the hunt. William the Conqueror, physically intimidating in his colossal height and strength, was the bastard son of Duke Robert II of Normandy. He succeeded to the duchy at the age of eight, and had mastered it by the time he was twenty. In England he governed with the same frightening efficiency, discarding the native language, confiscating vast areas of land from the inhabitants, and ruling through an imported alien aristocracy whom he established in fortified castles. Spasmodically the conquest was resisted by the ealdormen of the Old English, the Celtic tribes in Wales, the wild Malcolm Canmore in Scotland, and the Danes of Lincolnshire and Yorkshire, descendants of the Viking invaders. In a terrible vengeance William swept through the West Country, devastated Yorkshire and onwards to the gates of Durham, chased Hereward the Wake from his refuge in the Isle of Ely, and in 1072 marched as far

publice qu bina eu no erant ad miteend ad alena pñ
teuia ea in fui ſuſpenſi i ſint xxxvij. dio ver. ſet   cᵖt
uiles pe non ad mitterent ad teuiu eiu m d' i t ſepiuſ

pmē ē moð mqnmō lus tu̇ptatñi ftī tō tātoal
̇ tenitacōms ̇egulȧib͛ hat ficat ō fula ̇ſȯne
̇i dictu̇ teh· aliaᶊu· i· ſiaō tinen abitⁱs dnolꝭ

A Londres lvir p̃ soiourner
is loec fu tot le p̃ner·

il loec par maledic languiſt
t morut auu dieu uouſiſt

north as the Tay, where no English ruler had penetrated since the Romans left.

For this work William virtually created a professional military class. With the estates of the conquered at his disposal, he made the holding of land conditional upon the obligation of military service. Not only the lay magnates and tenants-in-chief had to put knights into the field at his command, but the bishops and abbots too, who previously had been exempt from the service due from the Saxon thegns. A typical order was sent in about 1072 to Aethelwig, Abbot of Evesham:

> I order you to summon all those who are subject to your administration and jurisdiction that they bring before me at Clarendon on the Octave of Pentecost all the knights you owe me, duly equipped. You also, on that day, shall come to me, and shall bring with you, fully equipped, those five knights which you owe me in respect of your abbacy.

24. Drawing of the seal of William the Conqueror. For many centuries the great seals of England have borne an equestrian motif.

The tariff tended to rise, because from Peterborough and Gloucester, apparently the richest of the abbeys, Henry II would demand sixty knights, and the same number from the bishoprics of Canterbury, Winchester, Lincoln and Worcester. William rapidly extinguished the class of Saxon thegns, who had held land by virtue of their rank, and replaced them with mounted knights who fought with specialised weapons and underwent military training as a condition of their tenure. Other knights held no land but were simply attached to the royal and baronial households as professional soldiers. Although each knight was responsible for his own horses, armour and weapons, every substantial household came to require its own marshal for the supervision of the stables and the maintenance of a military establishment. For the marshal of the King the responsibility was especially heavy, and it is likely that although his status continued for some time to be relatively modest, the actual importance of his office was transformed by the introduction of knight service and the conditions of Norman rule.

William also required horses for his hunting. When the monkish chroniclers bewailed his passion for the chase, they did not consider the importance of hunting in a primitive economy. In the summer months it was necessary to kill enough game for immediate needs and also a reserve to be salted for consumption in the winter. Even by William's time tillage and habitation had encroached upon the forests and seriously reduced both the refuge of the game and the supply of timber which an island people needed for their ships. There was a good case for the preservation of what was there and for re-planting where possible. But William's zeal for hunting went beyond economic necessity. He made it 'the royal sport' which, almost without exception, it continued to be until it was domesticated by racing. 'As greatly did he love the tall deer as if he were their father.' (Anglo-Saxon Chronicle.) In practice this meant that only he and his household were allowed to kill them, and savage penalties, including blinding, were inflicted upon hungry peasants seeking food in villages lying within the forests that he reclaimed.

The Normans also caused hardship and depopulation by enlarging their estates at the expense of the surrounding countryside. According to John Stow, writing in the sixteenth century, Henry I 'built his manor Woodstock with a park which he walled about with stone, seven miles in compass, destroying for the same divers villages, churches and chapels, and this was the first park in England. He placed therein, besides great store of deer, divers strange beasts to be kept and nourished, such as were brought to him from far countries, as lions, leopards, lynxes, porpentines, and such other.' Gifts or purchases of wild beasts continued in such number that eventually a royal menagerie was established in London, with keepers lodged in the Lion Tower. Its supervision then came under the Master of the Horse, who had to sign the bills for the large quantities of meat consumed by the animals.

23 (opposite). Edward I riding to London, on what may have been a roan. The illustrator was obviously more concerned with impact than accuracy.

CHAPTER THREE

Ellis of Rochester

The Master of the Horse was not known by that title until the fourteenth century, and by that time some of the offices of the Saxon and Norman household had become embryonic state departments. Even in the *Constitutio Domus Regis* the financial affairs of the Crown were already so complex that their administration was in the course of leaving the household to become a separate office of the Exchequer. It showed the chancellor on the way to developing a similar independence, and a hundred years later he too held an independent office: not as head of the writing-office, whose importance declined with the spread of literacy, but in his original function as royal chaplain and 'keeper of the king's conscience', through which he still exercises his equity jurisdiction in Chancery. By the thirteenth century the three great courts of common law – Exchequer, King's Bench and Common Pleas – had all acquired an individual existence: not wholly divorced from the household, since all government and all justice belonged to the King, but having now a fixed location in London, regular sessions and their own code of procedure.

When the machinery of government thus passed into the impersonal hands of civil servants, the great offices of the household were soon elevated to a largely ceremonial status. The office of the bed thegn was shared between the Lord Great Chamberlain, today the sixth officer of state with responsibility for the Palace of Westminster, including the Houses of Parliament, and the Lord Chamberlain of the Household, who has authority over most of the palace servants and appoints the doctors, chaplains, musicians and tradesmen who attend the sovereign. Until censorship was abolished in 1968 he was also the licenser of plays. The office of the Steward, originally the disc thegn, had become hereditary by 1200 and for a time was vested in the earldom of Leicester. In 1399 it was inherited by Henry IV, who by descent, marriage and usurpation laid his hands on many principal sources of power, and since then the post of Lord High Steward has been created only for special occasions, usually when a peer was to be tried by the House of Lords, a privilege now abolished. Here too, as with the bed thegn, there has been differentiation, because within the household the Lord Steward has preserved a continuous existence as the officer primarily responsible for the domestic arrangements of the court and, as president of the Board of Green Cloth, for its finances. He, like the Lord Chamberlain, is appointed by the sovereign and holds office at his or her pleasure, both salaries being paid from the Privy Purse. They have deputies and a staff for everyday administration. In modern times a measure of parliamentary control over the household has been exercised by the appointment of politicians, usually government Whips, as Treasurer, Comptroller and Vice-Chamberlain. They change with the ministry.

A similar evolution took place within the stables, where the Constable and the Marshal soon became titular hereditary officers. The first hereditary Constable was

Miles of Gloucester, Earl of Hereford, who was appointed in the reign of Stephen (1135–54), and the office remained in his family for nine generations until the male line became extinct. It then passed to the future Henry IV, through his wife Mary de Bohun, and on his accession it ceased to be hereditary. During the fifteenth century it was held by several powerful nobles, but in 1514 Henry VIII withdrew it after Edward Stafford, Duke of Buckingham, had claimed that certain manors in Gloucestershire and Monmouth were permanently vested in the office. Seven years later Buckingham was executed for alleged treason, and since then it has been revived only for coronations, when the Lord High Constable attends the monarch and assists at the reception of the regalia.

25. Map of Great Britain drawn in 1255 by Matthew Paris. He obviously had only a hazy idea of the topography of Britain, though he noted important landmarks of the time, among them London, Bristol, St Albans, Dover, Windsor, Pontefract and York.

26. Wood-engraving of the effigy of one of the Earls of Pembroke, hereditary Marshals of England, in the mid-13th century.

The dignity of Earl Marshal had been vested in the earldom of Pembroke by about 1200, and it then passed through several families before in 1672 it was conferred upon the Howard Dukes of Norfolk, who have held it ever since. The Marshal has long ceased to have any responsibility for the royal stables. Today he organises coronations and all great state occasions, at which he settles questions of precedence; and as head of the College of Arms he appoints the heralds, a function arising from the old Court of Chivalry at which he presided under the Constable.

The gradual reorganisation of the administrative machine did not mean that the royal household ceased to participate in government. It was not questioned in the Middle Ages that the King should govern through his *familia*, the kinsfolk and personal ministers and advisers he chose to have about him. When part of the original 'family' hived off into separate, self-regulating departments like Chancery and Exchequer, this merely led to an intensification of household activity. The new departments developed their own traditions and procedure. They grew to be attached to their own methods and routine, and if not actually resistant to the King's will, they were often slow in executing it. Thus for the sake of swift, efficient administration the household developed new resources to replace those which had gone 'out of court'. The instrument was the Privy Seal, used by the Crown to authenticate its documents now that the great seal was in the possession of the chancellor; and the centre of activity was the 'Wardrobe'. Even in the thirteenth century the King's chamber was the only place private enough for the discussion of confidential business and the storing of treasure; and the Wardrobe was a closet leading off the chamber where the King kept his robes, his jewels and plate and any documents or instruments that he wished to keep especially secret. (In schoolboy histories it is related as a joke against poor King John that he lost all his treasure in a crossing of the Wash. In fact this was a very serious matter as it represented the instruments and sinews of government.) Centralised administration through the Wardrobe was developed by the able Poitevin ministers who controlled the government during the minority of Henry III, and it largely organised and financed the wars of the following reign.

Unlike the successors of the bed thegn and the disc thegn, the horse thegn never went out of court to establish his own department. From the late Hanoverian period to the twentieth century the Master of the Horse changed with the ministries, but the appointment had still to be personally acceptable to the sovereign; and today, when the Royal Mews is maintained at public expense, he is himself still a household officer whom the sovereign appoints. Under the Angevin kings, when other offices were becoming state departments or titular dignities, the Keeper of the King's Horse (still referred to as marshal in many of the documents) remained within the household as a working officer, his salary and expenses paid from the Wardrobe even if the accounts eventually went to the Exchequer. He had supervision of the deputy keepers or marshals who looked after the King's equestrian business in different parts of the country, and the records show him stocking forests, protecting his master's hunting rights, maintaining the royal studs, buying horses both at home and abroad and, not least, enforcing the King's demands on individuals and institutions under obligation in return for land or privileges. The upkeep of the royal stables being a national concern, essential to good government and the defence of the realm, people were constrained in various ways to contribute to it.

The Patent Rolls for the reign of Henry III (1216–72) illustrate these activities. In 1217 the abbot and monks of Beaulieu are reminded that King John had placed some horses in their care and keeping, and they are to have them ready for the new

27. King and messenger in the early 13th century. Messengers had to be good horsemen and mostly received their orders through the stables department. The letters they carried were generally written by a scribe or clerk on parchment and sealed with wax. Edward III employed 12 messengers at 3d a day; they were given an allowance of 4s 8d a year for shoes.

King's use when he comes of age – until then, of course, the abbey has to bear the expense of maintaining them. From money entrusted to them the Bishops of Bath and Salisbury are to deliver 30 marks to 'Robert de Bruer, his son John, and Geoffrey de Cressy, knights serving in Gascony', with a further 10 marks to each of them for the purchase of horses (1226). In 1232 the mayor and bailiffs of London are directed to assist 'Richard the king's marshal' in buying three Lombard horses that were available for purchase, to advise him in paying a reasonable price for them and then to bring them to the King. In 1244 the sheriff of Wiltshire is told of works to be carried out, at the expense of the county, at the royal estate at Clarendon. These include 'a new stable for the king and queen extending lengthways from the south wall next the gate as far as the old hall which is now a stable for the king's horses; two chambers partitioned off at each end of the stable to keep the king's and queen's harness in.' The Queen also had 'a new stable roofed with slate' at the manor of Woodstock, and a chamber was to be erected adjoining the King's stable at Winchester 'to contain three beds [presumably for the grooms] and the harness.' Later it fell upon the sheriff of Hampshire to 'make a tower at Freemantle between the king's and queen's chambers, and another kitchen anew, and a stable for 80 horses.' On the other hand, exemption from such obligations might be a way of rewarding loyalty or seeking favours. In 1270 'out of devotion to St Edward and special favour to the said abbot and convent' Henry freed the abbey of Westminster from the duty of supplying 'livery' [provisions, fodder or clothing] for the King and his marshals; and in the following year John le Faulkener, clerk of the household, was likewise quitted of livery service for himself and his heirs, 'so that no steward, marshal or other of the king's household, or any other or their baggage shall be housed or tarry there without the licence of the said John.'

Permission to hunt or victual in the royal forests was another privilege in the King's gift, a valuable one since it conferred not only sporting rights but access to food and fuel. In 1227 Henry confirmed a grant of Richard I permitting the Bishop of Bath and Wells and his successors to hunt with hounds throughout Somerset on condition that they did not molest stags or does. Significantly, the original grant was witnessed by 'William the marshal' as well as by three bishops: the preservation of game in the forests was among his many responsibilities. Usually, therefore, permission was restricted to 'free warren', the right to hunt smaller animals like the hare, the badger and the fox. This was granted, for instance, in 1229 to Ranulph Brito for taking the hare and the fox in certain parts of Northamptonshire and Buckinghamshire, 'without any interruption from the foresters and verderers'; and in 1253 to Richard de Thany and his heirs to have 'eight harriers and 20 brachets' to hunt 'the hare, the fox, the badger and the cat' in the royal forest in Essex, so long as they do not intrude upon the King's warrens. From reports from his keeper of this forest Henry was satisfied that his own rights would not be affected if the abbot and monks of Coggeshall were allowed to enclose certain woods and heaths, 'provided always that the doe and her fawn have free entry and exit, and that the foresters of the said forest, on horseback and on foot, shall be able to go in and out to survey the said woods and heaths and keep the king's deer and make all attachments of vert [vegetation to protect the deer, and the right to cut it] and venison and do all else pertaining to their office.' (Calendar of the Charter Rolls, Westminster, 1257.) Some grants seem to have been genuinely charitable, as the issue from Woodstock in 1234 'to the Hospital of St John without the east gate of Oxford, and the brethren there, of the right of sending a sumpter horse twice daily into the forest of Shotover for dry wood and underwood to cook the portions of the poor of the said hospital, and to warm the poor themselves.'

The gift in 1233 of an oak tree in Windsor forest to Henry Gothmund, ostler of the royal household, in recognition of his service in the *mariscaltia*, may have meant more to him than it does to us, but it is early evidence of an attitude that has persisted over the centuries, that loyal servants in the royal stables should be suitably rewarded when they could no longer work. Long before there was any such thing as a pension scheme or a welfare state, the Masters of the Horse were importuning the Treasury to allocate money to men worn out in the Crown's

service, or, after their death, to their widows. We shall find evidence of this later on. Meanwhile, Richard the Marshal, and his heirs and assigns so long as they did not become 'men of religion', were given a property in Northamptonshire 'to hold by rendering at Christmas four horse-shoes', and this as a nest-egg while Richard was still in service. Among many such bestowals the Patent Rolls mention a grant to Adam le Scott, a groom of the sumpters, or baggage horses, 'who has been in the king's service for 20 years and is debilitated more than usual', of 'the first escheat that falls in, to wit of 4d. a day, or 2d. or 3d. at most' (1251); to John le Naper, King's huntsman, a gift of land for long service (1259); to Thomas de Tytlington, keeper of the King's palfreys, the post of 'usher of the conventual kitchen of St Swithun's' (1261); to Gilbert atte Pirie, for long service, a life pension of 1½d. a day 'which William atte Forde, keeper of the king's destriers, lately deceased, used to receive at the Exchequer.'

An incidental charge on the stables arose from the enlarging menagerie, as in 1237 '18s. 7½d. laid out by the king's order on the expenses of two of the king's leopards and of their keepers, with four horses and grooms', and three years later a writ 'to find the king's lion and his keeper their necessaries for so long as they shall be in the Tower of London', and William, the said keeper, 'to have 14s. that he expended in buying chains and other things for the use of the lion'. But the breeding and acquisition of horses possibly had more attention than anything else. In 1217 there is reference to a stud-master representing the King at Rochelle; John de Gyse and a farrier receive £10 for keeping the King's horses at Waltham, Adam de Guildford is in charge at Tewkesbury, and in London arrears of £31 18s. 9d. were paid in 1226 to a horse sergeant whose wage was 6d. a day. Tardiness in payment was all too common, and in 1236 an order was given the Wardrobe to disburse

28. Mounted messengers. The man with an axe is a forester encountered along the route.

29. Entry from the Patent Rolls (which recorded the directives of the king) in April 1260, mentioning Ellis of Rochester (de Roffa) as Marshal of the King's Horses.

40 marks for horses purchased for the King at St Ivo's fair at Canterbury but not yet paid for. Halingrat, a crossbowman, is sent abroad to buy 'better and more handsome horses' in Gascony or Spain, and in 1251 Henry paid 35 marks to William de Chaeny for a bay, the sum apparently to be found by the diocese of Winchester.

In the latter part of the reign, roughly between 1257 and 1269, the rolls introduce Ellis of Rochester, variously described as the King's Farrier or Sergeant or Keeper, and finally as Marshal of the King's Horses. This relatively unknown man earns his place at the head of this chapter because he seems to epitomise the long line of Keepers or Marshals who ran the stables in the early mediaeval period. Probably he was of yeoman stock, as most of them were, because although in 1265 he was granted the lands in Cosham of 'Peter de Cosham, who was an enemy of the king and Edward his son during the late disturbance', his reward in lieu of pension was only to such modest appointments as doorkeeper and chamberlain to the Bishop of Winchester and the sergeantry of the pantry and vintry at St Swithun's. His loyalty is proved by his service throughout the anxious period of Henry's conflict with the barons and Simon de Montfort, and he was entrusted with many responsible tasks at this time. In 1260, for instance, a royal mandate was issued to the constable of Dover Castle 'to cause three destriers, seven breastplates, two pairs of steel spurs and four pairs of trappings for barded horses which Simon de Monte Forti, Earl of Leicester, caused to be brought into England and which lately by the king's order were arrested in that port, to be delivered to Ellis de Roffa, marshal of the king's horses, to take to the king in London, as he has enjoined on him.'

Routine references to Ellis show him receiving 11 marks for a palfrey bought for the Queen; finding necessaries 'for the king's charger staying at Beccles to be shod and for his smith, so long as they remain there'; reimbursed of £15 0s. 3d. for harness bought in London for the King's palfreys and chargers for the Easter festival of 1268; claiming 5 marks from the sheriff of Hampshire, 'out of the issues of the county', for a hauberk, or coat of mail, a gift from the King; paid 9 marks to buy a palfrey and a pack-horse for Edmund Crouchback, the King's second son, and claiming £5 6s. 3d. from the Exchequer for the purchase of more harness for the King.

In 1268 Ellis was granted 'simple protection without clause for two years', a standard procedure for indemnifying royal servants against challenges or enquiries into their activities, but he must have died or retired soon after this, since he disappears from the rolls shortly after paying £12 14s. 0d. for bridles, saddles 'and other small harness' on the King's behalf. In 1272 John Gilmeyn is named as Marshal. Loyal, honest and energetic, Ellis has quite an important place in the history of the stables, and it is reasonable to regard him as typical of the early Marshals and Keepers until military pressures gave a new importance to the equestrian establishment and elevated the status of the office.

30. *Detail from a 13th-century manuscript showing a man on a 'sumpter' or pack-horse. In Norman times sumpters were used for carrying equipment of the Household. Later they pulled carts.*

31. *Man leading sumpters. For protection on his journey he carries a long-bow.*

The Brocas Masters

From the accession of Edward I (1272–1307) England was intermittently at war, against the Welsh, the Scots or the French, for almost two hundred years, and the immediate effect on the stables establishment was the expansion of the studs at home and even more numerous purchases abroad. Constitutionally, the wars further demonstrated the inadequacy of the feudal array – the Norman military system which required landowners, as a condition of their holding, to attend the King's wars in person and to supply a specified number of armed knights from their tenantry. The conditions of service made it impossible for the Crown to keep an effective army in the field for any length of time, and it became more expedient to allow the landowners to commute their service by money payments which were used to raise troops by 'indenture' or financial contract. The Crown also extended the classes on whom some military or financial obligation might be laid. By 'distraint of knighthood', first levied by the ingenious Poitevins in 1224, men with land of a certain annual value, usually £20, were forced to become knights, with the feudal obligations which this entailed, or to pay a fine in lieu. The cost of equipping his armies compelled Edward I to impose his demands on men of even lower status, and the Statute of Winchester (1285) required every man to keep armour and weapons appropriate to his position: a purposely vague definition with a subtle appeal to social snobbery. In 1345 every man with land worth only £5 was called upon to serve and to equip his retainers to serve with him, and both Edward II and his son tried to make towns responsible for providing soldiers for the army.

This military reorganisation laid a further burden on the Keeper of the Stables. He had always been responsible for arranging accommodation when the Court was in transit, and it is not for nothing that the phrase 'harbingers of doom' came to describe the 'herbingers', the household officers who rode ahead to pre-empt billets at a minimum price. They were followed, very close behind, by the 'purveyors', who bought up food and other necessaries at something less than the market rate. The Keeper and his deputies also had to ensure that the King actually received the number of soldiers his indentures had paid for, and even as late as the sixteenth and seventeenth centuries the Master of the Horse's department still had the duty of issuing writs for distraint of knighthood on landowners who ignored or challenged their obligations.

Principally, however, the Keeper had to find horses. At home the royal studs became so numerous that deputy Keepers were appointed for areas north and south of the Trent, under whom individual stud-masters maintained the breed. Purveyors were commissioned to furnish the necessary sustenance, and inspectors came to ensure that studs were being properly kept, the stock maintained at the required level and unsatisfactory mares disposed of when they became a burden on the royal purse. From Berwick in 1292 Edward I issued a writ of aid for one year 'for Richard

Foun, whom the king is sending to various parts of the realm to view the king's studs, select colts therefrom, put them in halters and break them, as he is further instructed by word of mouth.' (Possibly there are indications of a family connection here. Richard Foun may have been a kinsman or descendant of 'Thomas le Ferun', who, in 1260, as keeper of the King's horses was paid £30 for 'maintenance of himself and the horses lately at Canterbury while the king was beyond seas'.) The locust energies of the purveyors fell harshly on people living within range of royal studs, and sometimes it was necessary to propitiate these local interests. In 1311 Richard de Fryton, parson of the church at Hadleigh in Essex, was given a grant for himself and his successors of 'a tenth of the foals, the issue of the king's stud in the park of Hadleigh, which is within the limits of his parish'; and at the same time Roger Fillol, king's yeoman, was 'to have in each year every eighth foal' from the Hadleigh stud.

But it was also necessary to replenish the stock from abroad, and for this purpose the Crown employed merchants thought to have an eye for horseflesh and opportunities for successful bargaining. It was a satisfactory arrangement all round since the King saved travelling expenses, the merchants doubtless took their percentage, and it was no bad thing for a merchant to have done the Crown a favour. The King sent his own agents too, and in the entries in the Patent Rolls it is not always possible to distinguish them from the merchants; but the frequency of these entries shows how important the acquisition had become. Here are a few examples from Edward I's early years when he was seeking to subdue the Welsh: safe conduct for certain servants whom William, son of Glaye, is about to send to Stryvelyn fair to buy horses; safe conduct for Benevenutus of Bologna and John de

32. Groom helping a rider to mount. In the Middle Ages, dwarfs were often employed as stable-hands. In the 17th and 18th centuries, boys who wanted to be jockeys would stunt their growth by rubbing their backbones with the grease of moles, bats and dormice.

33. Philip III of France, from whom the royal stables purchased 'great horses' for Edward I's wars. As Vassal of Gascony Edward paid homage to him in Paris before leaving France for his coronation.

Graunt, merchants, bringing to England 30 horses which Henry de Lacy, Earl of Lincoln (a warrior ally of the King) bought beyond seas; request to the mayor and bailiffs of Whitstable to permit Nutus de Florentia, King's merchant, who has bought 20 horses for the King, to bring them and their keeper across when they come to the said port; safe conduct for Donelin de Florentia, merchant, or his men, until Easter, to bring over 12 horses of value to the use of William de Bello Campo (soon to be anglicised as Beauchamp) and others; request to the bailiffs of Whitstable to permit the following to bring horses of value: Nutus, merchant of Florence, 10; Matthew de Columbariis, 20 for the King's use; Galvanus de Ferrara, 40.

This Matthew would seem to be a merchant, and Columbariis a place. But in the following year, 1277, when he and his men were sent 'to parts beyond seas to buy 20 horses of value for the king's use', he is described as the King's Sergeant, so probably he was a household officer in charge of the royal dovecotes, *columbariae*. He must have known his bloodstock too, because Edward employed him on several missions, including the purchase of 40 horses from Philip III of France. Donelin, the Florentine merchant mentioned above, was also commissioned to bring back 18 'great horses' from France with Philip's consent, and in 1282 Nutus of Florence and Burgess his brother were given a safe conduct to bring home as many as 80 horses acquired abroad. In the same year sundry unnamed merchants landed with 'great horses' after travelling through the territory of the Count of Holland and Zeeland.

The next King, Edward II (1307-27), attempted unsuccessfully to complete his father's conquest of Scotland, and the quest for horses continued. Thus we find Bynde Bonaventure and his brother Philip going to Lombardy to obtain 20 war-horses and 12 mares for the King; William de Guernun, merchant, and Dominic de Rouncavalles, King's Sergeant, to Spain; Albertinus of Bologna 'beyond seas' for war-horses, and John of Mildenhall, King's Sergeant, and Blaise Aldebraundini, King's yeoman, also 'beyond seas'; William of Toulouse, merchant, to Navarre. This William was later paid £602 6s. 8d. for horses he had acquired – a sum apparently appropriated from moneys set aside to pay the Crown's dues to the Papacy.

Edward had a stud in Essex, with John of Redmere as keeper, and that he also had studs in Middlesex, Bedford, Buckinghamshire, Oxfordshire and Berkshire may be inferred from an order to the sheriffs of these counties in 1313 to give protection to 'Thomas de la Garston and John Bowyer, king's sergeants, whom the king is sending with his horses, and also for the keepers of the horses'. Purveyors were active in gathering supplies, notably one Robert of Doncaster, described as a 'king's clerk'. In 1311 the sheriff of Surrey and Sussex was ordered to help him when he was sent into those counties 'to purvey a shipload of hay and 5000 horseshoes and nails, and also a ship to transport the same to Boulogne'. He was appointed to acquire for the King's horses 500 quarters of oats and hay, straw and brushwood, to the value of £30, to purvey oats, hay, litter, beans and peas for the king's palfreys, and on another occasion to 'provide divers kind of victuals for the household for which the king is at present unable to pay'. Other purveyors were Maurice Dragheswerd, King's Sergeant, appointed to buy harness for the carts and sumpter horses of the household officers; John of Reading, who with the same Maurice bought harness for the King's horses and carts, and John of Mildenhall, authorised to buy shoes and nails. The incidental hazards of the royal employment are indicated in a terse report that Philip of Warendon 'whilst on the king's service, guarding one of his horses, lost an ear by its bite.' (He was duly compensated.)

In this reign of Edward II we meet for the first time the Brocas family from

whom came the first Masters of the Horse to be known by that title. On the tomb of Sir Bernard Brocas in Westminster Abbey it is incorrectly stated that they 'came into England with the Norman king William'. They were an ancient Gascon family, and in their homeland they probably had long experience in the breeding and training of horses. Gascony and Guienne had been under English rule since the marriage of Henry II to Eleanor of Aquitaine in 1152, and the Brocas family had been loyal to England throughout the sporadic risings to overthrow this foreign domination. It was apparently this loyalty that ruined them and compelled Arnald de Brocas to come to England with three sons and other relatives early in the fourteenth century. Arnald himself was 'slain in the king's service in Scotland, probably at Bannockburn in 1314, and his sons were taken into the Royal Household. John, the

36. Horseman in the mid -13th century. The horse is probably a Breton, which horse-merchants were sent to 'purchase overseas for the king's use.'

eldest, was by 1314 a *valettus* of the King's chamber, a rank below knight, esquire or *serviens* (sergeant) and equivalent to groom. Bernard, the second, was rector of St Nicholas, Guildford, from 1324 until his death in 1368, but he was a lawyer and man of affairs rather than an ecclesiastic, and he held administrative posts in Gascony as well as at the English court. The third son, Arnald, was by 1330 sergeant to the new King, Edward III (1327–77), and Master of the Horse to John of Eltham, the King's younger brother. He soon disappears from the records, so probably he either returned to Gascony or died young. Two other members of the family, perhaps cousins, were also in the royal service. Simon Brocas was educated at Cambridge as a King's Scholar and was still an officer of the Household as late as 1376; and Menauld Brocas was by 1335 keeper of the King's horses north of the Trent, and soon afterwards he is mentioned as deputy to his relative John. An entry in the Patent Rolls in August 1343 records the appointment of 'William le Ferrour, king's yeoman, to have the custody of the king's great horses in the same manner as Menaudus Brocas, now deceased', at a wage of 3*d.* a day.

We do not know how this resourceful Gascon family, evidently in high favour with Edward II, survived his overthrow, in which many of his former servants were brought down with him; nor how they survived the palace revolution of 1330 when Edward III rebelled against the influence of his mother Isabella and executed her paramour Roger Mortimer. John Brocas was in charge of the cavalry department for Edward's wars against the Scots and the French, and military necessity caused a constant re-stocking of the studs. A separate keeper was appointed for studs north of the Trent, counties were laid under contribution for their maintenance, purveyors gathered supplies at the lowest price they could pay, and merchants and royal officers were once again busy in the foreign markets. In 1334 protection and safe conduct were granted to Arnold Garcy of St John and three others 'going to Spain and other foreign parts to buy war-horses and other horses for the king', and this is just one example of many of the kind. The urgency is shown in a pardon issued in 1338 to 'John Brocas, king's yeoman, who from the time at which the king assumed the governance of the realm to July 11 last has purchased warhorses, coursers, hobbies, colts and other horses, with spurs, saddles, bridles, horse-cloths, halters and other things required for the horses, of any account which he is held to render to the Exchequer or elsewhere of the receipt of the said horses and things of the king's stable. . .' Similar 'pardons' were issued to Brocas in 1346 and 1350. Edward was forestalling enquiries into the work of his agents from

subjects who complained of the cost of his wars, and especially of their adverse effect on the wool trade.

Good horses were expensive. In 1330, when the only enemies were the Scots, Brocas purchased for the King three *dextrarii* or *destriers*, the chargers who carried the mounted knights to war. He paid £120 for 'one called Pomers, of a grey colour, with a black head'; £70 for 'one called Lebryt, dappled with grey spots', and £50 for Bayard, 'of a bright brown bay, with the two hind feet white'. The housings for about a hundred of these chargers required 441 ells of canvas and 360 ells of woollen cloth, which must come from Candlewick Street in London; while the cost of provender, shoeing, bridles and headstalls was in the usual way shared among the counties. For the upkeep of 30 horses for 60 days the sheriff of Wiltshire had to find £40 12s. 6d., about 5½d. a day for each horse. Magnates with military ambitions, or the hope of profitable ransoms, might be generous with individual contributions. In 1340 the King acknowledged his indebtedness to William de Monte Acuto (Montacute or Montagu), Earl of Salisbury, for £246 13s. 4d. 'for the price of horses taken for his use, with promise to pay the same at Christmas'. The maritime counties had to make a special levy for 'the bridges, hurdles, boards, rafts and other things necessary for the shipping of horses' when the King finally took his host abroad. There was occasional repining at these exactions, so that in 1343 William de Framesworth, recently appointed Keeper of the studs south of the Trent, was instructed to 'bring all the king's horses, lately in the custody of Edmund de Tidmarsh beyond the Trent, to Westminster Palace to be kept there, pursuant of an order of the council made for the avoidance of grievances caused to the people as well by the keeping of them in divers counties of the realm as by the keepers of the same.' But this seems to have been only a gesture, since later in the year Roger de Normanvill, King's yeoman, was appointed to the custody of the 'horses, mares, colts and stud beyond the Trent in the same manner as Edmund de Tidmarsh', with a commission to make purveyance for their necessaries.

John Brocas himself went with his son Oliver to Gascony to acquire horses for the campaign that ended in the great English victory at Crécy (1346), and by this time the 'King's yeoman' of 1338 had become a knight: an honour perhaps conferred as much for his work in putting his department on to a military footing as for his valour in the field – he commanded a considerable force at the siege of Calais. It was doubtless at this time that the Master of the Horse came to be known by this title. The change from *custos equorum regis* to *magister* was one in name only. The

37. While the king and his courtiers generally travelled on horseback, the royal ladies rode in carriages. The most luxurious vehicles (as in this illustration from the Luttrell Psalter) had four wheels and were pulled by several horses, one behind another. They were driven by one or two postilions carrying whips. The beams, on which rested the arched framework, and the carved wheels were richly painted and gilded. Inside were tapestries and embroidered cushions, and the windows were hung with silk curtains.

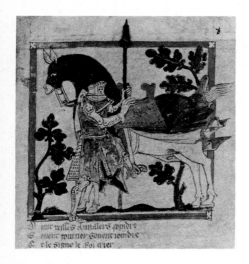

38. *This spirited – if somewhat fanciful – picture of an armed knight mounting his horse is from a romance written to celebrate the opening of the Hundred Years War in 1337, at the time when Menauld Brocas was keeper of the king's horses north of the Trent.*

simplest explanations are often the best, and it is likely enough that it was felt to be appropriate to an officer whose responsibilities had grown with the war. Within the household a knight could not be classed with men of the sergeant class who had held the office previously. Brocas, too, was a substantial landowner, with estates at Clewer, Windsor, Eton, Dorney, Boveney, Cookham and Bray.

Crécy stimulated Edward's appetite for further conquest, and writs of purveyance continued to fall upon the counties, along with commissions to investigate alleged abuses of the system. In 1347 Bochard Rolf was directed to make purveyance for 'the king's horses coming day by day from the north to Calais', and the net was flung wider with a licence to a pair of agents 'to go to Scotland to buy horses, broken and unbroken, mares, oxen and cows from the men of that land'. To prevent fraud by the purveyors, regular audits were carried out by clerks of the chamber, but the Crown was often in debt to its servants for disbursements that had not been repaid. In 1348 the executors of Edmund de Tidmarsh secured an admission that £314 17s 9d. was due to his estate for expenses not refunded, and they also obtained recognition of further claims in excess of £90. Overdue refunds were not the only risk. In 1350 Brocas was a member of a commission 'touching the persons who broke a dwelling at Cheltenham, wherein some of the king's horses at arms in the custody of William de Framesworth were lodged, and killed the king's sergeant John de Sherwood there, who afterwards received these persons well knowing of the deed, and those who killed there one of the king's horses worth £40.'

As the war dragged on, with the inevitable interruption of trade, it became increasingly unpopular. After Poitiers (1356), with the prospect of huge ransoms for the captured French king and many of his nobility, Edward began to reduce the military establishment and concentrated instead on the enlargement of Windsor Castle, where William of Wykeham was surveyor of works. So Sir John Brocas had to preside over the disbanding of the great cavalry force he had helped to build. It had always been his duty to thin the studs of horses that were no longer of service, but now the reduction was much more drastic. In 1357 he was ordered to sell the stud in Windsor Park, and to survey the other studs, 'to withdraw horses, mares and colts not suitable or useful to be kept for service and sell these', and at the same time to replace keepers and purveyors 'found to be insufficient or incapable'. Several of the northern studs were found to be afflicted with murrain and these were closed at once. A general break-up followed the Treaty of Brétigny (1360), which acknowledged English suzerainty over much of France. The proceeds were to be given to William of Wykeham, and it is to the dispersal of the studs that the rebuilding of Windsor Castle is due. But old retainers were not forgotten, even if their pensions often went on the county rates. A palfreyman, William of Tutbury, where there was to be a flourishing stud in later times, received a grant 'for his long labour in the king's service, and because he is so feeble and broken by age that he can labour no longer, of 2d. daily towards his sustenance and 10s. for his robe and 4s. 8d. for shoe leather, yearly, out of the issues of the counties of Bedford and Buckingham.' The record of many such awards shows that in his concern for faithful service Sir John Brocas instituted the high traditions of his office.

Brocas died in about 1371, before the resurgent French began to make inroads on the depleted English garrisons and Edward III, in the last transports of senility, sat his termagant mistress Alice Perrers on the judges' bench. It is generally believed that Sir Bernard Brocas, his eldest son, became Master in addition to the many other appointments that he held. He fought at Crécy and probably also at Poitiers and the Black Prince's victory at Najara in 1367, and he was a man who attracted legend. Sir

39. Beaulieu in the New Forest. A
royal hunting lodge and then a
Cistercian abbey founded in 1204 by
King John, it was at one time
among the king's important studs
south of the Trent.

40. Beaurepaire at Sherborne St
John near Basingstoke in
Hampshire. There is nothing visible
left of the original house built by Sir
Bernard Brocas and named after the
Brocas home in Gascony. But it is
more than likely that the moat was
there in his day.

Roger de Coverley was told that he was 'the lord who cut off the King of Morocco's head'; and in another story it was on behalf of his loyal henchman Brocas that the Black Prince wooed the Lady Joan Plantagenet, 'the Fair Maid of Kent', whom he himself was to marry.

Detached from these romantic suppositions, Brocas had a career of solid achievement during which he was a household officer, an ambassador, Constable of Aquitaine, Captain of Calais, and representative of Hampshire in the House of Commons in ten parliaments between 1367 and 1395. Finally he was chamberlain to Anne of Bohemia, first queen of Richard II, and his tomb in St Edmund's Chapel at Westminster is magnificent in spite of eighteenth-century embellishments and false ascriptions.

Numerous entries in the Close Rolls show a keen eye for property development and legalistic nuances, and compared with his father, this Brocas was perhaps more interested in acquisition than in disinterested service. A second generation often fattens on the dedication of the first. Sir Bernard's most gratifying acquisition through his second marriage, was the hand of a king's ward and substantial heiress, Mary, the daughter of Sir John de Roches and the widow of Sir John Borhunt. Through her he obtained estates and manors in Hampshire to which he added by

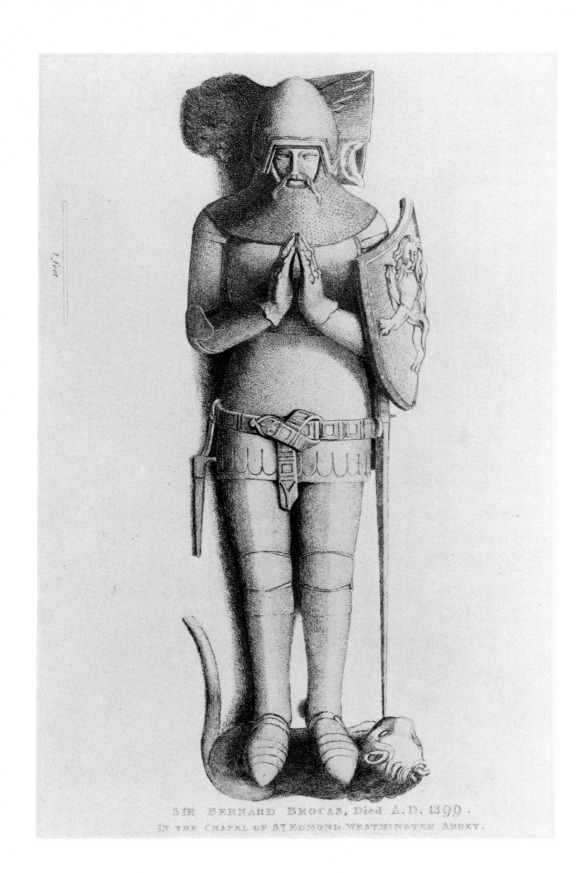

SIR BERNARD BROCAS, Died A.D. 1399.
IN THE CHAPEL OF ST EDMOND WESTMINSTER ABBEY.

1 feet

purchase in 1353 the lordship of Beaurepaire, near Basingstoke. A deed of enfeoffement in 1378 shows him to have been possessed at this time of manors at Beaurepaire, Farnham, Hoo, Bradley, Hanington, Froyle and Broxhead, all in the county of Southampton, Horton and Cheddington in Buckinghamshire, Peperharow in Surrey, Polingfold near Ewhurst on the Surrey–Sussex borders, and other substantial interests which he proceeded to augment in subsequent years.

His second marriage also brought him the hereditary Mastership of the Royal Buckhounds, which came through his wife's tenure of the manor Little Weldon in Northamptonshire. This 'hunter's manor' was held in 'grand serjeantry' (conferring rights for the performance of certain duties) as part of vast royal estates in Rockingham Forest. With its castle, Rockingham was a midland bastion of royal power as well as a hunting resort, and Little Weldon had been held *in capite*, at least since the reign of Henry II, by tenants who maintained 'running dogs' for the king's sport. (The land is now in Pytchley territory.) A grant made in 1216 to Hamon le Venour set forth his obligations and established a hereditary ownership which could be transmitted through the female line. From about the time of Bernard Brocas the Master of the Buckhounds was to receive a salary of £50 a year, chargeable on the sheriff of Surrey and Sussex but seldom enforceable under the weak Lancastrian government.

Bernard's son, also Sir Bernard Brocas, was executed in 1400 for his part in a rebellion in the name of Richard II, the murdered Plantagenet. In Shakespeare's play, Fitzwater tells the Bolingbroke usurper:

> My Lord, I have from Oxford sent to London
> The heads of Brocas and Sir Bennet Seely,
> Two of the dangerous consorted traitors
> That sought at Oxford thy dire overthrow.   *Richard II* V vi 13.

This is not quite correct since Brocas and three other conspirators, captured at Cirencester, were taken to Oxford and sent to London, where they were tried and executed. Their gruesome fate is described by Froissart, a Frenchman who spent several years at the English Court during the fourteenth century, in his Chronicle (IV, p. 668):

> The Mayor of London and the lords who had assisted in the judgement came to the Tower of London, where they seized the four knights of the king, Sir Bernard Brocas, the Lord Marclais, Master John Derby, receiver of Lincoln, and the Lord Stelle, steward of the king's household. They were brought into the Court and each tied to two horses, in the sight of all in the Tower, who were eye-witnesses of it as well as the king [Henry IV], who were much displeased and in despair; for the remainder of the king's knights that were with him looked for similar treatment, so cruel and revengeful do they know the Londoners.
>
> Without saying a word, these four were dragged from the Tower through the streets to Cheapside, and on a fishmonger's stall had their heads struck off, which were placed over the gate on London Bridge and their bodies hung on a gibbet.

The new king cancelled the forfeiture and attainder, so that Brocas's descendants were promptly restored to their possessions. After a century of prominence in national affairs the family settled on their estates as country gentlemen, serving through several generations as sheriffs and parliamentary representatives of their county of Hampshire. With some vicissitudes the hereditary Mastership of the Buckhounds remained with them until it was sold and extinguished in the seventeenth century. The family continued, however, in their loyalty to the Crown, and a Brocas fought gallantly against the Cromwellians who butchered the Royalist garrison at Basing.

42. *Seal of Sir Bernard Brocas, showing his crest: a Moor's head in profile crowned.*

41 *(opposite). Effigy of Sir Bernard Brocas from his tomb in St Edmund's Chapel, Westminster Abbey, where he was buried after the magnificent funeral accorded him by Richard II.*

CHAPTER FIVE

The Stable Knights

The Brocas family inaugurated a new era in the history of the stables. The new type of Master was of a higher social standing, and politically more important, than earlier keepers like Ellis of Rochester whose work seems to have been with horses and nothing else. As a result of Edward III's military ambitions Sir John Brocas was at the head of a much larger equestrian organisation than anything that had been known before; and a familiar consequence of the expansion of any government department is the growing detachment of its senior officials from routine administration.

With his pugnacious Gascon antecedents John Brocas was perhaps a horseman all his life, or at least until his great establishment was broken up. But he was also a Household officer close to the King, and he held other posts – he was Chief Forester of Windsor, Constable of the castle at Guildford and Keeper of its park – which helped to provide him with a salary appropriate to his professional services. His son Bernard, as we know, had even more distinguished appointments, and with Bernard, the Master's actual responsibility for the stables seems to become less intimate. He was a knight belonging to the smaller landowning class whose members might be saddled with duties, and rewarded with patronage and sinecure emoluments, without as yet any fear that they might become powerful enough to challenge the Crown's authority. They represented their counties in the Commons, as Bernard Brocas did for nearly thirty years, and the Crown had numerous ways of commanding their loyalty. They might be sheriffs, or receive the new fourteenth-century office of justices of the peace, or be appointed to judicial commissions like *oyer* and *terminer*. They might be constables or keepers or captains of castles or forests that they seldom saw; and there were dignities available within the Household, among them the Mastership of the Horse. The Masters were no doubt capable horsemen and experienced in the management of horses, but their post was becoming more nominal than at any time since the Norman Conquest. In fact they may have approximated to the horse thegns of the later Saxon period: trusted Household officers, with considerable influence and esteem in their own localities, whose duties at Court were largely exercised through deputies.

Administration through this rising class of knights was the style of government attempted by Richard II and practised also by the Lancastrian kings who supplanted him on pretence of restoring older methods. With the possible exception of the Earl of Warwick (d. 1439), whose presumed Mastership is uncertain, all Masters of the Horse were drawn from this knightly courtier class until the middle of the sixteenth century.

Richard II (1377–99), son of the Black Prince, succeeded his grandfather Edward III at the age of ten. His coronation, in the year of his accession, saw the first appearance of 'the King's Champion', who offered combat to any who dared to

43. Richard II riding with his knights, among whom at various times were Russell, de Clifford, Murrieux and Redman.

44 (overleaf). Richard II and the Duke of Gloucester at Plechy (Plashy) Castle, near Dunmow in Essex. The illustration, from Froissart's Chronicles, gives a wonderfully detailed view of courtly life in the late 14th century, when the Mastership of the Horse was established. The horses were probably palfreys – amblers used for travelling, hunting and hawking – or Barbs imported from North Africa via Spain (whence came 'Roan Barbary', Richard II's favourite horse.)

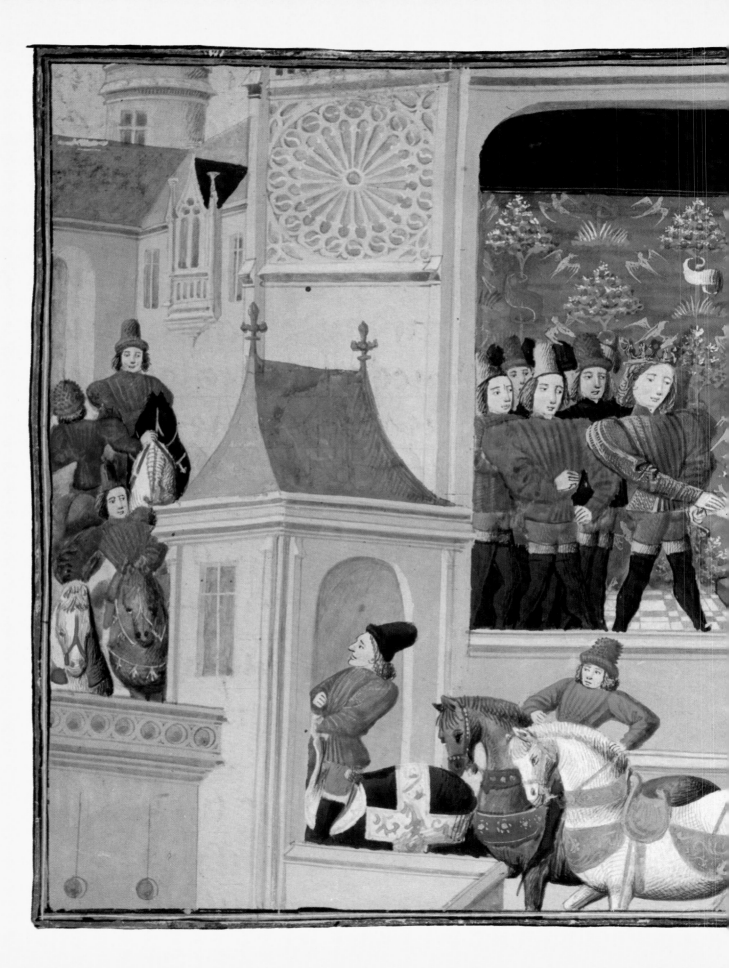

challenge the King's right to the throne. The Close Rolls record the petition of 'John Dymok, knight, in right of Margaret his wife for their manor of Scrivelsby' to 'have on the eve of the coronation one of the king's destriers with saddle and harness of iron and full armour, such as the king would wear in battle, and being so armed and mounted to ride before the king in the procession, crying to the people thrice in the hearing of all men that if any man would deny the king's right, he was ready to deraign the same by his body.'

Dymoke's petition was contested by Sir Baldwin de Freville but was upheld in the court of the Lord High Steward, and the appointment became hereditary in his family. This Dymoke died soon afterwards, but Froissart reported that at the coronation of the next king, Henry IV, 'when dinner was half over, a knight of the name of Dymock entered the hall completely armed and mounted on a handsome steed, richly barbed with crimson housings. The knight was armed for wager of battle, and was preceded by another knight bearing his lance. He himself had his drawn sword in one hand, and his naked dagger by his side.' To introduce the champion into the hall was one of the coronation duties of the Lord High Constable. This ceremony was enacted at every coronation until 1820, being discontinued with the accession of William IV. The champion in 1820 was Sir Henry Dymoke, and the current Master of the Horse allocated to his performance the sum of £118 18s. 6d. out of the total of nearly a quarter of a million that the celebrations cost.

Richard II, 'that sweet lovely rose', was described by a chronicler as 'fair among men even as another Absalom'. Born at Bordeaux during one of his father's incessant campaigns, he inherited the terrible Plantagenet temper but not the inclination for military exercise. A clutch of reactionary, war-fed uncles urged him to restore England's waning prestige in France, but Richard's courage was of another sort. His tutor, Simon Burley, taught him to believe in 'regality', the rights and duties appropriate to a king, and he instantly proved it when in his fifteenth year he rode out to meet Wat Tyler's rabblement at Smithfield and, while the politicians and the professional warriors dithered, outfaced them by his instinctive confidence in a sacred office. It was the supreme moment in a reign that in harsh political terms was a failure and ended in a solitary death in a northern castle.

Historians have given conflicting interpretations of Richard's aims, but in essentials his policy was to undermine the traditional influence of the barons and to make the Chamber the principal machine of government. He worked through the Signet Office, which in subsequent years was to make an important minister of the secretary who kept its secret seal. His trusted advisers were 'King's Knights', men like Wiltshire, Bagot, Bushy and Green, the faceless men of Shakespeare's play who are denounced as 'caterpillars of the commonwealth', 'shallow jesters and rash bavin wits' that misled the King and corrupted his morals and his judgment. But they were far from being 'favourites' in the pejorative sense. Wiltshire had been a soldier under John of Gaunt and seneschal of Gascony, and he was already a man of distinguished service when Richard made him Chamberlain of the Household and, later, Treasurer. The other three had served in their own districts as sheriffs, justices of the peace and royal commissioners. Bushy, a Lincolnshire knight, sat in nine of Richard's parliaments and was Speaker in three of them; Green was from Drayton in Northamptonshire and Bagot from Warwickshire, where he had acquired the castle of Baginton. They were members of the King's Council and loyal instruments of his Household policy. At his fall Bagot was imprisoned and later released, and the other three were judicially murdered when Henry Bolingbroke marched into Bristol in 1399.

45. *Richard II's funeral in 1399. The body of the deposed king, who had been put to death in Pontefract Castle, was carried from the Tower of London on a simple litter drawn by four black horses and escorted by four knights all in black. His last Master of the Horse, Richard Redman, having transferred his allegiance to the new king, may have been involved in organising the funeral.*

The background of these men is important, as it was from this class – gentry who would support the Household against baronial opposition – that Richard appointed his Masters of the Horse. There seem to have been four of them: Thomas de Murrieux, by 1377; Thomas de Clifford, by 1388; John Russell, from 1391 to 1398; and Richard Redman, 1399.

Not much is known of the first two in their capacity as Masters. Murrieux (or Moreaux, or perhaps even Morers – a William Morers, Marshal of the King's Household in 1381, may have been a kinsman) came of a Suffolk family who had held a fee of the manor of Thorpe Murieux, a few miles east of Lavenham, since 1200. His father, also Thomas, was High Sheriff for Suffolk in 1355. Murrieux's wife Blanche was the natural daughter of John of Gaunt by Catherine Turneford. In 1382 he was made Constable of the Tower for life and in the following year he was granted a wardship in Billingsgate. He received commissions of *oyer* and *terminer* in his native county, and in 1384 he was appointed 'to buy in England, at the king's price, and to bring to him all the king's horses needed for his present expedition beyond the seas.' (In the early years of the reign there were several small and fruitless expeditions to France and Flanders, but there was never sufficient money to equip them properly. Eventually a truce was sealed by Richard's marriage in 1396 to Isabelle, the French king's daughter, who was only seven years of age.)

Unlike Richard's other Masters, Thomas de Clifford came from an old family who had been barons of Westmorland for several generations. Thomas, born in about 1365, was governor of Carlisle, Warden of the Marches and keeper of the forests north of the Trent. He is mentioned as a Knight of the King's Chamber, and in 1388 one Richard Maisemore was ordered to 'buy and deliver to Thomas de Clifford, Master of the King's Horse, or his deputy, as many horses as may be wanted for the king's use.' At about this time he was temporarily banished from Court in the baronial reaction headed by the Lords Appellant, but in 1389 he was appointed King's Escheator in Ireland. An escheator was a collector of forfeits declared to be due to the Crown under feudal law or for other causes, and such an

46. Skipton Castle, Yorkshire, home of Sir Thomas de Clifford. A substantial part of this impressive stronghold, built on a rock overlooking the town, is still as he would have known it in the late 14th century.

appointment was recognised to be an opportunity for the collector to line his own pocket. In 1396 allegations of dishonesty were made against Clifford, but by that time he was dead, apparently killed in Germany in 1391. An inquisition into his possessions was held at Skipton in the following year, and the wardship of his estates was assigned to Queen Anne, the King's first wife.

John Russell was a knight of Worcestershire, and in 1378 he received £12 for the thirty days he spent as a representative of the county in the parliament held at Gloucester. He was also a member in later parliaments, but the significant date in his career was in November 1387 when he received a grant from the King 'that he might stay with him': that is, he became a 'King's Knight' and an officer of the Household. A licence in 1388 to crenellate his two manors in Worcestershire is evidence of his rising status and esteem, and in the following year an agreement was drawn up 'between Sir John Russell knight and William Hitchcock chaplain, to whom the king has granted the priory of Deerhurst for the life of Sir John during the war with France.' They are to pay the prior £10 for the first year and £5 for the next year, and they are to 'perform the services of the church'. The indenture is to become void at the end of the war and they are thereupon to surrender their interest, but Russell was still in charge ten years later, when custody was transferred to Master Richard Wyche for the reason that 'the possessions are dissipated and the divine services not held on account of the infirmities of John Russell, knight, farmer [one who pays a fixed sum for the taxes and revenues of a property] of the priory.'

Several entries in the rolls refer to grants and protection given to Russell for his services, and in January 1398 the customary 'discharge', exempting him from enquiry into his transactions, was made to him as 'long keeper of the king's great horses, in consideration of his good and gratuitous service in that office, in buying or getting horses by gift or otherwise from the king's lieges, from archbishops, bishops, abbots and priors on voidance of their sees and houses, as well as forfeited horses, and also in receiving chariots, carts, saddles, reins, standards and other things belonging to the said office.' The discharge is made 'notwithstanding that he is retained to stay with the king for life, in peace and war, for an annuity of £50'. Russell was at the same time granted exemption from serving on juries and commissions or holding any other office 'against his will'. This concession was presumably made because of the infirmity which led to his being relieved of his responsibilities at Deerhurst priory. In 1399 he was one of the knights appointed to assist the Duke of York in administering the kingdom during Richard's absence in Ireland, but at least by June of that year he had been succeeded as Master of the Horse by Richard Redman.

Redman was Master for only a short time: not because he was loyal to Richard and fell with him, but because he transferred his allegiance to the Lancastrians and was useful to them in other ways. The Redmans were northern gentry with estates at Redman in Cumberland, Levens in Westmorland and Harewood in Yorkshire. Richard, born not later than 1360, had early experience of the Border skirmishing to which the family had been long accustomed. In 1388 he received the grant for life 'of all lands and tenements which the king has in the town of Blencogo' and two years later he was retained for life 'to stay with the king', became sheriff of Cumberland and was granted lands in Heversham and Hutton Roof. In the following years his service to the King is attested by several 'pardons, grants and commissions', and in June 1399 he is preparing for the King's expedition to Ireland, John Hitton being appointed 'to buy at the king's charges sufficient horses for the king's use', and to deliver them to Redman as Master of the Horse. He still had time

47. *Seal of Thomas de Murrieux, from a quitclaim dated 1364.*

in that year to seek permission to stage a joust at Carlisle before accompanying Richard to Ireland.

Redman thus was a typical member of the gentry who rose in the royal service and was rewarded for his work; we do not know why he was a maggot in the apple and deserted Richard in the crisis of 1399. He was well enough rewarded for his treachery, because in 1401 Henry IV confirmed him, as a King's Knight, in the possession of the lands which Richard had granted him at Blencogo (Blencowe) not exceeding the value of £10 yearly. Immediately after the usurpation he was a member of a mission sent to treat with the Scots and try to persuade them not to support any of the pseudo-Richards who were putting themselves at the head of northern discontent. In 1404 he became sheriff of Yorkshire, and clearly he was among the trusted supporters on whom the King relied to hold the north against the powerful Percys of Northumberland. He received commissions of array to raise bowmen and men-at-arms, and in 1404 he was empowered to exact fines and forfeits from men implicated in the Percy rebellion that ended at the battle of Shrewsbury. From 1405 to 1421 he represented Yorkshire in the Commons, and he was Speaker in the parliament which met at Northampton in 1415, succeeding Chaucer's son Thomas. He helped to mobilise the army that fought at Agincourt, but himself was among the 'gentlemen in England now abed' who remained behind. He died in 1426, a man whose treason had prospered, but representative of the class that served the Royal Household and, among other duties, had nominal control of the stables. A grandson, also Richard Redman, was to be successively bishop of St Asaph, Exeter and Ely; and through the marriage of his daughter Joan to Sir Thomas Wentworth, Redman was a direct ancestor of the great Earl of Strafford.

'Forgiveness, horse. Why do I rail on thee?' In Shakespeare's play Richard II delivers a dramatic apostrophe when he learns from a poor groom of his stable that Henry at his coronation rode on Richard's favourite horse, Roan Barbary, 'that horse that thou so often hast bestrid.' The speech is characteristic of Richard's rhetorical, self-dramatising habit, and it should not be taken as evidence of any great affection for horses. The equestrian activity of the reign was less than in Edward's time because the country was never seriously at war, but it follows the familiar pattern of agents sent to acquire horses; abbeys and counties forced to bear part of the cost; payments to men no longer capable of active service; and harbingers and purveyors busy victualling the studs and their keepers. The entries so closely resemble those of previous reigns that there is no need to give further examples of them. A small departure from the usual pattern, illustrative of the Englishman's traditional xenophobia, is a protection granted in 1378 to a French saddler, John de Beaune, 'working in London and in fear of molestation by his rivals'.

The reasons for the fall of Richard II do not concern us here, and we should better understand them if we could read the mind of Richard Redman. The charge of trying to exercise 'personal government' unhelpfully employs a modern phrase to describe the traditional process of centring the administration on the officers of the Wardrobe. An equally traditional objection to this process was heard when an interfering minor cleric called Haxey complained in 1397 that too many bishops were spending too much time at Court. Richard had several high-ranking ecclesiastics among his advisers and he told the Commons, who had recently submitted a petition against the growing expenditure of the Household, that they had no business to 'misprise and take on themselves any ordinance or governance of the person of the king or his hostel or of any persons of estate whom he might be pleased to have in his company.'

This was an assertion to the sovereign's right to choose his own counsellors and servants, the Master of the Horse included. But Richard by this time was losing control of events. He had been shattered by the death in 1394 of his beloved Queen, Anne of Bohemia, razing the palace of Sheen where she died and striking a peer in the Abbey during her funeral. His cousin Henry Bolingbroke, heir to the Lancaster estates of John of Gaunt, swept aside a man seemingly bereft of the will to resist, and after a pretence of abdication Richard was silently put to death.

The reign of Henry IV (1399–1413) was as careworn as Shakespeare has depicted it. There was no immediate change in the system of government, and in continuing to rule through his household knights Henry met the same opposition from the barons and parliament as Richard had. This continuity in the administration was shown in the appointment of Robert Waterton as Master of the Horse in place of Redman. He even belonged to the same class of northern gentry.

The Watertons were a loyal Lancastrian family who had served in the household of Henry's father, John of Gaunt, and held estates in return for their service. Hugh Waterton had been a squire in Henry's own Household, acting as his Chamberlain and Keeper of the Wardrobe. He was treasurer of Henry's London establishment in Fleet Street, where in 1381 the upkeep of the stables accounted for £113 in a year's expenditure of £237. In 1390 he accompanied Henry to Prussia to join the Teutonic knights in a crusade against the infidels of Lithuania, and in a party of 70, including 11 knights and squires, his brother Robert was marshal. A third brother, John, joined them on a similar expedition in 1392, but John and Robert came home when Henry decided to push on to Jerusalem.

When Henry landed at Ravenspur in 1399 to claim his Lancaster estates and win a kingdom, Robert Waterton was keeper of the castle at Pontefract. Like other Lancastrian tenants, he sided with the usurper, and he brought out 200 foresters to greet him as he made his way inland through Pickering and Knaresborough. It was to the castle at Pontefract, where Waterton was custodian with Henry's half-brother Sir Thomas Swynford, that Richard was brought after his deposition. Shakespeare's account of Richard's murder by Piers of Exton was only one of several versions current at the time. Mediaeval usurpers always had problems with their predecessors, since enemies of the new regime habitually declared that the true King was still alive and paraded some supposititious character as the focus of rebellion. Men claiming to be Richard made their appearance in Wales, Scotland and parts of England. The usurper's only course in such circumstances was to exhibit the body of the late King to prove that he was dead; but it had to be the 'clean' corpse of a man who looked as though he had died of natural causes, not the mutilated body of one who had obviously been murdered. Poison was a risky method as its ravages might be difficult to conceal. Starvation was safer, except that a strong man could resist it for an inconveniently long time. Earlier in the century it had been attempted on Edward II, who was kept for months at Berkeley, starved, lying in darkness among his excrement and racked by any torture that would not leave an outward mark. Obstinately he would not die, and his eventual murder, by a red-hot iron thrust into his bowels, was not, as has been alleged, a symbolic comment on his esoteric habits but a way of killing him that would not show when his body was displayed to the public. History has not established how Richard II died, but it is likely enough that Robert Waterton knew.

Like Redman, he defended the King's cause in the north against the Percy rebellion. In 1403 he was a member of a commission 'to assemble all men within the counties of York and Northumberland to go with the king to resist Henry Earl of Northumberland and other traitors who have risen in insurrection', and after

49. Detail of Redman's belt from his effigy (overleaf).

50. Seal of Richard Redman, showing his crest: a horse's head couped argent crined or.

51 (overleaf). Effigy of Richard Redman and his wife in the church of All Saints, Harewood, Yorkshire. Dressed in full armour, he wears the SS collar of Lancaster, and his head rests on his crest.

Shrewsbury he was sent to fetch to the King the Lady Elizabeth Percy, wife of Henry Hotspur slain in the battle, 'and to take horses for the expedition'. He received substantial goods, including 'five colts of the age of two years', from the forfeiture of Northumberland's brother the Earl of Worcester, who had been beheaded for his part in the rebellion. But this could be perilous service, and when in 1405 he was carrying messages from the King to the Earl of Northumberland, he was detained in the Earl's castle at Warkworth and only released when his brother John stood surety for him.

In the following year he had a reversal of another kind, being among the knights and squires whom Henry was compelled to dismiss from the 'continuous council', the group of close advisers and officials who supervised the everyday running of the government. The Commons were always complaining of the expenditure of the household, which had risen as high as £25,000 in a year, and Henry undertook to reduce this by half, economising by dismissing the 'alien' members, mostly the foreign cooks and grooms who had come with his unpopular second wife, Joan of Brittany. The Commons' demand that he also dismiss knights and squires from his council was an attempt to weaken his dependence upon the *familiares* who had been one of the causes of the unpopularity of Richard II. Waterton's inclusion in their number shows his closeness to the King, and he was one of the witnesses of the will when, in 1409, Henry was taken ill and feared that he was dying.

Waterton continued to receive many favours from the King. As well as Master of the Horse he was 'master of the king's running dogs called harthounds', steward, master forester of the 'parks and foreign woods of Spofford and Hayley, co. York'. He had received through his wife the manor of Brotton in the North Riding, and further acquisitions during this reign included 'the manor of Wallewykgraunge with all other lands, etc., within the liberty of Tyndale, called Talbotland, co. Northumberland', and the manor of Methley in the West Riding 'with its appurtenances lying between the waters of Calder and Aire'. This was in 1412, and at the same time a licence was issued for the Queen to grant him 'her estate in the manor of Helaugh, co. York, which she holds for life as parcel of her dower'.

Rewards of this kind were frequent for King's Knights who had done good service, and the Master of the Horse habitually received other appointments to supplement whatever remuneration went with the office. Even though they were largely nominal, the posts given to Waterton suggest an interest in hunting and open-air activities, but it is evident that with all his other responsibilities, both as landowner and as King's servant in the north, he cannot have been personally very active as Master of the Horse. The records do indeed show that most of the stables' transactions at this time were carried out through deputies, with the Master exercising, at best, a distant supervision. Except during wars and emergencies, this had become the common practice.

Such an emergency was about to arise with the resumption of the Hundred Years War, but by that time Waterton had been succeeded as Master by his brother John. He continued in the royal service until his death in about 1425 – one of his last commissions, recorded in the Patent Rolls of 1423, being to 'purvey carriages to convey from Pountfreyt castle to the Tower of London, David, first-born son of the Earl of Athol, Alexander, Earl of Craufurd, Alexander, lord of Gordon, John de Lyndesey, Patrick, first-born son and heir of Sir John Lyon, Andrew Grey of Foullys, David de Ogilby, Sir Wilhan de Rothnane, David Meignez and William Olyfaunt, lord of Abirdalgy, hostages for the release of James, king of Scots'. His effigy in the church at Methley shows him in armour and wearing the SS collar of Lancaster, so named because it bears a reversed 'S' device.

53. *Methley Hall, Yorkshire, home of Robert and John Waterton.*

52 *(opposite). Close-up of Robert Waterton's effigy from his tomb in St Oswald's Church at Methley in Yorkshire. Carved in alabaster, it is, though mutilated, one of the finest examples in existence of a mediaeval portrait. The curled beard and the turban decorated with roses proclaim a man of fashion; the SS collar identifies allegiance to the Lancastrian cause.*

CHAPTER SIX # Games on Horseback

At least when he entered his knightly phase, the Master of the Horse was expected to take part in the extraordinary form of entertainment – a mixture of military combat, the niceties of chivalry, the heady artistic imagination, for the professionals a way of getting rich, and perhaps also just good clean fun – that was known as the tournament or joust. A king or wealthy nobleman who did not occasionally stage a tournament was guilty of failing to 'keep his estate', or live in a manner befitting his status. Ellis of Rochester had probably been only an *écuyer*, a squire who accompanied his master to the mimic field, but the Brocas knights and their successors had more prominent roles, and over the years Masters would be chosen for their jousting skill. Furthermore, although the whole household played its part in the staging of these extravaganzas, the stables department had a large share of the work and responsibility.

Chaucer's *Canterbury Tales*, begun in about 1387, has in Book IV of *The Knight's Tale* a spirited account of a mediaeval tournament. Palamon and Arcite, Theban cousins closely bound in knightly fellowship, are made captive by Theseus, Duke of Athens. Theseus has defeated and married Hippolyte, hard-running Queen of the Amazons, and the two young men become bitter rivals when they both fall in love with Emilia, her beautiful and more domesticated sister. When he comes upon them mauling each other in a forest glade, Theseus sagely points out that they cannot both have the girl:

> She may not wedden
> Both at once, though ye fighten ever-mo,

and one of them, like it or not, 'moot go pipen in an ivy-leaf'. The only honourable course is for them to enter the lists for love of their lady, and each may choose a hundred knights to support him. Arcite, with the celestial aid of Mars, the god of war, defeats Palamon in the combat but is cheated of his prize by Venus, who has been backing the other side. She and her father Saturn persuade Pluto, lord of the underworld, to promote an earthquake in which Arcite is thrown and crushed by his frightened horse. Before he dies Arcite gallantly bestows Emilia on his old companion.

The story is of course an absurd conglomeration of mediaeval chivalry and classical legend and mythology, and Chaucer gently reflects upon the Knight's intellectual capacity in relating it, but it is instructive on the splendour and elaborate formality of a tournament. Chaucer tells how the knights, the squires and the spectators rode to the lists on richly caparisoned horses, accompanied by musicians creating a battle-din on pipes, clarions, trumpets and kettle-drums. Bets are taken on the outcome, and then Theseus announces through a herald the laws of combat. Because

it were destruction
To gentle blood to frighten in the guise
Of mortal battle now in this empyre,

he decrees that no one shall bring into the action darts, axes, daggers or short-swords and staffs, and the wounded and the fallen are to be carried to safety before they can suffer serious hurt.

The *Chronicles* of Froissart contain several descriptions of this knightly exercise. He tells of a sumptuous occasion at Smithfield in 1390 when the English Court was determined to emulate the lavishness of a celebration held to mark the French Queen's arrival in Paris. Sixty knights, 'accompanied by sixty noble ladies richly ornamented and dressed', were to tilt for two days in the presence of the court, with

54. Knights fighting to the death. Needless loss of life in tournaments was condemned by kings and popes. Henry II suppressed them altogether; Richard I restricted them to five districts: Salisbury and Wilton; Warwick and Kenilworth; Stamford and Warmington; Brackley and Mixbury; and Smithfield in London.

sint com il lauoient deuise. En
sint sen issent del chastel li dui
rois. et li autre chrs auec els. et
uiegnent enla place la ou li afai
res estoit encomenciez. li rois ar
tus estoit enla place. et li bons
chrs. et li morholt. cil troi ne por
toient mie armes. aincoins esto
ient uenuz entele maniere meer
mes que li ros artus   estoit
uenuz. et missire blyo. et missire
gau. qui molt cointement esto
ient armez come gtune bachel

Issire gau. tout premieremt
encomence cele uate. et le
isse core tout maintenant a vn
chr de noubellante qui chr no
uel estoit. et le fiert si durement
en son uenir quil na force ne po
oir quil se tieng en sele. aincois
uole atere tout erraiment. et blyo
se dresce maintenant a vn au
tre. et le fiert si roitement del
glaiue quil le fait uoler aterre
et lui et le cheual. et si al greuez
molt durement de celui cheoir.

prizes bestowed upon the champions chosen by the ladies. The procession to the lists was headed by squires on barded (armoured) coursers, followed by the sixty ladies on their palfreys, each of them leading a knight with a silver chain, 'completely armed for tilting'. At the lists the squires mounted the knights upon their coursers and 'the jousting continued, with great courage and perseverance, until night put an end to it'. Many were unhorsed and many lost their helmets, and alas for patriotic esteem, the prize of a crown of gold was awarded to a French challenger, the Count d'Ostrevant, 'who far eclipsed all who had tilted that day'.

Tournaments were first heard of in England in the reign of Stephen, and the chronicler Geoffrey of Monmouth was not very complimentary about them:

> Presently the knights engage in a game on horseback, making a show of fighting a battle, whilst the dames and damsels looking on from the top of the walls, for whose sake the courtly knights make believe to be fighting, do cheer them on for the sake of seeing the better sport. (*Historia Britonum*.)

56. Knights entering the lists, engraved from a 13th-century manuscript. Their banners are held by the king-of-arms.

Originally tournaments were a method of cavalry training, a knight cultivating his skill by learning to fight at the side of other knights in close formation. But with the flowering of the code of chivalry they developed into sporting and social occasions with an increasingly elaborate ceremonial, and they became almost a way of life for professional combatants who rode from one court to another in pursuit of the rich prizes that were to be won. William Marshal, Earl of Pembroke, who became a senior statesman and Regent of England after the death of King John, began his career as a landless 'knight errant' fighting at tournaments, doing valiant deeds in the Holy Land and selling his strong right arm to any faction that would employ him. The realities of mediaeval knighthood have been enveloped in a romantic haze by Geoffrey of Monmouth, followed later by Sir Walter Scott. It was Geoffrey who immortalised the Arthurian legend and created the cult of the knight in shining armour ever anxious to succour the aged, fight with dragons or rescue helpless damsels.

The ritual of the tournament helped to put a spurious gloss upon this picture, but it was a dangerous pastime until a code of rules reduced the risk to life and limb. The clergy frequently condemned it, partly on ethical grounds but partly also because it occupied the energy of wealthy and talented horsemen who should have been dedicating their knightly devotion to crusades against the infidel. The clergy preached against these 'detestable fairs', and in 1179 the Pope refused Christian burial to knights who were killed in the lists. Kings too had their doubts, since the gathering of large numbers of knights might be a cloak for conspiracy and sedition, and tournaments might develop into the private wars which William the Conqueror had expressly forbidden in England. But enthusiasm for the sport could not be restrained, and warrior kings like Edward I not only wanted to take part in it

55 (opposite). Preparations for a tournament. This illustration from a French romance, drawn in the mid-14th century when the office of Master of the Horse was created, shows the kind of activities that the officers and servants of the stables would have been involved in at the time.

57, 58 and 59 are engraved copies from a contemporary Life of Richard Beauchamp, Earl of Warwick. In 57 (above) Beauchamp is seen taking part in a melée of knights.

*58. Beauchamp (wearing the bear and ragged staff crest of Warwick) at Verona,
jousting on foot with a knight called Sir Pandolf, whom he, 'sore wounded on the left shoulder'.*

themselves but saw in it a valuable training-ground for martial prowess. Opportunely combining military art with financial advantage, kings gave permission for tournaments to be held at certain times and places in return for a specified fee and sureties for proper organisation and the keeping of the peace. Fees were graded according to rank, Richard I requiring 20 marks from an earl, 10 from a baron and 4 from a landed knight. These precautions were not unreasonable, because irresponsible young noblemen attending a tournament with their personal following could easily become a social menace. The rules were often broken in the heat of local rivalries and ancient family feuds, and at certain tournaments held in the reign of Henry III the English combatants were determined to humble the pride of the French courtiers who came over to England on the King's marriage to Eleanor of Provence.

Even when the joust was no longer fought *à outrance*, to the utmost, it was impossible to prevent the infringements that occurred in the passion of the moment. A knight suddenly and unceremoniously unhorsed would be provoked into vigorous retaliation, and observers wrote of some very bitter hand-to-hand struggles in the later stages of the combat. With victory offering substantial rewards in prizes and prestige, devotion to the code of chivalry did not exclude some forms of 'gamesmanship', and certain knights had a reputation for breaking the spirit of the law. Froissart tells of a tilt between a French and an English knight in which the Frenchman angered the partisan spectators by lacing his helmet so loosely that 'it was held by one thong only'. This meant that it fell off when struck, so that the adversary was unable to break his lance upon it; and the Englishman's supporters complained that 'he does not fight fair . . . Tell him to put himself upon an equal footing as his opponent.'

In the vocabulary of the tournament 'the lists' meant the area in which the contest took place, surrounded by galleries for the onlookers. For the famous *pas d'armes* at the Field of Cloth of Gold in 1520 the area was 900 feet by 320 feet, but it might often be smaller than this. The fighting could take several forms. The crudest was the mellay, medley or *mêlée*, like the contest between Palamon and Arcite, in which large bodies of knights fought a free-for-all. By 1400 this was being superseded by the safer and more sophisticated 'tilt', in which two combatants rode at each other from opposite sides, separated by a wooden barrier. The barrier reduced the risk to both horse and rider, and to kill or wound a horse was a disgrace subject to severe penalties: the beast might be more precious than the man. The purpose of the tilt was to break one's lance on the opponent, and this required the striking of a firm, full blow that was not very easily achieved when it had to be aimed at an angle on a man riding past in the opposite direction. Lesser marks could be scored by 'attaints' – blows hitting the opponent's head or body without splintering the lance. The tilt might be followed by 'running at large' in the lists by knights armed with spears. Other forms of jousting included tourneying with the sword, again on horseback, and fighting on foot at the barrier. In the 'carousel' companies of knights, some mounted and some in chariots, disported themselves in races and manly exercises whose purpose was spectacular rather than combative.

The tournament acquired its own rules and rituals, and a code of 1466, attributed to John Tiptoft, Earl of Worcester, attempted to regulate tilting by official 'laws of the game'. The ritual stimulated, although it did not create, the science of heraldry, which occupies itself with armorial bearings and the right to display them. 'Poursuivants' are apprentice heralds learning their way through the thicket. At the joust each combatant was too heavily disguised in his armour to be personally recognisable, but he and his horse bore blazons, or heraldic devices, that revealed

59. Beauchamp unseating the Red Knight at the tilt. The word tilt is from 'toile', the stretch of cloth which at the beginning of the 14th century was introduced to separate the two opposing knights. In the mid-15th century it was replaced by wooden boards.

The Combate in SMITHFEILD betwixt the same IOHN DE ASTLEY and Sʳ PHILIP BOYLE, 30 Ian: An: 1441,

60. *Joust at Smithfield before Henry VI, 1441, in which John Astley, an English esquire, killed Sir Philip Boyle, a knight of Aragon. Combatants on foot were allowed a certain number of blows, and the one who stood up longest was the winner.*

him to the initiate, and it was the duty of the heralds to announce his identity as he rode into the lists. At the tilt each knight was accompanied by a 'squire of honour', and it was laid down, at some loss of prompt medical attention, that when a knight fell from his horse, only his squire should go to his assistance. Also important in the ritual was the fiction of the champion who, with fellow-knights of his choice, was the defender of the queen or great lady presiding over the ceremony, or maybe of a castle or a tree or a fairy bower or whatever ingenuity the promoters had devised. The champion and his fellows were the '*tenants*', or holders, who issued a challenge to '*venants*', the men who came against them.

Until the fourteenth century the horse favoured for jousting was the 'destrier', or charger, which in size and speed probably corresponded to the cavalry horse of modern times. The heavy Norman stallions, Andalusian chestnuts and mares from Flanders had been adequate for feudal warfare, but the crusades failed largely because European knights were outrun and outmanoeuvred by the swift Arab horsemen. Richard I therefore brought home oriental stallions of the Favell and Lyard stock, running horses 'swifter than dromedaries', and these lighter mounts brought some brisk action to the joust. But reality broke in when the victories of Crécy and Poitiers were won by archers whose clothyard shafts penetrated the knights' chain-armour and made them ridiculously vulnerable in battle. Their response was to clothe themselves from head to toe in plate-armour and thus to require horses large enough to carry the enormous weight. It has been estimated that by 1500 a mailed knight, with his saddle, weapons and bards, weighed 32 stone, or a fifth of a ton. His mount was the ancestor of the heavy horse (possibly the

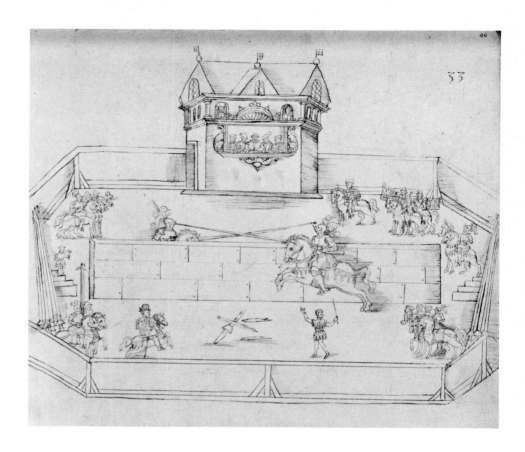

61. Drawing from a late 16th-century manuscript in which are recorded the important 15th-century jousting ordinances of John Tiptoft, Earl of Worcester. One of his rules was that 'whoso striketh a horse shall have no prize.'

Percheron) later used only for agricultural purposes, and a joust conducted by this combination of cumbrous man, half-blind and almost totally deaf, riding a cumbrous beast, provided poor sport for the spectators. Many 'courses' might be run at the tilt without a positive blow being struck. But as we shall see, by the time of Henry VIII the original military and sporting objects of the tournament had given way to a rich and formalised entertainment that was artistic rather than athletic.

The cost of the mediaeval tournament was enormous, and often disproportionate to the resources of the kings and nobles who promoted it. In the royal Household the work and expenses were shared among several departments. The stables, under the Keeper of the Horse, were responsible for mounting the King and his family, squires and attendants, together with their saddles, harness and sumptuous trappings. The armourer provided the armour and the weapons, and the sergeant of the tents furnished the spectators' galleries, the housings, pavilions and scenic 'properties' needed to give the entertainment its fictional setting. In time this work was shared with the special 'revels' department set up in the chamber to supervise the plays, dancing and other amusements of the court. With heralds, musicians, trumpeters and pages also to be supplied with the lavish clothing appropriate to the occasion, and cooks and serving-men to provide the banquets which always followed in the evening, it may seem that the staging of a tournament was a gross extravagance in time and money.

But a man's mightiness was judged by the estate that he was able to maintain, and kings and nobles could not afford to dispense with the outward symbols of magnificence. The need for economy had to be balanced against the ostentation that was a sign of a man's wealth – or at least of his credit rating – and therefore of his political strength. Tradesmen might have to wait for their money, and foreign bankers might be called upon for loans, but a king had to make his subjects conscious of the difference between himself and them. We can see some equivalent when contemporary ministers of the Crown are chauffeur-driven in expensive cars to meetings at which they discuss equality of sacrifice. Authority must hedge itself with splendour. Thus the Wardrobe accounts are full of requisitions for clothes and jewels and finery. Edward II, for instance, ordered his treasurer to assign to William Cassonces, clerk of the Wardrobe, £115 for the purchase of 'sixteen pieces of cloth for the apparel of ourselves and our dear companion, also furs, against the next feast of Christmas', together with thirteen pieces of cloth for corsets for the queen and her ladies, 'with napery and other things of which we stand in need'. Henry V paid 12d. a day to the eighteen minstrels who accompanied him to France in 1415, and Richard III marked his usurpation in 1483 with a lavish order for doublets of purple and tawny satin, gowns of cloth of gold and velvet, stomachers, cloaks, spurs of gilt, banners, 'three coats of arms beaten with fine gold for our own person; five coats of armour for heralds, lined with buckram; forty trumpet banners of sarsanet, etc.'

Kings were forced to this extravagance by the magnificent establishments maintained by their nobility. In 1315 the household expenses of the powerful Earl of Lancaster amounted to £7957 13s. 4½d., of which £3405 was spent on the pantry, buttery and kitchen. 'Expenses in the earl's great horses and the keeper's wages' were £486 4s. 3¼d., and there was an item of £8 6s. 8d. 'for horses lost in service of the earl.' Clothing for the knights, officers, squires, grooms, archers, clerks, minstrels and carpenters cost £1079 18s. 3d. All this was for an ordinary peaceful year without any special expenses like a family wedding or betrothal. Faced with expenditure on this scale, the King had always to try to outdo it. It is a simple fact of mediaeval politics that the royal Household must not appear to be shabby, mean or frugal, especially when his own citizenry might put the monarch to shame. John Stow's *Survey of London*, written in Tudor times, describes some of the shows promoted by the wealthy guildsmen of London. At the coronation of Henry III's Queen in 1236 the citizens rode to meet her 'clothed in long garments embroidered about with gold, and silks of divers colours, their horses gallantly trapped to the number of 360, every man bearing a cup of gold or silver in his hand, and the king's trumpeters sounding before them.' To celebrate Edward I's victory over the Scots in 1298, 'every citizen according to their several trade made their several show, but specially the fishmongers, which in a solemn procession passed through the city, having amongst other pageants and shows four sturgeons gilt, carried on four horses; then four salmons of silver on four horses, and after them six and forty armed knights riding on horses, made like luces of the sea, and then one representing Saint Magnus, because it was Saint Magnus' day, with a thousand men.'

Stow tells also of an entertainment devised for the young Richard II at the first Christmas of his reign, when 130 citizens in festive disguise rode through the city with minstrels and torches: first 48 esquires, then 48 knights in gay colours, and 'then followed one richly arrayed like an Emperor, and after him some distance one stately attired like a Pope, whom followed 24 cardinals, and after them 8 or 10 with black visors, not amiable, as if they had been legates from some foreign princes.' But the solemn youth to whom all this was offered needed no instruction in the importance of display.

62 (opposite). Engraving of the effigy of Richard Beauchamp who died in 1439. It is said to be the finest example in England of an armed warrior of the period. His splendid tomb, gilded and richly decorated, is in the church of St Mary's, Warwick.

63 (overleaf). Knights and ladies riding to a tournament at Smithfield, from Froissart's Chronicles. For many centuries Smithfield was London's horsemarket, as well as being a centre for tournaments and racing.

1 Feet

RICHARD BEAUCHAMP, EARL OF WARWICK, Died 1439.

from his Monument in the Lady's Chapel St. Mary's Church, Warwick.

CHAPTER SEVEN

Agincourt

'Now thrive the armourers', and many other tradesmen too: when Henry V (1413–22) revived the traditional claim to the throne of France, the whole of England was drawn into his preparations. It happens that the campaign of Agincourt is better documented than any other foray of its kind. Although the archers won it, it was primarily a cavalry engagement, as all mediaeval battles were, for the simple reason that the upper classes fought on horseback. Thus the Master of the Horse had an important function in mounting and equipping the monarch and his household servants. But the campaign has a wider interest in showing the organisation needed when a mediaeval kingdom went to war.

Henry demanded the restoration of all the territories lost since Edward III's triumphant Treaty of Bretigny, and he claimed the crown by descent from Isabella, the adulterous Queen of Edward II. He picked his occasion well, because France was torn by the vicious rivalry of the families of Orleans and Burgundy, and Charles VI, the King, was prematurely senile and had fits of insanity in which he supposed himself to be made of glass and went in fear of breakage. The diplomatic parleying that preceded the war has a modern ring of total insincerity, Henry protesting that he was making war only for the sake of peace and the absolution of his conscience. He bade Charles 'think of eternity' if England's outrageous demands were not accepted.

Until they dragged on long enough to interfere with trade and impose an intolerable burden of taxation, mediaeval wars were not unpopular. The nobility and the knights, and even the common soldiers, stood to make considerable sums from ransoms and plunder if the war went well; and even those not personally engaged might benefit from the spending money thus obtained, as well as from the profits they earned from equipping the campaign. Thus parliament made a grant, albeit a meagre one, and the clergy a much larger one, possibly to avert the confiscation of their lands and revenue that would have followed if they had not. But Henry's invasion was principally financed by borrowing on the security of future taxation and the expected profits of victory. Cardinal Beaufort, the canny Bishop of Winchester, was sufficiently hopeful of the outcome to invest in a loan of £35,000 out of a total of £110,000 which Henry borrowed from his subjects for the Agincourt venture. The bishops altogether contributed £44,243, and the City of London over £32,000. Because of the immediate success of the campaign, most of these loans were repaid, but at his death Henry was heavily in debt.

The troops were raised largely by indenture – wealthy nobles contracting to put into the field an agreed number of archers and men-at-arms, to be paid from the Exchequer when the King could afford it. The Duke of Clarence, the King's brother, contracted to provide 240 men-at-arms and 720 mounted archers, and lesser nobles made proportionate contributions. Each of these private contingents

64. The Battle of Agincourt, showing the death of the Constable of France (lying in foreground). The French standard and his horse, trapped in the same colours, lie beside him. Four Masters of the Horse are thought to have been present at the battle: John Waterton (Master at the time), Sir Henry Noon, Sir John Styward and John Beauchamp of Powyck.

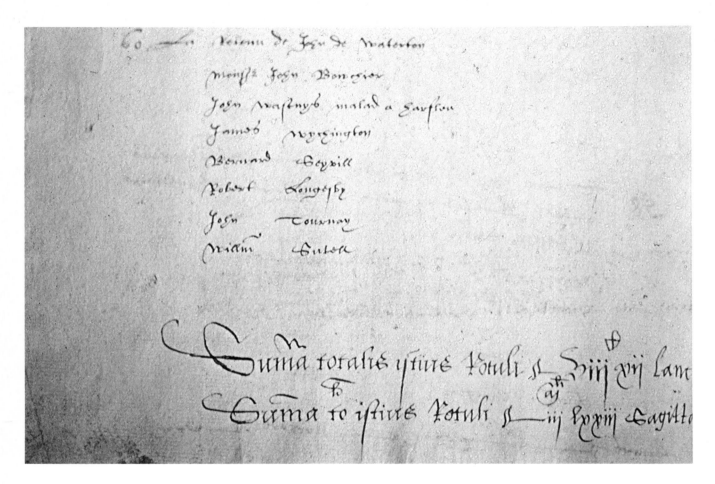

65. *The retinue which John de Waterton took to Agincourt, from a manuscript in the College of Arms. His men-at-arms were John Wastnys, who was taken ill at Harfleur, John Bowchier, James Wychington, Bernard Seyvill, Robert Longesby, John Tournay and William Sutell.*

had its complement of horses, a duke being allowed 50 for his own use, an earl 24 and a knight 6; and also a proportionate number of specialist troops, grooms and tradesmen, together with tents, arms and equipment and baggage animals for their transport. Since the Crown would ultimately have to pay for all this, it was important to ensure that the nobleman fulfilled the terms of the contract. Henry did not even trust his own brother, and among many similar commissions issued at the time we find one to 'Richard Redman and the king's clerk John Strange to supervise the muster of the men-at-arms, armed men and archers going with the king in his present voyage beyond the seas in the company of the king's brother Thomas Duke of Clarence, and to certify thereon to the king in person.'

Mediaeval figures are seldom reliable, but it is estimated that some 10,000 fighting men assembled at Southampton, along with the smiths, grooms, cooks, pages, surgeons, chaplains and other tradesmen needed for their material and spiritual support. Their horses numbered about 25,000, and their sea transport, which had to be provided by the King, consisted of about 1500 craft of assorted types and tonnage, some hired, some supplied by the Cinque Ports in fulfilment of their charter obligations, many appropriated from their owners without compensation. Three ships were damaged by fire in the Solent, and as there had never been enough shipping to carry all the armour and equipment, some of it had to be left behind.

In addition to his knights and archers Henry travelled with a personal retinue of

66. *Retinue of John Styward,
Esquire for the Body (three men-
at-arms): Edmund Hardys,
William Manston, Thomas Baker.*

926 men (Harleian MS. 782), including John Waterton, who as Master of the Horse was responsible for their horses, baggage and equipment. For the discharge of these duties Waterton was accompanied by 60 grooms; John Othvin, yeoman, surveyor of the stable; Nichol Harewood, clerk of the stable; Ranulph Appleton, clerk of the king's avenery (the officer in charge of provender for the horses); a garnetor (or granator, who supplied and issued grain, straw and oats) and 11 yeoman purveyors; Gerard de la Strade, groom of the horses; and 12 smiths and nine saddlers. The retinue also included miners, gunners, armourers, three heralds, the sergeant of the tents and pavilions with a staff of 27, a physician and 20 surgeons, 86 yeomen of the household, 120 ordinary labourers, carpenters, clerks, chaplains, wheelwrights, 15 minstrels and, not least, the commissariat – yeomen of the poultry, the bakery, the pantry, the buttery, the spicery, the napery and the scullery.

By the time it was brought to battle in the cornfields by the village of Maisoncelles, the English army had been depleted by losses at the siege of Harfleur and the casualties suffered during a long march in rainy autumn weather. In his *Ballad of Agincourt* Michael Drayton said that the English were outnumbered by ten to one, and Shakespeare's Earl of Westmorland (who in fact had been left at home to guard the Scottish border) puts the French numbers at 'full three-score thousand.' The actual odds were about five to one, 30,000 against 6000. But Shakespeare did not invent the 'little touch of Harry in the night'. On the eve of battle Henry rode along the lines to encourage his men and share their prayers. He

was mounted on a small grey horse, and pages followed him leading his other horses, among them a magnificent snow-white charger. In his battle dispositions Henry commanded the centre. On his right was the Duke of York, formerly Earl of Rutland and Duke of Albemarle (Aumerle), who according to some accounts betrayed the rising in which the younger Bernard Brocas lost his life in 1400; and on the left Lord Camoys, a veteran soldier who had married the Lady Elizabeth Percy, Hotspur's widow. In three hours' fighting the French were routed, losing some 7000 killed and 1500 prisoners, including Jean Boucicault, Marshal of France, and the Dukes of Bourbon and Orleans. There would have been more prisoners to swell the ransom money if Henry had not for tactical reasons ordered them to be killed. His force was so heavily outnumbered that he could not spare the men to guard them if the French should rally. The English losses, which Shakespeare, following the Tudor chronicle, puts at 30, were probably not more than 500. John Waterton's accounts for 1415 show a reduction in the number of the King's horses of 135 (from 233 to 98) and we can assume that most of these – which included names such as Lyard Strickland, Bayard Chaucer, Morell Kene, Sorell Tavistock and Grey Cornwell – were lost during the Agincourt campaign.

A ransomed prisoner remained in honourable captivity until his family and tenants got together the sum demanded for his release. Bourbon and Boucicault never were ransomed and they died in England. Charles of Orleans, who had married the young Queen Isabelle, Richard II's widow, was put in the custody of the invaluable Robert Waterton at Pontefract. Fearing he might escape, Henry thought it unsafe for him to leave the castle to hunt at Methley and ordered Waterton to forbid it. 'I will that the Duke of Orleans be kept within the castle at Pontefract without going to Robert's place or to any other disport; for it is better that he lack his disport than we be deceived.' (Cottonian MS. Vesp. fiii.) Orleans,

68 and 69. Where it was impracticable to use carriages, the nobility rode in litters drawn by two horses between shafts, as in this illustration from a 15th-century manuscript. The Master of the Horse's department may have provided Queen Katherine with a similar vehicle and escort for her journey to Vincennes in 1422.

67 (opposite). Another version of the battle, drawn about 1440. It is more accurate than the picture on page 86, as the soldiers are wearing brigandines and bassinet helmets rather than the later plate armour and sallets. Henry V can be seen by the English standard.

70. Arms of Sir Henry Noon: or, a cross engrailed azure. In Henry V's retinue at Agincourt he was listed as Henry Noon, Esquire.

obliged to console himself with writing graceful verse, was not released until 1440.

Henry had not the strength to follow up his victory by marching on Paris and he returned home to raise another army. Normandy took two years to conquer, and at the Treaty of Troyes (1420) he was recognised as regent and heir to the French throne. He married the King's daughter Katharine, who came to England to be crowned and to make a progress through the loyal Lancastrian north. Their son Henry was born at Windsor in December 1421, and a few weeks later a commission was issued to 'William Parker to take men and horses and other things for the office of the stable of the King's household for the present voyage of the King's consort, Katharine, Queen of England, to France'. But their reunion was brief because Henry's health broke down under the strain of harsh campaigning and in August he died at Vincennes of an enteric disorder, leaving his infant son the impossible task of holding what he had won.

The English possessions in France were too large and too widely scattered to be retained without the intensive garrisoning which no mediaeval country could afford. Inspired by Joan of Arc – the Witch of Domrémy – the French gradually pushed the invaders out, and when Guienne was lost at the battle of Châtillon in 1453, only Calais remained.

John Waterton ceased to be Master soon after Agincourt and he was followed by Sir Henry Noon, whose family lived at Shelfanger, near Diss, in Norfolk. He had been water-bailiff of Wiggonhall and gauger (exciseman) of Lynn, and he probably developed a concession granted to his late father to enclose 310 acres for a park on the family estates. In the tradition of loyal 'King's Knights' he received other grants of land, including a third portion of the manor of Chipping Norton. Noon had fought valiantly at Agincourt and for other exploits at Henry's side he was given the castle, lands and lordship of Condé-sur-Noireau in Normandy. Since he is mentioned in 1421 as a King's Knight going to France in the royal service, it is possible that he died abroad as his will was tested at the prerogative court of Canterbury in the following year. His military career suggests that his duties as Master were mostly performed overseas.

Meanwhile Redman and the Watertons were as zealous as ever in government service during a period when the country was still in arms. In 1419 there were fears of a diversionary raid by the King of Castile and Leon, and Redman was among those commissioned to make an array for defence against him on the ground that he had 'prepared a great armada of ships and vessels of Spain . . . and proposes to invade the king's realm.' For the Normandy invasion of 1417 John Waterton was commanded to supervise the muster at Southampton of certain knights and archers raised by the Earl of Salisbury to proceed to Harfleur, and 'to certify thereon to the king and council'. Robert Waterton's name appears on several commissions for the defence of the realm during the King's absence abroad, and in 1421 he had the delicate task of raising loans when the King 'was unable to pay the wages of soldiers going to France with him'. He was further required to guard the prizes of war, a responsibility with which he should by now have been familiar. In 1422 a commission was issued to William Troutbeck to collect eight French prisoners from the Tower and 'take them to the castle of Flint with all possible speed and take horses and carts for their carriage and fencible men for their safe conduct . . . and the like to Robert Waterton to take six to Pomfret', which had evidently established itself as a gaol for high-class prisoners.

The Patent Rolls for the same year also have interesting examples of the work of the stables functioning through deputies. This was a commission to 'John Long to go to any parts of England and treat with the king's lieges who have any destriers,

71 (on left). Letter from
Henry V concerning the Duke of
Orleans, taken prisoner at
Agincourt. 'Wherefore I wolle that
the Duc of Orliance be kept stille
within the castel of Pontfret with
owte goyng to Robertis
[Waterton's] place or any other
disport, for it is bettre he lak his
disport than we were deceyved.'

72. Pontefract Castle, Yorkshire,
which under the Lancastrians was
one of the most powerful fortresses
in England, and the centre of
activity for Richard Redman and
Robert Waterton. Richard II was
murdered there in 1399. It was
dismantled in 1649, after being held
by the Royalists during the Civil
War.

coursers and other horses for the king's stud, and cause them to come with their
horses before the Master of the King's Horses and agree with him on a price for the
horses for the king's use, and receive the price from him if they can agree, or else
their horses back again with reasonable prices'; also to 'Robert Merefyn to take men
and horses and other things for the office of the stable of the household. The like to
David Gower.' These show, incidentally, the King's desperate and continuing need
for horses for his war. But as Sir Henry Noon was abroad at the time, it is unlikely
that he ever inspected for valuation the horses that Long, Merefyn and Gower
found for him. In the turmoil of the fifteenth century the Masters would have to rely
increasingly on their permanent staff for the routine activity of the stables.

CHAPTER EIGHT

The Fifteenth Century

The loss of France was followed by the Wars of the Roses (1455–71), but these emblematic wars were only a concentrated and particularly bloody phase in a century of civil disturbance that lasted from the Percys' rebellion in 1403 until Henry VII's defeat of Perkin Warbeck in 1497. Henry V promoted a brief diversion when he took his father's advice to 'busy giddy minds with foreign quarrels', but his French escapade only aggravated the bankruptcy that was the persistent cause of the weakness of the Crown. It was impossible to maintain a system of Household government through the Wardrobe when bills and loans went unpaid for years and were even dishonoured when presented to the Exchequer. This financial embarrassment enabled the barons to make inroads upon a system they had always detested.

The withdrawal from France brought home a bunch of para-military bandits who had prospered by ignoring the chivalric code of mediaeval war. Their lawless roaming in search of rape and plunder stiffened the French resolve to be rid of the English hooligans and on their return they attached themselves to the baronial households. If their influence on the English civil wars has been exaggerated – they were not significantly numerous and their numbers naturally diminished – this has been due to some misunderstanding of the term 'livery and maintenance'. A liveried man wore his master's badge, but his 'livery' meant only his upkeep as a member of the household; and 'maintenance', which strictly meant the exercise of improper influence in litigation, was not far removed from the pardons, discharges, exemptions and protection granted to royal agents against civil processes or financial loss incurred in their master's service. It became an abuse only when it turned into armed intimidation of sheriffs and juries, and this was a consequence of Lancastrian 'lack of governance'.

Much depended on the character of the monarch, and Henry VI (1422–71) was not the right man for a turbulent age. He never had much in his favour. He came to two thrones when still a cradled infant and for fifteen years his affairs were directed by ambitious and contentious regents who wished to pursue the French war, or else to abandon it, with a primary concern for their own interests. His royal mother, the dowager Queen Katharine, was bedded by, and may have married, Owen Tudor, a clerk of her household. This association founded the Franco–Welsh dynasty that was seminal of England's greatness, but Henry was not to know this. Its present happening violated a rigorous social code which expected ex-queens not to co-habit with wardrobe clerks from an inferior and subjugated race.

But Henry was also unfortunate in his own person. Bookish and pious, he preferred monks to politicians, and his educational foundations at Eton and King's have proved more enduring testimonials than his father's glamorous performance at Agincourt. An enforced marriage did nothing for his happiness or his stability. It

73. Hunting the fallow buck, from a 15th-century manuscript. This was the kind of 'disport' that the Duke of Orleans and Waterton would have enjoyed.

was arranged for him in 1445 when the peace party were dominant at court and looking for a French alliance, and the bride was the 16-year-old Margaret of Anjou. She was beautiful, intelligent and high-spirited, and when she tired of her faltering husband, she threw the residue of her unused vigour into defending the crown which Henry seemed to be throwing away. But instead of trying to balance the factions, she threw all her weight into one scale, and the ferocity of this 'she-wolf of France' brought bitter personal hatreds into the struggle. Henry reacted by falling into a torpor which contemporary medicine diagnosed as insanity, and possibly he was to some degree schizophrenic. In normal health he was by no means apathetic, and he was proud of his smart blue hunting-coat, but he had periods of withdrawal which disabled him from ordinary communication, let alone leadership. Even at the sight of his first-born son he sat in an indifferent trance, displaying none of the

74. Leeds Castle, Kent. In 1423
Queen Katherine (de Valois)
received it as part of her dower, and
it was here that she fell in love with
Owen Tudor. On her death in 1437
it was granted 'at farm' to Sir John
Styward. Another Master, Sir
Henry Guildford, was its constable
in the 16th century.

age-long pride of fathers who have done so little of the work. He was deposed after the Lancastrian rout at Towton in 1461, and briefly restored in 1470-1. But soon his body was on exhibition to the citizens of London, another victim of the sudden illnesses that overtook imprisoned kings.

In this disorderly period of fluctuating loyalties there are fewer specific references to the Master of the Horse. First there was a long minority, Henry not being allowed the full exercise of his authority until 1437. Always in retreat from his debts, he moved frequently from one residence to another, carrying his Household from London to Kennington or Eltham or Sheen. In these circumstances warrants and documents might be signed or witnessed by officers who did not necessarily hold the offices for which they spoke, and it is therefore easy to attribute too much influence to the regular members of the King's itinerant Court.

Henry seems to have had four Masters, three of them Beauchamps, but the first is doubtful. This is Richard Beauchamp, Earl of Warwick (1382–1439), the Warwick of Shaw's *Saint Joan*. The Beauchamps were an old family who claimed descent from the legendary Guy of Warwick, slayer of the dun cow of Dunsmore, the winged dragon of Northumberland and the Danish giant Colbrand. By right of the manor of Kibworth Beauchamp they held the hereditary office of keeper of the king's pantry, and at the coronation of Henry III's Queen Eleanor in 1236 Walter de Beauchamp received the knives and salt-cellar as a fee for his service. They had acquired their earldom in 1268, and Richard Beauchamp was a very grand mediaeval person, excelling alike in deeds of chivalry and the grimmer realities of war and diplomacy. Succeeding his father in 1401, he was confirmed in his possessions after doing homage to Henry IV and in 1403 he was retained to serve the King with 100 men-at-arms and 300 archers, leading them against the Percys at the battle of Shrewsbury. Later he made a pilgrimage to the Holy Sepulchre, a leisurely two-year journey graced by jousting and other ceremonious deeds, and in the next reign he was an important figure in Henry V's designs on France.

In 1414 he was Captain of Calais, and the indenture indicates the cost of maintaining this sort of military establishment. Warwick was to provide in peacetime, 'for the safeguard thereof', 30 men-at-arms and three knights, 30 mounted archers, 200 foot soldiers and 200 other archers, 'all of his retinue'. For this he was to receive for himself 6s. 8d. a day, for his knights 2s. each, for the rest of his horse 1s.; for every mounted archer and foot soldier 8d., and for every archer on foot 6d. The garrison was also to contain at the King's personal charge 40 crossbowmen, 20 carpenters and five masons, 'besides bowyers, with other officers and pensioners'. But in the event of war, Warwick's provision was to rise to 140 men on horseback, 60 knights, 150 mounted archers and 184 others, and 100 foot soldiers. He was seconded, perhaps surprisingly as Henry's negotiations with the French king were already in progress, to attend with certain bishops at the Council of Constance, called to discuss much-needed reforms in the Church, and during his stay he slew 'a great duke' who challenged him at the joust.

After attending the King at the siege of Harfleur, he was sent home in charge of prisoners and other booty, so that he was not at Agincourt. But he was prominent in the Normandy campaign, sharing the command with Henry and the Duke of Clarence and receiving the capitulation of Caen and Rouen. He helped to arrange the peace treaty and the King's marriage to the Princess Katharine, and Henry in his last dispositions bequeathed to him the care and education of his infant son. This was later confirmed by the council, who also acquiesced in his demand for special authority to chastise his pupil when necessary and to remove from his presence any associate whose influence might not improve him. The responsibility, seemingly disciplinary rather than academic, may have kept Warwick in England during the early years of the King's minority, but he was too good a soldier to have been unmoved by the evident deterioration in France even before Joan of Arc made her over-publicised debut. In 1426 commissioners were appointed to 'take at Dover the muster of the 100 men-at-arms and 300 archers, retainers of Richard Earl of Warwick, who are about to proceed to France, and to certify the council of the sufficiency of their array, both as armaments and horses.' The provisioning of the armies in France was also within his concern. In 1430, compensation – although no more generous than exemption from the next instalment of taxes – was granted to 'merchants who lost their goods at sea' when a Calais-based ship owned by Warwick was 'driven by enemies over the sea in sight of Dover Castle', and broken and battered on the rocks with total loss of cargo and crew. Warwick was personally in Normandy in 1431, when he captured near Beauvais a notable prisoner, Poton de Xaintrailles, and in 1437 he was made Lieutenant of France and Normandy: the sort of last-ditch appointment given to men of approved valour and service by politicians who sense the crunch of breaking ice. He set sail from Portsmouth for the last time, and there was a sort of grandeur and pathos in this final voyage. 'Discerning great danger by a coming tempest', he caused his wife, his son and himself to be bound to the mainmast of the ship, 'to the intent that if they perished and were after found, yet by his coat-of-arms, discovering who he was, they might have been buried together.' This coat-of-arms was painted by 'a peculiar officer-at-arms called Warwick Herald who had a grant from him'.

The ship came safely to port, but Warwick died at Rouen less than two years later, his end hastened, it was said, by the humiliations he saw around him. His career is worth this brief notice as it illustrates the splendid variousness of mediaeval man. But was he ever Master of the Horse? The record kept at the Royal Mews says that he was, and there is no proof that he was not. He was much too eminent a personage to have been expected to bother with routine administration and a man who, with war approaching, could have left the captaincy to a lieutenant, Sir William Lisle, while he journeyed to the Council of Constance would not have been disturbed at leaving the stables to be run by experienced deputies. But if he was Master, he was the first peer to be appointed to the office, and there would not be another for more than a hundred years: a significant, and as yet isolated, breach in the sequence of King's Knights. The supposition that he was Master of the Horse may have been derived from a mis-reading of an appointment that followed the

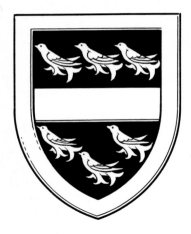

75. Arms of Sir Walter Beauchamp: gules, a fess between six martlets.

death of Henry V. Humphrey of Gloucester, the king's brother, was appointed protector of the realm, and Warwick, by Henry's will, 'master' of the infant King: meaning, of course, his guardian and tutor.

If he ever was Master of the Horse, it was not for long, because there is mention in 1429 of Sir Walter de Beauchamp as the 'late Master'. This man, probably a cousin, studied law and was a knight of the shire for Wiltshire. After serving at Agincourt he was elected Speaker of the Commons in 1416. In 1425 he was engaged by his distinguished relative to argue his claim of precedency against the counterclaim of Sir John Mowbray, the Earl Marshal. The dispute, which occupied several days of parliamentary time, was terminated by the restoration of Mowbray to the forfeited dukedom of Norfolk. It is possible that Warwick rewarded the services of his counsel and kinsman by transferring to him the Mastership of the Horse.

We should be on firmer ground with the next Master, Sir John Styward, who held office approximately from 1430 to 1441, if we could be more certain of identifying his name. It was spelt also Stiward, Stuward and Steward, and it was one of the many surnames gradually adopted from a man's occupation. As almost every gentle household had a steward (Malvolio was one), the name was common, and so was the forename John. It is more than likely that our Master is the John Styward (spelled thus in the list of Masters in the Royal Mews) who as an Esquire for the Body took a retinue of three men-at-arms to Agincourt. His name appears eight years later in the Patent Rolls for 1423, when he received a grant of £40 a year as King's esquire. This may have been his salary for acting as Keeper of the Stables to Katherine the Queen Mother, who had been granted a residence at Baynards Castle in Surrey. Among later appointments he became in 1428 steward of 'all the rents, issues and profits in the town of Framesden and elsewhere in the county of Suffolk', and next year he was captain of 'the king's tower of Rysbank in the parts of Picardy'. In 1435 he was commissioned to take muster of troops raised by Edmund Count of Mortmain, and to survey the soldiers left on his death by John Duke of Bedford, Captain of Calais.

These and similar entries may not all refer to the same John Styward, but these were the duties habitually given to men of his type, while the everyday work of the stables was done by men of lesser rank, such as John Talbot, sergeant-at-arms, and John Hexham, clerk, who in 1430 were ordered to commandeer shipping and bring it to Sandwich 'to embark 3600 horses to France'. The number is so large as to be unrealistic, just a bureaucratic figure in the books, but similar issues continued throughout the 1430s in the hope of turning the tide in France. Domestic requirements also had to be attended to, and in 1442, the King's Sergeant, Wake, is commissioned to 'buy horses for the King's saddle, car and carriage, palfreys, coursers, *carrehors*, *chariot hors*, *somers*, and *hakeneys* for reasonable payment'. Two years later he is ordered to 'take horses to conduct the King's Consort' and in the same year the Patent Rolls also show a commission 'to Richard Lokwode, King's saddler, to take workmen for the King's wages'.

We are familiar, too, with Masters of the Horse and similar officials who are entrusted with the care of political prisoners. Stiward was constable of Leeds Castle in Kent, where for a while he lodged Lady Eleanor Cobham, wife of Humphrey of Gloucester, during the trial of her associates on charges of necromancy and treason. She was herself accused of seeking the King's death by the traditional method of sticking pins into his wax image, and when she was to be brought to London for her examination Stiward was directed to 'provide wheat and other grain for the staff of the castle, and carriage for the same, and horses and other carriages by land and

76 (opposite). Windsor Castle in 1450, from a manuscript at Eton College. In the foreground is the old church which pre-dated the college chapel. Inside are Eton's founder, Henry VI, and his Queen.

Est Anglia l[z] in comitat[?] [?]dibn[?] [?] north
folch[?] south folch[?] grantebg[?] [?] dunani[?]
bedford[?] Et duos Epat[?] no[?]Wicen sem
[?] Elien[?]

Epscus l[z] epm london[?] comitat[?] hertfo[?]

water, to convey to London those persons who are in the castle by the king's command, and thence back to the castle.' The Duchess was sentenced to life imprisonment, first at Chester and later at Kenilworth.

Sir John Beauchamp of Powyck, a son or a nephew of Sir Walter, became Master in about 1442. The office was granted to him for life in 1450, and he probably kept it until Henry's first deposition in 1461. His frequent witnessing of documents proves him to have been already a regular member of the King's itinerant court. On the extinction of the direct Warwick line in 1446 Beauchamp put in a bid for the reversion. 'A voice and a language was had and moved in divers parties among people' that he should be the new earl, but a commission of peers disallowed his claim in favour of Anne Beauchamp, the late earl's daughter. By her marriage the title passed to Richard Neville, famous as 'Warwick the King-maker'. In compensation Beauchamp was given a barony, becoming in 1447 Lord Beauchamp of Powyck 'for his good service to Henry V and the king'. His life appointment as Master of the Horse was unusual in an office that depended so much on the royal pleasure.

Beauchamp's tenure coincided with an attempt to reduce the expenditure of the Royal Household, and so he found it an uphill struggle to supply the horses which the King needed with the approach of civil war. As one of many hopeful attempts he is found in 1448 issuing a commission to William Gervys 'to purvey as many horses as shall be necessary for the king's saddle and for the king's coach and other carriages, by due valuation between him and four good men of any town where such horses shall be, for reasonable payment to be made by the Master of the King's horses.' There is a hint of scraping the barrel here, and more frequently Beauchamp was being importuned for arrears. Thus in the same year a licence was granted to three merchants to take for themselves £120 from the customs due on a forthcoming shipment of wool; this being on the petition of John Spering, one of the merchants, 'shewing that on the coming of the queen to England [which was in 1445] he was commanded by Lord Beauchamp of Powyk, Master of the King's Horses, to go to divers parts overseas and purvey horses for the king, and prompt payment therefor was promised to him on return; which horses he purveyed.'

It was the practice of the stables department to submit periodic summaries of their accounts to the Treasurer of the Household before they were filed by the Exchequer. This casual record of receipts and of horses, saddles etc., either purchased or acquired by other means, would not satisfy the conditions of a modern audit. So far as it is trustworthy, Beauchamp's summary for the years 1449–58 shows how very little he was able to spend. Receipts for part of the period ending in 1456 were £44 8s. 8d., while purchases for the King over the full decade were given as £20 for a palfrey, Lyard Roos, bought from Lord Roos; £4 13s. 4d. for a bay from John Skelton; 16s. 8d. for a trotter from John Foster; 40s. for a grey trotter, Lyard Canterbury, from Richard Canterbury; £4 6s. 8d. for a sumpter from Richard Miller; £4 for a sumpter from William Norton, a member of the Household; and £6 13s. 4d. for a morello from the Abbot of Darley.

Fortunately the Master was able to record the receipt of a much larger number of horses as gifts: 14 palfreys, 15 trotters, 8 sumpters and 4 hackneys received from a French count; 26 palfreys and 4 trotters from the Canon of Wells; and 'diverse gifts' from the Abbots of Malmesbury and Jervaulx. Money was paid also for saddles, harness and other trappings, but the expenditure is startlingly low for a ten-year period and it suggests a meagre response to the numerous commissions issued for the purchase of horses. Beauchamp, incidentally, had troubles of his own at this time. When a meeting of the Order of the Garter was held at Windsor, his absence

77 *Lady in a carriage, from a late 15th-century manuscript. It shows Flemish horses, which were imported into England for the royal studs from the Middle Ages onwards.*

was excused 'because he was so much out of order in his feet that he could neither walk nor ride'. When Edward IV was on the throne he regularly sent excuses for not attending, possibly because age and infirmity were spreading from his feet to other parts.

Economies in household expenditure, with consequent effect upon the organisation of the stables, were made necessary by the Lancastrians' perennial shortage of money. Henry V, dying in the middle of an uncompleted campaign, left debts of £30,000, and his son, saddled with a regency and an unsuccessful war, was never solvent. In 1433, even before he came of age, a debt of £168,000 was more than three times the normal revenue, and the Household itself was costing £13,000 a year against an income of only £5000. The estimated annual deficit was some £30,000, and the interest charged on loans would make its reduction very difficult. There were frequent petitions for the payment of arrears in salaries and payments to tradesmen, mostly on the unreal assumption that 'good and sad rule' in the Household would bring about the necessary economies.

Thus the Household ordinance of 1445, following upon a parliamentary commission, aimed to reduce expenditure by restricting the allowances made at Court and the number of persons entitled to receive them. The chief target was 'bouche of court', the entitlement in food, fuel and lighting granted to officers and servants of the Household. The Master's department was crucial in this, since the avenor, now in effect the clerk of the stables, had record of the people present at any time. An itinerant Household was recognised to need ready facilities for transport, and the stable had provision for 60 horses for the King and his immediate entourage, including 6 for the chariot and 18 for the sumpters who carried the tents and heavy baggage. The Master himself had only two horses, which raised him no higher than the avenor, the farrier or the clerk of the carriages. As many as 126 horses were needed for 'the chariots', and the stable had also to maintain mounts for the purveyors and other lower officials; together with 16 sumpters to carry the appurtenances of the butlery, pantry, scullery, counting-house, every and other departments, including the professional and personal equipment deemed necessary for the *asmoigner* or resident chaplain.

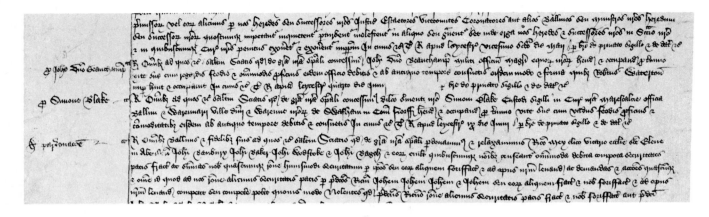

78. Entry from the Patent Rolls of 1450 showing 'Grant for life to John Lord Beauchamp, Knight, of the office of Master of the King's horses, with the usual rewards, fees and profits as Robert Waterton had the same.'

The ordinance of 1445 tried, like others before and since, to exclude all who on various pretexts laid claim to bouche of court to which they were not at that moment entitled. The specific prohibitions indicate the abuses to be prevented. Visitors and non-resident officials were having their horses stalled and fed at the King's expense: so there shall be 'no horse lodged within the king's gates but the king's own, and that sojourn be lodged from the king's court five miles at the least; and that there be no man keep no horse at the king's cost than be appointed, and that none other officer have no horse standing among the king's.' (Harleian MS. 642.) Families and domestic pets were being kept there too, it seems, since 'neither children, dogs nor ferrets' were to be at the Court without express permission, and people were also forbidden to leave their carriages or baggage at Court when not in attendance. Purveyors and yeomen of the stable would 'lose their wages and their horsemeat when they be out of court', unless they should be absent in the King's service 'and that the avenor record it truly in his daily accompt'; and none were to feed daily in the hall 'but such as be appointed'.

These, no doubt, were standard rebukes to standard abuses that quietly returned after a few months of official zeal. By 1449, only four years later, Household expenditure was up to £24,000 a year, the total debt was £372,000, and the King was paying 33 per cent on his borrowings. When in 1453 Henry fell ill and took little interest in what was going on, the great council of peers found it easier to recommend that the household 'be abridged and reduced to a reasonable and competent fellowship, as may worshipfully be found and sustained in the same'. So 'after ripe and sad communication', and discussions with royal officers, the great council nominated the persons to be employed in the Household, with the right of 'eating in the hall', chambers and elsewhere. These resolutions were never operative, as Henry soon recovered his health, but they methodically recite the establishment to be sanctioned for the stables, the chamber, the counting-house, the bakery, the pantry, and so on. Lord Beauchamp of Powyck, as Master of the Horse, was one of the two barons allocated to the Household, and he was allowed one squire and three yeomen as his personal attendants. The stables establishment of 22 comprised the avenor, two clerks, two yeomen purveyors, two footmen, one yeoman 'garnetor', a sergeant farrier and his yeoman, a yeoman of the horse and 11 yeomen and grooms of the stable. Reductions were also made in the number of attendants permitted to the Royal Family: 424 for the King, 120 for the Queen and 38 for the infant prince. Attempts were made to control the abuses of purveyance, and finally the Commons were invited to 'establish an ordinate and a substantial rule' in the Household that should keep it out of future debt.

But economy in royal Households might be obtained at too high a price in prestige and the appurtenances of power. Kings must be more magnificent than their subjects, and the Earl of Warwick was ostentatious 'wherever he stayed or passed the night. And when he came to London, he held such a household that six oxen were eaten at a breakfast, and every tavern was full of his meat; for anybody who had any acquaintance in his household could have as much boiled and roast meat as he could carry on a long dagger.' (Sixty years later the Duke of Buckingham probably signed his own death-warrant, under a different sort of king, when at Epiphany he gave entertainment at Thornbury to 319 guests at dinner and 279 at supper.) In his periods of withdrawal Henry VI cared nothing for his appearance, and even at his short restoration, following years of wandering and detention, he was 'not worshipfully arrayed as a prince, and not so cleanly kept as should seem such a prince'. Edward IV, a handsome extrovert, had much political acumen when he stirred himself to use it, and he achieved a successful compromise between the conflicting demands of economy and magnificence.

At Court the vital economy was to prune the horde of hangers-on, and this is the repeated refrain of all the Household ordinances. With this achieved, through the services of the avenor of the stables in keeping a check on the horses and servants housed there, the King might live in appropriate splendour. Although Edward never succeeded in curbing the appetites of the ravening kinsfolk who came to Court with his beautiful but calculating Woodville Queen, he banished the memory of his predecessor's drab regime. It is said that he thought so little of Henry's educational foundations at Eton and Cambridge that he contemplated destroying them, but in fact he spent generously on both, and he began the rebuilding of St George's Chapel at Windsor. The new device of printing furnished his library with books, he hunted, jousted and feasted, and European visitors were impressed by the polished manners of the English Court. In 1467 Edward staged at Smithfield one of the most spectacular jousts of the century, between Lord Scales, the English champion, and the bastard son of the Duke of Burgundy.

But shrewd as he was, Edward had his problems, with followers to be rewarded, a growing family and predatory in-laws, and it was some years before he was able to achieve a small surplus. His intentions were formulated in the Black Book of the King's Household, which was compiled during the 1470s by a chamber official, probably Sir John Elrington, the cofferer. It was incomplete and its principles were never observed in the precise terms laid down, but it indicates the way in which the King with his lords and his experienced officers thought the Household should be run, an early exercise in the 'organisation and methods' studies adopted in modern businesses. Outwardly the Court was to be splendid, and the book makes nostalgic reference to the glittering court of Edward III, 'the house of very polity and the flower of England', the epitome of what such things ought to be. But a distinction was made between the *Domus Regie Magnificiencie*, the small upstairs department where strangers would be impressed by the gracious living of the King and his lords, and the *Domus Providencie*, the sombre world below stairs where the work was done on minimal allowances. Squires and yeomen were paid no more than they had been in Edward II's Household ordinance in 1318, and the counting-house was to receive daily statements from the offices which fed and provisioned the household. There was to be a careful watch on the number of attendants which noblemen and ministers might bring with them and the 'diets' to which they were entitled. Unfortunately the Black Book details all the indoor offices down to the laundry, and the two loaves and one pitcher of wine that might be claimed if the King chose to cleanse himself on Saturday night, but it says nothing of the stables, the woodyard and the other departments outside. In practice, however, Edward worked on an ordinance of 1478 which largely repeats that of 1445 but is stricter in its control of hangers-on. The annual cost of the Household was reduced to £11,800, compared with the £13,000 estimated in the Black Book, and Edward was the first English king since Henry II to die solvent.

Edward had two Masters of the Horse, Sir Thomas de Burgh, who probably took office soon after Edward came to the throne in 1461, and after 1479 John Cheyne. Edward had immediately to replace the 40 horses from the royal stables killed at Towton, where also the King's chaplain lost his prayer-book. One of the few direct references to de Burgh's role as Master occurs in the Patent Rolls of 1465, when a grant was made to 'Thomas Delamere, esquire, in repayment of £84 in which the king is indebted to him for divers horses, iron saddles and shields for tournaments bought by him for the King's use and delivered to Thomas de Burgh, Knight, master of the horse.' But he must have done his work in the stables satisfactorily because he rose to wealth and influence in the usual manner of favoured household knights. His father acquired by marriage an estate at Gainsborough, and de Burgh sought to dignify the property by enlarging the old manor house into a hall. Loyalty, however grasping its motives, was precious to Edward during the 1460s when Henry VI was still alive, Margaret of Anjou was trying to raise men and money in the cause, and any sudden shift in the baronial alliances might lead to a restoration. De Burgh thus moved upwards by gradual steps, becoming Steward of the Duchy of Lancaster and Constable of Lincoln Castle, receiving the forfeited lands of William Tailboys of Kyme, and representing the county of Lincolnshire in the parliament of 1467–8.

These advances did not please his neighbours, who regarded him as an arrogant Yorkist *parvenu*, and this private feud helped to initiate the insurrection which sent Edward in flight to Flanders and caused Henry's short restoration in 1470–1. In 1470 Richard Lord Welles and Willoughby, whose sympathies were Lancastrian, joined with his son Robert and his brothers-in-law Sir Thomas de la Lande and Sir Thomas Dymoke of Scrivelsby to drive de Burgh out of the county. They made his return more difficult by burning Gainsborough Hall to the ground and carrying off its contents. Edward, on his return to England, took a stern vengeance, summoning Welles and his son to London and promising that their lives would be spared if they emerged from the sanctuary of Westminster Abbey. He then revoked his promise and had them beheaded, and Dymoke, too, was executed.

De Burgh bounced back again, in the manner of his kind, and when in 1475 Edward raised an army for a pretended war with France, Burgh, still Master of the Horse, provided 16 spearmen and 160 archers, a sure sign of his opulence. In 1478 he was promised on the death of the Duchess of Norfolk, the King's long-lived aunt who had been four times married, the stewardship of the castle of Somerton, the lordship of Boston and several other manors in the county. When in the same year Edward disposed of his dangerous brother George of Clarence, reputedly drowned in a butt of malmsey, Burgh was appointed to make an inquisition of his estates in the county 'and to take the same into the king's hands'. Still in 1478, he was granted the temporalities of the bishopric of Ely during a vacancy in the see. Further lordships and stewardships continued to pour in upon him, and the only setback to his aspiration was the reluctance of the Knights of the Garter to admit him to their fellowship, his election being proposed and rejected for several years before he was eventually successful in the following reign. De Burgh's capacity for survival was remarkable in these precarious times because although he supported Richard III and in 1484 received estates in Lincoln, Gloucestershire and Nottinghamshire 'for

79. The great hall of Gainsborough Old Hall, Lincolnshire, rebuilt by Sir Thomas de Burgh in the late 15th century.

80. *Detail from the effigy of Richard Beauchamp, Earl of Warwick.*

81. *Gentlemen in a stable-yard. This exquisitely-painted illumination is from a manuscript executed for Edward IV between 1473 and 1483, when Sir John Cheyne was Master of the Horse.*

82 *(overleaf). Field of Cloth of Gold, 7 June 1520. The painting, at Hampton Court, is a composite view of the happenings which took place at Ardres over a period of seventeen days. The Master of the Horse, Sir Henry Guildford, is riding behind the King, on the left. An earlier Master, Charles Brandon, is on the grey horse to his right.*

his good service against the rebels', he managed to ingratiate himself with Henry VII and in 1487 was summoned to parliament as Lord Burgh of Gainsborough. He died in 1496, doubtless to seek honours in a higher sphere.

If the *Complete Peerage* is to be believed, John Cheyne differed from previous Masters of the Horse in not being a knight at the time of his appointment: he was only knighted after the battle of Bosworth in 1485, when he fought on Henry of Richmond's side. He was the younger son of John Cheyne of the Isle of Sheppey, and he climbed by the usual Household ladder, having been a squire of the body in the 1460s. The reason for his further advancement was the patronage of the Woodvilles, but he was only a squire when in 1479 he and Robert of Oswestry, another King's servant, were granted 'the presentation to the parish church of Myvote, in the diocese of St Asaph, at its next voidance'. Nor was this a very lavish reward for a man who in 1475 had accompanied the King to France and remained there as a hostage. Edward had revived the traditional claim to the French throne, but he had no real intention of fighting, nor of spending all of the grant that parliament had made towards his non-campaign. He was only interested in getting a profitable treaty. Terms to his liking were agreed when he met Louis XI on a wooden bridge thrown over the Somme at Pecquigny, and Cheyne and Lord Howard were left behind as hostages until the English army re-embarked.

In 1478 Cheyne displayed the mettle which possibly led to his appointment as Master of the Horse. A tournament was held to celebrate the wedding of the King's brother Richard of Gloucester to Anne Neville, daughter of Warwick the King-maker. On a horse arrayed in 'a footcloth of goldsmith's work' he fought a duel with Sir Robert Clifford, a household knight. (Ashmole MS. 856.) They fought on foot and the contest became overheated, but Cheyne showed such chivalrous consideration that the heralds awarded him a special prize for his restraint.

When Edward died in 1483, he left his brother Richard of Gloucester in charge of his family and his kingdom during the minority of the boy King Edward V. This is not the place to enter the controversy about the subsequent events. Within a few weeks Richard announced, with the support of ecclesiastical lawyers supposed to know about such matters, that Edward IV had entered into a pre-contract of marriage before he married Elizabeth Woodville, so that the new King and his young brother were illegitimate. He therefore had himself proclaimed King as Richard III. Edward and his brother were already in the Tower in protective custody, and neighbours often saw them playing in the gardens. Suddenly they were seen no longer.

John Cheyne had none of the doubts that have agitated some recent enquirers. Perhaps he was naive, perhaps he overpaid his debt to Edward IV and the Woodvilles to whom he owed his advancement from Kentish obscurity. But he was among the loyalists who that same autumn rose against the man 'calling himself king'. They failed, and Cheyne was attainted and went to France while men like Thomas de Burgh were rewarded for their good service against the late rebels. Ironically, it was Sir Robert Brackenbury, the Constable of the Tower who allegedly refused to kill the young princes, whose service against the rebels was rewarded with the lordships, manors and rents in 'Rompneymarsh, late of John Cheyne, Robert Cheyne or Cheyney, and of Humphrey Cheyne, of the yearly value of £50 18s. 1d.' But Cheyne returned with Henry Tudor and fought with him at Bosworth, and he fought against the Yorkist adherents of Lambert Simnel two years later. If this was treachery, it was of a different kind from Richard Redman's; and his old opponent in the lists, Robert Clifford, also joined Henry and was employed by him as an agent to spy out Yorkist plots. Cheyne was made a privy

Cy commence le ixe liure
de rustican qui traitte
du prouffit qui vient de
toutes les bestes que len
nourrist aux champs·

Prologue~

Euant co li
ure que nos
auons ordon
nez appert as
sez des chaps
et de leur labourage· et
des vignes· et des arbres
des iardins· et des prez et

des bois· et de tout leur prou
fit· et des choses qui apper
tiennent a delectatione·
tant en verdure come en
merueilles dherbes· et de
arbres fruittes par adres
ce· Mais en ce ixe liure
nous traicterons desbes
tes qui sont nourries es
villes pour prouffit et
delectation· et affin que
lanciennete ne viengne
en ignorance· Nous
debuons scauoir que sico

councillor and Knight of the Garter, and as between 1487 and 1495 he was summoned to parliament by royal writ, he is held to have become Lord Cheyne. But he died without issue in 1499, when his honours became extinct. He was buried in Salisbury Cathedral, where his tomb was recently opened and his skeleton measured. He was found to have been seven foot tall.

In his few months on the throne Richard III employed two Masters of the Horse, the brothers Thomas and James Tyrrell, a name anciently associated with the death of kings. Thomas held the office for only a short time in 1483 before giving way to James. They were grandsons of Sir John Tyrrell, who fought at Agincourt and was Treasurer to Henry VI and Speaker of the Commons in three of his parliaments. The brothers were staunch Yorkists, James being present at the final extinction of Lancastrian hopes at Tewkesbury in 1471, where he received his knighthood. They both received grants from the estates of the fallen Clarence and were entrusted with the customary responsibilities of confidential members of the Household – although it was a departure from the norm when in 1482 Thomas Tyrrell and others, including the King's uncle the Earl of Essex, were licensed 'to found a fraternity or perpetual guild of two guardians and the brethren and sisters of the parishioners of the parish church of Ultyng, co. Essex'. Thomas appears to have died soon afterwards, his widow marrying William Brandon, father of the future Duke of Suffolk.

The interesting question, of course, is whether Sir James Tyrrell, after Brackenbury's supposed refusal, murdered the princes in the Tower. According to the traditional version Tyrrell was disappointed at his lack of further advancement and was willing to do anything to put Richard in his debt. One of his two accomplices may have been a servant from the royal stables, as he is described as John Dighton, horsekeeper, 'a big, broad, square, strong knave'. Rewards certainly followed, although he may not have regarded them as adequate for his dangerous service. He received commissions to array the men of Wales when the Duke of Buckingham turned against the King, and he was a commissioner for the Duke's forfeited estates. He benefited from the estates of another rebel, Sir John Fogge, and he was made Steward of the Duchy of Cornwall for life, sheriff of the county and sheriff of lordships in Shropshire and Wales. Richard's continuing confidence in him – although some reports suggest that his allegiance was wavering – is shown by his appointment to commands in Glamorgan, and then a posting to Guisnes near Calais, in the weeks before Henry Tudor's invasion.

On the other hand, apologists for Richard point to the favour shown to Tyrrell by Henry VII. He received a general pardon, and although he lost the post of Chamberlain of the Exchequer, he was made sheriff of Glamorgan and Constable of Cardiff Castle, at a salary of £100 a year. His presence at such ceremonies as the signing of the Treaty of Etaples, the creation of the young Prince Henry as Duke of York and the reception of Catherine of Aragon show him to have been a courtier of some eminence, but his luck ran out in the end. As lieutenant of Guisnes he was implicated in 1501 in the escape from England of the Yorkist Earl of Suffolk and he was beheaded on Tower Hill in the next year. On the eve of his execution he is said to have confessed to the murder of the princes, but in the Tudor period no great reliance is to be placed upon such pre-scaffold declarations.

In Richard's reign the two brothers do not seem to have been particularly industrious as Masters of the Horse, and Richard's last despairing cry at Bosworth, 'My kingdom for a horse', may, authentic or not, be taken as a fitting epitaph of the Middle Ages, when the strength of the kingdom was bound so closely with the strength of its equestrian establishment.

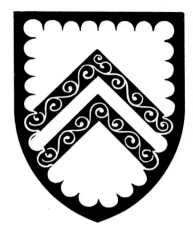

85. *Arms of Tyrrell: argent, two chevrons azure, a bordure engrailed gules.'*

83 (*opposite, above*). *Henry VIII riding to the Great Tournament of Westminster in 1511. He wears a robe of cloth of gold trimmed with sable, a crimson hat, bejewelled and edged with gold, and a gold chain set with precious stones. In his right hand he holds a shattered tilting stave. His grey horse is trapped in gold with a full bard of blue.*

84 (*opposite*). *Henry VIII at the tilt. Attached to his helm is a gold 'cointrise' (lady's sleeve or scarf) given to him by Queen Katherine who watches (at left) from the tilt gallery, under a golden canopy. The King tilts against a 'venant' or answerer, against whose helm he shatters his stave.*

86 (*overleaf*). *Effigy of Sir John Cheyne, in Salisbury Cathedral. Seven foot tall, he carried Henry of Richmond's standard at the battle of Bosworth, where he is said to have been unhorsed by Richard III.*

CHAPTER NINE

Tudor Display

The first Tudor, Henry VII (1485–1509) was a thrifty king but he understood the importance of maintaining a magnificent Court. The first parliament of the reign petitioned that his Household 'be kept and borne worshipfully and honourably, as it accordeth to the honour of your estate and your said realm, by the which your adversaries and enemies shall fall into the dread wherein heretofore they have been.' The clue to Henry's success was sound finance, because men will be loyal when the Crown is the most reliable paymaster in the land. But he spent liberally on his Court, intending that the King should be seen to be wealthier and more prestigious than any of his subjects, and it was in the Tudor period that English monarchs were for the first time addressed as 'your Majesty'.

Henry promoted spectacles, just as he accumulated jewels and plate and erected gracious buildings, as a necessary investment in the business of being a king. He did not take much part himself, and his state horses had to be starved to make them amenable to his rather cautious equestrianship. But he staged a costly tournament when his second son, the future Henry VIII, was made Duke of York, and an even grander one in 1501 for the wedding of his elder son Arthur to Catherine of Aragon. (Within a few months the young bridegroom was dead, and after a papal dispensation had armoured them against specific threats contained in the Book of Leviticus, Catherine married his brother Henry in 1509.) This wedding tournament astounded a girl brought up in a stiff Spanish court unfamiliar with the boisterous make-believe of the English and their national genius for pageantry. The knights entered the arena in pavilions, which were portable tents with symbolic decorations or heraldic bearings. One represented 'a red dragon, led by a great giant having a great tree in his hand', another 'a mountain of green with many rocks, trees, stones and marvellous herbs on the side, and on the height a goodly young lady in her hair, pleasantly beseen'. During the indoor festivities on the following day a castle of singing boys was drawn into the hall by two lions, a hart and an elk: each animal propelled by a man in its forelegs and another 'in the hinder part, secretly hid and apparelled, nothing of them seen but their legs, which were disguised after the proportion and kind of beasts that they were in.'

For his Master of the Horse Henry VII appointed Thomas Brandon, whose brother William had been killed bearing Henry's standard at Bosworth. In 1487 he was put in command of an armed force to go to sea against the King's enemies, but his chief employment was as a diplomat. He was present at the negotiations for the Treaty of Etaples in 1492 and went on an embassy to the Emperor Maximilian in the following year. He also attended the King in negotiations with the Archduke Philip. The customary favours came his way: the wardship of lands in Oxfordshire during the minority of Richard Fiennes which he tried to retain when Fiennes came of age; custody of a park in Hampshire with 'five marks yearly for his expenses in

conveying water in pipes and carts in summertime for the deer and game in the park'; and the manor of Southwold in Suffolk. As Master he performed the traditional duty of leading the riderless horse at Henry's funeral:

> First came riding through the City of London the sword bearer and vice-chamberlain of London with two of the masters of the Bridgehouse to set the crafts in array. Then came the King's messengers, two and two, with their boxes at their breasts, trumpeters and minstrels. Then the Florentines, Venetians, Portingals, Spaniards, Frenchmen, Easterlings. Then gentlemen ushers, chaplains having no dignity, squires for the Body. Then the aldermen and sheriffs. Then came riding two heralds in coat armour, a knight mourner on a courser trapped with black velvet bearing the King's standard, whose name is Sir

87. Part of the armour garniture (i.e. it breaks down into small pieces) of Henry VIII, made in the Royal Armouries at Greenwich. The borders are etched in gilt with designs by Holbein.

Edward Darrell, after whom came knights, chaplains of dignity as deans and others, the King's Council and Knights of the Garter not being lords, the Chief Justice of Common Pleas, Chief Baron, Chief Justice of King's Bench, Master of the Rolls; then the Crouched Friars on foot, the four orders of Friars singing; the canons of all places of London singing. Then came riding all the temporal lords and barons on the left hand and the abbots and bishops on the right. Then rode Sir Davie Owen bearing a steel helmet with a gold crown, Sir Edward Howard [second son of the Earl of Surrey, treasurer] armed with the King's harness, his face discovered and bearing the King's battle-axe head downward resting on his foot; Sir Thomas Fynes bearing a rich armour embroidered with the arms of England; the Mayor of London carrying his mace. Then came the chariot bearing the corse. Then followed the Duke of Buckingham, Earls of Arundel, Northumberland, Shrewsbury, Surrey, Essex, and other, to the number of nine, being Knights of the Garter; then nine henchmen on coursers trapped with black velvet the three foremost bearing caps of maintenance which three Popes had sent the King, the next three bearing rich swords point downwards, the seventh bearing target of the arms of England otherwise called a shield crowned, the eighth a helmet with a lion of gold on it, the ninth a spear covered with black velvet. Then followed Sir Thomas Brandon, Master of the Horse, leading a courser trapped with black velvet embroidered with the arms of England; then Lord Darcy, Captain of the Guard, with the Guard and many other gentlemen. (Harleian MS 3504f. 264b.)

Apart from this, there is little mention in the records of Brandon's connection with the stables. Sir William Willoughby was appointed 'master of the king's dogs called harriers' with wages of one shilling a day 'out of the issues of the counties of Bedford and Buckingham' for himself, and wages for the huntsmen and grooms and $\frac{3}{4}d$. a day for the feeding of '36 running dogs and nine greyhounds out of the subsidy'. Sir Giles Daubeny was put in charge of the king's harthounds, and in 1486 a grant was made to 'William Ferrour, king's servant, of the office of marshal of the king's mares, called the stud, and of his young horses as well' in Warwickshire. This was during the minority of the Earl of Warwick, who as a Yorkist claimant to the throne was already in the Tower and was to remain there until his execution. It may not be altogether fanciful to suggest that this William Ferrour was a descendant of the Ferraris, or man of Ferrara, mentioned in the Patent Rolls of Edward I. Quite a few of the men who as grooms or keepers brought foreign horses into England remained to look after them and eventually settled with their families.

In the few months after Henry's death in April 1509 Brandon received several favours from the new King. He was appointed to the offices of warden and chief justice of all the royal forests, parks, chaces and warrens south of the Trent; steward and surveyor of all lands in Devon, Cornwall and Somerset, and master of the hunt in all chaces and parks there, that had passed to the King on the death of his grandmother, the Countess of Richmond; and Marshal of the King's Bench. But he did not live to enjoy this further prosperity as he died in January 1510 and was buried at Blackfriars. In February the King appointed Sir Thomas Knyvet 'knight of the body, to be during pleasure Master of the Horse, *vice* Sir Thomas Brandon deceased, with profits as enjoyed by Sir Thomas Brandon or Sir John Cheyne.'

When Henry VIII (1509–47) cultivated magnificence, a conscious theory of kingship was only a secondary consideration. In his monstrous egotism he did it primarily to please himself. The tournament, which had been raised to a sophisticated art at the Burgundian court in the fifteenth century, was an exercise worthy of his talent for self-glorification. On New Year's Day 1511 he and his Queen rejoiced in the birth of a son and heir whom they called Henry Duke of Cornwall, and as part of the national celebration of this event a tournament was held at Westminster seven weeks later.

DV·TRES VALIENT
CHEVALIER MONSIEVR
THOMAS·BRANDON·CHLR·DV
T·RESNOBLE·ORDRE·DE·LA·IARITIER
ET·GRAND·ESCVIER·DE·LA·ROY
NOSTRE·SEIGNIEVR·FVST·INSTAILE
LE·DIXSIEME·IOVR·DV·MAYLE
XXII·ANN·HENRICI·VII

Tournaments no longer had much to do with military training. Soldiers nowadays were professionals of a different kind, and the massive armour of the mounted knight did not protect him against the gunpowder that was now being widely used in war. Nor did the tournament have much to do with sport: its conventions had reduced it to a lumbering game of, literally, 'hit or miss'. But it was still valued for other reasons. With its elaborate ritual and processions it emphasised the gradations in society, and politically it built up a king's prestige by allowing him to display his wealth and splendour. The Westminster tournament of 1511 cost £4000, compared with £2300 for the building of the nine-hundred ton ship the *Great Elizabeth*: which reflects the scale of values current at the time. Maximilian I, the Holy Roman Emperor, was not himself a warlike person, and he

88. Garter stall-plate of Sir Thomas Brandon, in St George's Chapel, Windsor. He was Master of the Horse (Grand Ecuyer) during Henry VII's reign.

89. Chanfron (face-piece) and crinet (mane-cover) from the silver and engraved armour made for Henry VIII c. 1514.

was usually in such financial straits that he had to clothe his attendants in black wool. But he realised the importance of keeping up the right sort of reputation, and so he commissioned books to celebrate feats in hunting and the battlefield that he never actually performed. In general, jousting was regarded as the 'assay and proof' of true nobility, a means of preserving chivalrous ideals and avoiding the sin of idleness.

If it had been no more than this, the tournament could have been regarded as a relic of outworn feudalism. But it had developed into a medium of full artistic expression in which the tilt, based on an allegorical situation, was enriched with music, poetry, spectacle and dance. The allegorical situation was not new. Edward III, for instance, had devised plots centred on the Round Table, or played at being a knight defending the Church against the infidel or an ascetic wrestling with the seven deadly sins. This at least gave some pictorial variety to what was becoming a very monotonous sport. The idea of bringing other arts into its service was further developed in the fifteenth century by René of Anjou, whose daughter married Henry VI, and particularly at the court of Philip the Good of Burgundy. Englishmen had been astounded by the artistic richness of the ceremony at Bruges in 1486 when Margaret, daughter of Edward IV, was married to Charles the Bold.

Henry VIII, being 'lusty, young and courageous', and also exceedingly vain, approved of the principle of this sort of entertainment but expected the emphasis to lie upon the outdoor proceedings, in which he would take the leading part. Henry jousted, as he did everything else, with the intention that he should win. It would not be wholly just to attribute this to the emotional immaturity that he never outgrew. He was, obviously, one of history's supreme chauvinists. But monarchy was still a very personal thing, with a close identity between the individual and the national interest. England's prestige would benefit as much as his own if Henry were able to justify his boast to be a tenth among the 'Nine Worthies', that strange selection of heroes containing men as diverse as Joshua and Julius Caesar. On his immediate flank Henry had an extra spur to his ambition in his infuriating brother-in-law James IV of Scotland, ruler of a barbarous people but extraordinarily adept in horsemanship and jousting, music and letters – all the arts of war and peace.

At his own coronation tournament Henry had been obliged to be a non-participant, sitting with the Queen in a tilt gallery while the Lady Pallas lengthily presented the challenging knights as scholars defending the tree of knowledge. But in 1511 he was the leading challenger, the focus of an entertainment on which, he hoped, all Europe had its eyes. A pictorial record of this tournament has been preserved in a contemporary scroll now in the possession of the College of Arms. It shows the procession that took place on the second day, with the knights and their attendants entering and leaving the lists, and the only action picture is of the king splintering his lance. The scroll has been reproduced, with a learned historical text, by Sydney Anglo in *The Great Tournament Roll of Westminster* (1968).

As leader of the four challengers or *tenants* Henry appeared as the knight Noble Coeur Loyal, and he was supported by his Master of Horse, Sir Thomas Knyvet (Vaillant Desyr), Sir William Courtenay (Bon Vouloir) and Sir Edward Neville (Joyeux Penser). The setting on the first day was a forest 'pageant' measuring 26 feet by 19 feet, and 9 feet high. The champions entered inside it, and it was drawn by a golden lion and a silver antelope, each ridden by a lady in blue and silver damask. That day Knyvet, who broke five lances, was awarded the prize for the 'best doer', but Henry, who had already ridden more courses than anyone else, obliged with a virtuoso mounted display. 'Notwithstanding that the horse was very courageous and excellent in leaping, turning and exceeding flinging, he moved no more upon him than he had held a soft and plain trotter.'

90. *Sir Thomas Knyvet as Vaillant Desyr in the Westminster Tournament. Riding under a crimson and blue pavilion carried by pages, he wore silver armour and a blue surcoat set with golden letters 'K' (for Queen Katherine). His white horse is trapped in crimson and plumed in russet-red and yellow.*

Next day the challengers came to the lists each in his own pavilion, a canopy held at each end by squires, and the answerers, or *venants*, were led by Charles Brandon, later Duke of Suffolk. They entered in a tower preceded by a gaoler with a key, and each emerged bearded and in the habit of a 'recluse or a religious person', throwing off the disguise when he had received the Queen's permission to answer the challenge. (Convention required the *venants* always to obtain from the Queen or the presiding lady permission to enter the tilt, and it was a favourite device to appear initially as a person far advanced in arthritic decrepitude. At a joust in 1514 the King himself came on with Brandon dressed as hermits in long beards of silver damask.) The Master of the Jousts and leader of the procession was Sir Edward Guildford in his capacity as chief armourer, and the stage-manager was Richard Gibson, sergeant of the tents. In his book Anglo prints the detailed accounts, for lath, canvas, dyes, wax, satin, damask, silks, provisions, etc, that had to be purchased to get this extraordinary show on the road. In the procession Knyvet, being one of the challengers, could not take his proper place as Master of the Horse, but he had a deputy styled 'le Grand Ecuyer'. This is believed to have been Matthew Baker, a man with long service in the Royal Household. He rode upon 'a lusty courser' and was described in a contemporary report as 'right well and sadly [soberly] appointed and like a man of good age and sadness'.

Henry was in high spirits, having run 28 courses, broken 12 lances and scored ten attaints, and at the banquet in the evening he wore a costume that had 887 small gold pieces stitched on to it. Knyvet had 893 pieces and had gone to the trouble of forming some of them to read Vaillant Desyr (his name in the joust) on his codpiece. He had literally to fight in defence of his honour when some of the 'rude people', over-exuberant after the free drink they had taken, burst into the hall and began to snatch all the gold and jewels they could reach, even those guarding the modesty of Valiant Desire. There were some violent scuffles but the King and his guests took the intrusion in good part and the evening ended happily enough. But the sequel was tragic. Nine days later, on 22 February, the infant prince died at Richmond. The history of England might read very differently if Catherine had been able to give Henry a surviving son.

Henry sought to kill his grief by violent action, the only way he knew. He hastened his preparations for his intended war with France, and in the spring he was displaying his characteristic energy in a tournament at Greenwich, piloting the good ship Fame with a cargo of Renown to be defended against privateers. A year later, again at Greenwich, the script required Knyvet to appear all in black in a pavilion called Castle Dolorous. This was gloomily prophetic for him, as will be seen in the next chapter. The year 1513 saw Henry in France fighting a real war rather than a mimic one. But he was accompanied by a huge retinue and all his usual domestic comforts, and his famous victory in the battle of the Spurs had something of the hollowness of a tournament since the French wanted to preserve their army and voluntarily left the field. Jousting continued when Henry came home again, but for some reason the allegorical settings disappeared and were never revived. The costumes and the trappings were still spectacular, but the tournaments were no longer adorned with speeches and drama and other romantic effects.

The most spectacular event of the reign was Henry's meeting with the King of France, Francis I, at the Field of Cloth of Gold in 1520. The ostensible purpose was diplomatic, as Francis hoped for England's neutrality, if not an actual alliance, in his intended war against the Emperor Charles V. But Henry had close commercial and personal ties with Charles, who was Catherine's nephew, had already met him for informal discussion at Canterbury, and would meet him again when the jamboree was over. The real purpose was showmanship. As the senior and most experienced of three young rulers, Henry was determined to display himself in all his glory.

The preliminaries were far from chivalrous, since each side suspected the other of treachery. A neutral meeting-place was fixed at Ardres, just outside the English territory round Calais, and the numbers to be present were settled after some haggling, and in the event were exceeded. In her detailed study of the meeting (*The Field of Cloth of Gold*, 1969) Dr J. G. Russell says that the English had 5832 personnel and 3217 horses. Henry brought most of his nobility with him, 34 peers and 132 knights, being fearful what they might get up to if he left them at home, and he was personally attended by 200 yeomen, 70 officers of the chamber, 266 from the Household and 205 from the stable and armoury. The nobles too brought their retinues, Cardinal Wolsey being supported by 300 servants and 150 horses; and it was noted that although he himself rode in Christ-like imitation upon a humble mule, the beast was richly caparisoned in scarlet and gold. He always, Polydore Vergil said, 'longed like a peacock to display his many-coloured tail', and as this was an official mission he was able to award himself £12 a day for food. Lesser people were not so fortunate, and many had to pawn their lands or pledge their revenues in

Legrant   Esquie   Le maistre

order to be there. In the first scene of Shakespeare's *Henry VIII*, which describes the splendour of the occasion, Lord Abergavenny speaks of

> Kinsmen of mine, three at the least, that have
> By this so sicken'd their estates that never
> They shall abound as formerly.

For his own lodging Henry had a palace erected that was of brick to a height of eight feet, with a further thirty feet of painted wood, and a covering of canvas painted to look like slate. Other temporary dwellings were less secure and were rocked by the winds that blew so unseasonably throughout those June weeks. Harbingers and purveyors had gone out in advance to pre-empt the food and lodgings required for the English host, and the elaborate preparations for Cloth of Gold give an instructive picture of the Royal Household in migration. The vice-

91. Matthew Baker, who acted as stand-in for the Master, Knyvet.

121

admiral, Sir William Fitzwilliam, arranged the Channel transport; the sergeant of the tents, still the hard-worked Richard Gibson, was assisted by the 'revels' office in providing the scenic apparatus; a sergeant of the cellar – a knight who was a sheriff and a member of parliament – supplied the drink, his expenditure for the month being £1568 1s. 11¾d.; the wardrobe bought the wax and sugar that ornamented the dishes, and some forty boxes were needed to transport these confections from England; the poulterer produced swans, capons, green geese, snipe, herons, curlew, storks, bitterns, peacocks and gulls to give variety to banquets that normally consisted of three courses with three dishes in each; William Cornish, master of the children of the royal chapel, led them in musical accompaniments to the feasting and wrote a carol for them to sing at the joust; among the many duties of the steward's department was the provision of rushes to strew the floor. Yet the whole enterprise could have faltered without the spicery, which seasoned and preserved the food before it came to the table. The deep-freeze has not been the only cause of stunned and undiscriminating palates.

In anticipation of the meeting Henry had instructed his agents to find horses fit to match his skill. This was not easy, since he had been known to wear out eight horses in a single day's hunting, and one of the heavy animals that carried him in full armour had needed a hedgehog under its tail before it would move beneath his weight. Europe was scoured for horses, especially the prized Neapolitan coursers that combined speed, strength and elegance. Henry had eight Italian grooms in the royal stables, experts from a country now supreme in breeding. Although Charles had sent him some Spanish horses to cement their diplomatic understanding, he rode at Ardres upon a morello (bay) courser that was a present from the Duke of Termoli, and Francis rode a Mantuan from the Gonzaga stud. Henry's mount was trapped in fine bullion 'pounced and set with antic work of Roman figures' and gold bells the size of an egg. Behind him came the Master, Sir Henry Guildford, leading the King's spare horse in the traditional manner of the office.

The portly Guildford, who was Master from 1515 to 1522, was an unlikely choice since he was no great horseman and his talents were more conspicuous in domestic entertainments. His father, Sir Richard, had been Master of the Ordnance and Comptroller of the Household to Henry VII. He had himself been a squire of the body at Court and had designed masques and pageants, appearing in one of them as Robin Hood. He promoted the revels when Tournai was captured during the campaign of 1513, and he was appointed Master at a salary of £40 a year: a trifling sum, but he had properties in Warwickshire, and as Constable of Leeds Castle in Kent, while living at Benenden nearby, he had entertained Charles V during the private negotiations that preceded Cloth of Gold. He was therefore a valued confidential servant of the King, and his appointment as Master at least meant that Henry would not be outshone in equestrian activity. At Cloth of Gold Guildford was one of the small party consisting of Wolsey, the Marquis of Dorset (acting as Constable and carrying the Sword of State) and the ambassador to Paris, that escorted Henry to a private business discussion with Francis. But apart from these formal duties that belonged to his office, Guildford seems to have contributed more to the social celebrations than to the administrative preparations. These were carried out by his half-brother Sir Edward Guildford, who had organised the famous joust in 1511 and was still chief armourer.

For all the show of gallant civility, and the determination of the French not to give offence to their visitors, the festivities were to some extent competitive. The English were amateurish compared with the French, most of whom were hardened veterans now, in serious practice for the Italian campaigns that lay ahead. It was

92. Francis I of France. At Cloth of Gold he vied in splendour with Henry, riding on a lavishly-trapped Mantuan stallion from the Gonzaga stud.

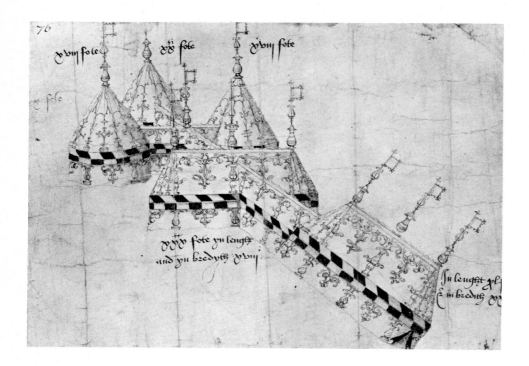

generally agreed that the French were better mounted. At the tournament, a *pas d'armes* that lasted fourteen days, Henry and Francis issued a challenge with a body of knights from both sides, but it was designed as a display of varied equestrian talents and there was no attempt to devise an allegorical situation. Allegory was confined to the emblems or mottoes which the combatants wore on their horses. Henry's bay had a device signifying England's mastery of the narrow seas, while Francis had a different device each day to signify his conquests in matters of the heart. The French Constable, the Duke of Bourbon, had a courser that could jump its own height, and Guildford's modest performance in the arena was outmatched by his counterpart, the Italian Galeazzo San Severino, who gave a special display on a Spanish jennet and found no one to answer his challenge. Although a generous observer noted that Henry performed 'supernatural feats', making his horses 'fly rather than leap, to the delight and ecstasy of everyone', Henry was the eternal schoolboy who tried too hard at everything and failed to achieve very much. He won the archery contest, but there was a dangerous moment when he engaged the long-nosed lecher Francis in a try at wrestling and was thrown to the ground: a trick, the English said, Francis employing an illegal throw known as the '*tour de Bretagne*'.

Dr Russell has estimated the cost to the English at £8839 2s. 4d., some £1400 in excess of the original budget. Fodder for the horses alone amounted to £575. The formal negotiations ensured the continuance of a French pension to Wolsey and confirmed the betrothal of the Dauphin to Henry's daughter Mary, a scheme that came to nothing. Perhaps the most gratifying result for the English was a tilt between Francis and Henry's cousin the Earl of Devonshire which gave Francis a black eye and an abrasion to the nose. Possibly more significant was the presence in the French retinue of a dark, sloe-eyed girl of thirteen named Anne Boleyn. With her sister Mary she had been sent by an ambitious father to be educated at the court of France. Francis punningly called Mary 'the English mare' for the number of

le grand escuyer galliot

times that he, and others, had ridden her. Anne learned to play her cards more discreetly.

Henry lost some of his interest in tournaments after this. Possibly he could no longer afford them, and anyway the flush of youth was over and he had other problems on his mind. Jousting continued desultorily until the end of the century. Leicester and Essex liked to display their skill, and 'checks' have survived which record the hits made when Essex was at the tilt. But Elizabeth was nervous of the risks, and to James I even this mimic show of violence was abhorrent. The hazards were still quite serious in spite of the heavy armour and blunted weapons. Early in Henry's reign Sir William Compton was thought 'likely to die' after an accident, and another of the King's sporting companions, Francis Bryan, lost an eye. There was an anxious moment at a joust in 1524 when Henry himself forgot to close his visor and Suffolk's lance 'broke all to shivers' and 'the King's headpiece was full of splinters'. It was by just such a splinter that Henry II of France was fatally wounded at a joust in 1559, and after that it was felt that there were safer ways of showing equestrian skills. The coming fashion was *haute école* with its fascinating variations of the *manège*, such as the capriole and the *levade*.

One of his subjects said that Henry spared no pains to 'convert the sport of hunting into a royal martyrdom', and he did not relax his energies in the chase when his interest in tournaments was waning. Hunting may even have played some part in his wooing of Anne Boleyn. He rode with her in the woods round Hampton Court and Windsor where earlier he had hunted with Catherine of Aragon, and it was observed that they would often detach themselves from the main body and ride off side by side, accompanied only by the Master of the Horse and a few attendants.

In 1528 Henry formed his own hunting pack, known as the 'privy buckhounds'. Later in the century a Brocas descendant attributed this to 'the sinister persuasions of divers of the servants of the said king, seeking their own private gain'. It is true that, among other sinecure appointments, the first Mastership of the buckhounds went to George Boleyn, Viscount Rochford, possibly as a reward for having a sister whom the King was hoping to seduce. The Master's salary was £33 6s. 8d., and the work was done by sergeants who received 9s. a month, equal to the cost of providing 'chippings', or dog biscuits, for the hounds. It is likely, however, that the hereditary establishment was no longer adequate for modern requirements, and Henry may also have been influenced by the fact that the direct male line had died out in 1512 and the mastership had passed to the husbands of two Brocas daughters. It is not clear whether the two packs were incorporated or continued as separate establishments, but the Brocas family alleged that Queen Mary later suppressed the privy pack, although it was revived under Elizabeth I. By this time the hereditary pack had reverted to the Brocas name through intermarriage within the family.

In his enthusiasm for the hunt, and his determination to emulate anything done by Francis I, Henry began in 1538 the building of his hunting-lodge at Nonsuch in Surrey. But it was to be much more splendid than that: a country palace modelled on the chateau which Francis had built at Chambord. The village of Cuddington, with its church and its farms, was destroyed to make room for a park of 1200 acres to hold 1000 deer. The foundations were laid of stone brought from the dissolved Merton Priory, and a force of 520 masons and labourers built a fantasy palace, part-Gothic and part-Classical, with high towers that enabled non-participants to view the progress of the hunt. It took three years to complete the inner court, and Henry did not live to see the fulfilment of his dream. But Nonsuch was the favourite resort of his daughter Elizabeth, although not of her courtiers who, despite the lavishness of the conception, had to sleep in tents in the grounds.

95. Sir Henry Guildford, by Holbein, who painted portraits of several of the great officers of Henry VIII's household. This shows Guildford wearing his Garter collar and holding a staff of office, probably as Comptroller.

CHAPTER TEN A Problem of Precedence

Towards the end of the reign of Henry VIII the administrative reforms of Thomas Cromwell completed the long process of taking the machinery of government 'out of Court', so that the officers of the Royal Household no longer had a dual responsibility as ministers of state. Ministers continued to enjoy Household sinecures to supplement their salaries, but they had no political authority by virtue of these appointments. Cromwell's reforms affected the Master of the Horse less than some of his colleagues as his department had never been 'political' to the same extent. But these changes created an uncertainty about his precedence within the Household that has bedevilled the office ever since.

All this was still in the future when Henry was enjoying physical sports with his early Masters, the nautical Knyvet and the unathletic Guildford. There exists from this time an 'order to be had when the King goes to Battle'. (Cottonian MS. Tib. E. VIII.) The office of Constable had not yet been relegated to ceremonial duties at coronations, and it was also customary in time of war to appoint a marshal to be in command of the army, as Charles Brandon was appointed for the invasion of France in 1513. The order requires them to 'send out riders to discover the countries together as the army draweth nearer every day'; and they are to be accompanied by 'one marshal or other valiant man, conjoin'd with good esquierye, of good men and horse', and sufficient ammunition 'for to succour the distress (if need be) of the spyers'. Harbingers, purveyors, the sergeant of the tents and the steward follow with their train, 'to discipline the lodging'. The battle dispositions are then laid down, and here 'the Master of the Horse ought to bear, or cause to be borne, the king's standard unto the time of the battle; then he must bear it himself.' Whether it had been among the Master's traditional duties actually to carry the royal standard in battle is one of those uncertain things, but undoubtedly he was expected to be present and to fight. Although primarily an officer in the navy, Sir Thomas Knyvet was appointed standard-bearer to Henry VIII, 'in the same manner as Sir John Cheyne', before he became Master of the Horse, and presumably he combined the two offices.

The family came from Buckenham in Norfolk, and his mother was a sister of Sir Thomas Tyrrell. His part in Henry's tournaments has already been described, including the loss of treasure from his codpiece, and while he was thus acting as a fighting companion to the King, his department was administered by George Lutkyn, or Lovekyn, whose name appears, as clerk of the stables, to receive harness, hatters, headstalls, etc. for 18 coursers, 'one courtant, a trotting gelding, and 22 hobbies and ambling geldings'. By his marriage to a daughter of the Duke of Norfolk Knyvet acquired the use of possessions in England, Wales and Calais, and the Lord High Admiral, Sir Edward Howard, as a brother-in-law. In 1510 he, Howard, Charles Brandon and Edward Guildford were licensed to 'fit out a ship

Cloth of Gold do not thou dispys
Though thou be mached with Cloth of fries.

Cloth of friez be not thou to bould
Though thou be mached with Cloth of Gold.

Trotter Sculp

not exceeding 250 tons burthen, and take it beyond the straits of Morocco, free of custom': a valuable concession if their commercial gains came up to expectation. But Henry's determination to make war on France interrupted such proceedings, and in July 1512 the Exchequer was instructed to grant Knyvet £50 'for revictualling the army on the sea'. Commanding the *Regent*, the largest ship in the English fleet, he was lying off Brest alongside his brother-in-law when he was grappled by the *Maria de la Cordelière*. A fire on the French ship caused both to blow up with the loss of almost all their men, and Knyvet became the only Master of the

96. *Charles Brandon, Duke of Suffolk, and Mary, Queen of France (sister of Henry VIII). The inscription is a satirical reference to Brandon, who represents cloth of frieze aspiring to be 'matched' with Mary who is cloth of gold.*

Horse to have lost his life in a naval action. Howard was so distressed that he vowed not to look upon the King's face again until he had obtained revenge, but he too was killed next year when chasing French galleons out of Whitstable Bay.

An incident in the career of Knyvet's younger brother is instructive on the tight-knit organisation of the Royal Household. Sir Edmund Knyvet was sergeant porter and keeper of the King's gates, a useful Court appointment whose main function was to prevent the smuggling out of silver, napery, food, clothing and everything portable. During an altercation in 1541 Knyvet struck a servant of the Earl of Surrey, for which he was brought before the Court of the Verge, an ancient court under the Lord High Steward with jurisdiction over offences committed within the precincts of the royal palaces. He was sentenced to imprisonment, the forfeiture of his estates and the amputation of his right hand. For the execution of this sentence sergeants from several departments of the Household were required to be present with their particular contributions: the sergeant surgeon provided the instruments, the woodyard the block, the cook a knife, the farrier the searing-irons, the ewery a basin and cloths, the chandlery dressings, the cellarer refreshments for the official spectators, and so on. In the end Knyvet was pardoned, having declared that he could no longer give service to the King if deprived of his loyal right hand, but the ceremony shows the importance attached to the keeping of the peace in the Household. This was emphasised by the attendance at the solemn rites of all the departments for which a reason could be found.

According to official tradition, Thomas Knyvet was succeeded as Master by Sir Charles Brandon, who in 1514 was made Duke of Suffolk, but this is not certain. The son of Henry VII's standard-bearer and nephew of a previous Master, he already had several lucrative appointments. With his fierce black beard he was irresistible to women and also 'most acceptable to the king in all his exercises and pastimes'. There is no reason why he should not have become Master in addition to his other posts, but there is no specific evidence of it. In the *Letters and Papers of Henry VIII*, a valuable source for the reign, the only recorded reference is that in May 1513 he received £1000 for embroiderers, saddlers, gold-drawers, silkwomen 'and other necessaries' for the stables. On the other hand, when Sir Henry Guildford was appointed Master in 1515, the warrant granted him the post 'at £40 a year in the same manner as Sir Thomas Knyvet, Sir Thomas Brandon or Sir John Cheyne'. There is no reference to Suffolk or to any immediate successor to Knyvet. There is a lacuna here. Perhaps the office was temporarily unfilled, or perhaps Suffolk did hold it and his name was inadvertently omitted from the new warrant. It has been suggested that Sir Nicholas Carew held it for a short time before his longer tenure that began in 1522, because there is a reference to him as Master in May 1515, six months before the appointment of Guildford.

Anyway, Suffolk was soon to disgrace himself. In the treaty that concluded the war with France, Henry's sister Mary, who was seventeen, was married to Louis XII, the widower King of France, who was fifty-two, and she drove the old man into his grave within three months. An anonymous squire at the French court tells how 'the good king, to please his young wife, changed his whole manner of life; for where he had been wont to breakfast at 8 o'clock, he had to take his *déjeuner* at noon, and instead of going to bed at 6 o'clock in the evening, he often did not get to bed before midnight. So, towards the end of December, he fell ill of a disease which defied all human remedies.' It was perhaps Mary's most expedient way of reducing her marital commitments. But in Paris a few months later she was secretly married to Suffolk, notwithstanding that in England he had both a real wife and a 'contracted' wife still living.

The ecclesiastical authorities smoothed over a little matter of trigamy in an accommodating spirit which they were not to show to Suffolk's sovereign a few years later, but Henry was furious, as he had every right to be. Dynastic marriages were important, and having played one round in the diplomatic game, Mary should have held herself available for the next. He deprived Suffolk of many of his posts, and if Suffolk was ever Master of the Horse, this could have been one of them; and it could explain the reference to Carew, who might have been a stand-in until Guildford took over. Suffolk meanwhile was not long in returning to Henry's favour, since Mary was able to return to England with valuable jewels and plate, property of the French Crown, which she had acquired during her brief stint as a royal bride. Suffolk was personally too congenial to Henry to be consigned to permanent disgrace. He became Steward of the Household, and as an old man he did useful service on the Scottish Marches and led the army that captured Boulogne in 1544.

Sir Henry Guildford was more at home in domestic revels than on the back of a horse, and most of the references to him as Master show him either as a provider of entertainments or as a trusted servant engaged in other business. He was one of the councillors before whom Buckingham was indicted for treason in 1521, he procured the evidence against a Kentish priest said to be in possession of seditious bills, and after Cloth of Gold he accompanied Henry at the more fruitful conference with Charles V at Gravelines. The letters he received from Erasmus certainly had nothing to do with horses. On earlier visits to England the eminent sage, always much concerned about his health and his creature comforts, had been disappointed of the preferments that he regarded as his due, but he was still hoping to be invited back. A letter to Guildford in May 1519 discloses the strange frailties of a noble mind:

> Where in school or monastery will you find so many distinguished and accomplished men as from your English Court? Shame on us all. The tables of priests and divines run with wine and echo with drunken noise and scurrilous jest, while in princes' halls is heard only grave and modest conversation on points of morals or knowledge. Your king leads the rest by his example. In ordinary accomplishments he is above most and inferior to none. Where will you find a man so acute, so copious, so soundly judging, or so dignified in word and manner? Time was when I held off from royal courts. To such a court as yours I would transfer myself and all that belongs to me if age and health allowed. . . . That king of yours may bring back the golden age, though I shall not live to enjoy it, as my tale draws to an end. (Erasmus, *Epistles*, 417.)

Guildford was deaf to these hints and blandishments, or his employers were, but he must have been a man of parts, and no little influence, for Erasmus to have chosen him as an intermediary. In 1522 he was transferred to his father's old post of Comptroller of the Household, which no doubt he found more congenial to his talents. When the issue of Catherine's divorce was at a critical stage, he was one of a deputation commanded to wait upon her and ask her to agree to the dissolution of her marriage. When they retired in some disarray, Guildford was heard to say that it would be as well if all the learned doctors who had recommended this solution were tied in a cart and bundled off to Rome to explain themselves. Before Anne Boleyn could take her revenge he resigned his Household office.

Sir Nicholas Carew, his successor as Master of the Horse (1522–38), was one of the knights and squires of the body who had shared Henry's lighter pleasures since the early days. In this reign the most favoured of 'the King's Knights' were not the sober, industrious men of the recent past. The new men received their lavish sinecures for supporting the King in his 'exercises and pastimes', and they seldom occupied themselves in the 'grave and modest conversation' which Erasmus claimed to have discovered at the English Court. They were essentially playboys, poetasters and revellers, dashing on a horse and even quicker in the bedchamber. Although he later inclined towards piety, William Compton lived for years in adultery with Lady Anne Hastings; William Carey eventually led Mary Boleyn, now ageing, into the respectability of marriage but died of the plague soon after; Francis Bryan, whose sonnets were praised by Sir Thomas Wyatt, earned from Cromwell the title 'Vicar of Hell' for his backslidings. Later he wrote a sour treatise on the life of a courtier, in which he had spent his entire career. Edward Neville, who had been Master of the Buckhounds, was another who grew weary of the Court, embittered by his detestation of Cromwell.

Nicholas Carew perhaps was of better calibre than some of these, and over the years he received more responsible appointments. He was a privy councillor, sheriff of Surrey and Sussex, an envoy on special missions to Francis and the Emperor, a special commissioner to the north when a Scottish invasion was expected. Employment on foreign embassies was a frequent activity of the Masters of the Horse at this time: Thomas Brandon, Guildford, Carew and later Sir Anthony Browne were all used on confidential business overseas, and it is reasonable to suppose that they had some diplomatic flair. Carew would have needed it when, on going to France to inform the French King of his admission to the Order of the Garter, he had to borrow a mule on his arrival as there were no horses available.

Carew lived in some splendour at Beddington in Surrey, where he once entertained the King. He held sufficient offices to be able to maintain this opulent state, but his first love was the horse and he probably valued his Mastership for its own sake. At the conclusion of a joust in 1517 he ran the lists on a blindfold horse, covered like his mount in blue satin, and carrying in his hands a huge green tree. In the following year, when French ambassadors were to be entertained at Greenwich, he and Guildford each received six yards of blue cloth of gold 'towards a base and trapper' to decorate their performance. During a brief resurgence of the allegorical idea he was among the knights chosen to attack a Castle of Loyalty, a timber building 50 feet high surrounded by ditches; and he led a band of coursers at the tournament that followed Anne Boleyn's coronation. He seems to have kept a watchful eye on the King's stables, where his assistant was one Richard Hampden, appointed 'overseer and yeoman of the king's horses' under his authority, and keeper of the stables in Buckingham's old manor of Thornbury. Carew also received the reversion of 'the office of the king's otter-hunter, with money for the keeping of six otter-hounds and 12 hounds'.

A temporary setback in his career in 1519 foreshadowed the coming re-organisation of the Household. Ostensibly the cause was over-familiarity with the King. The young men who rode and jousted and drank with Henry, played tennis with him and gambled with him at dice and shovel-board, could not help being familiar, and they took advantage of their privileged position to mock the staid deportment of more conservative courtiers. So by order of the Privy Council Carew, Bryan, Neville, Sir Edward Guildford the armourer and two others were sent away from Court to look after their provincial sinecures, Carew being dispatched to be Lieutenant of Calais, 'sore to him displeasant'.

This banishment did not last long, and a man as volatile and irascible as Henry, always quick to take offence, was quite capable of dealing with over-familiarity. The real causes must be found elsewhere. Some of the banished had recently been in France, and they were overtly pro-French when Henry and Wolsey were inclining towards an alliance with the Emperor Charles V. But a more pressing reason was

97. Sir Nicholas Carew. 'His first love was the horse, and he probably valued the Mastership for its own sake.'

the need to cut the expenditure of the Household by reducing the work performed through deputies. The chamber appointments of the offenders were filled by four 'sad and ancient knights' chosen by Wolsey at cheaper rates, while they themselves had to attend to other responsibilities for which previously they had been paid but done no work.

Henry then instructed Wolsey to draw up plans for a more systematic reform. When the Court was at Greenwich, Henry was housing and feeding upwards of a thousand people a day, not all of whom had any right to be there. A survey made at the beginning of the reign found about 170 people under the authority of the Chamberlain, who controlled the regions 'upstairs': squires of the body who sat outside the royal bedchamber at night, the bedchamber staff, servers, doctors, musicians and ushers. Below stairs the Steward, with a staff of 220, directed about

25 departments, and in his domain there were various ancient anomalies that demanded to be rationalised. For instance, the acatry, which handled the meat supplies, provided mutton, but lamb came from the poultry. The Master of the Horse then had a staff of 60, but the number of servants was increasing all the time – the 60 in the stables became more than 100 within 30 years. In theory, expenditure was supervised by the Board of Green Cloth, consisting of the Treasurer, the Steward, the Cofferer, the Comptroller and a group of clerks, but the departments were unable or unwilling to submit accurate and prompt accounts.

In 1526 Wolsey produced the Eltham Ordinances (Harleian MS. 642) to set the Household in 'honourable, substantial and profitable order'. On paper this scheme made a resolute attempt to cut out the officials who, with their servants, obtained free board and lodging while their work was done by deputies; and to retain at Court the financial experts, such as purveyors and auditors, who were too often absent on other work. Sir Henry Guildford, as Comptroller, did indeed make some drastic reductions: the gentlemen of the chamber decreased from 112 to 12, the grooms from 69 to 15, the servers from 45 to 6. There were to be checks on officers taking meals 'in corners and secret places', that is, in their own lodgings, where they entertained their own guests at the King's expense. Duties were to be more carefully regulated, and improvements were projected in the sub-life of the kitchens, where the porters and lower menials worked naked; spaniels were the only dogs allowed to the ladies, and no other animals were to be brought in without permission. But very little of this was put into action. The dismissed officials began to creep back, the Green Cloth still had no effective authority, and Henry himself, while consenting to economies below stairs, was reluctant to have his own entourage diminished. Comprehensive reform had to await the organising genius of Thomas Cromwell.

But before he could put into effect his plans for 'abridging the king's house', Cromwell had to take public administration out of Court. Edward IV had initiated a last flourish of Chamber activity. He elevated the office of the secretary, previously a mere household clerk, and revived the secret seal as an instrument of personal policy. With this went a system of 'Chamber finance' which under Henry VII made the treasurer of the Chamber responsible for the collection of the greater part of the revenue. Henry appreciated the importance of ready money in preventing a renewal of the Wars of the Roses. Thus the Exchequer continued to collect the customs and parliamentary grants, but the income from Crown lands, the feudal dues, fines, the profits of justice and various other moneys were paid directly into the Chamber, where the accounts were regularly audited by the King himself.

But the defect of Chamber and Wardrobe administration through private seals had always been its dependence upon a king with the strength and ability to maintain it. It could not last indefinitely with the increasing scope and responsibilities of government. Henry VIII began his reign by butchering Empson and Dudley, two expert and conscientious agents of Chamber finance. It was a popularity-seeking gesture that indicated growing resentment of the system and showed that it could not continue in the way that it had been used in the previous reign. It was weakened immediately during Henry's early playboy years, and Cardinal Wolsey, who as Chancellor was not a Household officer, showed little interest in preserving it. It perished finally with the reforms of Thomas Cromwell, who saw that the administration of public affairs could not rest for ever upon the personal accidents of an energetic king and an efficient Household, imponderables that could not be guaranteed. In any case the Reformation, which brought the Church and its vast estates under the Crown, created new responsibilities beyond the capacity of the ancient Household. The details of Cromwell's far-reaching reforms need not concern us here, but, briefly, he set up six statutory courts to administer the royal finances; he converted the old 'inner ring' of councillors into an institutional Privy Council with a clerk and a formal procedure; he took the seals out of the Household and virtually out of the government machinery; and he raised the secretary into a public – that is, non-Household – officer who, because his duties were not defined, might undertake any responsibility.

These reforms did not imply any weakening of royal authority. A king who claimed to have resumed control of a national Church for centuries usurped by foreigners was stronger than his many pious predecessors who had consented to the usurpation; and statute itself, until the Commons began to place a novel interpretation upon it, was a declaration of the royal will duly confirmed in parliament by the peers and representatives of the realm. Through the office of Secretary, Cromwell retained the flexibility in control that the King had formerly exercised through the Household, and Elizabeth's multi-purpose employment first of Burghley and then of Walsingham was a tribute to his foresight. Again, it was of course the King who chose the members of the Privy Council, although in time the holders of certain offices would establish a right to be included. Nor was the Household itself substantially diminished in authority. Cromwell's reforms withdrew it from the national administration, and of itself it would never again be an organ of government. But a Court appointment was not for the individual a bar to political office, and the Household was still a springboard for men of ambition or a profitable pasturage in later years. The middle rank of the Household, the working officers, were a mixture of courtiers, careerists and civil servants, as in effect they always had been. The Court was still *Domus Regis*, the place where the great men of the kingdom were to be found, where ambassadors were received and crucial decisions taken. Its prestige did not suffer when it was disentangled from administrative machinery which it could no longer operate. Instead it now became more attractive to men of wit or social grace or artistic accomplishment who had no great interest in politics and government.

Cromwell's reforms left the Master of the Horse as a great Household officer appointed by the sovereign. Immediately, however, there was a setback that has had tiresome consequences. In 1539 Cromwell prepared a Statute of Precedence whose object was to establish the new status of·the Secretary. It ranked him immediately below the high dignitaries of the state and the Household, with precedence over barons and bishops who held no office. This is the significant paragraph:

> And it is enacted by authority aforesaid that as well in all parliaments as in the Star Chamber, and in all other assemblies and conferences of Council, the lord chancellor, the lord treasurer, the lord president, the lord privy seal, the great chamberlain, the constable, the marshal, the lord admiral, the grand master or lord steward, the king's chamberlain, shall sit and be placed in such order and fashion as is above rehearsed, and not in any other place. (Letters and Papers of Henry VIII.)

It will be noted that the Master of the Horse is omitted from the list: as a result of which his precedence has been subject to periodic challenges, even during the tenure of the Duke of Beaufort in the twentieth century. The omission may have been due to a clerical oversight, which in those days was common enough. It is possible, however, that the statute was drafted at a time when the office was vacant, between the disgrace of Sir Nicholas Carew and the appointment of Sir Anthony Browne as his successor. No permanent exclusion was intended, since Browne was one of nineteen members of the Privy Council present at a meeting in 1540 at which

98. Cole Park, Malmesbury, site of one of Henry VIII's great studs. In Tudor times it covered a considerable area and was divided into various paddocks, such as Townleas, Ratborne, Campsfields, Barne Meade and Conigre.

the council appointed a clerk; and as Master he appears in his rightful place in a warrant of the same year authorising the appointment of a second secretary:

> His Majesty ordaineth that in all Councils, as well in his Majesty's Household as in the Star Chamber and elsewhere, all lords, both of the temporalty and clergy, shall sit above them [the secretaries]; and likewise the treasurer, comptroller, master of the horse, and vice-chamberlain of His Highness's Household; then after that to be placed the said principal secretaries . . . (Ibid.)

This clearly recognised the Master, who was not then a peer, as a senior officer of the Household, and gave him his place in the hierarchy. But it did not entirely rectify the earlier omission, since a statute has greater authority than a royal warrant.

Carew by now had gone. In a more carefree time he had tilted at a Castle of Loyalty, but real castles of loyalty were harder to maintain, and since the upheaval of the Reformation, England had become a dangerous place and Henry VIII a dangerous man. During his diplomatic journeys to Europe while the 'divorce' was being discussed, Carew had come to feel that Catherine of Aragon was being badly treated. He was never a Boleyn man, except for immediate tactical purposes, and he had no regrets when Henry transferred his affections from Anne to Jane Seymour. In 1536 Jane was lodged with Carew during the proceedings which brought Anne to the scaffold, and she rewarded him later with a brooch of gold. In the same year he supplied 200 men to the force sent against the Pilgrimage of Grace, and he was present at the christening of Prince Edward. But Henry was becoming neurotic about his own safety, and in 1538–9 he made a purge of his dynastic rivals. The chief object of his fears was the Marquis of Exeter, a Yorkist claimant to the throne as a grandson of Edward IV, and Carew and Edward Neville were known to have made visits to him at his home at Horsley. Early in 1539 Chapuys, the Emperor's ambassador, reported that 'on 31st Dec. the Grand Escuyer, Master Caro, was taken prisoner to the Tower . . . It is presumed the King will not have forgotten to charge [the commissioners] to take the most beautiful diamonds and pearls and innumerable jewels which he formerly gave to the said Escuyer's wife . . . The office of Escuyer has fallen to Master Brun.' Carew was accused of having traitorously corresponded with Catherine of Aragon before her death and encouraged a scheme to marry Exeter's son to Princess Mary, the daughter whom Henry had disinherited. The formal charge against him was that he had known Exeter to be a traitor but had failed to inform the King. On the scaffold he attributed his fall to his neglect of true religion and he urged the spectators to read evangelical works and attend to their own spiritual regeneration. There is nothing new in brain-washing. Another victim was Edward Neville, the *Joyeux Penser* of the 1511 tilt; and Exeter himself was the former Earl of Devonshire who had given Francis I a black eye at Cloth of Gold.

In attempting his household economies Cromwell had first to deal with Henry's disinclination to reduce his own comfort and magnificence. Henry was anxious to revive his body of 'spearmen', or gentlemen pensioners, that had lately been disbanded. These were young men of good family and sterling physique whose presence fortified the royal image on ceremonial occasions. There was an element of shrewd policy in it too, as these youths would be hostages for the loyalty of their families. Henry wanted 100 of them, and although Cromwell beat him down to 50, it brought that many additional servants into the establishment. The number of other servants was also larger than had been projected in the Eltham Ordinances, so Henry managed to protect his amenities. But Cromwell went to the heart of the matter by establishing the authority of the Green Cloth, with a new officer, the Lord Great Master of the Household, in charge of it in order to overcome the traditional rivalry between the Steward and the Chamberlain. The effect of his changes was to set up a Household system working independently of royal intervention and under the control of officers of Privy Council rank. He did not succeed in wholly abolishing waste, and the parsimonious Elizabeth was to be horrified at what she found. But at least he curtailed it, and his arrangements did not neglect the minutiae of administration. The financial officers were to meet at 8 o'clock each morning to scrutinise the previous day's accounts and purchases and the menus prepared for dinner and supper. Clerks were appointed not merely to make a record of those eating at table but to inspect the private chambers to see that no unauthorised meals were taking place there. Even the permitted perquisites were regulated – the feathers from the poultry, the skins and heads from the meat and fish. The yeoman of the bakehouse was allowed to make what use he might of the cinders from the ovens.

The revised structure of the Household has given us one of the fullest surviving records of the staff, their duties and their remuneration. It is contained in a document originally printed as though it were part of the Eltham Ordinances, but the names of some of the personnel – including Browne, who is mentioned as Master of the Horse – indicate a later date, probably about 1544, after Cromwell's death. It specifies the members of the Household entitled to 'bouche of court', the allowance of food, fuel and light; those not having bouche of court but allowed to dine and sup in the Household; and so on through all the familiar gradations. (The complexity of the arrangements is, one would have said, self-defeating, were it not that such gradations were felt to be very important. Much time and money must have been spent in seeing that they were observed.) Browne was at this time, as well as being Master of the Horse, captain of the gentlemen pensioners, and it is in this capacity that he appears as a gentleman of the privy chamber entitled to bouche of court and a salary of 200 marks (£133 6s. 8d.). His salary as Master was a half of this, £66 13s. 4d., and together with the avenor and 'the Esquires Quyre' (the squires of the stable, later to be known as equerries) he was to receive three 'messes'. A mess was originally a course served at a meal, and it only later came to mean also a company of men who fed together. The Master was 'to sit in his own chamber at his meals', meaning that he did not, like some of the officers, take his meals with the King; the avenor and squires were to sit with him, together with some of the gentlemen pensioners, and he was to be waited on by his own servants. A single mess was estimated to cost £358 9s. 4¾d. a year, but the document contains the inconsistencies that we have to regard as inevitable. Elsewhere Sir Anthony is said to be entitled to four messes, not three, costing £368 9s. 4¾d. each. The Great Chamberlain had three messes at the same cost, and the secretaries two at £406 each, but the 'chirurgeons' only one mess at £66. The King's diet for the year' cost £1520 12s. 4d.

Details of the food to be served show that the consumption was colossal. For instance, the menu served to the chief officers each Sunday, Tuesday and Thursday comprised at dinner a first course of bread, ale, wine, flesh for pottage, beef, mutton, veal, 'swan or other dish', capons, conies, friands (delicacies) and fritters; followed by a second course of heron, kid or lamb, cocks, plovers, snipe, rabbits, larks, 'tart or other dish', fritters, fruit and butter. At supper there was a first course of bread, ale, wine, flesh for pottage, mutton, capons, conies and 'doucettes'; and a second of lamb, larks, rabbits, baked meats, butter and eggs.

Particulars of the stables establishment (Eltham Ordinances) show a provision of 109 horses and mules for the King, of which 30 were coursers, and a further 10 for the officers: three each for the Master and one of the squires and two each for the avenor and another squire. Their hay, litter and oats, with a sum of £45 for shoeing and nailing, cost £769 12s. 4¾d. a year. The stables had further to maintain 66 hackneys for 'divers officers' such as clerks, grooms, purveyors, farriers and baggage-men, one of them being for the King's fool, and the cost of feeding and shoeing these was £301 12s. 6d. Although no costs are estimated for this, the department had also to provide stabling for the horses of the senior officers and distinguished visitors, and of their servants. Privy councillors, the secretaries and the Vice-Chamberlain, for instance, were each entitled to stabling for eight horses and three beds for servants. The entitlement for dukes and bishops when attending the Court was, respectively, 24 and 16 horses and nine and six servants.

The annual charge of wages, board-wages and 'other allowances' for all officers of the stables and the avenery was estimated at £1132 10s. 2½d.; the allowances including in many cases the cost of livery coats and, for the Master, 'one cart for the

99. Sir Anthony Browne, one of the most energetic and influential courtiers of the 16th century. Henry VIII showed exceptional confidence in him by confirming him as Master of the Horse for life.

HE, LYVYNGE, WAS ALL AT ONE TYME, AND TO HYS
DEATHE: MASTER OF THE HORSE TO KYNGE HENRY
THE EYGHT: AND AFTER TO KYNGE EDWARD THE SYXTHE·
CAPYTAYNE OF BOTHE THEYRE MAIESTIES GENTLEMEN
PENTIONERS, CHEEF STANDARD BEARER OF ENGLAND,
IVSTICE IN ONOVR OF ALL THEYRE FORRESTES, PARKES,
AND CHASES BEYOND THE RYVER OF TRENT SOWTHWARD
LEVTENAVNT OF THE FORRESTES OF WENDSOR WOLMAR
AND, ASHDOWNE WYTH DYVERS PARKES, AND CHASES
SOWTHWARD ONE OF THE EXECVTORS, TO KYNGE HENRY
THE EYGHT· ONE OF THEYRE MAIESTES HONORABLE
PRIVEY COVNCELL· AND KNYGHT AND COMPANION OF
THE MOST NOBLE ORDER
OF THE GARTER ❦

HE ENDED HYS LYFE THE SIXT OF MAY, IN THE SECONDE YERE OF KYNGE EDWARD THE SIXTHE 1548,
AT BYFLET HOWSE IN SVRREY, BY HIM BVVLDED · AND LYETH BVRED AT BATTELL IN SVSSEX, BY ꝗ
DAME ALICE HYS FYRST WYFF: WHERE HE BEGAN A STATLY HOWSE, SENCE PROCEDED IN BY HYS
SONNE AND HEYER ANTHONY VICECOVNT MOWNTEGVE · CHEEFE STANDARD BEARER OF ENGLAND·
LEVTENAVNT OF THE FORREST OF WYNDSOR, WYTH OTHER PARKES · ONE OF QVENE MARYES HONORABLE
PRIVEY COVNCELL · AND KNIGHT AND COMPANYON OF THE MOST NOBLE ORDER OF THE GARTER · ꝗ
HE HAD BY DAME ALICE DAWTHER TO SYR IOHN GAGE: KNYTGHT OF THE NOBLE ORDER OF THE GARTER·
CONTROWLER TO KYNGE HENRY THE EYGHT : AND CHAVNCELLER OF HYS DOWTCHY OF LANCASTER·
AND AFTER LORD CHAMBERLEYNE TO QVENE MARY · CONSTABLE OF THE TOWER OF LVNDON·AND ONE
OF THEYRE HONORABLE PRIVEY COVNCELL · SEAVEN SONNES · ANTHONYE OF HIS PROPER NAME, WILLYAM,
HENRY, FRANCIS, THOMAS, GEORGE AND HENRY BROWNE · HE HAD ALL SO BY HER, THRE DAWGHTERS ✚
MARY, MABELL, AND LVCY · HIS SECOND AND LAST WYFE, WAS THE LADY ELYSABETH GARRET: AFTER
COVNTES, OF LYNCOLNE: AND ONE OF THE DAWGHTERS, OF GERRALD, ERLE OF KYLDARE: BY WHOE HE
HAD TOW SONNES: EDWARD, AND THOMAS: WHYCH DYED BOTHE, IN THEYRE INFANCIE ✚

100. The ruins of Cowdray. Browne began work on the house in the 1530s, and by the time that Edward VI visited it in July 1552 it was one of the most luxurious private houses in England. 'At that goodly house,' wrote Edward, ' . . . we were marvellously, nay rather excessively, banqueted.' It was destroyed by fire in 1793.

carriage of his stuff at the king's removing'. The Master's fee, as already mentioned, was £66 13s. 4d. The avenor was paid £40, and five squires (compared with the two for whom horses were provided) £40 or £20; but their entitlement to bouche of court meant a substantial increase in their real wages. With 97 lower officials and servants, the total establishment amounted to 104; and we shall find in later documents a possibly surprising consistency in the numbers of the establishment, just over a hundred permanent officers and servants at a ratio of roughly one man per horse. There was also an unspecified and probably fluctuating number of 'weekly helpers', men without regular employment.

The ordinances go on to indicate what the King expected for his money. First, the Master was to appoint what he regarded as an appropriate quota of squires, officers and keepers to attend the King at Court or on progress, the number depending upon the occasion. Secondly, the King required the daily attendance at Court of the avenor, three squires, the clerk of the avenery, one surveyor, one purveyor, one yeoman garnetor, the yeoman of the stirrup, the yeoman farrier, the yeoman saddler and 10 footmen.

Later provisions are directed against waste, thieving and idleness. At least two squires or surveyors are to keep daily observations on the feeding of the horses appointed for the King's own use, 'without any waste, bribing or giving away any part or parcel thereof'. If the horses 'do not eat the said daily allowance of half a bushel . . . then the overplus of the said oats is to be saved daily for the King's use'; and the supervisors are to keep a careful check upon this and submit a reckoning to the Master and the avenor, who in turn are to render a monthly statement to the counting-house. Similar provisions insist that other members of the department 'do daily give their attendance upon the coursers and young horses', supervising their feed and retaining the surplus for further use; and that the servants in charge of the carriage-horses and sumpters shall observe like discipline.

The wage-bill for the department also includes modest provision, totalling less than £75, for 'medicines and drinks given to horses', and for repairs and 'divers necessaries' for the sumpters and the carts. In fact the whole document – except perhaps in the particulars of the food to be consumed – is in a tone of aspiration rather than achievement. A new reign was soon to bring new problems, and the very frequency over the years of these Household ordinances suggests both optimism and impermanence. Heads of large departments have an occupational longing for the unattainable. But it is useful to have at the threshold of the modern period at least an outline of the duties and organisation of the Master's department.

Browne, the last of Henry VIII's Masters, was appointed in February 1539 at the usual salary of £40 a year, and the increase to 100 marks in the Cromwellian ordinances – if accurately recorded – was an acknowledgment of Tudor inflation. He was a veteran of the Household who managed to stay in Henry's favour for twenty-five years. He had been knighted for his valour in the assault on Morlaix, and as a squire of the body he was frequently seen in the lists. The Eltham Ordinances named him as one of six gentlemen-in-waiting attendant on the King, and he was employed on several diplomatic missions, among them a visit to the court of Cleves in 1539. Misled by a flattering Holbein portrait, and perhaps by Cromwell's anxiety for a Lutheran alliance, Henry had decided to marry Anne of Cleves, and Browne was sent as proxy for the well-seasoned bridegroom. At the ceremony he was handsomely garbed with leg 'arrayed in white satin for the purpose of being thrust into the bed of the princess, in token of the real husband's rights over his wife'. (G. R. Wright, *Sir Anthony Browne and His Descendants*, 1866.) As Master he was present, leading the horse of state, when Anne arrived in England to meet her real husband, and he was a witness soon afterwards to Henry's distaste for this new marital possession.

For the exercise of his duties in the stables Browne was granted lodgings at Hampton Court, and he is recorded as receiving £80 10s. 11½d. as payment for 'certain stuff, workmanship and carriage'. On another occasion he was instructed to obtain 'clothes, bits and other necessaries' for a certain Madame de Tamps 'who wished to have a horse from the king'. On the death of his brother-in-law, the Earl of Southampton, he succeeded him as master of the king's harriers with '3¾d. a day for the keep of a horse, and ½d. a day for each of the 36 running dogs and nine greyhounds'. The revival in the 1540s of Henry's military ambitions then obliged him to prepare the Household for war. He was himself sent to York to confer with the Scots commissioners in the hope of dissuading them from intervention, and he also took part in negotiations for an imperial alliance. Although, like his sovereign, he was no longer a young man, Browne accompanied Norfolk's army against Scotland in 1542, when James V died of a broken heart at the news of Solway Moss, and in 1544 he went as Master when Henry invaded France. It was an old man's expedition, with the aged Suffolk once more at its head.

In the last of the many Court revolutions of the reign Henry was persuaded by the Protestant party, with the Seymours at their head, that the Catholic Howards were plotting a religious and political reaction. Browne, who had walked the tight-rope for so many years, would not lose his footing now, but he must be sure that the safety-net was in position before he would venture. In a letter written in August 1545 to Sir William Paget, son of a rural catchpole and secretary of state, Sir John

Russell spoke of him as 'a man most unreasonable, and as one whose words and deeds do not agree together . . . and one that will blame every man for that fault and yet will do worse himself. I would he were here where he should have want both of good meat and drink.' (Letters and Papers of Henry VIII.) To be mistrusted by jackals like Russell and Paget is to no man's discredit, but Browne discreetly wavered until Henry's mind was made up before he took a stand against the Howards and appeared at their trial. He was not unrewarded. Henry had earlier shown exceptional confidence in him by confirming him as Master of the Horse for life. In 1546 he received with his son a 'joint patent' as standard-bearer at an annual fee of £100. He also received a legacy of £300 in Henry's will, and he was appointed to be one of the guardians of the young Prince Edward and his half-sister Elizabeth. It was perhaps because of these many tokens of royal favour that Browne was entrusted with the most delicate of all his missions. He was believed to have such a firm hold on Henry's fickle temper that 'when it was certain that the king's maladies were incurable . . . Sir Anthony was selected for the dangerous and unpleasant duty of telling the monarch of his approaching end' (G. Wright, *op. cit*). In his role as guardian, Browne went to Enfield in the company of the future Duke of Somerset to tell the King's children of his death, and he then rode to London for the proclamation of Edward VI, who was destined to rule for only six years (1547–53).

Browne was fortunate in living at a time when the loot of the monasteries was available for distribution among loyal supporters of the Crown. From the

101 (see also 102 and 103). Engraving made in 1788 for the Society of Antiquaries, by S. H. Grimm, of Tudor paintings commissioned for Cowdray by Sir Anthony Browne. This one shows the Siege of Boulogne (1544), an occasion notable for the use of wooden cannon which were constructed as fakes, complete with fireworks, because the real ordnance was stuck in the mud. Browne's camp is on the hill at top left.

dissolution he received lands in Surrey owned by Chertsey Abbey, St Mary Overy in Southwark and the priories of Guildford and Merton. In Sussex he received the ancient Battle Abbey, where he pulled down the church, the chapter-house and the cloisters and established himself in the abbot's lodgings. As châtelain he installed the young bride of his later years, Lady Elizabeth Fitzgerald, orphan daughter of the Earl of Kildare, to whom the poet Earl of Surrey addressed loving verses. From his brother-in-law Southampton, who was killed in action against the Scots, he inherited the magnificent Cowdray estates at Midhurst, and after his own death in 1548 his son, later Viscount Montague, moved there from Battle.

The story goes that once when Browne was feasting with his family at Battle, a monk appeared and pronounced a curse upon them: 'By fire and water thy line shall come to an end, and it shall perish out of the land.' Since this prophecy took seven generations to come to pass, it is permissible to suspect coincidence rather than long-range divination in its eventual fulfilment. However, in 1793 the eighth Lord Montague, a young man of 24, tried, against urgent warnings, to shoot the rapids on the Rhine in a small boat, which disappeared and was never seen again. When his servant came home with the sad tidings he found that Cowdray House had burned down. The estate then passed to Montague's sister, who later had two small boys. The final scene was at undramatic Bognor in the year of Waterloo. The two children went boating on a calm sea, and when the boat heeled over, both were drowned, leaving no one to succeed to the title.

102 (overleaf, left). The encampment of Henry VIII at Marquison before the siege of Boulogne.

103 (overleaf, right). The meeting of Henry VIII and Sir Anthony Browne on a hill between Calais and Marquison.

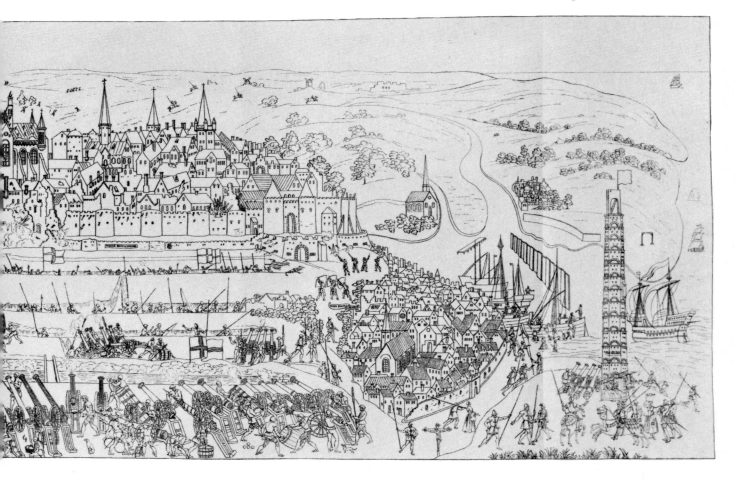

THE CAMPING OF THE KING AT MORGUISON.

THE MEETING OF THE KINGE BY S. ANTONY. BROWN. VPON. THE HILL. BETWENE. CALLIS. AND. MORGVISON.

CHAPTER ELEVEN

Mid-Century

Although easily tired by the breathlessness of his fatal malady, Edward VI loved his hunting, and the privy buckhounds establishment was fully maintained for his sport. Indeed he was encouraged in it, for so long as he was hunting or had his head down among his pious books, the politicians were free to pursue their own affairs. These were gilded hours for the Protestant profiteers; not least Sir William Herbert, Master of the Horse from 1549 to 1552, later first Earl of Pembroke of the second creation. Not appointed until December 1549, he received the post for life at a salary of 100 marks, plus the arrears outstanding since Browne's death, although he had done nothing to earn these.

After a career of astonishing deviousness, even by Tudor standards, Herbert came to his final rest in St Paul's in 1570. It is instructive to see how he did it. Originally a squire of the body to Henry VIII, he was granted lands from the dissolved abbey of Wilton, where he began to build the mansion. As a privy councillor under Edward VI, he supported the early religious changes and helped to quell the Cornish rising in 1549. Backing Northumberland's conspiracy against Somerset was a profitable investment, rewarded with the presidency of Wales, Somerset's estates in Wiltshire and an earldom, bestowed, according to the citation, on one who 'both in King Henry's time served well in wars against France, and in office at home also served the King many times.' Backing Northumberland again – this time in his bid to keep Queen Mary off the throne – proved to be less judicious, but in a typical sixteenth-century somersault he hastily declared for Mary and in 1554 commanded the force that put down Wyatt's rebellion. The erstwhile Protestant was soon on easy terms with Philip of Spain, and he was made governor of Calais a few months before it was lost. In the next reign, sensing the changing wind, he was a Protestant once more and became Steward of the Household; but finally he had to use the practised nimbleness of a lifetime of intrigue to extricate himself from a charge of aiding the Catholic Duke of Norfolk in an intended marriage to Mary Queen of Scots.

Such a busy man had little time for his duties in the stables, and he surrendered his patent to Northumberland in 1552. An Exchequer warrant to pay £651 to Edmund Standen 'towards the provision of such furniture as is requisite for the king's majesty's stables' may mean that Standen was the responsible official who did the work. More characteristic of Herbert's real interests was an order to the Lord High Admiral to deliver a royal ship, the *Minion*, 'to the Master of the Horse, taking order that the ordinance of the same, or the value thereof, may be answered if the ship perish out of the king's service'. (Acts of Privy Council, June 1550.) His department did, however, have to meet a heavy bill outstanding from Henry's French wars. There was a warrant in 1550 authorising the payment of £5000 to the Earl of Warwick (later Northumberland) and the Master of the Horse, 'by them

borrowed for the furniture of the king's army last sent to Calais, and £252 due for the interest of the same'. (Ibid.) Probably Pembroke's proudest moment, so far, was his lavish entertainment of the King and his retinue at Wilton in 1552. The vessels at the royal table were of beaten gold and 'all members of his household, down to the very least, ate off solid silver.' (Cal. State Papers, X.) As a parting gift Edward received a travelling-bed, decorated with pearls and precious stones, made to fold up and to be carried by a mule.

Since the fall of Somerset in 1549 the country had virtually been ruled by the Earl of Warwick, who was acclaimed by advanced Protestants (mostly foreign immigrants) as a 'most faithful and intrepid soldier of Jesus Christ'. This

104. Armour made in the Greenwich Armouries, c.1550, for Sir William Herbert. It was worn by him at the Battle of St Quentin in 1555.

105. *William Herbert, 1st Earl of Pembroke. He was described by John Aubrey as 'of good natural parts but very choleric . . . strong set but bony, reddish favoured, of a sharp eye, stern look.'*

106. Sir Edward Hastings. He was not very active in the stables, being more concerned with political matters during Queen Mary's unhappy reign.

faithfulness he dutifully displayed by annexing property from the see of Durham and adding it to the estates of the ancient earldom of Northumberland, recently extinct, to create a new dukedom for himself. Northumberland had come a long way. He was John Dudley, eldest son of the Edmund Dudley who as an over-zealous tax-gatherer had been sacrificed to public demand by Henry VIII. The boy, aged nine, was adopted by Sir Edward Guildford, the chief armourer, and brought up at Calais when Guildford was in charge of the garrison. He married Guildford's only daughter, Jane, who bore him five sons and two daughters, and they gave the forename Guildford to the fourth son.

Knighted in 1523 for service in the French wars, Dudley soon recommended himself to Henry VIII. He was Master of the Horse to Anne of Cleves, warden of the Scottish Marches, Lord High Admiral, and governor of Boulogne, which he

107, 108. The old stables (now known as Washern Grange) in the grounds of Wilton House. They are all that is left of the abbey, pulled down by William Herbert in the 1540s, but parts of his Tudor mansion can still be seen in the present house.

helped to capture. On Henry's death he was created Earl of Warwick, and after the success of his intrigues against Somerset he began to make plans for a future in which he saw himself as a second Warwick the King-maker. On acquiring his dukedom he transferred the Warwick title to his eldest son John and in 1552 made him Master of the Horse, 'which patent the said William [Herbert] has surrendered to the intent that another patent be made to John Earl of Warwick.' Warwick was appointed for life, at a fee of 100 marks, 'as fully as Henry Gulforde, knight, or Nicholas Carow, knight, or any other enjoyed the office'. Like all the Dudley family, Warwick was attainted for suspected complicity in their father's succession plot, but although he was pardoned he died in 1554 and the Warwick earldom passed to his brother Ambrose. The keystone of Northumberland's plot was the marriage of his son Guildford to Lady Jane Grey, who as grand-daughter of Henry VIII's sister Mary had a claim to the throne if superior claims could be set aside, and Northumberland persuaded Edward to sign a will to that effect. The survival of

YOW THAT THESE BEASTS DO WEL BEHOLD AND SE
MAY DEME WTHE EASE WHERFORF HERE MADE THEY BE
WITE BORDERS LKE WHERIN[...]
71 BROTHERS NAMES WHO LIST TO SERCHE TE GROVN

109. Inscription in the Tower of London, carved during John Dudley's imprisonment there with his four brothers in 1553. It shows the bear and ragged staff, badge of the Earls of Warwick, and the double-tailed lion of the Dudleys. The verse and the carved border are interpreted as roses for Ambrose, gilly-flowers for Guildford, honeysuckle for Henry, oak for Robert (Latin 'robus' = oak).

true religion could only be assured, he said, by the disinheriting of Mary, the obstinately Catholic daughter of Catherine of Aragon.

This conspiracy to annexe the crown to the Dudley family was Northumberland's undoing. It foundered at once on the determination of the English people to follow the legitimate succession and be ruled by 'King Harry's daughter': Mary Tudor, the brave, dumpy little woman who was to flood the court with massing priests and Spaniards and burn three hundred Protestants for the safety of their erring souls. It was from Protestant East Anglia that she began her triumphant progress to London, and at sour, ungentle Cambridge that Northumberland realised that the game was up and threw his cap in the air for Queen Mary. He had always, he declared, been a true son of the Catholic Church, even when he was growing fat on its plundered treasure.

When the issue was still undecided and she reviewed her scanty troops at Framlingham, the men fired their guns and proclaimed their loyalty so loudly that

Mary's palfrey reared in panic and she had to complete the inspection on foot. It was an ill omen for a reign in which very little went right, but despite all its anxieties and upheavals a proper establishment had still to be attempted. There must be festivities at the coronation and at the Queen's wedding with Philip of Spain in Winchester Cathedral; and after that the supercilious Spaniards must have horses for their sport in a landscape much different from their own.

The Patent Rolls record in May 1554 the 'grant for life, in consideration of his service, to the queen's councillor Edward Hastings, knight, of the office of Master of the Horse, in the queen's disposition by the attainder of John Dudley, knight.' Third son of the first Earl of Huntingdon, Hastings had held Buckinghamshire for Mary during the critical days in 1553 when Northumberland was trying to build up support. He had been labelled in the previous reign as 'a hardened and detestable Papist', and he was devout but argumentative in his beliefs, swearing 'by the Lord's foot' that his was the true and only faith. Although he regarded Mary's Spanish marriage as unwise, he rode to Blackheath to face the rebels whom Sir Thomas Wyatt had raised against it. This rising would have given the crown to Princess Elizabeth, Henry VIII's daughter by Anne Boleyn, and Hastings was dispatched to Ashridge to enquire into the nature and extent of the illness which, she said, made it impossible to obey the Queen's summons to come to London. She came.

On the death of the Earl of Bedford in 1555 Hastings was granted the following life appointments: 'steward of the Duchy of Cornwall (40 marks), steward of the borough and manor of Bradnynch, co. Devon, and of all lands in Cornwall and Devon reputed parcel of the said duchy, and warden, keeper and steward of the Stannary court within the said counties (£20), rider and master forester of the forest and chace of Dartmoor, co. Devon.' He was licensed 'to appoint at his pleasure one of his servants or friends to shoot in any crossbow and handgun at any kind of game, fowl or thing, and to keep such crossbow, etc. in his house', provided that no person thus appointed shot in the royal forests or in any other forest without leave of the owner: and he was licensed also to keep '100 persons, gentlemen or yeomen' wearing his livery, badge or cognisance, without penalty under the statutes forbidding retainers.

A warrant issued in 1555 may suggest the difficulties he encountered in his official duties. It empowers him and his deputies 'to take in the Crown's name in all places within the realm for reasonable money as many palfreys, hobbies and ambling geldings as he or they shall think requisite from time to time for the furniture of the royal stable or to be employed by way of gift or otherwise to ladies and noblemen within the realm and parts beyond seas.' A blanket licence like this seems to indicate lack of a coherent policy or of money to support it, and too much is left to unguided individual discretion. The efficiency of the stables department had been steadily declining under recent Masters, and Hastings, for all his idiosyncratic merits, was not the man best fitted to restore it. The privy buckhounds were disbanded, the royal studs were not very well maintained, and there was not enough money to make necessary purchases abroad. The department needed the driving force of a Master who was really interested in horses, if only to keep the sergeants and other deputies up to the mark, and as a privy councillor close to the Queen, Hastings had other things on his mind. As proof of his influence the Earl of Derby once desired him to 'move the queen not to grant the lieutenantship of Lancashire and Cheshire to the Earl of Shrewsbury in preference to the writer'. Increasingly involved in the personal concerns of the sovereign, he surrendered his office in 1557 on becoming Lord Chamberlain. After serving in France he was created Baron Hastings of Loughborough, with lands and offices to support this new dignity.

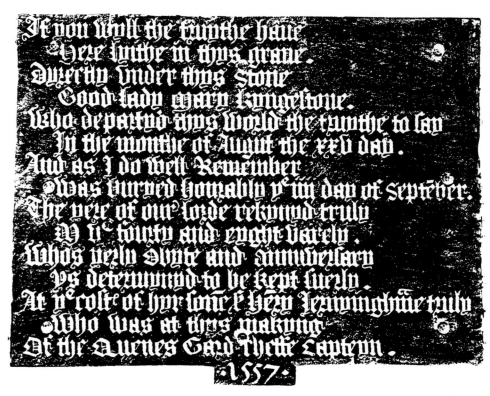

110. Memorial tablet in Leyton Parish Church, London, inscribed by Sir Henry Jerningham to his mother, Lady Mary Kingston. Her second husband, the wily Sir William Kingston, was Constable of the Tower during Anne Boleyn's imprisonment, and Lady Mary attended the Queen at her execution.

Hastings was too loyal a Catholic to approve of the religious changes that followed Mary's death, and he retired to a hospital which he had built for the poor. He was briefly imprisoned for continuing to attend the mass and he eventually compromised by taking an oath of subscription to the new religion. He died without issue in 1573, a prey, it was said, to melancholy thoughts from which he sought consolation in playing chess. He would not have found consolation in the intense Puritanism of his nephew Henry, third Earl of Huntingdon, of the long, thin, persimmon face, who had married a daughter of Northumberland.

Following Hastings's resignation in 1557, Sir Henry Jerningham was appointed Master of the Horse. He was the last Master to have both begun and ended his tenure of office as a knight: although a peerage would probably have followed if Mary had not died the next year. On the day of his appointment he received an annuity of £300 in addition to the income of the office. Mary had cause to be grateful to him as he had been her first important adherent in defiance of Northumberland's intrigues in 1553. It was a decisive declaration of loyalty as Jerningham was a squire of Norfolk, a county exposed by geography to the importation of novel doctrines. When travelling to Yarmouth to make recruits he found that six of Northumberland's ships were taking refuge from heavy seas. His passion and eloquence won the crews to Mary's side, and they brought with them their heavy naval ordnance, the first guns the royalists possessed.

As soon as Mary was established on the throne she rewarded him with the manor of Wingfield in Suffolk. Later he was granted some of the estates of Lady Jane Grey's father, and after he had been made constable of Gloucester Castle he received lands and perquisites at Tewkesbury. But he only became Master in the middle of a war, and within a year Mary was dead. Like Hastings, he was too staunch for the old beliefs to have any expectation of office under Elizabeth I.

CHAPTER TWELVE Elizabethan Masters

On the day that Mary died, 17 November 1558, Robert Dudley, Northumberland's son and future Earl of Leicester, 'being well skilled in riding a managed horse', rode to Hatfield on a snow-white steed to tell Elizabeth I that she was Queen, and the first act of her reign was to make him Master of the Horse. They had been fellow-prisoners in the aftermath of Northumberland's conspiracy, and the curious attachment that sprang up between them then lasted until Leicester's death: probably never a sexual one, nor even a romance *manqué*, because Elizabeth was a queen and Leicester had a wife, but a strange personal alchemy that disturbed other courtiers and made foreigners for a time take Leicester more seriously than he deserved.

With his dark gypsy looks he was handsome enough, and cunning in flattery, but except in his expert horsemanship he was a second-rate person. Affection did not blind Elizabeth to his faults, and it was not until the end of his career that she gave him anything worthwhile to do – a military command in the Netherlands – and he lost no time in making a mess of that. She liked having him around, however, and by making him Master she could always command his attendance at her side. But he had to wait five years for his earldom, and he was the last Master of the Horse not to have been a peer at his appointment. This is a significant consequence of Thomas Cromwell's changes. Now that they were no longer entangled in public administration, the heads of the Household departments might safely be titled persons, often privy councillors, while the active work was done by high-grade professionals. But the efficiency of a department would still depend upon the interest and enthusiasm of its titular head. Leicester was not much interested in routine and paper-work, but he did care about horses.

With his instinct for ceremonial he delighted Elizabeth with a brilliant coronation. They often hunted together, and sometimes she was seen riding pillion behind him on the same horse. No one was surprised when her first gift to him was the castle of Kenilworth, built early in the twelfth century, rebuilt by John of Gaunt and passing to the Crown with all the other Lancastrian appurtenances. Leicester extended and adorned it, partly at the expense of unpaid traders and craftsmen, and here in 1575, 'having completed all things for her reception', he entertained the Queen for seventeen summer days: 'with excessive cost', Dugdale says in his *Antiquities of Warwickshire* (1656), 'and variety of delightful shews'. It was the most celebrated carnival of the reign, full of artificial pomps loved by Tudor Englishmen, including 'a Savage Man with Satyrs' deputising for the more familiar quarry in the hunt. 'Hither came the Coventry men, and acted the ancient play, long since used in that city, called *Hocks Tuesday*, setting forth the destruction of the Danes in King Ethelred's time; with which the Queen was so pleased that she gave them a brace of bucks, and five marks in money.' Robert Laneham preferred the

imported Italian acrobat with his 'sundry windings, gyrings and circumflexions', and no doubt fun was had by all.

There was a deer-hunt among the revels at Kenilworth, but the fact that for half a century England was ruled by female sovereigns had some effect on equestrian development. For one thing, riding had to be much slower. Although Mary and Elizabeth were both capable horsewomen, they had not the stature or the strength to ride large horses over long distances or at any speed. For the sake of the royal image, attempts were made to conceal this. Elizabeth rode a palfrey, not the courser on which she appears in contemporary prints, and it was sitting side-saddle on a palfrey that she spoke rousing words to the troops at Tilbury in 1588. Again, she loved hunting, especially at her father's architectural extravaganza at Nonsuch. Early in the reign Leicester told the Lord Deputy of Ireland that she wanted some native horses 'for her own saddle' and they must be 'good gallopers, which are better than her geldings, which she spareth not to try as fast as they can go. And I fear them much, but she will prove them.' There was no real truth in this. Elizabeth was fearless, as Queen Victoria was, but she cannot have ridden fast by male standards, and this slowed the hunt as her companions had to adjust their pace to

111. Seal of Elizabeth I, dated 1559. The horses she rode were generally palfreys or Spanish jennets (from 'Zenata', a Barbary tribe noted for their horsemanship). The Queen kept a stud of Barbary horses at Greenwich.

112. At Kenilworth in July 1575 Robert Dudley staged a lavish entertainment for Elizabeth. It lasted seventeen days and among the attractions were a floating island on the lake, fireworks, Italian tumblers, and a Triton riding on an eighteen-foot mermaid.

113. Kenilworth Castle. Originally part of the royal manor of Stoneleigh, it was founded in the reign of Henry I, rebuilt by John of Gaunt, and given to Robert Dudley by Elizabeth in 1558.

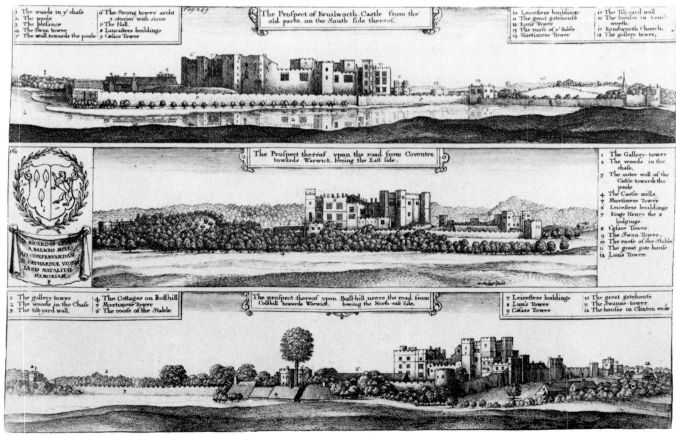

hers while she proceeded side-saddle on her palfrey. At the kill the sport might be tepid indeed. The deer were driven up and down within a netted space while Elizabeth lurked behind a well-screened butt and awaited the moment to pick off the victim with her arbalest. The Queen's example encouraged her sex to take part in a sport that had become much safer and slower – and easier – and in Shakespeare's comedies we find ladies present at the chase, not as spectators or incidental decoration but as participants. Thus hunting tended generally to become a more sedate activity, with growing emphasis on horn-blowing and other associated rituals.

Tilting went into a gradual decline, possibly slowed by the perennial youthfulness of Sir Henry Lee. Elizabeth had no great taste for it, but she recognised its usefulness in creating an image of regal splendour. A week's jousting followed the coronation, and here Lee, formerly a clerk in the royal armoury, appeared as the Queen's traditional champion. He was so elated with his performance that he vowed to renew the challenge every year on the day of the Queen's accession, and this, with occasional gaps, he continued to do until 1590; 'being by age overtaken' (he was then 60), he resigned and instead was appointed master of the ordnance. He was to live another twenty years, a prosperous landowner and builder, rich enough to be chosen for the financially crippling honour of acting as host to the Queen and her entourage.

Records exist of jousters appearing as Arthurian knights, long-haired Irish kerns, savages from the unknown lands beyond the sea or whatever role might be devised for them by their household sages. In one tilt there was a 'frozen knight', but the particulars of his ingenuity do not survive; in another the knights were accompanied by 'Amazon' attendants 'with hair hanging down to their boots'. Although there was no longer the rich, many-sided pageantry of the tournaments of Henry VIII, poetic wit could express itself in the *impresa*, the motto or device by which a combatant proclaimed his identity, his lineage, his immediate hopes and his future intentions. These elaborations kept the heralds busy and provided an outlet for the literary fecundity of the age. The Queen sat through much of this, it being part of her duty to listen to squires long-windedly explaining the significance of their master's 'disguising' before she could give them permission to proceed. A tolerance for tedious entertainment has long been one of the burdens of royalty; and for Elizabeth there was the consolation that each squire who mounted the steps to her gallery bore her a rich present from his master. It must have been agreeable enough, because she decreed a further tournament to be held annually to celebrate the defeat of the Armada. But with inflation, the lethal price-rise of the sixteenth century, jousting became financially as well as socially obsolete. It no longer made sense to employ great horses that had become useless in war and might be better employed in drawing carriages or ploughs. For nimbler horses, too, alternative employments were already being foreshadowed by the popularity of 'Bankes his curtal'. This was the bob-tail Morocco belonging to a Scottish showman, John Banks, which could dance and make numerical calculations: prodigies mentioned by several contemporary writers, including Shakespeare in *Love's Labour's Lost* (i. ii. 57) and possibly in *All's Well That Ends Well* (ii. iii. 65).

While jousting gradually languished and disappeared in its own preciousness, racing began to extend its appeal and thus to create a need for rules and organisation. It is impossible to say when or where racing began, because it is a primitive human need to run or jump or fight or ride more successfully than other people. The Romans raced in chariots, but the Arabs apparently raced on horseback even earlier than that, motivating their mounts by depriving them of drink and then

114. Queen Elizabeth arriving at Nonsuch Palace, which was built by her father and was the favourite residence of her later years. The turrets to the east and west were five storeys high. The two-storey structure between them was 'adorned with a variety of statues, pictures and other antick forms of excellent art and workmanship.' Two rooms in the inner courtyard were set aside for the Master of the Horse.

spurring them to the nearest water: just as the modern greyhound needs the inspiration of an electric hare. Wherever there was a stretch of open country, men would always be likely to race their horses for a wager, and a chronicler records this sort of thing happening in England in the time of Henry II, usually at Smithfield, which was London's horse-market. Richard I made his knights race their stallions at Whitsuntide for a purse of 'forty pounds of ready gold', and Edward III had 'running horses', or racers, in his huge equestrian establishment. A code of rules, if only to settle disputes and prevent cheating, would obviously be necessary, but development was surprisingly slow and there is no record of even a tentative organisation until a meeting was established at Chester in about 1512. Races were also held at Croydon, Doncaster and Newmarket, and although the sport did not become widely popular until the reign of James I, horses were now being bred especially for racing. Pedigrees were more carefully studied, and this would be the origin of the English thoroughbred.

Leicester had an honourable part in all this activity. He was Master from 1558 until his death thirty years later, the longest tenure of any Master until the Duke of Beaufort in the present century; and in 1572 he resumed control of the buckhounds which he had briefly held in his father's day. The amount of attention a Master gave to his duties depended on his personal interests, and it was in horsemanship that Leicester particularly excelled. He was never happier than when displaying his talents in the *manège*. Since, in spite of all the honours and favours he received, he was always short of money, he was no doubt attracted too by the perquisites the office brought him through the placing of contracts for supplies and materials and the appointment of huntsmen, stud-masters and keepers.

His principal responsibility was to purchase, breed, train and equip the large number of horses the Household needed for a variety of purposes: chargers for war, 'great horses' for the joust or for pulling the unsprung coaches that were coming into use in Elizabeth's reign, coursers for the squires and gentlemen, palfreys and amblers for the ladies, cobs and rouncies for the lesser servants, mules and sumpters for the baggage. Good horses were valuable creatures, breeding mares especially. Henry VII had forbidden the export of the better breeds, except by licence procurable at a suitable fee, and his son had made it a capital offence to steal one. It was a serious matter if a good horse fell ill or died through malnutrition, but it could easily happen when veterinary science was still undivorced from horology, and the fodder was poor because there was not enough corn in it. When Biondello describes the nag on which Petruchio rode to his wedding (*Taming of the Shrew* III. ii), he tells us how many things could go wrong with an Elizabethan horse – glanders, lampass, the fives, the yellows, the staggers, the bots. Accounts sent to Leicester early in the reign by the keeper of the royal studs mention payments for dressings, poultices and medicines for glanders, the stranglion, chafed legs, sore eyes and inflamed belly. Malt and brimstone were among the favoured remedies.

Leicester was always trying to improve the royal stables by acquisitions from abroad, but he was handicapped by Elizabeth's enforced parsimony and his own shortcomings in other areas. Foreign envoys made him presents and bribes when the international situation required it, but they knew that he did not really count. He might persuade the Queen's heart but he would never influence her decisions, and she would never be made accessible through gifts offered to him. Thus when in 1564 he asked the ambassador in Paris to procure the services of Hercules Trinchetta, an Italian trainer who 'gave place to no other in the breaking of young and rough horses', the reply only suggested what the French court would like in return. The French King told his own ambassador about the fighting mastiffs that the English bred so well, 'and two or three pretty curtals . . . that would gallop', not to mention some geldings for the Queen Mother. Export restrictions imposed by other countries also hampered Leicester's efforts. When on one occasion he tried to buy twelve Spanish jennets, he could only offer dogs in exchange, and his envoy in Aragon had to report that the deal was a non-starter. The best he could offer was a couple of skins that might make a jerkin and some harness. Leicester was again unsuccessful when he suggested to Sir Francis Walsingham in Paris that there must be some trainer-breeder left masterless by the decimation of the French nobility at the Massacre of St Bartholomew, and he offered a wage of £30 a year with free food, drink and stabling. Walsingham replied that he could find no Frenchman to come for that money, and £50 would be a more appropriate figure.

However, Leicester was not always defeated in his attempts, and his agents in Europe were able to make some useful purchases that enabled foreign breeds to cross with the native strains: barbs for their speed, or Spanish jennets whose mares bred the best palfreys. A happy purchase for ceremonial occasions was a group of six Hungarian horses acquired in the Netherlands in 1581, greys with tails dyed orange tawny, 'of light shape and good of travel'. They were favourites of the Queen on state appearances, with diamond pendants in their foreheads and their bridles studded with pearls.

But with imports costly and difficult to procure, the reigns of Henry VIII and Elizabeth are to be remembered for the careful improvement in the breeding at the home studs. Henry had so many horses that the royal manors at Eltham and Hampton Court could no longer accommodate them, and extensions were opened at Tutbury, within the Lancaster estates in Staffordshire, and in a park at the dispossessed abbey of Malmesbury. C. M. Prior (*The Royal Studs of the Sixteenth and Seventeenth Centuries*, 1866) mentions a Yorkshire landowner who urged the government to acquire Jervaulx Abbey, whose last abbot was hanged in 1537 for supporting the Pilgrimage of Grace. Other estates contemplated, such as the Stafford family estates at Thornbury 'which are fen grounds', were unsatisfactory compared with Jervaulx, where the King 'by good overseers, should . . . have the best pasture that should be in England, hard and sound of kind.' The horses there would have 'large and high grounds in summer, and in winter woods and low grounds to serve them', and the sturdiness of the northern breeds proved the quality of the pasture.

Although a small stud was opened at Ripon, native breeding declined in the confused reigns of Edward and Mary. Holinshed, the Elizabethan chronicler, was to lament that the 'noble studdery' erected by Henry VIII had failed when the officers, 'waxing weary, procured a mixed brood of bastard races, whereby his good purpose came to little effect'. Elizabeth enforced ancient statutes, originally military in their objects, that required landowners to maintain stables appropriate to their acreage and responsibilities, and she instructed Leicester to improve the quality of the royal studs.

He received plenty of encouragement in this work. In 1565, from his estate in Norfolk, Thomas Blundeville, a didactic gentleman of many purposes, dedicated to him *The Four Chiefest Offices Belonging to Horsemanship*. This was only one of Blundeville's hortatory productions. He wrote also upon logic, astronomy, government, and the education of young gentlemen for public service, whose principal qualification was that they should be good-looking. The four chief offices of horsemanship, he said, were those of the breeder, the rider, the keeper and the farrier. He commended Leicester for introducing an Italian expert, Claudio Corte, whose courtesy was equal to his 'perfection in riding', but the main purpose of his treatise was to urge Leicester to enforce Henry VIII's wise statutes for the encouragement of breeding, so that royal parks 'might not wholly be occupied to the keeping of deer, but partly to the breeding of horses for service'. In the event of invasion England would be poorly equipped in the cavalry arm, and the Master was advised to ensure that 'not only a sufficient number of able horses may be bred within the realm, but also that the same horses may be broken, kept, maintained and exercised accordingly.' In the matter of breeding Blundeville offered to instruct Leicester 'how to conceive either horse foals or mare foals, and of what colour you list to have yourself.'

Ten years later Leicester commissioned one Prospero d'Osma, who had a school of *manège* at Mile End, to report upon the royal studs and to propose remedies, as he feared that they had deteriorated through past mismanagement. Osma's report, which Prior analyses in some detail, is a fascinating mixture of old wives' tales and sound equestrian sense. He recommended that the entire Malmesbury stock should be moved to Tutbury (which was not done) because Malmesbury was divided and small and was situated in a damp clay valley which made the fodder injurious to good foaling. Dams reared on damp grass would mix mud with the food. In one of the parks at Tutbury, Castlehay, there was also a meadow that should not be used as the soil was sour with ferns and fungi.

Osma is full of advice on the principles of breeding. Ideally, he suggests, mares should be covered in mid-April, 'during an increasing moon and not when it is decreasing'. Covering should take place at night, and the stallion should not be given any human assistance in mounting: the best results were obtained when both partners were left free and spirited. A young stallion should not be given to a young mare, and it was also a mistake to suppose that the mating of a large animal with a small one would produce a medium-sized foal.

A mare should not be required to breed every year, since 'even soil needs rest to produce good fruit' and 'even iron is not eternal'. To make the point absolutely clear, Osma adds, 'There is a proverb which says that continuous fever kills a man, which is to say that flesh is flesh, and that continuous indulgence in one's desires will be very harmful in the end.' A stallion, however, was not in need of such discipline,

115. Robert Devereux, Earl of Essex, ill-advised and ill-fated, but nonetheless one of the romantic figures of the Elizabethan period. During his fourteen years as Master he did much to improve the royal studs.

The Right Honorable Robert Devoreux Earle of Essex and ewe Earle Marshall of England, her Maties Lieutenant and governor generall of the Kingdom of Ireland, Vicount hereford and bourgcher, Lord Feres of Chartley bourgcher and Iouan Mayster of her Maties Horse and of her Ordinance; Knight of the most noble order of the garter, and of her highnes priue Counsell, and Chauncellor of the Uniuersitie of Cambridge,

IRELANDE

The Ilands of Treceras, Coruo, S.t George, Trecera, Flores, Faiall, Pico,

The English Fleet,

ROAN

CADIZ

A. 1596

BASIS VIRTVTVM CONSTANTIA

HONI SOIT QVI MAL Y PENSE

Vertues honor, Wisdomes valure, Graces seruaunt, Mercies loue,
Gods elected, Truths beloued, Heauens affected, Doe a proue   Tockson fecit

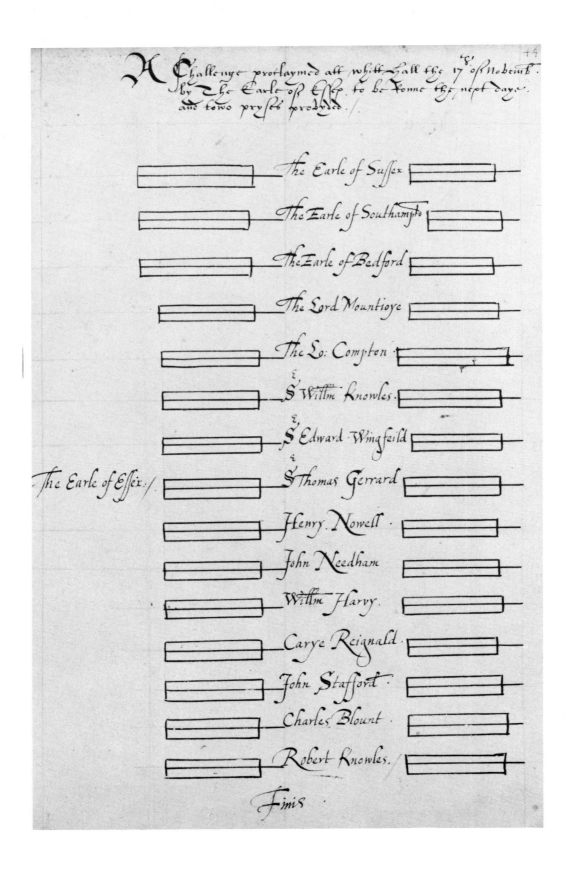

and if not burdened with other duties, 'can cover twelve mares (much to his pleasure) without suffering any damage.' It was only necessary not to weary him with unnecessary travel (Osma estimated that six resident stallions would be sufficient for the whole stud) and not to feed him on grass, which weakens the flesh. 'When a stallion mounts a mare under these circumstances, his reproductive substance is like water', and his offspring will be enfeebled. Stud work should begin when a horse was thirteen. Osma's recommended regimen was five years for rearing before the colt was ridden, a year for training, and seven years for general work: after which he should be 'ready to stand for service' and should be relieved of all other offices.

Osma urged that Thomas Eyton, the stud-master at Tutbury, should be directly accountable to the Master of the Horse for the execution of these principles, and at least his report led to closer supervision. Even if he was misguided in some of his proposals, he was right in emphasising the need for better management. Local objections that 'the nature of the soil will never breed good horse' were disregarded, coming as they did from tenants who were turned from their holdings, and until the Civil War Tutbury was a prosperous stud, with an increasing supply of Spanish and Moroccan mares. Its extent was over 14,000 acres, and Osma's list of the stock in 1576 was followed by further reviews at intervals of about twenty years. Tutbury also had its place in the political history of the reign. Its castle, today a ruin, belonged to the Earl of Shrewsbury, who was one of the nobles entrusted with the care of Mary Queen of Scots during the nineteen years she spent in England as a virtual prisoner. Elizabeth provided her with a household which was fitting to her station, and it was among Leicester's duties to supply her with horses. The rebellion of the Northern Earls in 1569 had the intention of releasing her, and Elizabeth, perhaps mistrustful of Shrewsbury's Catholic sympathies, sent the Earl of Huntingdon with 500 men to strengthen the garrison. Even this precaution was not enough, and for a time Mary was moved under closer guard to Coventry.

The size and cost of the stables establishment at this time appear in an estimate of the Crown's annual expenditure in about 1590 (Harleian MS. 642). This gives the Master's fee as 1000 marks (£666 13s. 4d.), 'a table furnished for the lords', meaning that he had first-quality entertainment at Court; and 'these offices in his gift', a list of 147 officers and servants. The Master's salary put him well ahead of the master of the buckhounds at £50 (a shilling a day for himself 'and the rest to sundry huntsmen serving his appointment'), the masters of the harthounds and the otter-hounds, each £13 6s. 8d., and the master of the harriers, £11 5s. 0d.; and in other departments the sergeant trumpeter £40, the master of the ordnance £151 11s. 8d., the sergeant of the tents £30, the master armourer £66 13s. 4d., the master of the mint £100. He profited, too, from the large number of places 'in his gift', whereby he could reward service and do favours. Among his subordinates, the chief avenor received £40 a year, six riders each £30, fourteen esquires each £20, sixteen footmen each £20, four coachmen each £18 5s. 0d., the sergeant of the carriages 1s. 3d. per day, the clerk of the stables and the three surveyors each 11d. per day, day. The lowest wage was 4d. a day paid to the four yeomen bit-makers. All these regular servants had certain rights of food and lodging at Court, and probably gained a great deal else in the clothing, food and fuel that made their unauthorised way downstairs. The total cost of wages alone was over £2100, without provision for the supply, equipment and feeding of the horses; and except that the Master's salary would have covered his duties there, no specific provision is made for the Tutbury and Malmesbury studs.

The relationship between a man's wages and his keep may be inferred from the

116. Jousting cheque, dated 1594, from a collection in the College of Arms. On the left is the name of the challenger, the Earl of Essex, who excelled at the joust.

household establishment of Prince Henry, son and heir to James I, in 1610, two years before his premature death (Harleian MS. 642). Footmen who earned £10 a year drew £30 for their board and £6 15s. 0d. for livery. For some other servants the board was equal to only half the wage, while others officially drew none at all. Henry's stable establishment was extremely lavish, with six grooms of the hunting horses each receiving £18 5s. 0d., seven groom sumpter-men the same, the groom of the bottlehouse (the hay store) £24 6s. 8d., and seventeen grooms of the coursers' stables £21 5s. 0d. each. Higher officials like the esquires, avenor and clerk to the stables were on lower wages but had a more liberal 'diet'. Among the prince's other servants was a surveyor of the works, salary unstated: a Mr Inigo Jones.

On Leicester's death Elizabeth appointed as Master the flamboyant Earl of Essex, the rotten apple of her declining years. As well as numerous other rewarding offices, she gave him serious work to do – naval expeditions to Spain, and finally the command of her troops against Tyrone in Ireland. This merely encouraged his flighty ambitions and in 1601 he attempted to raise the Londoners against the Court, failed, and died on the scaffold. But Essex was an efficient Master, zealous in acquiring good horses and looking after the royal studs. Contrary to Osma's advice, Malmesbury was not closed, and in 1596 Essex ordered Eyton to enquire into its administration, of which there had been further complaints. The blame fell on Thomas Baskerville, groom of the Queen's stud, who was accused of leasing one of the parks and neglecting the fences and leaving gates unfastened, so that the stock had mixed, with some unfortunate results. Baskerville offered the standard excuses – he had been ill, and slanderers were trying to deprive him 'of the poor living which I hold under her Majesty'. Apparently he was allowed to keep his poor living, because he was still submitting his accounts in the following reign. Two years later Eyton retired as chief stud-master and Essex took the opportunity to appoint Sir Robert Brett, who put Malmesbury in order and brought it closer to Tutbury's higher standards.

Elizabeth's third and last Master was Edward Somerset, fourth Earl of Worcester, who had been at Court for most of his life and was by now a senior statesman, a quiet supporter of the Cecils. Elizabeth is supposed to have said that he 'reconciled what she believed impossible, a stiff Papist with a loyal subject'. The stiffness of his Popery is in some doubt: the Jesuits had converted his wife and his daughters and eventually his son, and he was known to have no great regard for them. But undoubtedly he was conservative in religion, like his father, and in her constant search for a political equilibrium at her court Elizabeth used him as a balance to the aggressive Protestants like Huntingdon, of whom she had more than enough.

As a wealthy man with vast possessions around Raglan in Monmouthshire, Worcester had little need of the emoluments of the Master or of his perquisites. Nor did his tenure, which lasted until 1616, allow him much time to promote equestrian causes. He had ridden and tilted as a younger man, but in his time there was no official stock-taking of the royal studs: which is understandable because he was approaching fifty when he was appointed. Usually, too, he was occupied on graver matters. In 1601 Elizabeth sent him with other dependable men to try to dissuade Essex from his suicidal rising. At her funeral in 1603 he led her favourite palfrey behind the hearse, which was carried by six earls and followed by twelve nobles carrying banners. Six horses preceded it, draped in black velvet.

James I kept him in office, a tribute to his *gravitas*, and in 1605 he was a member of a special commission to examine the Guy Fawkes conspirators. In 1616 he was

made Lord Privy Seal when Buckingham became Master of the Horse, and once again his aptitude in difficult or revolutionary situations was shown in his appointment, with Bacon and Sir Edward Coke, to lead the enquiry that followed Raleigh's disastrous Orinoco expedition in 1618.

The old man was finally appointed Lord Chamberlain at the coronation of Charles I, but there is a more gracious side to his character than might be apparent merely from his association with formalities of state. His essential bond with Elizabeth was in their love of music, which meant as much to her as painting did to Charles I. He was a persistent champion of the great William Byrd, which required courage as well as taste since for years Byrd was kept in obscurity as a Catholic recusant. Worcester was also a patron of the drama. In 1601 he brought to Court a company that included the famous comedian Will Kempe, and he obtained leave for them to act in the public theatres despite an ordinance of 1597 that restricted this privilege to only two companies, the Chamberlain's and the Admiral's Men. Under the law, all actors, including Shakespeare, might be classed and punished as vagabonds unless they wore a nobleman's livery to protect them. James I ended this nonsense by putting all the existing companies under royal protection, and Worcester's company duly became Queen Anne's Men. Nor, finally, was Worcester lacking in orderly wit. Writing to Robert Cecil in the following reign, he offered his own diagnosis of the new King's persistent ill-health: 'Every day that he hunteth, he takes a new cold; for being hot with riding the chase, he sitteth in the open air and drinketh, which cannot but continue, if not increase, a new cold.'

117. Queen Elizabeth and courtiers on their way to a wedding. In the foreground is the 4th Earl of Worcester, who was known as 'the bald-headed Earl.'

CHAPTER THIRTEEN

The Early Stuarts

In the years between Elizabeth's death and the Civil War, James I (1603–25) and his son Charles I (1625–49) spent lavishly on the purchase of horses and the upkeep of their studs and stables. Whereas Elizabeth had been scandalised at the rising cost of her household and had ordered rigorous economies at the end of her reign, James and Charles maintained their royal estate in the face of inflation and constant parliamentary complaints about their rising expenditure. There was no longer any counting of the cost when imported horses were required, especially of the Neapolitan courser, a cross between a barb and an Andalusian. Politically this Stuart extravagance was disastrous, but it was to have an enduring effect on the quality and breeding of the English horse.

King James placed horsemanship first among the 'commendable' exercises that a prince should cultivate. He thought it 'most requisite for a King to exercise his engine, which surely with idleness will rust and become blunt'. In his *Basilicon Doron* (1599), a selection of kingly precepts written for a son who died before he could put them to use, James barred 'all rough and violent exercises as the Football; meeter for laming than making able the users thereof', but gave his approval to leaping, wrestling, fencing, running 'and such-like other fair and pleasant field-games'. Among these, 'the honourablest and most commendable games that ye can use are on horseback; for it becometh a Prince better than any other man to be a fair and good horseman. Use therefore to ride and tame great and courageous horses . . . and specially use such games on horseback as may teach you to handle your arms thereon; such as the tilt, the ring, and low riding for handling of your sword.'

Although personally he was wont to turn pale at the sight of a naked sword when bestowing an accolade, James continued in this high heroic vein. He praised hunting with running hounds as 'the most honourable and noblest' fashion of the sport, 'for it is a thievish form of hunting to shoot with guns and bows; and greyhound hunting is not so martial a game. . . . As for hawking, I condemn it not, but I must praise it more sparingly because it neither resembleth the wars so near as hunting doth, in making a man hardy and skilfully ridden in all grounds, and is more uncertain and subject to mischances; and (which is worst of all) is therethrough an extreme stirrer up of passions.'

His final words upon this matter contained a warning which he himself was to ignore when he came to the English throne: 'But in using either of these games, observe that moderation that ye slip not therewith the hours appointed for your affairs, which ye ought ever precisely to keep; remembering that these games are but ordained for you in enabling you for the office for the which ye are ordained.'

James preferred hawking and hunting to racing, and it was primarily for hunting that he made himself a comfortable home at Newmarket with enlarged accommodation for his horses and hounds. Lord Herbert of Cherbury thought riding a

WELBECK.

L'Ecurie voutée de pierre, les filiers de pierre, la mangeoire de pierre,
à l'Italienne, et une fontaine qui coule le long de la mangeoire, et se rend dans
une voute au dessous ou coule un petit ruisseau. Contre la teste de Chaque
Cheval il y a une petite cheminée pour chaleur du Cheval, laquelle
s'ouure ou se ferme, selon la chaleur, ou froideur; Elle est s'auec de
pierre de taille.

Le Grenier de l'Ecurie.

Il y a d'autres
quatre-vint   Ecuries pour
                     Cheualux.

A Diepenbeck del: Coruin au Cauberau sculp:

Nobilissimo Courser Napolitain

great horse, dancing, swimming and fencing were the fittest recreations for a
gentleman. He did not approve of 'running horses', or racing, 'there being much
cheating in that kind; neither do I see why a brave man should delight in a creature
whose chief use is to help him to run away.' Nor was he enthusiastic about hunting,
'that exercise taking up more time than can be spared from a man studious to get
knowledge; it is enough, therefore, to know the sport, if there be any in it, without
making it an ordinary practice.' But James had no intention of thus regulating his
pleasures, and his good humour did not fail when one day out hunting he fell
through the ice and had to be pulled out by his boots. His purveyors were a regular
but dreaded sight on the road through Royston to Newmarket, commandeering
food and transport at prices fixed by themselves. He had been on the throne little
more than a year when the local people begged 'that it will please his Majesty to go
back to London, for else the country [district] will be undone; all our provision is
spent already, and we are not able to entertain him longer.' James was indifferent to
considerations of this kind, and once he was arrived at Newmarket, it was difficult
to get him away again. To pleas that he return to London for public business he
invariably replied that he was in ill-health; although he was always well enough to
hunt. Not even the death of his Queen at Hampton Court would shift him: 'the

*118. Neapolitan courser at
Welbeck, from the Duke of
Newcastle's 'General System of
Horsemanship'. This big, strong
type of horse – bred from Barb
crossed with Spanish blood – was
much sought after in England in the
16th and 17th centuries, and there
were mares and stallions in the
royal studs at Tutbury and
Malmesbury. Welbeck Abbey was
to be the home of a later Master of
the Horse, the Duke of Portland.*

Burley Stables on the East side.

119 (opposite, top left). Accounts relating to the royal 'race' or stud at Tutbury, when the 1st Duke of Buckingham was Master.

120 (opposite, top right). Tutbury Castle, Staffordshire. Built on an 'alabaster hill' it was given to Henry IV by his father, John of Gaunt, and in the 15th and 16th centuries was an important administrative centre. The royal stud was in the surrounding area, divided into paddocks called Castlehay, The Trenches, Stockley, Rolleston, Little Parke and Obholme.

121 (opposite, below). The stables at Burley-on-the-Hill. In 1645 the house was burned down by the Roundheads but 'the stables escaped their malice, the effect of which remains to this day the noblest . . . building of this kind in England' (John Wright, 1648.)

122 (above). Henrietta Maria and her retinue on the road to Amsterdam, 1642: the journey from England having been arranged by the Master of the Horse's department. The Queen had fled to Holland, as she thought she was going to be impeached for selling some of the Crown Jewels to raise money for her husband's cause.

King continues still at Newmarket, and so is said will do till the funeral be past.' This levity did not please all his subjects. Francis Osborne wrote of 'this sylvan prince . . . dress'd to posterity in the colours I saw him . . . which was as green as the grass he trod on, with a feather in his cap, and a horn instead of a sword by his side: how suitable to his age, calling or person, I leave others to judge.'

There is a story, probably apocryphal, that it was on the course at Newmarket that James I first saw George Villiers, the future Duke of Buckingham, seeking to attract attention. Villiers was the son of an impoverished Leicestershire knight, and with possets to improve his sallow midlands complexion he was brought to court by a faction, including the Archbishop of Canterbury, that wanted to counter the influence of the Howards. Given a walking-on part in a Court play, he instantly fascinated the King. He was made Master of the Horse on Worcester's death in 1616, and with other and greater offices showered upon him and his horde of penniless relatives, he soon enjoyed a patronage and influence probably unequalled by any Court favourite.

It is a curious fact that the three Masters who perhaps did most to improve the bloodstock – Leicester, Essex and Buckingham – were unstatesmanlike people with little but good looks to commend them. Buckingham had two advantages that Leicester lacked: he served a monarch who had no inhibitions about economy, and he was vested with offices sufficiently important to make it worth while for foreign statesmen to seek his favour with handsome gifts, notably horses. Horses came, too, from aspiring Englishmen looking for rewards at Court of which he was now the principal dispenser. But as a Leicestershire man Buckingham was genuinely interested in horses, and it is likely that as Master of the Horse he served his adoring sovereign more efficiently than in any other of his manifold duties; and as admiral he was able to arrange the transport of his prizes and guard them from the pirates who preyed on less valuable cargoes.

James wrote ecstatically to Buckingham: 'God thank the Master of the Horse for providing me such a number of fair useful horses, fit for my hand; in a word I protest I never was master of such horses.' In his *History of the Royal Buckhounds* J. P. Hore suggests (p. 142) that not all these horses came from the royal studs officially maintained by the Master, which were 'lesser and more significant'. This might well be so to some extent, because English landowners were generous with their gifts and might also 'lend' mares to the royal studs. The difference here between giving and lending may be nominal, since private landowners had their problems in an inflationary age and the King's studs were better financed and better equipped. Buckingham himself certainly contributed horses in this way. A survey at Tutbury in 1628, just after his death, registered three mares with the 'Burley' prefix, originating from his establishment at Burley-on-the-Hill near Oakham. In 1620 he had married the only daughter of the Earl of Rutland, which brought him the rich estate of Helmsley in Yorkshire and made him a wealthy breeder in his own right.

In his official capacity Buckingham made surveys of the Tutbury and Malmesbury studs, nominating colts to be supplied to the King's stable at Charing Cross. He authorised the pack-masters to acquire horses for their sport as well as hounds, and gave them leave to pre-empt hay and oats at reduced rates. He also bought, or received, many fine horses from abroad. Whether these were acquired for the Crown or for his own personal use it is impossible to say, and in the long run it does not matter since many of the descendants had passed to the Crown by the end of the century. James thought that the sun shone from him and around him whatever he did, and these transactions cannot be reduced to a simple *meum* and *tuum* to prove that the Crown was being cheated. Buckingham may have taken certain horses to his own estates because he thought he could rear them better there, but they may have been given or sold or hired to the royal stud later.

However this may be, there seems now to have been a steady supply of stallions from abroad, and the six in use at Tutbury in the 1624 survey were all imported. Successive ambassadors in Madrid – Cottington, Doncaster and Rich – all supplied Buckingham with horses, and he was able to test the market personally in 1623. This was during the expedition in which he accompanied Prince Charles in quest of marriage with the Spanish Infanta. Buckingham knew that the scheme was very unpopular in England, and his notoriously boorish behaviour may have been intended to wreck it. But the prince became infatuated with a girl whom, like Pyramus with his Thisbe, he had seen only through the crannied walls that immured her from offending Protestant eyes. This caused the Spaniards to increase the gifts they were offering to persuade the English party to go home, and Buckingham obtained for the Crown 24 horses from the valuable royal stud at Cordova, together with foals, mules and camels; and a further gift of a dozen good horses for himself. It was more than a fair return for the 12 pacing nags that had been James's modest gift to the Spanish king; and if not all these horses found their way to Tutbury or Malmesbury, they went to private estates and mostly escaped the grasping fingers of the Cromwellian Commonwealth.

There remains the mystery of the 'Markham Arabian', reputedly sold to James for £164. Of the breeding quality of this horse there is no question, but its provenance is obscure. It is said to have been imported by Gervase Markham, a minor literary figure who was a soldier in the Netherlands wars before turning to poems (an inflated epic on Grenville and the *Revenge* is atrocious), plays, and books on horsemanship and country life. But the nature of the transaction has never been convincingly explained, and Markham's part in it, if any, is obscure. However, he wrote pleasantly on the nature of the hunt, which he saw in terms of the predatory hound pursuing the timid deer:

> Hunting is then a curious search or conquest of one beast over another, pursued by a natural instinct of enmity, and accomplished by the diversities and distinction of smells only, wherein Nature, equally dividing her cunning, giveth both to the offender and offended strange knowledge both of offence and safety. In this recreation is to be seen the wonderful power of God in his creatures, and how far rage and policy can prevail against innocence and wisdom. *Country Contentments*, 1611.

123. A little-known drawing of Robert Dudley, Earl of Leicester, which is probably truer to life than more formal paintings of him.

124 (overleaf, left). Jousting armour made for Leicester at the Royal Armouries, Greenwich. It is of russetted steel engraved with flower-patterned gilt bands.

125 (overleaf, right). Part of the funeral procession of Queen Elizabeth I, showing the Earl of Worcester leading the Palfrey of Estate, followed by Garter King of Arms and Lady Northampton, who was chief mourner.

126 (overleaf, right). King James I, an accomplished horseman who 'divided his time betwixt his standish [inkstand], his bottle and his hunting; the last had his fair weather, the two former his dull and cloudy.' This equestrian portrait is thought to be a good likeness of the King. The building in the background may be Nonsuch, where he spent much of his time.

The Earle of Worcester Master of the Horse leading the Palfrey of Estate, two Esquirts Kagroome attending to Lead him away.

A Gentleman Usher of the priuy chamber

William Dethick Garter Principall King of Armes.

The Lady Marchionesse of Northampton Principall Mourner assisted by the lord Buckherst Lord Treasorer and the Earle of Nottingham Lord Admirall.

Her traine assisted by two Countesses and Sr John Stanhop Vice-chamblaine.

It may not have been quite like that at the hunting of the stag 'Cropear' in 1624, which an observer thought to need 'nothing but bells and bonfires' to consummate it. A stag which gave good sport might often be preserved for future diversion, and the officer known as the 'sergeant of the toils', who carried nets to capture an elusive quarry, might have to use his apparatus to rescue it from the hounds.

James was absurdly extravagant in his administration of the privy buckhounds. His first action was to increase the staff of officers, grooms and yeomen prickers, and the cost rose from £164 in the last full year of Elizabeth to £642. By 1608 it was over £1000, with the head sergeant now receiving a wage of £51 (£1 more than his master) and £100 for the expenses of feeding the pack. Thereafter the cost tended to fall and was only £818 at the end of the reign, but James seems to have failed in an attempt to extinguish the old hereditary pack under Sir Pexall Brocas. In 1613 this was transferred to Prince Charles, with Sir Timothy Tyrrell as master, and Brocas was paid a *per capita* fee for the use of some of his hounds. But the ancient Brocas rights were not to be easily disposed of, and eventually the hereditary fees had to be restored. When the next Brocas sold Little Weldon, the hereditary manor, in 1633, the rights passed to the purchaser, Sir Lewis Watson, first Baron Rockingham, and they remained in the Rockingham family until a final amalgamation in 1707.

Charles I, as Clarendon says, 'abhorred all deboshry' and he kept a sober court, but in financial matters he was almost as imprudent as his father. Van Dyck's famous equestrian portrait showed Charles as he wanted to appear, for van Dyck acquired much of his reputation by studying the self-esteem of his sitters. The portrait subtly minimises Charles's lack of inches and gives a knightly aspect to an essentially non-military man. Charles was a diffident intellectual and he had the finest art collection of any English monarch, which was to be plundered, sold and dispersed after his execution. In 1628 he spent on buying the Duke of Mantua's collection part of the niggardly sum the Commons had grudgingly voted for a war. He tried hard to excel in the more vigorous exercises expected of a king, and he genuinely loved hunting, but the result was not always a success. Sir Philip Warwick, who was for a time Charles's secretary, says in his *Memoirs* that 'his exercises were manly, for he rode the great horse very well, and on the little saddle he was not only adroit but a laborious [hard-working] hunter or field-man: and they were wont to say of him that he failed not to do any of his exercises artificially but not very gracefully, like some well-proportioned faces which yet want a pleasant air of countenance.' His hunting was never allowed to interfere with his devotions. Clarendon says that 'he was never known to enter upon his recreations, though never so early in the morning, before he had been at public prayers; so that on hunting days his chaplains were bound to a very early attendance.' Warwick describes his practice at the other end of a day's sport: 'through the whole week, even when he went a-hunting, he never failed before he sat down to dinner, to have part of the Liturgy read unto him and his menial servants, came he never so hungry or so late in.'

Buckingham, still a royal favourite, continued to be Master of the Horse but now with ambitions of military glory. The early years of Charles's reign were occupied with constitutional quarrels and military disasters, and expeditions against Spain and France speeded the search for serviceable horses. Endymion Porter, a member of Buckingham's household, was warned by a cousin in 1628 that they were hard to find and unreasonable in price, but the cousin had found one 'like to be fit for the great saddle' at a cost of £30. A meeting of the Council of War resolved to put into operation

the four advices of Mons. La Broue, how to make horses acquainted with war – viz., that

127. Edward Somerset, 4th Earl of Worcester, Master of the Horse to Queen Elizabeth and King James I, and forebear of the Dukes of Beaufort.

the groom dressing him should be in armour, that provender should be given him on a drum-head, that while he is eating a piece should be discharged, and that he should be ridden against a suit of armour, which he may overthrow and trample under his feet.

Before the efficacy of these principles could be tested in the field Buckingham had been assassinated, and in October 1628 Lord Goring reported in a letter to the Earl of Carlisle that 'Marquis Hamilton is expected to-morrow, he shall presently be Master of the Horse.'

James Hamilton, third Marquis and later first Duke of Hamilton, is one of those enigmas familiar to historians, a man of immense contemporary reputation with no apparent foundation for it. Clarendon says that Charles was 'always an immoderate lover of the Scottish nation' and welcomed him for that reason; 'and then no man had such an ascendent over him, by the lowest and humblest insinuations, as Duke Hambleton had.' His father had come south after a political career in Scotland and had been given the earldom of Cambridge in the English peerage. The young Hamilton was only twenty-two at his appointment, and he was made a privy councillor at the same time. Perhaps he filled the gap in Charles's affections created by the abrupt removal of Buckingham, but the confidence reposed in him proved to be disastrous when trouble broke out in Scotland late in the 1630s. Between 1630 and 1634 Hamilton commanded a British contingent that fought with the Swedish army in the Thirty Years War, and on his return he was Charles's principal adviser in Scotland. His efforts were on the side of mediation, but the happy settlements he was always anticipating never materialised. He lacked credibility in Scotland through his refusal to take the Presbyterian Covenant, regarded in those parts as the only authentic token of patriotism and true religion. In 1648 he marched into England at the head of an army as hesitant and reluctant as himself, and when he was brought to trial after being routed by Cromwell at Preston, his explanations were as baffling to the judges as they have been to later historians. He even seemed uncertain whether he had been in England at all. He was executed in the following year: one of five Masters who have been beheaded, the others being James Tyrrell, Carew, Essex and, in 1685, the Duke of Monmouth.

Because of his other engagements Hamilton was a cipher in the stables, although the business was conducted in his name. Within a week of his appointment a warrant was issued to pay him '£400, on accompt, for provision of horses for his Majesty's use'; and six months later he was to receive a further £17 due on that account, and '£400 towards like provision thereafter', and shortly afterwards £200 for the repair of the stables at the Royal Mews. The excuse of military necessity had ceased by now. Between 1629 and 1640 Charles ruled without parliament and withdrew from his foreign commitments. In the need to stabilise his finances without parliamentary help he resorted to various shifts of technical legality but dangerous import, but he did not economise on the stables. In this he was to some extent justified as once the breed deteriorates, recovery is slow and expensive. Thus in 1630 Lord President Conway applies to the Master, as an encourager of good breeding, for an old stallion formerly belonging to Lord Gerrard; and later there is mention of delivery to the Lord President's steward at York of 'seven of the finest horses for shape and colour, and so suitable that the like are not this day in any one man's hand in England.' In the matter of horse-breeding Buckingham's death was already being felt.

Most of Hamilton's transactions concern his European ventures. Sir Charles Vavasour asks for employment in the name of 'the ever-honoured Queen of Bohemia', the King's sister, on learning that the Master is 'undertaking a charge for Sweden, and that there is other action afoot for Venice'; and there were rumours

that 'the king has engaged himself to send 10,000 men to the Swedish army.' They could only be volunteers, because there was no government money to pay them. Charles must meanwhile have been putting some pressure on Hamilton for more horses for the stables. In 1632 there is endorsement of an offer from Hamilton that 'if £7000 were yearly paid to him, he would furnish the king and queen with all provision for their stables, including those of Prince Charles and Princess Mary.' Nothing came of it, but the sum proposed was not unreasonable in view of the King's extravagant notions of what was due to his state. A warrant in 1630 for 'twenty of the king's hunting horses maintained on the establishment of the Master of the Horse' provided that each horse be supplied annually with

> a wattering head-stall and reins of red leather, a pair of pastrons, trammels, a double collar, a double reins, a white and green cloth, horse-houses lined with canvas and bordered with white and green cloth, a canvas hood, a leading reins, a surcingle of brown web, a horse-comb, a mane-comb, a sponge, a round hair-brush, 48 ells of canvas for a bag, a dusting cloth, a hunting snaffle, a girth and a stirrup leather. (State Papers.)

For his own use the King had ten saddles a year, richly jewelled, and according to their status the officers of his Household were entitled to 'certain provision of horses and accoutrements for the same'. So they always had been, but subordinates tend to set their own standards by those of their employer.

128 (left). George Villiers, 1st Duke of Buckingham. James I wrote to him: 'God thank my Master of the Horse for providing me such a number of fair, useful horses fit for my hand.'

129 (right). James Hamilton; 1st Duke of Hamilton. Clarendon wrote of him: 'He had more enemies and fewer friends in court or country than anyone else.'

CHAPTER FOURTEEN # Bloody Interlude

In military terms the English Civil War was quite a minor contest, with only about 140,000 under arms in four years and perhaps only 20,000 on either side at Marston Moor, its biggest battle. A parliamentary commander, Sir William Waller, spoke of it as 'this war without an enemy' (although he went on fighting it), and to the best men in both parties it was the suicide of a generation. It was brought about by bad statesmanship on both sides, the King's myopic obstinacy and John Pym's calamitous flair for instant politics. When eventually a military posture was taken up, it was in the belief that one sharp, swift battle would settle the business. Even so, some agonising decisions had to be made, and not everyone had the secure assurance of the Hampshire vicar who prayed with his congregation, 'O Lord, in Thee have I trusted: let me never be a Roundhead.'

Since for thousands there was no real reason for fighting at all, the initial enlistments followed the family and territorial allegiances that had divided the country for centuries. Tenants followed their master against a local and hereditary foe. Militarily this was not an effective way of conducting the war if it was to last for any length of time, because the tenant levies were reluctant to move far from their own counties and in any case had to be home in time for their annual duties in the harvest. It was inevitable that if the war continued, the professionals would take it over. A bubukled Huntingdonshire squire knew already where his 'Providences' were leading him, and the Scottish Covenanting army that entered the war in 1643-4, although Jehovah-demented in its recreational exercises, was disciplined and efficient in action under officers who had fought in the Thirty Years War. Thus there could be only one end to the conflict once the Royalists had failed in their three-pronged attack on London in 1643. But except in certain limited areas the war had remarkably little effect on everyday life, and some counties formed associations resolved to have nothing to do with it. There is an authenticated report of a Warwickshire squire out with his hounds who was astonished to meet an army drawing itself up for a pitched battle. He did not even know there was a war on.

The war has little to do with our present story, except that if the Stuarts had cared as much about warlike preparations as they did about hunting, hawking and caprioles, they might have crushed the rebels in the early months. Despite the pikemen and musketeers, the cavalry were the decisive arm in all the major battles, and it was here that the Royalists might have won. Charles's German nephew Prince Rupert, as yet little more than a teenager, was a devastating leader of cavalry, and the open countryside, only in few places the patchwork of hedged fields we know today, was ideal for his charges and pursuits. Most of the great peers and landowners were Royalist and they had the money and the household establishments to put out a formidable force. Among the opposition, too, there were peers capable of an immediate muster, although Pembroke's promise of forty horsemen,

ENGLAND'S ROYAL PATTERN; or the History of King CHARLES ye first from his Marriage to his Death.

The KING'S Declaration to his GENTRY & ARMY in Septembr 1642.

His Majesty soon after setting up his Standard took his March to Shrewsbury, a place very promising & and to preserve ye Liberty & Property of ye Subject with ye same care as his own just Rights, & that if it of great Moment, & having drawn all his Men to a Rendezvous He for ye first time caused his Militar yOrders for ye pleased God to bless his Arms He would maintain ye just Priviledges & Freedom of Parliaments & observe inviolably Discipline & government of ye Army to be read at ye head of each Regiment & then in a set Speech he made his famous the Laws he had Consented to the Parliament, that ye during ye War any of them should be violated he hoped God & Protestation, He declared that he could not suspect their Courage & Resolution seeing their Constancy & Loyalty Man would impute them to ye dulkness of ye War & not to Him. That when He willingly failed in these particulars had brought them together to fight for their Religion, ye & ye Laws He solemly promised them He would He would expect no Relief from any Man, or Protection from Heaven. But in this Resolution He hoped defend & maintain ye Church of England. He assured them it was His desire to govern by ye Known Laws of ye land, for the chearfull assistance of all good Men and was confident of God's Blessing.

the largest on the parliamentary side, shows on what a minor scale the war was to be fought. In theory the side with the preponderant number of wealthy landed magnates should have been able to strike an early decisive blow, before through casualties and lack of replacements the Royalist cavalry became a wasting asset. That they did not was due partly to Charles's indecisions and hesitant leadership which finally paralysed his cause, and partly to the peaceful sporting pursuits in which dedicated horsemen had lately been occupying themselves. In the military sense Charles had very little return for the money the Crown had been spending on equestrian activity. His hunters and 'pygmy baubles' lacked the strength and stamina of the 'great horses' for which the royal stables had latterly found little use. His wealthiest supporter, the Duke of Newcastle, who lent him £10,000 to meet the Scottish invasion in 1639 and is said to have spent altogether a million pounds in his

130. Charles I rallying his supporters at Shrewsbury in 1642 at the beginning of the Civil War, when the Royalist cavalry still had the upper hand.

master's cause, was an academic theorist, often mistaken, in breeding and the *manège*, and not an expert fighting soldier as his forebears would have been. After the slaughter of his Whitecoats at Marston Moor he went abroad and ran a circus at Antwerp. Thus the rebels were given time to gather and train their smaller troops of horse raised by yeomen farmers and the lesser gentry, and led by 'plain russet-coated captains, such men as had the fear of God before them, and made some conscience of what they did'.

After the war was over and the King was dead, two constitutional experiments were tried before, at the end of 1653, Cromwell was made Lord Protector. He at once caused himself to be addressed as 'Your Highness' and began to invest himself with semi-regal splendours. There were sound political reasons for this as the nation's wounds would be quicker to heal under the traditional symbol of the Crown even if a non-royal usurper was wearing it. But it was not to the liking of his old republican comrades, who found the Court overrun with russet-coated captains trying to wear the purple. Mrs Lucy Hutchinson, wife of a regicide colonel, declared that the poison of ambition had ulcerated Cromwell's heart, and 'his wife and children were setting up for principality, which suited no better with any of them than scarlet on the ape.' Although Cromwell was not by inclination an ostentatious man, he saw himself as representing the authority of the State and he consented to the revival of the protocol of the Stuart Court. Visitors and delegates were received by gradations of Household gentlemen before being ushered into the presence, where Cromwell stood 'in a handsome and somewhat awful posture', surrounded, it was noted, by 'at least thirty young fellows, his sons and attendants'. It sounds very like Richard II.

Whitehall was re-edified for his accommodation, and many of its customs too, these being the only model that anyone knew. Furniture, pictures and hangings from the old Court were brought out of store, including a red velvet chamber-pot from Greenwich, but so many of these items had been sold or destroyed that much had to be purchased afresh. Upholstery for a coach for the Lady Protectress cost £48, and when the family dined in state, there were separate tables for men of every degree as in former times. The Household had its chamberlain, steward, cofferer, grooms and menial servants, and inevitably it had its Master of the Horse.

This was John Claypole, from Northborough in Northamptonshire, who in 1646 had married Elizabeth, Cromwell's second daughter and favourite child. The Claypoles were typical of many yeoman families who acquired modest estates and the status of gentleman during the Tudor period. A great-uncle of the Master was surveyor of the royal stables in 1594 and was later knighted by James I, and his father, also John, was brought to trial for refusing to pay ship-money, and after fighting for parliament in the war was rewarded with local offices and a baronetcy during the interregnum.

The new Master led the horse of state alongside the coach in the portentous ceremony of Cromwell's inauguration as Protector, and at a still more elaborate investiture in 1657, when Cromwell was confirmed in his appointment with the right to appoint his successor, he again led the horse of state 'in rich caparisons'. The Claypoles were given apartments at Whitehall and also at Hampton Court, where Cromwell loved to retire at week-ends to hawk and hunt with the buckhounds. He did not keep an establishment at Windsor, but in order that he might enjoy his recreation at Hampton Court the Council of State had to buy back some of the surrounding properties that had been sold off. The re-employment of the royal mews in London had appalling consequences. It had become the home of a little colony of pathetic creatures, grooms, attendants and menial servants who had been

living there in squalor and penury since King Charles's Court left Whitehall. They were evicted to make way for the Protector's horses.

Mrs Hutchinson, ever charitable, dismissed Claypole and Cromwell's son Henry as 'two debauched, ungodly cavaliers'. Claypole had a mind of his own and spoke out against the tyranny of the Major-Generals through whom Cromwell governed the country when other constitutional arrangements broke down, but Cromwell knew his faults and favoured him with Court appointments because he was the husband of the beloved Elizabeth. Cromwell knew his daughter's failings too. At the time of their marriage he had written to Bridget Ireton, a daughter of more sober disposition, 'your Sister Claypole is, I trust in mercy, exercised with some perplexed thoughts. She sees her own vanity and carnal mind; bewailing it.' To his wife he wrote in 1651: 'Mind poor Betty of the Lord's great mercy. Oh, I desire her not only to seek the Lord in her necessity, but in deed and in truth to turn to the Lord; and to keep close to Him; and to take heed of a departing heart, and of being cozened with worldly vanities and worldly company, which I doubt she is too subject to.' Claypole later became a lord of the bedchamber and ranger of a forest in his native county, and he was elevated from the Commons to the Upper House that was restored in 1657. But he was a courtier rather than an administrator, and any improvements in the equestrian establishment were due to the Protector's own energy and interests.

The Tutbury stud had remained in existence throughout the war, and after executing the King, the regicide government planned to dispose of it as they were already disposing of the King's pictures. (It is not known what happened to the Malmesbury stud. Probably it was dispersed at the same time.) During the war, neglect and encroachment had despoiled many of the royal forests and parks, deer having been poached and killed by 'the people of the country in a continuous and

131. Great Seal of Oliver Cromwell, from a letter dated 4 March 1658.

132. Medallion portrait of John Claypole, Cromwell's son-in-law and his Master of the Horse.

133. Inventory of the King's horses at Tidbury (Tutbury) Race, made in 1649 after the Roundhead take-over. In 1650, six of the best animals were chosen for the Lord Protector and taken to Hampton Court.

134. Woodcut of Prince Rupert from a parliamentary tract of April 1643, aimed at discrediting the Prince. The Roundheads also made the spurious claim that Rupert was a warlock and his dog 'Boye', a standard white poodle (killed at Marston Moor), his 'familiar spirit'.

tumultuous manner'. The republican Colonel Ludlow saw no reason why he should not avail himself of royal pleasures and was 'very earnest to have some sport' at Windsor. He was disappointed because there had been no deer at Windsor for several years. But Tutbury had been expertly managed by Gregory Julian, studmaster to both James and Charles, and when parliamentary commissioners were dispatched there in 1649, they found 140 head of horse (a larger number than reported in earlier surveys by Essex and Buckingham) which they valued at £1982. At first the Council of State hesitated, being sensibly reluctant to disperse the stud 'in consequence of the great destruction of horses during the late wars'. They were content with dismissing Julian, who had obviously been unco-operative, 'to answer for his miscarriages'. But in the following year they decided to sell the horses, apart from six that were to be selected for the use of Cromwell, now supreme commander of the army. A further six had already been set aside for Lieutenant-General Michael Jones, whose victory over the Royalists at Rathmines had made Cromwell's blood-boltered expedition to Ireland unnecessary except as a mission of extirpation and vengeance. Even the sale of the remaining horses was delayed by priorities of purchase granted to other interested parties. It was a scruffy piece of racketeering, but on the other hand it was beneficial to the breed by distributing the Tutbury horses among a number of other studs.

Cromwell himself was a great lover of horseflesh, and although he had to forbid race-meetings because of the danger of mutinous assembly, he was too magnanimous a man to share the inhibitions of his Puritan fellows who suppressed mincepies as idolatrous and made an ordinance condemning Christmas as an occasion 'giving liberty to carnal and sensual delights, being contrary to the life which Christ himself led here upon earth'. Cromwell's favourite outdoor exercise seems to have been hawking, and even on his way home from the 'crowning mercy' of Worcester he paused to hawk in the fields near Aylesbury.

In practical terms he saw the need to replenish the country's stock of horses after the heavy wartime losses, and if he had not at the time been occupied with his campaigns in Ireland and Scotland, Tutbury might have been preserved, with the unbeaten Frisell's 33 colts. For his own recreation he retained a staff of grooms and huntsmen, and he aimed to improve the native breed by the purchase of light cavalry horses and the finest oriental stock. He told the Levant Company, with its trading interests in the Mediterranean, of 'his desire to be accommodated with some good Arabian horses to furnish England with a breed of that kind'. The company's agent at Aleppo was reminded that these 'must be of not mean or ordinary breed, but of such a race as may prove acceptable and be a fitting return to his Highness's notions'. Arabs were still hard to come by, and of four that he ordered at Aleppo only one was procurable. Cromwell also obtained Neapolitan coursers from Leghorn, and during negotiations for a French alliance Cardinal Mazarin presented him with four fine Arabs. Although his intention was to procure fighting horses rather than runners, he indirectly did much to promote the oriental stud that had such a fruitful effect on English racing.

Sometimes his zeal, or maybe his sense of divine protection, misled him. In 1654 the Duke of Oldenburg made him a present of six Friesland greys and he had to try them himself. The story is told by Colonel Ludlow, who resented Cromwell's regal progress through the parks and had seemingly forgotten his own eagerness to hunt in royal forests.

> The Duke of Holstein made him a present of a set of Friesland coach-horses; with which taking the air in the Park, attended only with his secretary Thurloe and a guard of Janissaries, he would needs take the place of the coachman, not doubting but the three pair of horses he was about to drive would prove as tame as the three nations which were ridden by him; and therefore not contented with their ordinary pace, he lashed them very furiously. But they . . . ran away in a rage, and stopped not until they had thrown him out of the box, with which fall his pistol fired in his pocket, though without any hurt to himself: by which he might have been instructed how dangerous it was to meddle with those things wherein he had no experience.

After an agonising internal illness, Elizabeth Claypole died at Hampton Court in August 1658, and it was believed that his grief hastened Cromwell's own death a few weeks later. He had been constantly at her bedside, uncharacteristically neglectful of business, and Clarendon has a version of what happened there.

> That which chiefly broke his peace was the death of his daughter Claypole; who had always been his greatest joy, and who, in her sickness, which was of a nature the physicians knew not how to deal with, had several conferences with him which exceedingly perplexed him. Though nobody was near enough to hear the particulars, yet her often mentioning, in the pains she endured, the blood her father had spilt, made people conclude that she had presented his worst actions to his consideration. And though he never made the least show of remorse for any of those actions, it is very certain that either what she said, or her death, affected him wonderfully.

Elizabeth was buried in the Henry VII Chapel at Westminster, and she was the only member of a regicide family whose peace was undisturbed at the Restoration. It was said that she had interceded with her father on behalf of certain Royalists the regicides wanted to condemn. Claypole was unmolested too. The Restoration was not vengeful – even Mrs Hutchinson's husband was reprieved – but Claypole's subsequent existence suggests an inadequacy that must have been recognised by all who knew him. Within the next few years three actions were brought against him

OLIVERIVS MAGNÆ BRITANNIÆ HIBERNIÆ ET TOTIVS ANGLICI IMPERII PROTECTOR
HVNC SVMMI ET TOTO TERRARVM ORBE CELEBERRIMI HEROIS
EFFIGIEM SVPREMO SVÆ CELSITVDINIS CONSILIO D.D.D.

by London traders for sums owing since the interregnum. It is unclear whether these were for work and supplies for which he contracted personally or as Master of the Horse. This is a recurrent uncertainty in the transactions of the Masters, and in the obliquity of Household accounting it is unlikely that they always knew the answer themselves. In 1670 he married the widow of a London merchant, but before long he was living with a woman who had been appointed maid to his infant daughter. He was soon forced to mortgage his Northamptonshire estates to his son Cromwell Claypole, Elizabeth's child, but received them back when the boy died unmarried. In 1682 he sold them outright to Lord Fitzwilliam for £5600, of which £4765 was immediately consumed by his debts. He died penniless in 1688.

If John Claypole was the most worthless of Masters of the Horse, there was for a few months in 1653 a Master who never saw the home stables. Prince Rupert, third son of the marriage of James I's daughter Elizabeth to the Elector Palatine, has possibly been overrated as a cavalry commander. His irresistible charges failed to make the best use of the Royalist cavalry when it might have won a victory sufficiently decisive to end the war with negotiations in Charles's favour. Rupert was not popular with his men, and his appointment to the chief command in 1642 was unwelcome. He was 'rough and passionate', Clarendon said, 'and loved not debate, liked what was proposed as he liked the person who proposed it.' In a laconic entry in September 1660 Pepys noted: 'This day or yesterday, I hear, Prince Rupert is come to court; but welcome to nobody.'

Taking to the sea after the Royalist defeat on land, Rupert fought off the coasts of Ireland, in the Mediterranean and the Caribbean until there were no longer any Royalist harbours to receive him, and possibly he was a better admiral than general. His use of the concealed time-bomb in naval engagements was a tactic ahead of his time. In 1653 he was forced to bring his only surviving ship to France, where the fugitive Charles II was maintaining a threadbare Court in Paris. It was in these circumstances that Rupert was appointed Master of the Horse. He had brought some piratical prize with him when he landed at Nantes, and Charles was keen to share it. A Court observer says that 'Prince Rupert flourishes with his blackamoors and new liveries, and so doth his cousin Charles, they having shared the monies made of the prize goods at Nantz; and in recompense Rupert is made Master of the Horse.' (Memoirs of John Evelyn, 1827 ed., Vol. V.) This caused ill-feeling in the exiled Court as the post had been expected by Lord Percy, who was made Chamberlain instead. Rupert's rewards did not answer his extravagant expectations. He 'goes little abroad out of the Palace Royal, because he wants a princely retinue, which I see no probability for him to have in France yet awhile.' (Ibid.) He was easily drawn into the factions that simmered in a Court with too little to do, and he tried to overthrow the influence of Edward Hyde, later Earl of Clarendon. According to Clarendon's own report, when he found this unavailing he told Charles that he was 'resolved to look after his own affairs in Germany, and to visit his brother in the Palatinate and require what was due to him for his appanage, and then go to the Emperor to receive the money that was due to him upon the Treaty of Munster.' It was an extraordinary episode altogether.

Rupert was in Germany from 1654 to 1660, occupying himself in scientific studies. On returning to England at the Restoration he fought at sea against the Dutch, joined the Royal Society and served on the Board of Trade. His temperament was somewhat quirky. A gentleman who served under him in the Civil War said that he was 'always very sparkish in his dress', a great beau as well as a great hero, and he was a magnificent sight riding into battle 'clad in scarlet, very richly laid in silver lace, and mounted on a very gallant black Barbary horse'.

135. Contemporary engraving by Pierre Lombart after van Dyck's painting of King Charles I under an archway: a plagiaristic attempt at making an heroic figure of Cromwell.

CHAPTER FIFTEEN

Restoration and After

As a boy of eight, Charles II (1660–85) had been taught to ride by the Duke of Newcastle and had shown high promise by his instructor's somewhat obsessive standards. His apprenticeship was abruptly removed from the preenings of the *manège* to life's grimmer realities when at twelve his father led him into battle, and at fifteen he was in nominal command of the Royal army in the west. After years of penniless exile he was brought home in 1660 by a people sickened of the tyranny and confiscations of God's elected Saints, and when he observed the acclamations that greeted his return, he sardonically remarked that it must only have been his own fault that he had been away so long.

Among his first actions was to restore the Crown's equestrian establishment, and he demanded the seizure of 'the seven horses of Oliver Cromwell, said to be the best in England'. It is not true that, as was at one time believed, Charles restored the English breed by costly purchase from abroad. He did indeed import when it was practicable, and he failed to revive the Tutbury stud as an intended gift to his first Master of Horse, George Monck, Duke of Albemarle, the great architect of a peaceful, legal Restoration. But the horses he was looking for, or their descendants, were not far to seek. The details of the Tutbury dispersal have not been discovered, but many of the horses had gone to private studs in the north and they were soon put at the disposal of the King.

Some of them were at Buckingham's estate at Helmsley, which in 1651 had been given to General Fairfax as 'a salve for a bad wound' he had received during the Yorkshire campaigns of the Civil War. At Naseby and other battles he had ridden a chestnut mare from whom he bred several good horses. Although he commanded the parliamentary armies, Fairfax refused to be a king-killer and retired from active politics when Cromwell marched against brother Protestants in Scotland. He presented one of his horses to Charles II for his coronation, and when in 1657 his daughter married George Villiers, Buckingham's son, he gave them Helmsley as a wedding present. In this way the Crown regained access to the magnificent stud that Buckingham had created, and the younger Villiers, now second Duke of Buckingham, succeeded Monck as Master.

Other horses from the great breeding activity of the early Stuart reigns had gone to the Sedbury estate, also in Yorkshire, of the Darcy family. Charles threatened reprisals against anyone found in possession of horses and other property that had been 'embezzled and taken away and detained from us by persons who had no right or title thereunto', and after some delicate negotiations, during which he pointed out that it had cost Charles's father up to £1500 a year to maintain the royal studs, James Darcy agreed to supply the King with twelve Sedbury colts a year for an annual fee of £800. Darcy had the mares, and he undertook also to provide the stallions. It was a profitable bargain for the King, formally concluded 'with the

136. *George Monck, 1st Duke of Albemarle, soldier and admiral, who 'supervised the stables as conscientiously as he did everything else'.*

consent of our Master of the Horse'. But like most financial agreements undertaken by the Stuarts, it was not punctually fulfilled. Later in the reign, and again under William III and Anne, Darcy's son was petitioning for payment of the fee, now several years in default. In 1689 he was complaining, too, that he had not received the complement of barb or Arab stallions he now needed to serve his many mares.

It was Charles II who established racing as the sport of kings. He constructed a course on Datchet Meads near Windsor, where Falstaff had once been carried in a laundry-basket, but Newmarket was the place he loved best and here he built a new house – or refurbished an old one – to accommodate the ladies and gamesters whom he always needed in his company. The diarist John Evelyn was not impressed by it:

Many of the rooms above had the chimneys in the angles and corners, a mode introduced by his Majesty which I do at no hand approve of. I predict it will spoil many noble houses and rooms, if followed. It does only well in very small and trifling rooms, but takes from the state of greater. Besides, this house is placed in a dirty street, without any court or

187

avenue, like a common one, whereas it might, and ought to have been, built at either end of the town, upon the very carpet where the sports are celebrated.   (22 July 1670.)

Evelyn and his companions went to see 'the stables and fine horses, of which many were here kept at a vast expense, with all the art and tenderness imaginable', and the course itself was 'mostly a sweet turf and down, like Salisbury Plain, the jockeys breathing their fine barbs and racers, and giving them their heats'.

Evelyn was no better pleased when next year, 21 October 1671, he

lodged this night at Newmarket, where I found the jolly blades racing, dancing, feasting and revelling, more resembling a luxurious and abandoned rout than a Christian court. The Duke of Buckingham was now in mighty favour, and had with him that impudent woman the Countess of Shrewsbury, with his band of fiddlers, etc.

There was indeed much to be complained of in the behaviour of the countess, who lived with Buckingham at Cliveden as his mistress, and when the husband challenged the lover to a duel, disguised herself as a page and led the lover's horse into the field. Like all principled men, Evelyn had welcomed the Restoration as the resumption of God's orderly intentions for Britain, but he had been disappointed by Charles's frivolity and refused to perceive the cold and cynical resolution which it partially disguised. Whereas James I had often gone to Newmarket to retreat from his responsibilities, Charles welcomed all the world to come and attend to sport or business with equal gravity. Thus racing prospered amid the coming and going of diplomats, ministers, ambassadors, courtiers and men of commerce as well as the 'fiddlers, etc.' deplored by Evelyn. John Macky, a top-grade spy before this had become an over-exposed activity, reported that there were contests there

every day during the season, of one sort or another; and great wagers are laid on the several horses besides the prizes run for, which are seldom under Four Hundred Pounds, and often above a Thousand.

However, there are sharpers at this as well as other diversions of England; a groom's riding at the wrong side of the post, or his riding crimp, or people's crossing the horses' way in their course, makes a stranger risk deep when he lays his money, except he can be let into the secret, which you can scarce believe he ever is.

Never was such a splendid show of fine horses at any review of an army made by the French king, or any other prince in Christendom, as here on these plains on a match-day . . . there is something so very noble in the whole pursuit of the courses that it animates even a by-spectator or stranger to share in their pleasure.   *A Journey through England* (1684).

Evelyn witnessed 'the great match' between the King's Woodcock, and Flatfoot, which belonged to a gentleman of the bedchamber, 'many thousands being spectators'.

The importance of Newmarket as one of the main centres of the Court's activity gave a boost to racing, which was its favourite recreation. The only drawback was that highwaymen found richer pickings on this road than any of the others leading out of London, and a gang of them even built a hutted settlement just off the road at Waltham Cross.

Evelyn, who was not censorious in all things, was captivated when he went to St James's Park

to see three Turkish or Asian horses newly brought over and now first showed to his Majesty. There were four, but one of them died at sea, being three weeks coming from Hamburg. They were taken from a Bashaw at the siege of Vienna . . . I have never beheld so delicate a creature as one of them was, of somewhat a bright bay, two white feet, a blaze . . . in all regards beautiful, and proportioned to admiration; spirited, proud,

137. Arab, Turk, Neapolitan and Barb, from engravings by Baron Reis d'Eisenberg at Wilton House. It is interesting to compare them with the Duke of Newcastle's horses on page 196 which were painted almost a century earlier.

nimble, making halt, turning with that swiftness, and in so small a compass, as was admirable . . . They trotted like does, as if they did not feel the ground. Five hundred guineas was demanded for the first; 300 for the second; and 200 for the third, which was brown. (17 December 1784.)

He went on to describe the embroidered saddles and housings, and reins and head-stall 'of crimson silk, covered with chains of silver gilt'. It is possible that Evelyn was witnessing the arrival of the famous Byerley Turk, though by some accounts the horse was taken when Budapest was recovered from the Turks in 1686. (Some of the horses known at this time as 'Turks',and which were actually Arabs, were so called because they were ridden by the Turkish soldiers and were captured from them.) The Byerley Turk was ridden by his master Colonel Byerley of the 6th Dragoons at the Battle of the Boyne in 1690 and then taken to his stud at Goldsborough in Yorkshire; the first of the three great sires that made the English thoroughbred. The second was the Darley Arab, bought for £300 by Sir Thomas Darley, the consul at Aleppo, and sent to his father at Aldby House, another Yorkshire stud. It is said that the sheikh who agreed to sell it tried to renege on the transaction and the horse was hijacked by some English sailors. The third great sire, the Godolphin Barb, was obtained in France by Edward Coke and acquired by Lord Godolphin.

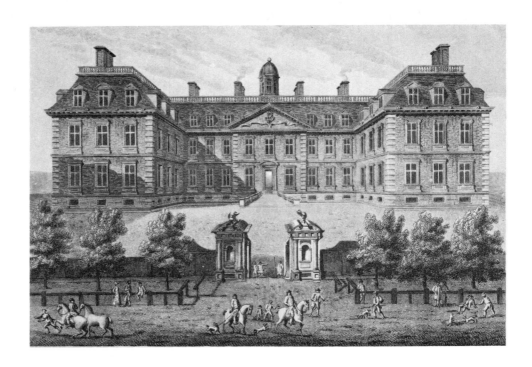

138. *Albemarle House, formerly Clarendon House, built on the north side of Piccadilly in the 1660s. Clarendon sold it for half its original cost to George Monck's son, Christopher.*

For interlocking reasons the growing enthusiasm for racing was accompanied by some decline in deer-hunting. This decline must not be exaggerated, and at least until 1800 more packs were kept for chasing deer than for hunting the fox, and there was no question of the sport's losing its fundamental appeal. Man, as Dr Johnson said, 'feels his own vacuity less in action than when at rest'; and although Johnson found it 'very melancholy that the paucity of human pleasures should persuade us ever to call hunting one of them', he nevertheless rode Mr Thrale's old hunter 'with good firmness' and sometimes 'followed the hounds fifty miles on end'. Indeed an Oxford don, William Somerville, was shortly to write *The Chase*, four books of Miltonic blank verse, in which he described hunting as 'the image of war, without its guilt'. But deer-hunting would never be revived on its former scale. The forests had been depopulated during the war years and the interregnum, and the acreage of woodland was steadily declining through the need to bring more land under cultivation. Fox-hunting, on the other hand, could take place over open country. The venturesome exercises of great hunts like the Pytchley and the Quorn did not become fashionable until the reign of George III. In 1700 the hunts were small runs undertaken by farmers and freeholders over their own lands: men like the Tory fox-hunter who came in for Addison's sleek metropolitan sneers. But even in this bucolic world of people 'who have always lived out of the way of being better informed', racing was becoming an alternative attraction. The farmers enjoyed the sport of entering their sturdy mounts for the hunters' plates of the kind which would later oblige Gibbon to abandon his books at Buriton and dutifully accompany his father to meetings at Stockbridge, Odiham and Reading.

On his accession Charles II allocated £1000 to have his forests re-stocked with deer, but he did not get as much sport from the royal buckhounds as his father and grandfather had done. It merely cost him more. The salary of the Master of the Buckhounds, which had remained at £50 for several generations, had to be raised to £400 and then to £500. This was because in the financial settlement at the

139. *Charles II leaving Hampton Court. The coach is of the type used before glass windows were introduced. It would have had a leather top and side-panels. The horses were probably Friesians.*

Restoration the Crown commuted its ancient feudal rights for a lump sum. These rights included purveyance, which had been a source of grief and dispute for centuries. It appears that the Master had derived much of his income from the profits he made on this, and now he had to be compensated. John Cary, who was Master of Buckhounds throughout Charles's reign, was additionally compensated by a licence which gave him the sole right to export hounds. Ostensibly this was to prevent unauthorised exports 'to the hindrance of our own store, the decay of the breed and prejudice of our game and sport of hunting'. The phrase about 'the hindrance of our own store' is revealing. The nature of the hindrance had been the regular thieving by the masters and head servants who caused valuable hounds to 'disappear', this being one of the perquisites of the underpaid official. But Charles was always short of money, and the high cost of his racing made it impossible for him to maintain the buckhounds at a full working pitch. The cost of the pack in 1662 was £2378, and much of it was unpaid, the officers lamenting that they were 'utterly undone'. In a further attempt at economy some liveries and allowances were discontinued; and although they were restored after renewed protests from the servants, it seems that they were seldom paid. Charles was always more liberal towards his horses and his women than to his household officers.

The Duke of Albemarle, Charles's first Master of the Horse, supervised the stables as conscientiously as he did everything else. His career had begun as long ago as the abortive Cadiz expedition of 1625, when he volunteered at the age of seventeen. He fought on the King's side until captured in 1644, but he was never a partisan, and the settlement of the troubled affairs of Ireland and Scotland occupied him until 1660, except for a short period when he was called away to fight three battles against the Dutch at sea. When on Cromwell's death his jackals began to scramble for the prizes, Monck and his Coldstreamers marched in from Scotland to restore the monarchy and a freely-elected parliament. Monck had to go to sea to fight the Dutch again, but his department was as efficiently run as was possible at an

The Effigies of the Duke Minjacke & Earle Coventry Viscount Vil- Knight of ye most Ho... ¶ Most Noble George of Buckingham Earle ...ler: Baron of Whaddon ble order of the Garter:

R. White sculp.

140. George Villiers, 2nd Duke of Buckingham. His appointment as Master was 'the frivolous appointment of a frivolous and untrustworthy man'.

unsettled time. Between 1640 and 1660 much property had changed hands, some of it legitimately so far as anything could be legitimate in years of lawlessness. The dispossessed returned to claim lands and houses whose occupants could show accredited titles, and Albemarle had to deal with several disputes of this kind. Lady Belhaven, whose husband had been Master of the Household in Charles I's time, claimed that her house at the mews had been granted to him by the late King's warrant, together with the keepership of the mews. Although appearing to be satisfied with the warrant that she produced, Albemarle sent soldiers to turn her out, as the property belonged to the Master of the Horse. When the persistent widow complained to the King, the law officers ruled that while the patent was good in law, the keepership had been granted to one Andrew Cole and could not be exercised by a deputy, which Lady Belhaven was claiming to be. She appears to have accepted that Cole's patent 'of the Mewskeeper's place and certain tenements' was legitimate, merely petitioning to be protected from 'the continued molestations which she suffers'.

In order to recover the properties and appointments that had formerly belonged to the mews, Albemarle seems to have acted somewhat arbitrarily towards the residents, even when, like Lady Belhaven, they claimed their titles from the previous reign. It is probable that when Hamilton, the nominal Master, was absent in Scotland, some rather lax transfers had been made, and Albemarle was determined to restore the full status of his department. When Gilbert Dawson was ejected from the keepership of St James's Park on suspicion of disloyalty, he claimed that he had been appointed by the late King, had held the post ever since and had done his best to help the Restoration. William Bedborough, Cromwell's stable-keeper at Hampton Court, was discharged for alleged fraudulent dealings, but his successor had to sue for possession because he would not give it up. In 1665 Hugh Fisher, trumpeter in ordinary, petitioned Albemarle to be allowed to remain in a house he had bought in the mews. He complained that the surveyor of the stables was threatening to turn him out even though he had been 'at great charge in cleansing it' after a maidservant had taken the plague. Next year Albemarle's brother-in-law, Sir Thomas Clarges, who had played an important conciliatory role during the Restoration, claimed unsuccessfully that five houses built at Forbury during the usurpation were part of his lease of the Abbey of Reading, and he demanded £160 as arrears of rent for the use of the houses by the Master's servants. The Attorney-General ruled that in the lease an exception had been made for the free ingress and egress of the King's officer and servants.

A warrant to the avenor to deliver two horse-liveries to the keeper of the privy purse is in the tradition of the Master's duty to mount the Household officers, and in 1663 a survey was ordered of 'the proportions of carriages and other furniture in the royal stables yearly required for the King and Queen and allowed to the officers and servants of the stables'. In the following year necessary repairs to the stables were estimated at £960 5s. 0d. An instruction to the Master to 'give in his account to the King only, who shall then grant a privy seal for furnishing the money for horses whereof he has given account' seems to be an attempt to stop the Commons looking too closely into Household expenditure, but with a sport-loving king like Charles economy was difficult to maintain. Sharp practice in the duty-free transport of horses in the Master's name was prohibited in a royal order to the farmers of customs: 'Although the transportation of horses is contrary to law, and daily refused to the most considerable men of France, yet . . . it is daily done by connivance, to the prejudice of the service and defrauding of customs. None are to pass in future without licence under the King's hand and that of the Duke of

141. James, Duke of Monmouth, one of five Masters who died on the scaffold. This fine equestrian portrait is said to have been his wife's favourite painting of him.

Albemarle, Master of the Horse.' (Cal. State Papers.) This apparently was effective, and Lord Aubigny was prevented from sailing with a ship carrying his horses until he had sent to London for a warrant. But the drain of money continued. The coronation had cost the stables over £1000, and on Albemarle's personal intervention a recent economy regulation was relaxed to 'continue all the horse and nag liveries of servants of the stables who personally attend the King and Queen, and also their ordinary riding wages and lodgings, anything signed in the late book notwithstanding.' The surveyor at Hampton Court claimed £1009 13s. 4d. for expenses incurred in a three-year period, and a king who could refuse nothing to his ladies was always requesting more horses and liveries as the Court entourage grew steadily larger.

On Albemarle's resignation of all his public duties in 1668 the Duke of

Buckingham became the new Master, the frivolous appointment of a frivolous and untrustworthy man. He was the 'Zimri' of Dryden's *Absalom and Achitophel*,

> Stiff in opinions, always in the wrong,
> Was everything by starts, and nothing long;
> But in the course of one revolving moon
> Was chemist, fiddler, statesman and buffoon.

Nothing material survives of his tenure, and when the Cabal ministry broke up and he was dismissed from all his offices, the Duchess of Portsmouth (Louise de Kérouaille, the most durable of Charles's mistresses and herself to be the mother and grandmother of Masters of the Horse) tipped the Duke of Monmouth for the post 'and offered to lay any wager of it'. A letter in February 1674 gave among the latest gossip the news that 'the King has thought fit to suspend the Duke of Bucks from the execution of his place of Master of the Horse, designing it for the Duke of Monmouth.' Monmouth was Charles's illegitimate son by Lucy Walters of Haverfordwest, and perhaps he was the only person Charles really loved. He was already a privy councillor and Captain-General of the forces, and with his new dignity a critic remarked that he was 'growing yet greater by an addition of home employments'. A warrant for him to 'admit and seat Harry Worth as a page of honour extraordinary without fee, to come into immediate waiting, and on the first vacancy to succeed to all the emoluments of that office' (State Papers) draws attention to the growing prestige of stables appointments. Young men of good family were beginning to seek the privilege of serving as pages. It is significant, too, that although good horses were still sought overseas, the native breeds were in demand for export. Monmouth tells the Prince of Strasbourg: 'I would have answered your letter sooner, had I not for some days past been hunting with the Duke of York in Sussex. I have ordered my people to look out for such a horse as you desire, though I must tell you they will have trouble to find one of the kind, they are so sought after by the dealers for export abroad.'

Monmouth involved himself in disloyal intrigues following the perjuries of Titus Oates in the Popish Plot, and Whig politicians put him forward as heir to the throne, claiming that Charles had been legally married to his mother but the marriage certificate had been lodged in a black box that had been stolen by the Pope. So he had to be deprived of his offices and sent out of the way, and in 1681 Charles, who did not distinguish himself in his choice of Masters, appointed the ten-year-old Charles Lennox, Duke of Richmond, his natural son by Louise de Kérouaille. Major Theophilus Oglethorpe was made Gentleman of the Horse and he and George Feilding were appointed commissioners until Richmond should reach the age of fourteen.

Charles died before Richmond was old enough to exercise his responsibilities, and the boy was at once deprived of them. Oglethorpe was made principal equerry to James II (1685–8), and after leading the charge against Monmouth's rebels at Sedgemoor he was promoted to Brigadier-General. In the revolution of 1688 he refused to fight against James, and his regiment was taken from him. For some years he went abroad, but eventually he returned to take the oath of loyalty to the new regime, bought the manor of Godalming and became MP for Haslemere. It is said that in later years his daughter Anne was mistress of James Edward, the Old Pretender.

Apparently to the disappointment of the Duke of Portsmouth, who had expected this reward for his long years as an acquiescent cuckold, James appointed as Master of the Horse one of his most loyal servants, George Legge, first Baron

142. Portrait of Prince Rupert, painted at the beginning of the Civil War, when he was in his early twenties.

143 (overleaf). Horses in manège: top, Neapolitan courser; second row, Turk and Russian; bottom, Spaniard and Barb. The picture was painted in Antwerp for the Duke of Newcastle, who taught Charles II to ride when he was eight years old.

144 (overleaf). Charles II leaving Nonsuch Palace. In 1670 he gave this favourite residence of the Tudors to the Duchess of Cleveland. Not long afterwards she had it pulled down and its contents sold to pay her gambling debts.

145 (overleaf). Charles II's Coronation Eve progress from the Tower to Westminster, 22 April 1661. The Master of the Horse, the Duke of Albemarle, rides behind the King, leading the Horse of Estate.

Prince Rupert.

Dartmouth, who had already held this office in James's private household before his accession. He had been a groom of the bedchamber and Master of the Ordnance, and Evelyn describes him as 'an active and understanding gentleman in sea-affairs'. The warrant for his appointment as Master of the Horse at 100 marks 'and all other fees, privileges, etc,' recites all the previous holders as far back as John Dudley. Sutton Oglethorpe was appointed master of the royal stud at a salary of £200. James had always been a keen horseman, and even when in exile at Brussels during the crisis of the Popish Plot he had asked for his hounds and huntsman to be sent over. 'I now begin to have plenty of stag-hunting, and the country looks as if the fox-hunting would be very good.' In the critical months of 1688, when his throne was slipping away, he sent regularly for reports on his kennels and stables. He cared for racing too, and early in his reign he was pleased to grant a warrant to certain Irish noblemen who 'to encourage the breed of horses there, have subscribed to raise a considerable sum of money to be employed for the maintenance of a plate to be for ever run for yearly' in County Down. They were incorporated in the name of the Governor and Freemen of the Corporation of Horse-breeders to make investments for raising money for the proposed plate.

Although a Protestant, and incidentally cousin and close friend of John Churchill, future Duke of Marlborough, Dartmouth was personally devoted to James and was Admiral of the fleet lying off the Thames when William of Orange brought over his invading army. When James considered that his throne was lost, he sent his infant son to Portsmouth with orders to Lord Dartmouth to ship him safely to France. Dartmouth's letter of refusal shows his patriotism and integrity. Having begged James to stand in defence of his rights, he says this:

> Pray, Sir, consider further on this weighty point: For can the Prince's being sent to France have other prospect than the entailing a perpetual war upon your nation and posterity; and giving France always a temptation to molest, invade, nay hazard the conquest of England, which I hope in God's name never to see.

Although he later swore his loyalty to William, Dartmouth was arrested on suspicion of conspiracy and lodged in the Tower, where he died in 1691 'suddenly of a fit of apoplexy, his lady being in bed with him.'

The abdication of James II and the accession of William III (1688–1702) immediately had the consequences which Lord Dartmouth had hoped never to see. On a cool assessment of all the possibilities, Dutch William took the throne to obtain an ally in his own country's defensive war against Louis XIV; and the presence in France of the exiled James and his family gave Louis a pretext for a war of restoration whenever he chose to take it. Thus the fighting that took place between 1689 and 1697 was virtually a war about the English succession; and France's renewed support for the Stuarts drew England into the larger European war that broke out in 1701. Except during the twenty years of Walpole's peace, England was almost continuously at war between 1688 and 1815, with France always the principal enemy: a period roughly as long as the Hundred Years War of the Middle Ages.

On the female side William had a personal claim to the throne as the son of Charles I's daughter Mary, but it was offered to him through his marriage to a descendant of the male line, another Mary, who was the daughter of James II by his first marriage. He accepted the throne in his own right rather than hers, refusing to be his wife's 'gentleman usher'. He was granted the title of King, which the English do not normally allow to their princes consort, and so continued to reign when Mary died in 1694. But he was made to understand that he was only King on

146. Queen Anne in procession to the Houses of Parliament. The Queen is in her state coach and is accompanied by an escort of Household Cavalry, a group of walking grooms or watermen, and Yeoman of the Guard. The rider nearest to the coach is probably Gold Stick; the Master of the Horse could be one of the attendants behind the coach.

147. Hampton Court at the time of Queen Anne. Horses can be seen in the Home Park at bottom left. The Mews is the furthest building away from the Tudor palace. Bushey Park is at top right.

148 (left). The 1st Duke of Richmond, who was appointed Master when he was ten years old.

149 (right). George Legge, Baron Dartmouth. He and Thomas Knyvet were the only two naval men to have been Masters of the Horse.

sufferance. The revolution of 1688 altered the tenure of English monarchs. No longer ruling by divine hereditary succession, they were removable at will if they deserted the Church of England or broke the law. The consequent financial arrangements marked a further stage in the separation of the Royal Household from the public domain. The sovereign's personal income was supposed henceforth to suffice for his domestic expenditure, while public expenditure was regulated by parliamentary grant. Thus although the King was still Commander-in-Chief of the forces and nominally in control of foreign policy, in practice the forces were now controlled by parliament, which made an annual grant for their upkeep. Nearly all the senior British regiments were founded between 1660 and 1702, and even the King's own Household guards had a separate establishment. This meant that the Master of the Horse still had to maintain stables and studs for the King's ceremonial, transport and sporting requirements, but, except for the King's own use, he no longer had to supply horses for military purposes.

A review of domestic expenditure made at the beginning of the reign allocated an annual figure of £16,400 19s. 3¼d. for 'the expense of his Majesty's stable' (Harleian MS. 5010). Salaries totalled £9067, with the Master receiving £1200, the avenor £260, seven equerries £256 each, the clerk of the stables £224, the riding purveyor £200, the yeoman saddler £183, three pages of honour each £156, two yeoman riders each £130, two surveyors each £120, and so on down to the messenger at £15. The master of the stud and surveyor of the race surprisingly had only £26, less than the £31 paid to the page of the back stairs. (Race in this sense had nothing to do with racing. It meant breeding or the production of offspring, and was thus equivalent to stud. Documents often refer to 'Tutbury Race'.) The establishment included farriers, grooms, coachmen, footmen, littermen, a coach-maker and a porter, and the total number of employees was 105, or roughly one man per horse, since provision was made for 102 animals: 12 for the Master, 42 for the coachmen and four for the Gentleman of the Horse, or senior equerry. There were 36 'hunters, coursers and pads' and two 'chirurgeon horses', two bottle horses and four simply called hunting horses.

A 'computation' made of 'the expense of the horse liveries' budgeted for an annual total of £5355 15s. 7½d., approximately one pound a week for each horse. It laid down the quantities of hay, straw, oats and beans to be purchased each month, with the estimated cost; and twopence a day as the likely cost of 'shoeing and medicining', although it was mentioned that hunters might be more expensive than that. The full budget allocated £1000 to 'the contingent charges in his Majesty's progress and removes' and £270 to the repair of his 'private ways'; and finally £708 as stipends and pensions to servants employed in the stables by Charles II but no longer in the King's service. Probably the calculations in this budget were based on the actual establishment and expenses of Charles II's stables, except that Charles had employed more equerries.

English courtiers who lost their posts to the new invaders felt that, even for a Dutchman, William was indecently partial to the Dutch, and there was some resentment of his Master of the Horse, Henry Nassau, Count of Auverquerque. Known in England simply as Overkirk, he was a Dutchman of ancient noble lineage, and with one exception he was the last Master to accompany his King in battle. He fought the Catholic Irish at Limerick and tried in vain to save a desperate day at Steenkirk in 1692. Later, as a Field-Marshal in both the Dutch and English armies, he was, despite his years, the only Dutch commander upon whom Marlborough could rely for consistently determined policies. He died in camp at Lille in 1708.

Overkirk seems to have suffered no serious mishap when, according to a news letter in 1691, 'a gentleman's coachman turned over the coach wherein was himself, Lord Churchill, Lord Portland and Mons. Overkirk, or the Duke of Ormonde, I am not certain which, but I do not hear that any great damage was done, only Churchill complained of his neck being broken; the King told him there was little fear of that by his speaking.' Whether for military needs or sport, warrants to the lieutenant-general of the ordnance requisitioned the delivery to Overkirk in 1690 of 400 Dutch saddles and subsequently of '530 hostlers, without caps, and 80 saddles'. Sporting needs certainly dictated an instruction to the Admiralty at the end of the year: 'The King would have you give order to the *Mermaid* to convoy six ships with horses and hounds to such port in Holland as Mons. Gatiquier, who is to take care of them, shall appoint, and to give notice thereof to Mons. Overkirk, who will tell you the names of these six ships and where they lie.' William enjoyed 'the divertisement of hunting' even when he was campaigning in the Netherlands. Overkirk's accounts show the purchase of horses for the stud at Hampton Court, but a more economical way of supplying these was confiscation from Roman Catholics, who for fear of armed conspiracy were forbidden to possess any horse worth more than £5.

Racing continued at Newmarket even though William had little time for personal participation. It was still, as Charles II had made it, as much a place for business as for pleasure. For the spring and autumn meetings it was not unusual for the whole Court to move there, and functionaries and theologians were dispatched from nearby Cambridge to depress the occasion with loyal and hortatory discourse. In the spring of 1698 Marshal Tallard arrived from France for discussions on the delicate issue of the Spanish succession, and as his arrival coincided with the spring meeting, away to Newmarket he had to go and the negotiations were conducted there, with races, hunting, hawking, dances, music and even cock-fighting to divert him if diplomacy became too solemn a matter.

It was on horseback that King William came to his death. On Sorrel, a favourite mount, he was ambling after the hounds at Hampton Court when a quarry was espied, he spurred the horse and it stumbled over a molehill. William was thrown and broke his collar-bone. This was followed by a chill, and his constitution, weakened after years in the battlefield and the camp, could not stand the strain.

William was succeeded by Queen Anne (1702–14), the late Queen's sister, and the new reign began with a political reshuffle to oust the Dutch favourites and the Whig ministers who were thought to be over-zealous for war. Overkirk, undeservingly, was among the fallen, and for a year a commission was issued to Sir Stephen Fox and two others to take care of the stables, with power to determine complaints relating thereto. But they were to refer important cases to the Queen, and the Crown reserved the fees and patronage of the office pending a new appointment. Relations with Scotland were delicate, and Edward Southwell, Clerk to the Council, was directed to find out the number of horses and quantities of grain being exported there. He was advised to ask the commissioners to get returns from the collectors, 'but if you think that too public a way, I will get the best information I can from the two collectors of this country and send it. The sort of horses that are generally sent for Scotland is small grey horses about 13 hands high very near. At present I hear they have put a stop to further importation into Scotland.' A more important consideration for the commissioners was the cost of shipping horses to the Continent on the outbreak of the War of the Spanish Succession. An estimate for the shipping and provisions for 285 horses for 90 days amounted to £8566 9s. 4½d., of which the largest item was for 2280 tons of shipping at 14s. a ton per month, £4788. Hay at 15 lb. a day for each horse would come to £748 2s. 6d., water casks, bound in iron, to £1781 5s. 0d., and 285 stalls floored with planks to £427 10s. 0d. To assist expected allies, licences were issued for Aurelio Capitoli and 10 grooms to pass to Holland 'to look after 38 horses which are going over for the Elector Palatine', and to four grooms, four boys and a footman, 'who are to convey 19 horses and some hounds from the Duke of Ormonde to the King of Poland'. The commissioners had also to find money for Anne's coronation, and these are sample items: 'To Sam Aubery for a state coach made to carry the ambassadors, and for the chair in which Her Majesty was carried, £250'; and £60 'for furnishing horses, etc. and £35 for providing shackles for the horses'.

In July 1703 Anne appointed as her Master Charles Seymour, sixth Duke of Somerset, a man of high principle and steady loyalty in an age when these qualities were not conspicuous among leading statesmen. The Queen valued him as a moderate, non-party man who would protect her from the extremists of either side. But he could be prickly too, and it is said that when his second wife tapped him with her fan, he rebuked her thus: 'Madam. My first duchess was a Percy, and she never took such a liberty.' In his early days as Master he was prepared to give up his office when he 'received a dissatisfaction occasioned by some pretences of the Lord Chamberlain'. Anne soothed his scruples and persuaded him to stay, and he had at once to try to restore the finances of his department, asking the Treasury for £9000 'upon account of her Majesty's stables, to defray the expenses' incurred during the year before he took office. The exigencies of war kept the stables short of money, and in 1710 Somerset was again applying to the Treasury, this time for 'payment of fees and gratuities disbursed, he having received no part of the £4000 a year allowed

to his predecessors'. Somerset resigned in 1712 after losing his place on the council, and the office was again put into commission, but the financial problems did not ease. In October the commissioners, Conyers Darcy and George Feilding, prayed the Treasury 'for the issue of £3000 for the tradesmen who supplied the liveries'.

Next year they sought £500 'for defraying the charge of 10 mares brought from Holland for her Majesty': probably horses returning from the wars now that treaties were being negotiated. These mares may have gone to stud, but it is likely enough that they worked in the hunting field first. Queen Anne was hailed by flatterers as 'the mightest huntress of her age'; Dean Swift went as far as proclaiming her to be 'a mighty hunter like Nimrod'. But this was an upholstered Diana following the deer in a chaise or a calash over grassy swathes cut in Windsor forest and levelled and drained for her safe approach. On the other hand, she was a genuine enthusiast who had learned horsemanship from her father, James II, and had hunted with him when, as Pepys complained, he should have been at his desk at the Admiralty. Not even the gout from which she suffered in later years could keep her from her favourite sport.

The royal kennels which Anne established at Ascot lasted until the present century, and she restored the annual payment of £2341 to the buckhounds, for 'salary and all manner of charges and expenses', after Treasurer Godolphin had tried to reduce it to £1000 as a wartime economy. Racegoers remember her gratefully too. In 1711 Somerset paid £558 19s. 5d. to 'sundry workmen employed in making and perfecting the round heat' for the first race-meeting at Ascot in 1711. Thus 'Royal Ascot' was begun, and Anne gave the Queen's Plate of 100 guineas, finding the money from the secret service fund administered by the Crown. In conjunction later with the Jockey Club, it became one of the Master's duties to supervise competitions for the sovereign's prizes and to adjudicate disputes.

150 (left). Henry de Nassau, Count of Auverquerque (Overkirk), the only foreigner to have held the office of Master.

151 (right). Charles Seymour, 6th Duke of Somerset, 'a man of high principle and steady loyalty in an age when these qualities were not conspicuous among leading statesmen'.

CHAPTER SIXTEEN

The Horsemen of Hanover

Queen Anne having died without an heir, the throne passed to the next Protestant candidate, George Lewis, Elector of Hanover, grandson of a daughter of James I who a hundred years previously had married a German prince. He had been a brave and efficient soldier in his youth, fighting for the Emperor in Italy and on the Rhine and helping John Sobieski to save Vienna from the Turks. He was at Neerwinden with William III and he brought five regiments of horse from his little Electorate to campaign with Marlborough in the Netherlands.

Hanover, where he had ruled since 1698, was one of many petty European courts refulgent with the diluted splendour of Versailles. Noblemen were numerous at these courts, and at Herrenhausen all members of the first ten gradations were aristocrats, including the pages and secretaries. Below them was a host of gentlemen ushers, tutors, physicians, fencing-masters, fiddlers, waiters, and so on down to the cooks, masters of the roast, lackeys and scullions. George Lewis had a Master of the Horse who was paid 1090 thalers a year, a little less than the High Chamberlain but twice as much as the barber. In the stables were some 600 horses; 20 teams of carriage horses, eight to a team; 16 coachmen, 14 postilions, 19 ostlers and sundry farriers, horse-doctors and stable attendants.

Although he told parliament of his satisfaction at being called to 'the throne of our ancestors', George I (1714–27) never saw himself as more than a temporary lodger who might be made to depart as suddenly as he had come, and he revisited Hanover as often as he could. In equestrian matters, however, he put England in his debt by bringing from his homeland the famous cream horses which drew the state coaches until for reasons of economy the breed at Hampton Court was dispersed in 1920. Some of these strange animals, with 'characteristic Roman noses and bright pink eyes', were milk-white albinos. White and cream horses were anciently sacred to the German tribes, for whom they provided a vocal source of divination. Tacitus noted in his *Germania* that 'it is peculiar to this people to seek omens and monitions from horses. Kept at the public expense, in these same woods and groves are white horses pure from the taint of earthly labour. These are yoked to a sacred chariot and accompanied by the priest and the king, who note their neighings and snortings.' The creams were sometimes called 'Isabels' from the tradition that in the fifteenth century Queen Isabella of Spain presented them to certain German knights in reward for service in the Spanish army. In 1714 they were still being bred in the royal houses of Schaumburg-Lippe and Gotha as well as Hanover. To preserve the stock, regular importations were made from the Hanover stud until breeding was begun in England early in the nineteenth century. It has been suggested, too, that some of the creams from Hanover were crossed with certain 'tiger-coloured' horses, apparently creams with darker spots, which had been presented to William III by the Landgrave of Hesse in 1695.

Yet while England was importing horses, the native breeds were being exported even to enemy countries. Louis XIV had his way in many things but he failed to create a home-bred stock sufficient for his vast requirements, and both he and his successor came to England for hackneys from Suffolk and hunters from Yorkshire. There is an instructive contrast in method here. Colbert, the energetic minister of Louis XIV, believed that state-controlled enterprise was the way to procure all things necessary and helpful, but horses, unlike the profitable silkworm, proved him wrong. He set up *haras*, or studs, throughout the kingdom which were to be nourished by state aid, and the great landowning families also received financial help for the upkeep of their *haras* on condition of allowing the government its pick. But the system simply did not work. At about the time of George I's accession in England the French government was confessing that the national horse-breeding service was not producing results: 'We are reduced to bargaining, money in hand, with Jewish merchants for all the requirements of the cavalry, the dragoons, the artillery and even the King's own household.' In the haphazard British system, with a free market in breeding, purchase and a rough-and-ready balance between import and export, no English Master of the Horse has ever had to make such an admission.

An analysis of the stables establishment at the end of Queen Anne's reign

152. *Herrenhausen, the palace on the outskirts of Hanover where the Hanoverian court resided from the 1660s and which was later transformed by the Electress Sophia, mother of George I. The stables are the second group of buildings at top left.*

(printed in the appendix to J. M. Beattie, *The English Court in the Reign of George I*, 1967) shows that there were still just over a hundred officers and servants, as in 1689, but it suggests a significant rise in the salaries, and possibly the status, of the senior members. The Master's financial emoluments were now £1267, and in addition to twelve horses he had a personal staff of thirteen footmen and grooms in the royal livery, all maintained by the Crown. With the right to lodging at Court when he needed it, these privileges had been for some time among the perquisites of the office. But Beattie states (page 100) that the Master also received gold plate to the value of £400 on his appointment, and that on the sovereign's death he was entitled to possession of the royal coaches and their horses. The replacement of these could be a considerable expense in the new reign, and if Anne's two commissioners, Darcy and Feilding, had not accepted a lump sum in lieu, George I might have had no coaches to meet him when he arrived from Hanover. The Master further enjoyed a lucrative patronage in the appointment to senior offices in the department, which he might either sell or bestow upon relatives and friends, or the sons of friends, or supporters of his political interests. There were direct financial opportunities as well. Although the regular fixed charges of the department were paid from the Privy Purse, through the Board of Green Cloth, extraordinary expenditure was paid from the Exchequer on accounts declared by the Master. This expenditure might include the provision of new liveries for the servants. The right to provide liveries had been acquired by the Master in a legal battle in 1694, so he must have thought it worth possessing. Possibly none of this was very new, the office having always given scope for various kinds of exploitation, but in the eighteenth century it was becoming a fine art. Not for nothing was the Master thought to have 'the handsomest employment in Britain'.

Since 1689 the wage of the equerries had risen from £256 to £300, and of the pages of honour from £156 to £260. They received 'diet' at Court when they were in attendance, the equerries having their lodging as well, and they all drew allowances for travel. As personal attendants upon the King – his outdoor companions as the gentlemen of the bedchamber attended him indoors – the equerries and pages were men of good family and some ambition. Employment at Court admitted them to influential acquaintances who might advance their careers in politics or the army. For this reason there was a steady turnover in these posts – to the advantage of the Master, who filled the vacancies – as the equerries and pages moved on to higher things. This is largely conjectural, but it is possible that in the social sense the equerries and pages were of a better rank than in earlier times. While it is true that the 'squires of the body' to mediaeval and Tudor monarchs were aspiring members of rising families, and often went on to high and responsible posts, the difference lies in the new stabilisation of society. Tudor England had lived for long on its nerves, Stuart England for long on its dogmatists and its bayonets. But now the great issues had been settled, or so it was thought: all passion spent, and man could be confident of his central place in a universe whose essential orderliness was evident to philosophers and bishops in equal measure. Since there were now no problems that might not be solved by exercise of the reasoning faculty, man could optimistically see himself as a perfectible creature without recourse to the parson or to acrimonious and divisive interpretations of scripture. This was an inevitable reaction to the strains and upheavals of the seventeenth century: a more realistic and sceptical mood, which Charles II brought home with him after the fugitive years. This mood spread through the higher and upper-middle levels of society and expressed itself artistically in all that we mean by the 'Queen Anne style' – Wren's buildings, the balanced Augustan prose, Bentley's

153. Stables, almost certainly in Hanover, of Ernest Augustus, Duke of York, brother of George I.

critical scholarship, the theatrical comedy in which the incidental bawdiness was so much less important than the language and the artistic control. Presently it penetrated into such an unobtrusive corner of society as the department of the Master of the Horse. The young men who sought employment there were not necessarily better than their predecessors but they were more certain of their roots and their intended destination.

The Duke of Somerset, who had supported the Hanoverian succession against Jacobite intrigues to enthrone the Old Pretender, was reappointed Master of the Horse, but he had a gift for resignation and within a few months he was gone again: this time over a matter of family pique, his son-in-law, Sir William Wyndham, having been accused of complicity in the 1715 rebellion. When on Marlborough's death this 'proud Duke of Somerset' proposed marriage to the widowed Duchess Sarah, he received the classic brush-off of all time:

> If I were young and handsome as I was, instead of old and faded as I am, and you could lay the empire of the world at my feet, you should never share the heart and hand that once belonged to John, Duke of Marlborough.

The King did not take long to discover that his income was falling short of his Household expenditure, and an annual £1000 for the keeper of the 'running horses' at Newmarket was an additional burden not included in the Master's establishment. On Somerset's resignation he put the Mastership into commission for the rest of the reign. The post had been expected by the accommodating Baron Kielmansegge in return for the attentions accorded to the monarch by his wife, and the appointment would have been consistent with George's practice of rewarding the visiting entourage. Alternatively, according to English observers, the fees and patronage went to swell the already considerable emoluments of the Duchess of Kendal. But

154. Sir Conyers Darcy at Newmarket in 1715. Darcy, who acted as a commissioner when the Duke of Somerset resigned the Mastership, is seen talking to a jockey.

probably the motive was economy; in 1712 Anne had done the same thing. Darcy, who had been avenor and gentleman of the horse as well as commissioner under Anne, was now reappointed, sharing the commission with Colonel Francis Negus. Darcy's dismissal in 1717 cannot be explained as a loss of George's favour for he soon returned to court as Master, and later Comptroller, of the Household, remaining in office until 1755. George was able to save a great deal of money by these arrangements, estimated by Beattie at £1179 a year. The commissioners were paid £800 a year each, but without the perquisites of horses, footmen, carriages and liveried servants; and when for ten years Negus was sole commissioner, this brought a further annual saving of £800. As though determined to make as little use of the English scene as possible, George seldom hunted outside the Royal Parks, and he never went out at all if the weather was bad. Thus he was able to make an additional economy by asking Negus to be commissioner of the buckhounds too.

Negus was an engaging person, destined for immortality in the drink named after him when a political discussion grew more heated as the wine passed round, and he suggested to the disputants that they should take more water with it. In the next reign he was given official charge of the buckhounds and he was also avenor of the stables. So in effect he was in charge of the royal sport and transport between 1717 and 1732, when he died in the saddle while hunting at Swinley. He was ranger of Swinley and Windsor: he represented Ipswich in the House of Commons; and he was continuously active in his underpaid duties even when the King was in Hanover and doing his hunting there. George trusted him well enough to summon him to Hanover in 1720 to explain what the politicians had been up to when the South Sea Bubble was about to burst. For his equestrian duties he was granted a lodging at Hampton Court. Thirty couple of buckhounds were maintained at £1000 a year, and by 1725 a deficit of £1200 was included in accumulated arrears of over half a million in the Civil List. Alexander Pope one day met the heir to the throne and some of his ladies out hunting near Hampton Court and remarked in a letter to Martha Blount what it must mean 'to eat Westphalia ham in the morning, ride over hedges and ditches on borrowed hacks, come home in the heat of the day with a fever, and (what is worse a hundred time) with a red mark in the forehead from an uneasy hat. All this may qualify them to make excellent wives for fox-hunters and bear abundance of ruddy-complexioned children.' The ladies were undaunted by these considerations, and Negus had to produce a constant supply of horses for their pleasure, mostly drawn from the stock of a hundred kept in the Royal Mews at Charing Cross. As commissioner for the Master he supervised the lower officers who looked after the buildings, the horses and the carriages. It is surprising how much he had to do. He not only had to provide hunting-horns but he had to see that the huntsmen knew how to blow them. His duties included the provision of medical care for men as well as animals – his accounts include a fee of ten guineas for the setting of a huntsman's broken leg. He had to find horses and hounds as gifts for distinguished visitors; feed the turkeys in Bushey Park; and in an additional post as superintendant of the royal menagerie he was responsible for feeding the resident tiger, which consumed six pounds of meat each day. Manifold tasks of this kind were under the general care of the Master when he existed, but as an under-salaried commissioner Negus seems to have attended to much of the work himself.

155. *Richard Lumley, 2nd Earl of Scarborough, a close friend of George II, who fought against the Jacobites in the rising of 1715.*

George II (1727–60) was a peppery little man who in his Lilliputian rages would jump on his wig and kick the pieces round the room. Like his father, he was a natural soldier, and on every possible occasion he would wear the red coat in which he fought with Marlborough at Oudenarde. He also shared his father's love for Hanover and distaste for the people and customs of England. Between 1729 and 1731 he was away in Hanover for two years, and in spite of a European war he managed eight visits between 1740 and 1755. Even when he could not be in Hanover, the Court at Herrenhausen was maintained in its full glory of chamberlains, marshals and equerries, and at the weekly assembly on Saturdays the whole Court advanced and bowed to a picture of their missing prince. In his disapproval of his English subjects George denounced their cooks, their confectioners and their actors, and added that 'no English coachman [could] drive, no English jockey ride, nor were any English horses fit to be ridden or driven.' He was fortunate however, in a sensible minister and a sensible wife, and he had chosen both of them well. Sir Robert Walpole won his confidence by promising a substantial increase in the Civil List and then guided the country through fruitful years of retrenchment and peace. Queen Caroline of Anspach was a shrewd, outspoken, masculine woman who tolerated George's indiscriminate affairs and never lost his love.

The King had always been at odds with his father, and the fact that the Mastership of the Horse had been neglected in the previous reign was sufficient reason for him to revive the office. In 1727 he gave it to a close friend, Richard Lumley, Earl of Scarborough, one of the band of would-be courtiers and ministers who had gathered round the heir at Leicester House. They were almost a 'shadow cabinet', sure that they would be rewarded at his accession. The buckhounds went to Negus at the old rate of £2341 for the establishment, but there were allowances for special duties like providing hunt breakfasts at Swinley. George also revived the mastership of the harriers, which had been in abeyance since James II. Wednesday and Saturday were George's regular days for hunting, and although he purchased nearby Cranborne Lodge, he was not very fond of Windsor and preferred Hampton Court or Richmond. He was also firm in the belief that the stag was the only

156. Racing at Newmarket in the early 18th century. The race is a 'Round' or 'Plate' Course, run for the King's Plate.

worthwhile quarry for a true huntsman. He told the Duke of Grafton that it was no fit occupation for a man of quality 'to spend all his time tormenting a poor fox, that was generally a much better beast than any of those that pursued him; for the fox hunts no other animal but for his subsistence, while those brutes who hunt him did it only for the pleasure they took hunting.' By this standard the difference between the fox and the stag is not very clear, but George revived the policy of paying the under-keepers of the forests a fee for each kill: 40s. for a stag, 20s. for a hind, and 10s. for a buck. No doubt this made them more diligent in warding off poachers. The mightiest huntress was the King's second daughter, Princess Amelia, a tomboy who cared for nothing but horses. She never married, and lived to a great age to exchange pretty compliments with Horace Walpole. Queen Caroline was never a hunting enthusiast but attended as a duty, riding in a chaise and enjoying the company of the waspish and epicene Lord Hervey, whose horse she provided. Another stern feminist, Lady Mary Wortley Montagu, was more robust in her opinions. Having taken up the chase in her sixties, she discovered herself to have 'arrived to vast courage and skill that way, and I am well pleased with it as with the acquisition of a new sense.'

Sexagenarians may take heart from this, but the sport had its dangers and frustrations, and also its rivals. In 1733 Frederick Prince of Wales missed a hunt at Richmond because he was on the cricket-field leading eleven men of Surrey against

eleven of Kent for a silver cup presented by himself. In 1751 he was to die very suddenly of a feverish cold, and it is possible that his resistance had been weakened by a blow on the head from a cricket-ball while he was fielding, less than attentively, in the deep.

Hunting, too, could be dangerous, and this seems to have been a bad time for accidents, especially the year 1734. When the dashing Princess Amelia was thrown, she was dragged some distance by her petticoat, which had attached itself to the pommel. Unafraid, she wanted to remount and continue, but the Queen insisted that she be bled, the universal remedy for any illness or mishap. Then a child of two was knocked from its mother's arms by a passing horse and 'a coach and six horses flying by at that instant, the babe was trodden to death and the woman miserably bruised.' On the same day the young Earl of Londonderry, only a schoolboy, was thrown and killed. The Duke of Cumberland, a son of the King, was thrown 'with a great effusion of blood from the nose'. Even Walpole, who acted as field-master after the death of Negus and hunted 'clothed in green as a ranger', had to be bled after a tumble, and he began to find the exertions of the hunt more than he could endure. One of the royal mistresses, the Duchess of Suffolk, could not understand why the ladies of the Court should be so fond of a sport when they 'have every day a very tolerable chance to have a neck broke'. There were also dangers from unbidden spectators. It was well enough when the Duke of Cumberland hunted

157. Cumberland Lodge, Windsor, formerly the home of the Park Ranger, Henry Frederick, Duke of Cumberland. The drawing by Thomas Sandby shows Barnard Smith, stud groom, lunging a horse, watched by the Duke of Cumberland (left) with three attendant gentlemen: Sir Thomas Rich, Lord Albemarle, and Sandby himself.

158. Horsemen at a cricket match.

159. The earliest known laws of cricket, drawn up in July 1727 by the 2nd Duke of Richmond and A. Brodrick (later Lord Midleton).

160. The 2nd Duke of Richmond and his wife Sarah. He married her when he was eighteen to settle a gambling debt incurred by his father, then rushed off for three years on the Grand Tour. On his return to London he went to the theatre and was attracted by a beautiful woman: who turned out to be none other than his wife.

with some boys from Eton College whose families were assembled to watch, because on that occasion the gratified onlookers made a collection to purchase books for the library. The trouble came from highwaymen who lurked in the woods waiting to pounce on casualties and stragglers, and this menace grew so serious that permits had to be issued to spectators wishing to follow the hunt, and the buckhounds had to be put under an armed guard.

Racing, too, was increasingly in need of regulation. Although rules already existed when the King's Plates were being run, formal regulations appeared for the first time in the Racing Calendar for 1739. The preface, issued by the Clerk of the Stables, stated them to be

> a copy of the articles relating to his Majesty's Plates, annually run for at Newmarket and other places by six-year-old horses, etc., carrying twelve stone, published by his Grace the Duke of Richmond, Master of the Horse, who, for the satisfaction of those gentlemen who desire the publication thereof, has been pleased to order James Adams, Esq., Clerk to his Majesty's Stables, to sign the said copy as an evidence of His Grace's consent.

What is interesting here is the reference to the 'gentlemen who desire the

161. *The 4th Duke of Devonshire, the only Master of the Horse to have been Prime Minister.*

162 *(opposite). Lionel Sackville, 1st Duke of Dorset. He became Master at the age of sixty-seven.*

publication thereof'. The Jockey Club, which was formed in the 1750s, was a protection society of wealthy owners who wanted to outlaw the unscrupulous. In 1739 some of them met at the Duke of Bolton's seat at Hackwood 'to consider methods for the better keeping of their respective strings at Newmarket'. By this they intended to stop the gate-crashers, and in the following year a statute was passed for better control of the meetings at Ascot.

The Earl of Scarborough was Master until 1734, and he was under constant pressure to find horses and money for the growing cost of equestrian sport. When it was decided to resume bonuses to the under-keepers for each kill, an order came to him from Walpole, as Lord Treasurer, to pay them 'out of any monies coming to your hands for the extraordinary expense of our stables'. This was unhelpful and unspecific, as the stable resources – though perhaps not the Master's own – were already overstretched. Another steady drain was the equipping of state visitors. Even the shifty Duke of Lorraine, who chose to arrive under the name of Count Blamont, had to be supplied with two Barbs from Tripoli, and a gift of four saddle horses.

Charles Lennox, second Duke of Richmond, who was Master from 1734 to 1750, was a grandson of Charles II and Louise de Kérouaille and son of the young Richmond who was appointed to the office at the age of ten. The new Master had the characteristic versatility of the eighteenth-century aristocrat. He had a law degree at Cambridge, he was commissioned in the Horse Grenadier Guards, and after being made a Lord of the Bedchamber in 1727 he was High Constable at George's coronation. He was a fellow of the Royal College of Surgeons and of the Royal Society. His menagerie at Goodwood, which included a 'Jack all', was chosen with a discrimination that drew the attention of zoologists, and horticulturalists came to see the trees he planted there. He was also an Elder Brother of Trinity House.

His fox hunts at Charlton, in the lee of Goodwood hill, were famous among the fraternity, and like many great landowners of the time, he was a patron of cricket. Thomas Waymark and the Surrey professional Stephen Dingate were among the cricketers he employed in his household, Dingate serving as his barber. Although apparently he was not a great player himself, Richmond ran a famous team at the little Sussex village of Slindon, where the manor-house had once been the summer palace of the archbishops of Canterbury. The 'England' team that played Kent in 1744, the earliest match recorded in *Scores and Biographies*, was virtually the Slindon side. It was built round Richard Newland, a local surgeon, and his two brothers, and Slindon might have occupied a greater place in cricket history even than Hambledon if Richard Nyren, originally a Slindon player, had not moved across the border to keep the 'Bat and Ball' on Broad-Halfpenny Down, and if his son John had not been the first great writer on the game. Richmond also led his private team in encounters against similar combinations, when the bets were heavy and the intervals were lengthy and much attended with food and drink. It is arguable that the detailed regulations drawn up between himself and Lord Midleton for a match at Peper Harow in 1727 constituted the first coded 'laws of the game' (J. Marshall, *The Duke who was Cricket*, 1961.)

But for all his talents, Richmond was an erratic man. His mother said that he was 'extremely rattle-headed', and Queen Caroline, whose judgment can never be disregarded, found him 'so half-witted, so bizarre and so grand-seigneur and so mulish' that his best intentions were as confounding in their effect as deliberate malice. His marriage at the age of eighteen to the thirteen-year-old daughter of the Earl of Cadogan was said to have been in settlement of a gambling debt, and the

state of indebtedness in which he passed the whole of his life was possible only to a man grandly indifferent to the hardship it brought to other people.

He was the last Master of the Horse to have fought at the side of his King on the battlefield, at Dettingen in 1743, but his performance in the office was not particularly distinguished. He applied for it when Scarborough retired and he had the Earl of Pembroke as a rival. According to Hervey, George 'was not averse to granting his request any further than he was always averse to giving anything to anybody'. He thought that all his English ministers were overpaid, and 'while employments were vacant he saved the salary'. But as there were two applicants, he had to make a decision, and Richmond's immediate reward for being the favoured one was a command to accompany his sovereign to Hanover.

In 1740 England entered the War of the Austrian Succession, and the King, now sixty-one, decided that his personal presence was necessary to ensure the safety of Hanover, to which many of his English ministers were, in his view, cynically indifferent. He set out with a baggage-train of 662 horses and a due complement of carriages and wagons, which Richmond had to organise, and there were immediate difficulties over rations and fodder. At Dettingen Marshal Noailles seemed to have the allied army in a trap, from which they escaped through the disciplined heroism of the English infantry. King George's energy and courage on the field were extraordinary, but he gave offence by leading his men in the yellow sash of Hanover. He also inflicted a personal slight upon his Master of the Horse by refusing to give him command of any of the Hanoverian contingent. This was not unreasonable since the Hanoverians were professionals and Richmond's military experience was confined to a guards captaincy, but he poured out his troubles in a disingenuous letter to the Duke of Newcastle. It had grieved him, he said, to have heard resentful mutterings about George's wearing the yellow sash instead of the red of the Order of the Bath. 'It hurts us on his account more than our own to see his great partiality to the Hanoverian troops, of which there are but too many instances.' He hoped that Newcastle will not think it 'from love of tittle-tattle that I say it, for I believe you know that is not my turn.' It is only because the King has been so good to him that he is obliged to report these things.

The letter goes on to disclose his real grievance, which was a personal one: 80 Hanoverian horses had been put in the charge of 'a puppy of a Very Grand Ecuyer', a Monsieur Freechappel, and this was such an insult to the Master of the Horse that he had felt obliged to tell his wife about it, although he made a point of never involving her in politics. Another letter a month later shows some smoothing of the ruffled feathers:

> I must say that things are rather mended. Mons. Freechappel does nothing now but the part of a head groom, that is taking care of all his Hanoverian horses, and I do all the functions of the Master of the Horse, that is of helping him [the King] into his voiture, and sitting in it by him and so forth . . . But the greasing of the wheels and all that is entirely under Mons. de Freechappel, so you see I have cloak enough to cover my discontents, but between your Grace and I, I can never forget what I think literally was a barbarous and cruel usage, which was that of not even letting this Freechappel so much as offer me a horse, upon a day of such consequence as that of the Battle ... Think of that day, and that the King's Master of the Horse must have been that day on foot if General Honeywood had not been so kind as to lend him a horse.

Although regimental sources contributed part of the immense train of horses and vehicles that accompanied the King into Europe, the war put a renewed strain on the Master's official expenditure. Richmond's accounts for the two years 1740–1 show that he began with £1868 in hand and received £15,500 from the Exchequer.

As he spent only £13,402, he finished nearly £4000 in credit. Approximate figures for disbursements in this period were: to the coach-maker and other tradesmen for goods delivered and work done, £2035; for new liveries, £3928; for the hire of coaches and horses, and travelling charges, £1142; for horses bought, £324; for the king's gifts 'in lieu of Plates at horse races', £1365; for salaries and overheads, £2761; for salaries of grooms and servants at the stud, £258; and 'for provisions and other contingent expenses', £1586.

This expenditure continued in the ordinary way during the war, but for 1743–4 Richmond made additional claims amounting to £21,551, of which £7208 was for purveyorage, forage and travelling charges, and £14,342 paid to Joseph Pouchard, the King's agent at Utrecht, for the hire of horses, purchase of coaches and 'other disbursements'. Extraordinary allowances of £1584 were also due when the King went abroad again in 1745; and after Richmond's death his duchess, as 'relict and executrix', put in a claim for a further £300 paid to Pouchard but not yet refunded (Lansdowne MS. 669).

When the 'Forty-Five' rebellion broke out, Richmond urged the immediate return of the English army from the Netherlands to save the kingdom, not from the Scots but from the French invasion which he and other observers mistakenly anticipated. He himself went as far as Lichfield to face the peril, but then he was mainly concerned by the news that his wife was coming north to join him, and he complained to Newcastle that she should have been prevented from doing so. At the end of the war he was sent on a special embassy to try to procure a more friendly relationship with France. He was at once worrying about his allowance for the expedition, demanding the sum of £18,000; and when Henry Pelham at the Treasury offered £14,000, with the suggestion that Richmond should make up the balance himself, he lamented that this would be a severe imposition on 'me, who never saved a shilling in my life, but on the contrary always was and still am in debt'. He wrung a small increase out of Pelham and set out for Paris with a retinue consisting of 52 horses and 50 retainers, including four coachmen, six postilions, five master-cooks and a confectioner.

Richmond died in 1750 and the office was widely canvassed. In one of his gossipy letters (1 September 1750) Horace Walpole says: 'The Duke of Richmond is dead, vastly lamented: the Duchess is left in great circumstances. Lord Albemarle, Lord Lincoln, the Duke of Marlborough, Duke of Leeds and the Duke of Rutland are talked of for Master of the Horse. The first is likeliest to succeed; the Pelhams wish most to have the last.' Albemarle had been at Dettingen, and also at the butchery at Culloden, and George always had a special regard for his comrades-in-arms, but the office went to none of these. The Duke of Newcastle, the most adroit political jobber of the age, was dissatisfied with the Duke of Bedford, his colleague as Secretary of State, and Lady Yarmouth, the King's German mistress, suggested that as Master of the Horse Bedford would have a post better suited to his indolent habits. But George, who was still grieving for Richmond—'I couldn't have lost anybody more affectionate, and a more sincere friend'—disliked Bedford and thought him unworthy to replace 'the poor man that is gone'. So crafty politicians still could not influence the appointment of a great officer whose duties brought him into close personal association with the sovereign, and the post went to William Cavendish, Marquis of Hartington and later Duke of Devonshire, who held it until 1755, when he succeeded to his dukedom and was made Lord-Lieutenant of Ireland. Devonshire is unique as the only Master of the Horse who has ever been Prime Minister, being First Lord of the Treasury for a few months in 1756–7, with the elder Pitt as leader of the Commons.

163. Granville Leveson-Gower, 1st Marquess of Stafford. During his tenure of office he helped to raise militia for internal defence.

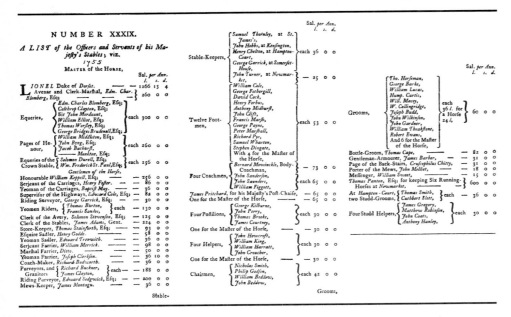

The adjoining 'List of the Officers and Servants of His Majesty's Stables, 1755', (R.M. Records) shows little change in the organisation of the Royal Mews since Queen Anne's time. It was possibly prepared for the guidance of the Master, Lionel Sackville, first Duke of Dorset, who was now an elderly man. Long ago, in 1714, he had been sent to Hanover to tell the Elector that Queen Anne was dead, and he then became First Lord of the Bedchamber. He had had a long career of service in the Court, and with the King no longer active in the fields of hunting or battle, the Mastership was a dignified reward.

Dorset resigned on receiving other appointments two years later, and George's last Master was Granville Leveson-Gower, Earl Gower, who was to be a valued Household officer in the next reign. The country was now at war again, but Pitt's policy was to leave the land fighting to subsidised continental allies while his navy strangled the French at sea and took possession of their colonies. The most notable event of Gower's term of office was the embodying of a militia for internal defence in the expected event of invasion. It differed from the feudal levies and indentured armies of the past, but it was not exactly a citizen yeomanry either, since its majors had to own property worth £300 a year and captains £200. Edward Gibbon belonged to it as a captain in the south battalion of the Hampshire militia, and he found himself condemned by this 'mimic Bellona' to 'a wandering life of military servitude' though the danger was over and this conscript home guard therefore was not called upon to fire a shot. Moreover, his temper was 'insensibly soured by the society of our rustic officers'. But Gibbon was a man of sedentary habit. When his father 'galloped away on a fleet hunter to follow the Duke of Richmond's fox-hounds', he had no wish to join him. 'The horse, the favourite of my countrymen, never contributed to the pleasures of my youth.' In this seemingly simple phrase the amplitude of Gibbon's irony spreads the joke over a surprisingly wide area. First it is at the expense of the author himself for being so unathletic and unfashionable. Then it seems to enlarge itself to take in the horse, which is felt to be a rather clumsy creature, and then the hard-riding men of the shires, who may be just a little stupid; and at the end, by some sleight of hand, Gibbon emerges in effortless superiority over both beast and burden.

164. The list shows that there were just over one hundred officers and servants in the stables establishment in 1755.

165. 'Beauty', King George III's cream-coloured charger. Intended as a coach-horse but found to be not strong enough, he was ridden as a charger until the King discovered that the upstart Napoleon Bonaparte was using cream horses from the Hanoverian stud to draw his carriage.

166 (overleaf). King George III returning from hunting at Windsor. In 1786 King George discarded the tricorne for a black velvet 'jockey' cap. It was about the same time that the royal buckhounds became the direct responsibility of the Master of the Horse.

CHAPTER SEVENTEEN

George III

Historians have lately ceased to belabour King George III (1760–1820) as a clumsy tyrant who tried to subvert the constitution by reviving Chamber government through 'king's friends', or *familiares*, and silencing opposition by unscrupulous bribes. If King George attempted anything, it was only to exercise the royal prerogative in the choice of ministers, and to maintain them in office by the arts of 'persuasion' of which Robert Walpole had been such a consummate master. In trying to preserve the personal choice that was still the King's constitutional right, he tended to dispossess the Whig grandees who in their various and fluctuating combinations had dominated the Court and the administration since 1714. He was not even very good at this, having often to put up with ministers he detested; and after the triumph of the royal electoral machine in winning a majority for the younger Pitt in 1784, he more or less gave up the attempt.

King George was a limited but immensely dutiful man. He was the son of the ill-fated Frederick Prince of Wales, that 'Fred who was alive, but now is dead', and he succeeded his grandfather, King George II, when he was only twenty-two. At that age his appreciation of the Crown's rights and responsibilities was theoretical, even academic, and he had to feel his way through some early obstacles and blunders. King George's supposed despotism was less corrupt than the methods by which Walpole and then Newcastle, the supreme wire-puller, had kept the Whigs in power for so long; and eighteenth-century despotisms were in any case tempered by the steady opposition of the 'country party', the solid men from the shires who were always suspicious of the Court and were quite incorruptible on major issues. It is true that obedient courtiers prospered under King George's régime, but when in history have they not?

Unlike his two predecessors, King George fairly claimed to 'glory in the name of Britain' (although in his long life he never went farther north than Cheltenham), and he was determined to be a model British king, frugal, disciplined and industrious. Soon after his accession, following a brief infatuation for Lady Sarah Lennox, youngest daughter of the cricketing Duke of Richmond, he married Princess Charlotte of Mecklenburg-Strelitz, and the Mews Journal has details of her reception (folio 6). If she comes up the river, 'on orders from St James's to the Stables, the creams, one of the bay horses, the black set and the equerries' set, must repair to Greenwich and conduct the Princess from the water-side to the house, and wait there for further orders.' Instructions follow for the footmen, attendants, coachmen and their liveries, and 'two chaisemarines with four hired horses ought also to go to bring the Princess's apparel with speed to London.'

Queen Charlotte was no beauty, but between 1762 and 1783 she bore King George fifteen children, an astonishing feat of sustained fecundity by them both. Their attendants were touched by their unswerving loyalty to one another,

167. This dashing horseman with strong Hanoverian connections, is William V of Orange, a grandson of George II, from whom he received his Garter. The walking groom is wearing a Hanoverian uniform, and the horse a Hanoverian bit.

something unique among Hanoverian monarchs. With its modest pleasures and a stiff, unyielding etiquette, their Court was uncomfortable and dull, but it was decent: a fact of some importance when profligate thrones were toppling all over Europe. The King habitually rose at six, worked at his papers for two hours before attending chapel, and then met his ministers: or on his hunting days, usually twice a week or more often when he was in the country, he would hunt until four. Even after a day of violent exercise, his dinner, which he took at four, consisted only of soup, meat with one vegetable, and fruit. Carpets he regarded as an unnecessary luxury, and when there was music at the palace, he was content to dance for hours to a single tune – which brings him bang into the twentieth century. The smears about King George, of which there were many, were mostly the invention of political opponents unable to obtain the offices they coveted. They mocked his shabby dress and homely ways. He was 'Farmer George', who looked and spoke like one of his own herdsmen and wondered how the apple got inside the dumpling. They said that when he hunted he always made his equerry go over first when he came to a difficult jump. They were pitiless about the malady, now thought to have been porphyria, which robbed him of his reason and for the last ten years of his reign

168. Francis Hastings, 10th Earl of Huntingdon. The Duchess of Hamilton wrote of him: 'I can never believe Lord Huntingdon will marry. He holds women in such a contemptible light that to be sure he will never trust one of us with his honour'. (He remained single.)

made it impossible for him to take any part in government. When driving at Windsor, they said he once stopped the carriage and held a conversation with an oak tree in the belief that he was addressing the King of Prussia.

To save expense, King George used St James's for ceremonial business only, and he lived at Buckingham House, called the Queen's House, which he bought from the Buckingham family at the beginning of the reign. He also abandoned Kensington Palace and Hampton Court, using Kew and Windsor as his country residences. But despite his personal economies he was always in debt, and this was to have its effect on the establishment of the Master of the Horse. In 1760 he surrendered the Crown's hereditary revenues in return for a Civil List of £800,000, which was £76,000 less than the sum for the last year of the previous reign. From this he had to pay ministers, judges and ambassadors, maintain a court with its lords and grooms of the bedchamber, its equerries and its stables, and bear the cost of the pensions and sinecure offices that served as retirement pay. When he came to the throne, he had three brothers and two sisters to provide for, and he would soon have the expense of his coronation and his wedding. Nor should he have been so philoprogenitive; he came to acknowledge that 'Heaven having blessed me with a numerous progeny' had contributed to his financial troubles, especially when his eldest son began to accumulate vast debts of his own. Within ten years the Civil List was in debt by more than half a million, and when in 1777 the debt had risen to £618,000, parliament reluctantly granted an additional £100,000 a year. These debts simply meant that government was becoming more expensive, not that the King was extravagant. For his own expenditure King George had a privy purse of £48,000 a year, increased to £60,000 in 1777, for which he was not accountable to the Treasury, and a further £5000 from the Duchy of Lancaster. But even the privy purse had to find various pensions and charitable gifts that properly belonged to the public sphere. When the Royal Academy was founded in 1768, the privy purse contributed £5000 to the initial expense and paid the first year's deficit of £370. There was also a secret service fund of £60,000, disliked by the parliamentary opposition because it too was unaccountable. In this reign it was no longer used for electoral manipulation, which was financed from the privy purse. It was mostly spent on sweeteners to foreign diplomats, but honorific pensions were paid from it too, including Dr Johnson's: not, one would have thought, a very sinister thing.

However, the Whigs believed that by pruning the Household and reducing sinecures they would be able to eliminate the placemen and dependants whose pliancy kept unpopular ministries in office. Edmund Burke's campaign for 'economical reform' was just another stroke in the Commons' inveterate hostility to the royal Household, and Lord Shelburne deplored the time wasted on 'the nonsense of Mr Burke's bill. It was both framed and carried through without the least regard for *facts*.' Shelburne was a cross-bench Whig who judged issues on their merits and was widely hated for his refusal to attach himself to any party. He was 'Malagrida' or 'the Jesuit of Berkeley Square'. But although he may have disliked some of the methods, Shelburne endorsed King George III's policy of aiming at a steady administration after the endless diversity of Whig family combinations which might at any moment overthrow settled government for the sake of domestic faction: as for instance in Carteret's unsuccessful coup against the Pelhams in 1746, when for a couple of days the Duke of Richmond was deprived of the Mastership of the Horse. Besides, public servants had to be rewarded somehow, and high-sounding sinecures, many of them survivals from the mediaeval Household, were as harmless a method as any. A lordship in the Board of Trade and Plantations, from which Gibbon enjoyed £750 a year 'without being called away from my library',

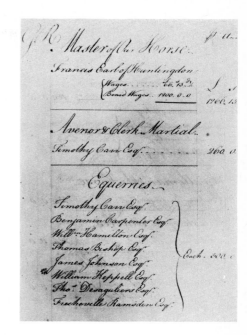

169. Page from the Establishment book of the Master of the Horse (the Earl of Huntingdon) in 1760.

170. *John Manners, 3rd Duke of Rutland, Master from 1761 to 1766.*

was described by Burke as admission to 'an Academy of *Belles Lettres*'. Locke, Prior and Addison had all sat there in their time.

The *facts* to which Shelburne referred demanded an administrative reform to complete the separation of the Crown's personal income from all the salaries and other charges that properly belonged to the domain of public expenditure, but this was not achieved until 1831. Burke himself was no reformer. 'When the poor rise against the rich,' he once wrote, 'they act as wisely for their own purposes as when they burn mills, and throw corn into the river to make bread cheap.' He was merely the spokesman for the aristocratic Whig group under Rockingham. If in 1782 Burke's honest purpose was to weed out political corruption, it was strange that he should at the same time be seeking two valuable sinecures for his son and various other endowments for his Irish kin. The first of the measures which he inspired deprived revenue officers of the vote, with the curiously undemocratic consequence that the electorate of Bossiney in Cornwall was reduced to one man; the second prevented the holders of government contracts from sitting in the Commons, a mere seventeen members losing their seats thereby; and his own Civil Establishment Act abolished certain sinecure offices at an annual saving of £20,000. The immediate consequence of this, since men must have their rewards, was an increase in the number of peerages. The younger Pitt, regarded as a correct and austere constitutionalist, created more new titles than anyone since James I. Reformers when they reap seldom look as wise as when they sow.

Among the offices abolished were the masterships of the harriers and foxhounds and also of the buckhounds, although the titles survived and the offices, which had always been under the general supervision of the Master of the Horse, were now brought under his direct control. An enquiry was started into Civil List expenditure and the Treasury requested the Master, the Duke of Montagu, to propose economies. He duly submitted a list of offices with their duties and salaries, 'in order to retrench every unnecessary and superfluous expense, if such should be found; and to make such other savings in his department as shall appear consistent with his Majesty's service and the dignity of the Crown.' He thought that 'there is not an equal necessity for the continuance of all the officers upon the list', but he asked that in the event of reductions the present holders be allowed to retain their salaries for life. 'Their salaries are not very considerable; but if taken from them, may occasion great inconvenience to some, and even distress to others of them.' Montagu further suggested an economy totalling £1913 8s. 0d. from the abolition of the prizes given for the 18 King's Plates, 'as the object for which they were at first given is fully obtained, namely, the encouraging the breeding of light horses for speed.' But as no reply was received from the King or the Treasury, the Plates continued. (RM Letter Book, 51–2.)

King George had already in 1779 abolished the post of first equerry and directed that £30 of the salary of £260 paid to the pages of honour should be earmarked as fees for the servants who taught them to ride (RM Letter Book, 194). The reductions made in consequence of the reforms of 1782 fell upon the equerries as well as the humbler servants. They were reduced to five in number, and a letter survives telling Lieut.-General Matthew that he has been 'omitted in the list of those that are retained'. From Naples in January 1783 came a letter from another of the dismissed equerries, Sir William Hamilton, husband of Emma, the English plenipotentiary there from 1764 to 1800:

I can assure you, sir, that my pecuniary loss is what gives me the least concern. The exigency of the times should induce every honest man cheerfully to contribute his mite for the service of the public; but their Lordships of the Treasury, by utterly depriving me of the honour of waiting upon my Royal Master (an honour which I have enjoyed whenever it was in my power for upwards of twenty-seven years) have, if I may be allowed to make use of one of our celebrated poets, robbed me of that which not enriches them and makes me poor indeed. (RM Letter Book, 209.)

With the abolition of the Household offices of the cofferer and the treasurer of the chamber, the accounts of all the Household departments were subject to public audit by the Treasury, and the pressure for economy grew stronger when Britain was involved in the long war against the French Revolution and Napoleon. Parliamentary committees on finance in 1797–8 imposed further 'regulations tending to establish checks, or to effect retrenchment, in the Master of the Horse's department'. Ten years later David Parker, clerk of the stables, was giving assurances that 'the strictest economy has been adhered to in every branch of it'. The establishment for the year 1807 (RA Letter Book C/239–40) now includes the Master of the Buckhounds with a provision of £2000 for his responsibilities and a further £300 'for the breakfasts at Swinley Lodge' that were important to the sport. The huntsman at £125 and the six yeomen prickers at £104 each also belonged to the buckhounds' department, which heretofore accounted for £3049 of the total wage-bill for the establishment of £13,490 for 114 officers and servants. The wage-bill of William III's stables in 1689 was £9067. Allowing therefore for inflation and the addition of the buckhounds' department, a total of £13,490 in 1806 suggests that the reforms of 1782 had some effect and that a fairly strict economy was being maintained.

So much for the structure and finances of the department in King George III's long reign; we can now look briefly at the men who held the Master's office and then at some of the routine work that went on under their supervision. King George had eleven Masters, the Duke of Montrose serving twice, and although he would never have surrendered his right of personal choice, there was doubtless on occasions some consultation with the ministers. These Masters were mostly courtier peers of no great political importance, but their wealth and social eminence could usually guarantee a block of compliant votes in the Commons. The fact that they were not politicians of the first rank gave them the opportunity, if they chose to take it, to run their department efficiently, and although there were some indolent exceptions, it is clear that many of them did. Continuity in the administration was provided by the official who acted as clerk of the stables and secretary to the Master, and for much of the reign this was Parker, a loyal and efficient servant who had to handle a mass of varied business. Continuity of another kind, in experience of the actual work to be done, came through the long-serving equerries, men who had worked their way to senior rank in the department and had no wish to move on. Such a man was Richard Berenger, senior equerry for many years until his death in 1782. He was well liked all over London, despite a certain fecklessness in financial matters. 'Mr Berenger knows the world,' was Dr Johnson's conclusion after they had agreed upon the impracticability of conducting an intelligent discussion on an empty stomach. Berenger wrote two books on horsemanship and also a quantity of minor poetry, so that Hannah More found him 'all chivalry and blank verse and anecdote'. But eventually his money ran out and he had to take refuge in his official residence at the Mews, where the bailiffs could not get at him, and there he remained until David Garrick arranged a composition with the creditors.

The first Master was Francis Hastings, tenth Earl of Huntingdon, a descendant of the Hastings who served Queen Mary I. He had been Master in King George's Household as Prince of Wales, but now on being appointed groom of the stole, he

171. Francis Seymour Conway, 1st Marquess of Hertford, Master for only a few months in 1766.

resigned after only six months, and his death in 1789 without legitimate issue caused a legal battle over the succession to the earldom that took forty years to settle. But in his short term of office he took one very important step (RM Journal, folio 1), having evidently found his department in some confusion.

> The first two or three months were employed in arranging the officers and servants and settling the establishment of the stables and in making out warrants. No regular offices for the clerk of the stables being kept in the late reign, it was with great difficulty that any books or papers to give any proper light into the business of this department could be procured from the person who did the business in the late reign. Much time therefore was spent in searching for precedents and rules for conducting the affairs of the Master of the Horse. To prevent which in future, an office was established in the Mews in which business of the stables was to be transacted, the accounts regularly kept, and records of every material transaction that may serve as precedents or rules to go by in like cases. Instructions for this purpose, signed by the Master of the Horse, were given to the clerk of the stables.

The scantiness of the earlier records is a sure enough indication that hitherto the Mews had not been good at its paperwork, and the lack of recorded precedents had obviously made it difficult to handle the business with the required efficiency. Thanks to the admirable Huntingdon a journal was kept and many of the letters were copied and filed. That is why it now becomes possible to give fuller details of the work of the department.

From 1761 to 1766 the Master was John Manners, third Duke of Rutland, father of the Marquis of Granby whose dashing feats at Minden were commemorated in inn-signs all over the country. He was Master for the coronation in 1761, although he is not mentioned in Horace Walpole's account of the equestrian solecism that marred the dignity of the occasion. 'The Champion acted his part admirably,'

Walpole says, 'and dashed down his gauntlet with proud defiance,' but Lord
Talbot, the Lord High Steward, was not so fortunate. He had patiently trained his
horse to leave the hall backwards in deference to the King's Majesty, but the animal
had so accustomed itself to this regressive motion that it entered the hall the wrong
way round and showed royalty its rump. Rutland also supervised the construction
of the gold state coach, now used only for coronations, which may still be seen in
the Royal Mews.

> Several designs and drawings, made for that purpose and shewn to the Master of the
> Horse, were examined, and the approved parts thereof thrown into one by Mr Chambers,
> surveyor to his Majesty's Board of Works. This coach being long in building, the old
> state coach, which had been built in the reign of Queen Anne, was obliged to be made use
> of until the new one was ready (RM Journal, folio 2).

The panels were painted by a Florentine artist, Giovanni Cipriani; 'a very
beautiful object,' Walpole thought, although full of 'improprieties'. The coach
weighed four tons, cost £7661 18s. 11d. and needed eight of the cream stallions to
draw it.

Rutland was concerned about the accommodation available for his department
and in 1764 he asked the Treasury to build 'proper coach-houses' at the Green
Mews, there not being sufficient space because of 'the increase of carriages for their
Majesties' service'. It was not until 1775 that these were built, but Rutland also
demanded repairs to houses occupied by servants which were becoming 'ruinous
and decayed'. It seems, however, that he may not have been very attentive to his
accounts because his successor, the Earl of Hertford, was required by the Treasury
to make an estimate 'of the several sums wanting to discharge the debt in your
office, distinguishing the several heads on which the same is due'. Some of this debt
apparently went back nearly three years (RM Letter Book 1–2).

Francis Seymour Conway, Earl of Hertford, was Master for only a few months in 1766 before moving to another Household office as Lord Chamberlain. He was a nephew of Sir Robert Walpole, but perhaps his principal recommendation to the government was that he had five sons sitting in the Commons. Peregrine Willoughby, Duke of Ancaster, had a much longer tenure, until 1778. He was one of the early lovers of Liz Armistead, who passed through many noble hands, including the Prince of Wales, Grafton, Derby and Dorset, before becoming the wife of Charles James Fox. Ancaster had a formidable wife who had the temerity to sit down in the presence of Queen Charlotte, which Court regulations did not allow, and something of her imperious manner appears in the directions which he dispatched from the Mews concerning repairs that had become 'absolutely necessary' at the stud at Hampton Court.

Between 1778 and 1780 the Master was Hugh Percy, first Duke, by the third creation, of the ancient title of Northumberland. By birth he was a Yorkshire squire called Smithson, but he took the family name and title on marrying the heiress to the earldom, and later he was made a duke. Northumberland was the quintessential courtier, adroit in the in-fighting of eighteenth-century politics, and he was equally willing to accommodate the mob. When as lord-lieutenant it was his duty to declare against John Wilkes's election for Middlesex, the mob were so incensed that he found it the better part of valour to drink the hero's health. His duchess was a courtier too and was present at the delivery of the Prince of Wales. The last worldly success of this Master was the grant of the barony of Lovaine, with a reversion to his son. 'They are crying peerages about the streets in barrows,' was Horace Walpole's thought on this. He served throughout nearly the whole of Lord North's long ministry, and as he had inherited the traditional Percy following he was able to be of some assistance to the government through his control of seven seats in the Commons. Now that the Court no longer made use of the palace at Hampton Court, Northumberland was willing to surrender to the Office of Works a coach-house and stable formerly used there by the Master of the Horse's family when the Court was in residence, but he made the sensible proviso that 'equal accommodation' should be provided if the Court should ever decide to return (RM Letter Book, 112).

George Brudenell Montagu, Duke of Montagu and fourth Earl of Cardigan, was Master until his death in 1790. He had taken the Montagu name and titles on the decease of his father-in-law, and he had formerly been tutor to the King's two eldest sons, who were to be brought up as 'examples to the rising generation'. It fell upon Montagu to carry through the unwelcome changes introduced in 1782, and he did this with tact and efficiency without surrendering anything essential to the royal service. He was obliged to submit regular reports to the Treasury on the expenses of his establishment, which in 1787 numbered 136 horses, including one state set of 12 creams and another of 9 blacks, 12 for the Master and 45 'hunters, road and manage horses.' The cost of their upkeep was £5138, or about £38 a year for each horse (RM Letter Book, 267). Montagu reported also on the scale of pensions allowed to servants and their widows, which ranged from £30 for a coachman to £15 for a 'by-helper', the widows receiving approximately two-thirds (RM Letter Book, 285–6.)

Montagu was succeeded until 1795 by James Graham, third Duke of Montrose, whom King George regarded as 'the best Master of the Horse ever in my service, and a man of a high sense of honour.' To him we shall return. On his appointment as Commissioner for India he was replaced by John Fane, tenth Earl of Westmorland, who after doing some excellent and ameliorative work in Ireland had been jockeyed out of the lord-lieutenancy on a change of government policy. Before Westmorland resigned in 1798, to become Lord Privy Seal for nearly thirty

173. Buckingham House, acquired in 1762 by King George III as a dower house for Queen Charlotte, and known as the Queen's House. From 1821 to 1825 it was reconstructed by King George IV, and became known as Buckingham Palace.

years, a mean little economy was forced upon him by a Commons select committee on finance: 'the practice of receiving New Year's gifts by any person in this department shall be discontinued, so that you may not send them as heretofore' (RA Letter Book B/32). A few months later Chesterfield, the new Master, was determined that if the Treasury proposed to be mean in small matters, they should at least pay the salaries owing to the servants (RA Letter Book B/32):

> Finding the arrears in the department of the Master of the Horse to be very considerable, and that the delay of the payment thereof is severely felt by the tradesmen as well as by the officers and servants under me: by those of the former, especially, who supply the royal liveries, there being now two years due to them; and of the latter, the livery servants in particular, many of whom are in great distress: I thought it incumbent on me to acquaint your Lordships therewith; and to request that money may be speedily issued for the discharge of one or two quarters of the said arrears, that both classes may be relieved from the inconvenience which they now experience.

Philip Stanhope, fifth Earl of Chesterfield, had been a co-recipient of those famous letters from his godfather which, in the view of Dr Johnson, 'teach the morals of a whore, and the manners of a dancing-master'. The other guardian of Chesterfield's youthful steps was the Rev. William Dodd, who was hanged for forging a bond for £4200 in his former pupil's name. Although there is evidence that Chesterfield was not always very diligent in his duties, he cared about his

174 (left). Hugh Smithson Percy, Duke of Northumberland, Master from 1778 to 1780.

175 (right). George Brudenell Montagu, 1st Duke of Montagu. He was responsible for carrying through unwelcome changes in the Master's establishment in 1782.

servants and he defended the rights of his office from encroachment by other departments. He was dropped, with a promise of the Garter, when the Addington government fell and the younger Pitt returned to power in 1804.

Francis Seymour, second Marquis of Hertford and Earl of Yarmouth, whose father had been Master for a short time in 1766, was one of the richest men in England, with a country estate in Warwickshire and a London house in Manchester Square, now the home of the Wallace Collection. Like Westmorland, he had enlightened views on Ireland, where he recommended an independent native parliament as the solution of the people's mounting grievances. But contemporary satirists were only interested in him as a cuckold of the Prince of Wales. It was one of the temperamental peculiarities of the Prince that he had reached the age of fifty before he had a regnant mistress younger than himself. The Marchioness of Hertford was already a well-built grandmother when the royal fancy discovered her, and it was soon a jolly family affair, with her husband chamberlain of the princely Household and their son vice-chamberlain. In the public prints, which enjoyed then a freedom of expression unknown for the past 150 years, the prince was displayed riding 'the old yellow chariot', and in the Lords a peer spoke wonderingly of her as 'a matured enchantress'.

Of Hertford as Master there is little recorded, and on Pitt's death in 1806 he was replaced, in a ministry dominated by the ailing and irresponsible Fox, by Henry Herbert, Earl of Carnarvon. Carnarvon lasted little more than a year, falling with a ministry that thought it possible to make peace with Napoleon after Jena and Austerlitz, and he tried to pluck the fruits while they were ripe. King George

disliked this short-lived ministry and he was evidently unavailable to the Master. In May 1806 Carnarvon caused Parker to write a letter to the King (RA Letter Book C/233) saying that he had seldom found 'a fit opportunity of communicating to his Majesty the affairs of the stables without soliciting an audience for the purpose, which he is unwilling to do lest he should thereby interrupt or set aside a more important business.' This guarded irony introduces Carnarvon's real intention, which was to acquire a vehicle on the cheap. He reported that there was a deficiency in the Mews establishment of one landau, and he suggested it might be filled with a landau for himself, 'as a close carriage never agrees with his Lordship, to be long in it at a time.' His proposal is that the King should buy a new one, and that an older one, now seldom used by the Court, 'would serve his Lordship very well'.

Montrose returned in 1807 and was Master until the end of the reign, serving the Prince Regent with equal loyalty when King George was no longer able to rule. During his first term of office Montrose had begun to make economies by reforming the administration. In 1792 he had reported a saving of £175 a year after discovering that the allowances for the feeding of the King's saddle horses were 'also sufficient for the keeping of a horse for each of the grooms' (RM Letter Book, 305). He 'conceived that the King's horses would be better fed if the allowance were abolished and the grooms were not permitted to keep a horse each, but to hire one when necessary for his Majesty's service'. In a year's trial Montrose had found that whereas the allowances for feeding the horses totalled £1670, the actual consumption cost £1166. It would not be possible to make the full saving implied in these figures since Montrose thought it necessary to make some compensation,

176 (left). John Fane, 10th Earl of Westmorland. In 1782 he eloped to Gretna Green with Sarah Anne Child, 18-year-old daughter of Robert Child of Osterley Park. Her mother forgave her, but her father left Osterley and the Child fortune to his second daughter, Sophia, who married the Earl of Jersey.

177 (right). Francis Seymour, 2nd Marquess of Hertford, whose house in Manchester Square, London, now houses the Wallace Collection.

178. The royal menagerie at the
Tower of London, which was
maintained there from the end of the
12th century until 1834, when the
animals were transferred to the zoo
at Regent's Park.

totalling £330, 'to the purveyors of his Majesty's stables for the loss they will sustain by the alteration, and also to the grooms in lieu to the advantage accruing to them from the allowance'. So the net saving was only £175, and it may not seem very much. But it was made in just one small area of the department's expenditure, the provender for the saddle horses, and with similar scrutinies made elsewhere, the saving began to reach a significant figure – especially as it probed the sensitive area of the employees' perquisites.

It would appear that King George would have liked to reappoint Montrose to the stables when Chesterfield departed in 1804, but Pitt wanted him at the Board of Trade, and had his way. Nevertheless the King 'had much conversation with him on the actual state of his stables'. He was almost morbidly conscientious about his duty to the people and the importance of keeping down his debts, which in fact rose not because the Crown was extravagant but because it was still being charged with public expenditure beyond its constitutional resources. Now, in the forty-fifth year of his reign, he was looking for economies in the stables, and he suggested that before Hertford's appointment was announced

> it would be necessary for Mr Pitt to get the Duke of Montrose to state the present advantages of that office, and to have the whole reduced to a fixed allowance in money, the use of one set of horses, the four footmen and such number of grooms as the Duke of Montrose might think reasonable. The coach-horses ought to have their full allowance of forage and straw, and the coachmen receive a proportionable allowance as in the rate established by that Duke in the saddle stable. If the Duke of Montrose should see Grey, the body coachman [Richard Grey, whose salary was £83 a year] who is an excellent and ever reasonable man, this may be easily settled. The Clerk of the Stables is an enemy to this proposal. (A. Aspinall, *Later Correspondence of George III*, Vol IV, No. 2854.)

This letter provides much illumination. It was dated 7.20 a.m., showing that even in

179. James Graham, 3rd Duke of
Montrose. King George III
regarded him as 'the best Master of
the Horse ever in my service, and a
man of high sense of honour'.

The favourite of the Fair.

the forty-fifth year of his reign King George was prompt and attentive to his business; and Montrose had evidently been trying to mend abuses in the stables. The average Briton is an honest man, but his blind spot has always been to regard as a legitimate perquisite anything he can quietly abstract from his employer. It would appear that the coachmen had been receiving a rake-off from the tradesmen who supplied the forage and straw: a practice immemorial among those who served menially in the royal stables. In his previous term as Master, Montrose had tried to prevent this, and he would prevent it again. But the hostility of the clerk of the stables suggests that he too was getting his percentage: not unreasonably, perhaps, since he was paid only £350 for himself and his assistant. The letter indicates also that the Master himself must accept some reduction in the number of personal servants maintained at the Crown's expense.

Montrose persisted in his reforming efforts and did what was possible in the circumstances; but a constructive settlement was impossible until in 1831 a firmer distinction was made between the Crown's public and personal expenditure. None the less he encouraged the King to follow up their discussion about the coachmen's perquisites, since it was clear that they had been under-feeding the horses and pocketing the balance from the fodder that had been ordered. King George instructed Parker that

> his Majesty is determined, from the abuse he has met from some of the sets of horses not being properly in order for work, that the same mode shall be adopted in the coach-horse stables as in the saddle ones, namely that each coachman shall have an allowance of £5 12s. 0d. per horse, in lieu of the bad perquisite of returning unused fodder to the purveyors; and to effect the horses being in future properly fed, agreeable to the work and state of each horse, that the body coachman shall see all the coach horses fed in the Mews, and in his absence the next senior coachman. (RA Letter Book C/205)

In his pursuit of economies Montrose also discovered that when horses had to be hired, he could get them more cheaply from the dealers than from regimental sources, and he ordered that in future the department should acquire them in this way 'instead of applying to the Second Regiment of Lifeguards for that purpose' (RA Letter Book C/250).

In such issues of financial and administrative importance the Masters were concerned personally, and here they did not just sign the letters. But in the meantime Parker and his humbler colleagues were carrying on the daily and ever-multiplying routine. The movement of the Court was the main concern, as it always had been, but this involved many things: the special problems of transport on ceremonial occasions; the travel arrangements for horses, especially those presented to the King by foreign governments; breeding, so that movement might continue in future reigns; the training of equerries, pages and grooms, as well as the breaking-in of horses and their conditioning for quiet behaviour in crowds; and provision for royal sport. The department had also to maintain its own internal regulations and discipline, and fight its battles against the Treasury and against other Household departments; and thanks to Huntingdon's sensible foresight, it was also compiling its precedents. A few examples from the voluminous correspondence will suggest the problems and show how the department dealt with them.

It was obviously a sound idea to record the arrangements for the coronation of 1761, so far as these concerned the Master of the Horse. It was just bad luck that there was not another coronation for sixty years, by which time London had become a larger and more populous city and much of the detail was no longer practicable. But the organisation for processions became formalised and more efficient, and the department took stock of the buildings and properties which it owned in London, Windsor, Bushey, Hampton Court and elsewhere. A document of 1766 setting out the stabling at the Mews, and recording by whose horse each of the 234 stalls was occupied, seems now to be of little consequence, but it was a useful thing for the clerk of the stables to have and it enabled him to answer queries and settle disputes (RM Precedents Book, 66–7). Diplomatic distinctions had to be maintained between ambassadors and visitors from abroad, and there is a memorandum (49–50) of 'the rules by which the ambassadors from the Barbary States have been supplied with an equipage'. On his arrival, an ambassador was to be met by a hired coach and six to take him to London, and while in London a coach or 'chariot and pair' is to be hired to attend him; with the addition of four horses for his country outings if the distance requires it. The memorandum adds that variations from these rules 'have always been deemed indulgencies and an extra service', and are not to be considered as a precedent.

Some of these 'indulgencies' were duly recorded as departures not to be repeated, and it was on this basis that in 1767 (RM Letter Book, 195–6) the Duke of Ancaster was able to instruct Parker to tell the Moroccan ambassador that

> I cannot, consistently with the Master of the Horse's orders and the rules established in this office, comply with your Excellency's desire by ordering three, or even two, saddle horses to attend you. The coachman that drives your Excellency came to me yesterday to signify your desire of having four coach horses added to the pair that constantly attends you, and three saddle horses to attend you for a few days next week into the country: the four coach horses I immediately ordered, and also one saddle horse, which your Excellency may command; but more than these I cannot order without particular orders from the Master of the Horse or one of the Secretaries of State.

180. Henry Herbert, 1st Earl of Carnarvon, Master for only a year.

Probably of value as a precedent, although it was filed in the Royal Mews Letter Book (250–1), were the special arrangements for the procession to St Paul's in April 1789 for a service of thanksgiving for the King's recovery from illness. An equerry wrote from Windsor to say that the King wished to have the coach new-lined with a figured velvet, 'patterns of which had better be immediately procured and sent hither for the King's choice'. A proposed 'addition to the hammer cloth did not seem to meet his Majesty's approbation, from the gold being so likely to be soon tarnished.' A note to this entry says that 'no figured velvet being procured, the coach was not new lined.' However the elaborate organisation went off well, with the Duke of Montagu's landau and six horses following the King's leading coach, which was drawn by eight creams. A footnote added that 'none of the footmen walked, but rode, properly dispersed, behind the several carriages.' Six helpers walked by the side of the royal coach, and others attended elsewhere in the procession. 'Only two tradesmen attended, viz. the coachmaker and the harness-maker, who walked behind their Majesties in laced coats of the 3rd sort, borrowed for the purpose.'

Some quaint little instructions found their way into the Mews records. In Rutland's time (1764) it was laid down that

> no person whatsoever dwelling within his Majesty's Mews shall presume to have himself, his wife, child or any other of his family inoculated for the Small Pox, before he has the permission of the physician or surgeon of his Majesty's household, and has also given notice of his intention at the office of the said Mews; in order that all necessary precautions may be used to prevent any ill consequences issuing therefrom.
>
> (RM Precedents Book, 48)

In 1785 Montagu orders the footmen to be careful not to allow wax from their

Nro.	Nahmen und Haar der Pferde.	Englisch Maaß.			Race der Pferde.			
		Alt.	Hand	Zoll.	Vater.	Mutter.	Groß-Vater des Hengstes	Groß-Mutter
9	le Prevenant ein Hundeschim melfar Wallach	8	15	1	Sampson, so aus England übersandt Englische Race	la Delicate	Sind nicht bekant	Dieselben
10	le bien Venu ein Brauner Wallach	8	15	–	Sampson, so aus England übersandt Englische Race	la Jolie	Sind nicht bekant	Dieselben
11	le Senateur ein Brauner Wallach	8	15	½	Sampson, so aus England übersandt Engl. Race	la Masquée	Sind nicht bekant	Dieselben
12	le Joli ein Fuchs Wallach	8	14	3	Hamptoncourt barbe, so aus England übersand Englische	la Constante	Sind nicht bekant	Dieselben
13	l'Amusant ein Rothschim melfar Wallach	7	14	3½	Hamptoncourt barbe so aus England übersand Engl. Race	la Chimère	Sind nicht bekant	Dieselben
14	le Resolu ein Brauner Wallach	7	15	¼	le Senateur Spanische Race	la Dangereuse	l'Andalous	l'Hermionne
15	le Fortuné ein Schwartz brauner Wallach	7	15	1¼	le Senateur Spanische Race	la Volage	l'Andalous	l'Hermionne
16	le Badin ein Brauner Wallach	6	15	1	Fox, so aus England übersand Engl. Race	la Proprette	Sind nicht bekant	Dieselben
17	le Robuste ein Brauner Hengst	6	15	1½	Fox, so aus England übersand Engl. Race	la Variable	Sind nicht bekant	Dieselben

181. Page from the Hanoverian stud book, 1781.

flambeaux to drop on to the carriages, which have been 'much defaced' thereby (107). A memorandum in 1789 (311) prescribes the duty of the Master and his assistants 'when attending the King at reviews, hunting, etc.':

> The Master of the Horse is to present the stirrup to the King on the near side of the horse when his Majesty mounts; and the equerry-in-waiting is to hold the stirrup at the same time on the off side; and they are to attend in the same manner when the King alights.

In the Master's absence the equerry will move to the near side, and 'the equerry of the Crown stable or the first yeoman rider, whosoever duty it may be to attend, is to hold the stirrup on the off side.' In 1808 Montrose ordered that horses at grass, both in London and at Hampton Court, 'shall have their feet pared, etc., on the 1st of every month, excepting it happens on a Sunday in which case it is to be done on the following day' (173). Now and again the outside world intrudes upon these domestic affairs. Following the Gordon Riots in 1780 Montagu submitted to the Treasury an account for 'bread, cheese and beer delivered to the 16th Regiment of Dragoons whilst on duty in the King's Mews during the late disturbances, amounting to £172 9s. 1¾d.' (RM Letter Book, 23). The Treasury instructed him to pay the bill and charge it to the incidental expenses of the department.

The importing of horses was a regular duty. The landing of creams from Hanover continued at intervals throughout the reign, and in 1787 the department paid £5 10s. 0d. for the arrival of four of them: four guineas for a lighter to bring them from the ship to Tower wharf, 17s. for 'the use of crane, tackle, straw, etc.', 4s. in wages for four men and 5s. 10d. for incidentals (RM Precedents Book, 119). In 1773 the King received the valuable present of a grey Arab called Dervish from 'Sheck Fearis of the Arabs of Eshead, Sheck Hussein and Meshaick of the Arabs of Saker,' who set their hands and seals upon this letter in 'the Year of the Hegira 1186':

> The subject of the present writing is, To testify concerning the within mention'd Horse and of his Race, Whose name is Dervish. His color is like the Wood Pigeon, white & Grey & was foal'd in the possession of Sheck Fasket: His Dam a Bay Mare of the Kohilan Race & his Sire likewise of the Kohilan Race of the Arabs of Sheck Mehemed Bey known to all the Arabs, & this Horse is famous Race renown'd among the arabs of Eshaad & the Arabs of Saker; And this is to certify moreover that being arriv'd amongst us a certain Englishman named George & requiring of us the said Horse, whose Age is seven Years & whose Race has never been mix'd nor ever conquer'd in War, we have conferr'd him this favour. (RM Letter Book, 201).

It was not always horses that had to be landed, and from India the Marquess Wellesley sent 'three cheetahs or hunting leopards' that were lodged in the menagerie at the Tower of London under the care of the keeper of the lions (RA Letter Book, B/47). Sometimes the gifts arrived along with representatives of the ruler who was presenting them, and Parker had a good deal of trouble on one such occasion. In 1800 he was told to send a coach and six to Ramsgate to fetch the ambassador of the Dey of Algiers, with a peremptory note from the Duke of Portland at the Home Office two days later to say that 'the public service will be hurt and the public expense enhanced unless Mr Charles Logie [interpreter] is permitted to proceed to Ramsgate' to overcome the linguistic difficulties (RA Letter Book B/124–8). From the same source Parker was told to land from a Danish ship some horses which the Dey intended as a present for the King, but next there came a message that the ambassador and his suite had travelled up river and were to be received at the Tower, and not at Ramsgate at all. His baggage included two lions and two tigers as well as the horses, and these were to be lodged in the Tower. What was obviously agitating the Duke of Portland at this time was that Chesterfield, then Master of the Horse, was not in residence, and he seems to have feared that the experienced Parker did not know his job. Through his secretary he says:

> When the day is appointed for the ambassador's audience of his Majesty, I shall give you notice, and request a leading coach and pair, with one of his Majesty's footmen to attend the same, for the conveyance of the ambassador to St. James's. And as it is customary to provide a hired coach and pair for the use of the ambassadors from the States of Barbary during their residence at this court, and as such carriage will be wanted to carry the ambassador to the Duke of Portland when he makes his first visit to his Grace, I submit to you whether it may not be proper to move the Earl of Chesterfield that a hired carriage may be forthwith provided for the ambassador's use, and the coachman to be directed to attend his Excellency's orders when wanted.

So there were limits to the instructions that outsiders, even a Secretary of State like Portland, might give to officials of the stables department. Protocol required certain matters to be handled directly through the Master, and Portland is clearly displeased at Chesterfield's absence from town. But Parker's inconveniences were not yet over. Again at Portland's request, he wrote to the customs officers requesting that the ambassador's baggage be inspected on a lighter lying at the wharf, instead of in the warehouse, a much lengthier procedure. The customs officers readily agreed and, Parker says, they 'immediately directed Mr Tahourdin, the surveyor of the king's warehouse, to lose no time in inspecting it on board the lighter, but he chose to delay it until the next morning, thereby occasioning great inconvenience to the ambassador and expense to the king.'

But Chesterfield was quite capable of standing up for his rights against bumbling officialdom or the improper assumptions of other departments. When on duty the royal servants were exempt from the tolls charged by the turnpike trusts, but in 1802 Chesterfield himself was stopped at Hyde Park Corner and at Kensington (RA Letter Book B/137). Parker had therefore to remind the turnpike commissioners that the King's horses and carriages, and also those of the liveried servants, did not have to pay tolls. The trouble, Chesterfield suggested, was that the administration of the turnpikes went up for auction annually and was often acquired by 'strange persons'. It would be convenient, therefore, if bidders were reminded at the time that 'none who wear the royal livery are liable to pay the said tolls'.

Rivalry between the Household departments was probably as old as Alfred's thegns, although they would unite against intrusions from the officers of state. In 1798 Chesterfield had a complaint from the parks commissioner about 'irregularities and abuses of every kind' (RA Letter Book B/90). The specific complaint was that royal grooms had used keys to the barriers to exercise their own horses on Buckbine Hill, 'a pasture reserved for the deer and for his Majesty's horses'; and that they had 'frequently, with circumstances also of wantonness, passed across the gravel walk at the head of the Serpentine river'. Such complaints often arose from the endless wrangling about protocol and precedence, and a typical dispute over a trifling issue was carried as far as the Earl Marshal himself. It began among the coachmen, over the precedence of their carriages when they awaited their masters at the House of Lords. The marshal's official deputy having refused to decide such a delicate matter, Montrose applied to the Duke of Norfolk, who in turn consulted the College of Arms (RA Letter Book C/257). The issue was blandly evaded, Norfolk replying that he could not find any precedents to guide him to a decision, except when carriages were 'on personal attendance on his Majesty, or public ceremonial, in neither of which the dispute you mention seems to have taken place'. It is perhaps surprising that such matters can have been of concern in the year 1808 when the country was engaged in a desperate war with Napoleon. Earlier, Chesterfield had made a point of discovering who were the proper persons to attend the King in the Master's chariot during his absences, which clearly were more frequent than they should have been. The Lord Chamberlain replied (RA Letter Book B/106) that it was his Majesty's pleasure that the Chamberlain himself and the Gold Stick-in-Waiting should ride in the chariot; and in their absence, their deputies. Montrose would not put up with nonsense of any kind, and possibly his motive in referring the coachmen's dispute to the Earl Marshal was to remove a long-standing irritation by exposing its absurdity.

Although most of the servants of the Royal Mews were dedicated to their work, the personal factor was always present and inevitably mishaps occurred from time to time. There might be drunkenness, occasional violence between the men, or

182. Philip Stanhope, 5th Earl of Chesterfield. 'He cared about his servants and defended the rights of his office from encroachment by other departments'.

negligent performance of duty. Indiscipline in the royal service could not be tolerated, but although the penalty in serious cases was always dismissal, compassion was felt for the erring individual. A petition from a dismissed coachman in 1796 indicates that on occasion pensions were granted to senior servants in such circumstances, and a coachman was a man who had graduated through the ranks. The nature of the offence is not indicated, but the petitioner, George Welch, does not contest the justice of his dismissal even though he claims that it was for a single offence by one who had 'never conducted himself in any way to incur your Lordship's displeasure' (RM Precedents Book, 284–5). His claim is for the refunding of disbursements he had necessarily made and for the payment of outstanding wages. He had paid £20 in fees on his appointment and a further £60 on furnishing his apartments, and he was owed his wages for eight months – unfortunately quite a usual thing for servants of the department. In his petition to the Master, the Earl of Westmorland, Welch says:

> That your Petitioner has great Reason to apprehend and fear that his Dismissal from His Majesty's Service will greatly prejudice his character and prevent him obtaining another

183. *One of Tipu's hunting cheetahs, sent from India by the Marquess Wellesley as a present to King George III.*

Employment whereby your Petitioner is in Danger of being exposed in Consequence thereof to Poverty and Distress for the Remainder of his Life.

Your Petitioner therefore most humbly submits the consideration of these Circumstances to your Lordship's well known Humanity and Generosity as the only Hopes your Petitioner has now left of ever obtaining any support and Maintenance and humbly to implore Your Lordship's Goodness and charity to attend to the unhappy situation in which your Petitioner is now placed in the Decline of his Life and most earnestly to intreat Your Lordship to recollect that under similar circumstances a Pension has theretofore been granted to a Person in a similar unfortunate Situation to your Petitioner. And should Your Lordship from a Consideration of your Petitioner's Situation consider him as an Object worthy of any Mark of Your Lordship's Attention and Favour so as to prevent the Calamities to which Your Petitioner will in future be exposed Your Lordship will confer a lasting Obligation upon him.

And Your Petitioner humbly implores Your Lordship will (in order to afford your Petitioner the immediate Assistance of which he will stand in need) give Directions for your Petitioner to be paid what shall appear to be due to him for Wages and Disbursements.

It is noted in the records that the wages and disbursements were paid, but as this old servant was not granted a pension, his solitary offence must have been quite a grave one.

Montrose too was insistent on discipline. He dealt forthrightly with footmen at Windsor who had been choosy about the horses they rode (RA Letter Book C/268). Two of the men had refused to ride a certain horse

on pretence that he was an improper one, as he had lately fallen down when one of the footmen was on his back; although the horse received no injury at all, but was as capable of carrying either of you as he ever was; that his fall was merely accidental, or owing to the carelessness of the footman who rode him . . . If any footman shall refuse to use any horse that may be allotted for him, his Grace will immediately dismiss such a footman from the King's service. For in a short time, if the footmen were permitted to use their own judgment, humour or prejudice, respecting the horses provided for them, there might not be a horse in the stable that they would *choose* to ride.

Montrose added that reasonable complaints would always be considered, and he could be just and compassionate. The nature of the matter is not recorded, but in 1807 he saved two men their jobs (RA Letter Book C/240). Parker was instructed to inform two named purveyors that he regretted 'finding himself obliged to remove them from their situations'. But two others, 'having been dismissed without being charged with any fault, ought to be restored to their former situations'. Montrose seems to have had no doubt of their guilt in whatever offence they were supposed to have committed, but since they had not been specifically charged, 'he conceives himself, in justice to the gentlemen last mentioned, compelled to adopt this painful resolution.'

Most of the business so far described consisted of internal matters conducted within the department. It was different when the King personally was involved, and even an impeccable civil servant like Parker cannot always conceal the rough edge of his exasperation with King George's fussiness and exigent attention to detail. It was worse for the equerries, each of whom had to be in personal attendance for a month at a time and had accommodation at Court during his turn. The turns came round more often now that the number of equerries had been reduced – Charles II had had eleven. When the King travelled, the equerry-in-waiting rode in the leading coach. In earlier times equerries had ridden on horseback alongside the coach, but Charles II had discontinued this as 'more expensive to them than necessary to the sovereign'. Junior equerries might have to attend the King on his more important journeys, but their special duty was in 'mouthing, managing and breaking the saddle horses, and preparing them for the King's riding'. But whatever its form, being an equerry was never a comfortable office during this reign, and George once remarked, apparently with some jocular satisfaction, that he had fewer applications for this employment than for any other in his gift. His simple sense of fun did not make it any easier. Nathaniel Wraxall says that

> it was his delight to mount his horse before the equerry-in-waiting could possibly be aware of it; often in severe and unpleasant weather, which rarely deterred him; always at an early hour. One of his equerries has assured me that, when thus surprised, he has been compelled to follow the King down Windsor Hill, with scarcely time to pull up his stockings under his boots. No place about his Majesty's court or person, so long as he retained his intellect, could indeed be less of a sinecure than the office of equerry. The appointments were very inadequate to the fatigue and exertions of the post.
>
> *Memoirs of my Own Time*, iii, 137.

The strain was felt by the young men who were subject to this whimsical authority. In 1794, during his first term as Master, Montrose caused Parker to write to Richard Wilson, Esq., about the undutifulness of his son (RA Letter Book B/298). Early in August, Wilson is warned that 'in consequence of the promotion of Mr Draper it falls to the lot of your son to be in waiting during the month of October.' The young Wilson was only a page, not a full-fledged equerry, and unless he was more attentive at Court, and improved his riding, he never would be. Parker writes:

> I embrace this opportunity to acquaint you also, that the Master of the Horse having learned that your son has not attended once this year at the Riding-house to learn to ride, I am directed by his Grace to acquaint you that he expects that the order for the pages to attend for that purpose, during their months of waiting at least, be strictly observed; as, otherwise, they may not be properly qualified to attend the King at reviews or on any other public occasion.

Unlike some monarchs, King George found pleasure in moving among his people, and although he expected the arrangements to be precise, he had a habit of interfering with them. The annual holiday at Weymouth, his favourite resort, was a portentous matter, and this was the sort of thing Parker might have to put up with. In 1797 (RA Daily Occurrences Book, 63–5) a letter was sent to the Treasury for the necessary finance, and the King made out 'in his own writing' a list of the servants who were to accompany the family. The expedition consisted of the King's landau, the equerries' coach, and three travelling coaches for the Queen. Some of the horses went as far as Bagshot before returning to Windsor, and the journey was completed by post horse. The whole business had to be organised again for the King's return in September, and after the Royal Family were safely home, 'the servants that attended from Weymouth to Basingstoke and Overton were conveyed from thence in the hired long coach which brought other servants from Windsor.' Parker closes this account with a note that 'the king paid the expenses of this journey, excepting the keeping of the horses and the servants' travelling expenses and lodgings, out of his privy purse; among which were the following bills preparatory to the journey . . .': namely, two bills of £59 15s. 6d. for jackets, etc., £40 19s. 0d. for hats, and £6 16s. 6d. 'for repairing footmen's furnitures'. But Parker was not yet done with royal outings in 1797, as in October the King decided to visit Admiral Duncan's fleet after its great victory at Camperdown. Unfavourable winds prevented him from going aboard and added to the confusion. When he decided to return, his carriage was to await him at Greenwich soon after noon. 'It may probably have to wait some time; but had better be too soon than too late.' If the carriage was already at Dartford, as the original instructions prescribed, a hobby groom would dispatch it to Greenwich. The allocation of charges for these outings was another of Parker's problems. In 1807 he was instructed (RA Letter Book B/132–3) that additional servants and horses accompanying the Queen to Weymouth were to be charged to her, but 'all extraordinary expenses incurred upon this service' would be 'defrayed by his Majesty'. A few days later an equerry was writing from Weymouth to clarify these rather ambiguous orders. The Queen's account was to be charged 'with what the keep of her Majesty's horses might fairly be supposed to amount to, had they been left at the Mews.' But in fact they were at Weymouth, and the King would meet the difference.

Finally there was the hunting. King George was not much interested in racing, which his Queen regarded as 'a vulgar business', and he kept no racing-stable of his own. But he hunted with the energy that he devoted to all his activities: not the fox, which went to earth too soon and spoiled the sport, but the deer, which might give a chase for some forty miles. As had become the practice in previous reigns, favourite deer would be saved from the hounds and carted off for another day. They were kept in the paddocks at Swinley 'in a style of invigorating luxuriance': Moonshine and Starlight, so called because they would outrun the day, Highflyer and Compton. Moonshine is said to have given sport for at least seven seasons, and there was a famous chase in 1797 when Compton, 'plunging into the immense sheet of Virginia Water, passed entirely through it'. Many of the retinue were ready to give up the pursuit after seeing the quarry's aquatic initiative, but the King 'absolutely insisted in getting the hounds forward, laying them on where the deer left the water, and speaking to them in a sporting-like style.'

Tuesdays and Saturdays were his hunting days, and 'critically exact to time', he would arrive sharp at 11, attended by his Master of the Horse, equerries and distinguished guests, and wearing the new fashionable cap that had replaced the three-cornered hat. Whereas earlier Hanoverians had confined themselves to the Royal Parks, King George hunted the whole countryside 'round Windsor, and although he was accompanied by a 'pilot', this was to restrain his impulsive enthusiasm and did not reflect upon his courage. He was known to brave 'the most dangerous leaps with the utmost indifference'. But the royal hunt was not fun for everybody. One of the equerries, Colonel Goldsworthy, has described what it was like to spend a long day in the field, 'fagging like mad', and come home to a refreshing draught of barley-water.

> Being wet over head, soused through under feet, and popped into ditches, and jerked over gates, what lives do we lead!
> Well, it's all honour, that's my only comfort . . . Home we come, like so many drowned rats . . . sore to the very bone, and forced to smile all the time! And then after that what do you think follows? 'Here, Goldsworthy,' cries his Majesty: so up I come to him, bowing profoundly, and my hair dripping down to my shoes: 'Goldsworthy,' cries his Majesty. 'Sir,' says I, smiling agreeably, with the rheumatism just creeping up all over me, but still expecting something a little more comfortable. I wait patiently to know his gracious pleasure, and then, 'Here, Goldsworthy, I say,' he cries, 'will you have a little barley water?' Barley water after a whole day's hard hunting!
> *Diary and Letters of Madame d' Arblay*, iii, 67.

Here no doubt Goldsworthy was speaking for all the King's long-suffering equerries, who had to share his frugality as well as his masochistic exercise, but his

Journey to Weymouth.

Rec.d a Letter from Col.l Fitz Roy, relative to Frere's going to Kew with his Men, Horses, &c.
See Letter Book B, Page 131.

Rec.d a Letter from the Queen's Clerk of the Stables, inclosing one from Gen.l Harcourt relative to Her Majesty's Horses going to Weymouth.
See Letter Book B, Page 131.

Isaac Taylor, Bye Helper, resigned his Place, and was succeeded by John Howard (immediately).

184. Page from the Master of the Horse's 'Daily Occurrences' book, 1801.

self-pitying complaint does not conceal his underlying affection. When King George had his first illness in 1788, it was Goldsworthy and two other trusted equerries, Colonels Harcourt and Greville, who were able to persuade him, by the promise of their personal attendance, to move from Windsor to Kew, where he would get better treatment. After this illness he had to give up energetic riding and he was only able to hunt the hare. But it was not only his own weakness but the fear of assassination by highwaymen or French-inspired revolutionaries that necessitated special measures for his security when hunting. The Earl of Sandwich, who was then in charge of the buckhounds, made the arrangements and requested the Treasury to charge the cost (RA Letter Book B/34 *et seq.*). The arrangements would hardly have been impressive against a determined attack. One George Gosden was to furnish two boys and two horses for the season, for £100; two yeomen 'prickers' were to attend the King home at all times after hunting, and if he should return in a post-chaise, a third yeoman pricker was to attend on a hired horse, which he was to charge to the stables. The two first prickers were to receive 20 guineas each for the season, and the third a retaining fee of 10 guineas with an additional one guinea when he was employed. The boys riding Gosden's horses were allowed a by-helper's livery, with boots, spurs, whips and capes, but it appears that the King himself was to be responsible for saddles and pistols for the two senior prickers and 'a pair of pocket pistols' for the third.

It is a sad little pendant to the reign. In early days King George was at the mercy of satirists obedient to his political opponents, but in the stress of a revolutionary war the people came to value his homeliness and fundamental decency as a symbol of the continuity of English life in a world turned upside-down.

CHAPTER EIGHTEEN

The Move to Pimlico

King George IV (1820–30) held no such place in his people's regard. In his golden youth he had thought of himself as Prince Florizel, a role appropriate to his liaison with the actress Mary Robinson who, although little qualified to represent innocence in any form, had had a stage success as Perdita. George was then a capable horseman, and he is said to have ridden from London to Brighton and back, a distance of 108 miles, in 10 hours. But he soon succumbed to the corpulence that ran in his family and that had partly accounted for his father's austerity and passion for regular exercise. As the Prince grew fatter, so did the ladies of his choice, and his debts increased in proportion. When he came of age in 1783, parliament agreed to pay his outstanding debts of £30,000, give him a further £30,000 for the acquisition of Carlton House and settle on him an income of £62,000 a year, augmented by £12,000 from the Duchy of Cornwall. The Prince had hoped for an income of £100,000 and simply spent according to his expectations. Over the next nine years he expended £1,300,000, which was equivalent to a year's yield of the land tax or half the annual cost of the navy. In 1795 he married his cousin, Princess Caroline of Brunswick, although he had previously gone through a form of marriage with Maria Fitzherbert which was illegal under the Royal Marriage Act of 1772. His first meeting with Caroline recalled Henry VIII's first sight of Anne of Cleves. He turned to a companion and said, 'Harris, I am not well. Pray get me a glass of brandy.' The marriage was disastrous from the start and led to a scandalous divorce soon after he came to the throne. Its difficulties were partly financial since parliament set up a commission to administer his debts, then totalling £630,000. The sum of £65,000 a year was set aside to meet them, and the Cornwall revenues were mortgaged for twenty-five years. He therefore began married life on £60,000, less than he had received when he came of age.

He justified his extravagance on the ground that lavish expenditure by the upper classes was the most effective answer to the egalitarian doctrines of the French, but he had a better excuse for his playboy self-indulgence. His brothers were allowed to travel and even to have some of their education abroad. They were also given useful things to do – York and Cambridge were in the army, Clarence was a naval officer, Kent had commands in the West Indies and Canada. But George, Prince of Wales, was kept at home without any state employment to occupy his energies: the same mistake as was to be committed with the future King Edward VII, and with not dissimilar results. The throne was injured by the scandals.

Much of the Prince's expenditure was on horses. He had his own stud and racing-stable and pack of foxhounds, and when between 1788 and 1795 he had a country estate at Kempshott in Hampshire, meets were among the entertainment provided for the French *émigrés* who sought refuge there. But it appears that the stables were not very well managed, and the Prince himself was already so gouty that he had a stout

185. The King's Mews at Charing Cross, where the National Gallery now stands. It consisted of the Great Mews (on the south side of what is now Trafalgar Square), the Green Mews, and Buckingham Mews.

lady, Nancy Stevens, to nurse him and help him out of the bath. In 1793 he sold his hounds, and soon afterwards his racehorses, following an unfortunate incident at Newmarket when a steward of the Jockey Club accused one of his riders of unfair practice. But in later years he was able to revive his establishment. He always had an expensive stock of hacks and hunters, and when in 1813 the famous Charlton hunt was broken up, the fourth Duke of Richmond presented him with the pack and he brought it to Ascot. When riding began to lose its attractions, he became an expert whip and drove his phaeton with skill and daring.

The nation had some return for the money the Prince of Wales spent upon his pleasures because as a patron of the arts he was a man of taste and discernment. His collection of pictures was comparable with Charles I's, and he helped to found the National Gallery by persuading parliament in 1824 to purchase the collection of John Julius Angerstein, a wealthy merchant of Russian extraction. He also helped to find new premises for the British Museum, to which he gave his father's library of 70,000 books. The expenditure of half a million on his oriental fantasy at Brighton was scarcely justifiable in time of war, but when he became King he employed Sir Jeffry Wyatville to transform Windsor Castle and John Nash to convert Buckingham House into a virtually new palace.

It was King George IV, too, who transferred the Royal Mews to their present site in Pimlico. There had been King's Mews at Charing Cross, where the National Gallery now stands, since very early times, but it was merely the place where the royal falcons were kept while they 'mewed' or changed their plumage. The stables were at Lomesbury (Bloomsbury). The mews at Charing Cross was probably built by Edward I, a king who loved field sports. An existing chapel of St Eustace was incorporated, and between 1274 and 1277 two solars were built for the falconers and the chaplains. Behind a wall that protected the mews from the road was a turfed garden that contained a lead bath bearing a metal image of a falcon. Water was brought by an aqueduct and poured into the bath through four brass taps shaped like leopards' heads. There were in addition dovecotes to provide food for the birds, kennels for the King's dogs and a shed for the cranes at which the gerfalcons were flown. A new gateway was soon added, with a stable for the use of the falconers, and on the accession of Edward II, 'an old building which was formerly the falconers' hall' was replaced together with its kitchen, spensery and garderobe. Repairs and alterations during the fifteenth century suggest that the mews was coming to be used as a pleasure-garden within convenient reach of the palace of Westminster. The master mason, Robert Westerley, built for £50 a new 'bower' with a winding stair, and in the garden was a 'hautepace' or 'spy-house', plastered and pargeted and painted green. It contained a window, four doors and a cupboard, and it would appear to have been an early gazebo.

But in spite of these recreational fantasies the mews continued to serve its original purpose, and the office of Grand Falconer, which Richard II created for his tutor Simon Burley, was one of the most coveted in the King's gift. (Charles II made it hereditary in Charles Beauclerk, Duke of St Albans, his son by Nell Gwynne.) But when in 1537 the stables at Lomesbury were destroyed by fire, Henry VIII moved the falcons elsewhere and accommodated his horses in an enlarged establishment at Charing Cross. By 1732 this building was so dilapidated that George II had it pulled down and built new stables designed by William Kent, architect to the Earl of Burlington. This was in the Classical style, with central columns and a pediment, but the space in front was too narrow for comfortable access, and the neighbourhood was getting overbuilt and overcrowded. When King George III bought Buckingham House he made use of the stables there, and in 1820 a new site was chosen in the gardens adjoining them.

Plans were discussed with the Master of the Horse, the Duke of Dorset, and approved in July 1822, but it was three years before the comparatively simple building was completed. Nash tended to be over-optimistic in his costing and imprecise in his specifications, so that his enterprises nearly always cost more than he had promised. Here, apart from a Doric archway, there was nothing ornate. A riding-school designed by Sir William Chambers was already on the site, and Nash did little to this. His design was for a large quadrangle, with further stabling to the rear, a porter's lodge flanking the gate, a house for the clerk of the stables and his assistant, and a house each for the equerry of the Crown stables and the veterinary surgeon. His estimate was for £49,124 18s. 6d., and the contract was won by the lowest of the seven tenders submitted, for £48,565. The highest of the seven was for £61,235, and even this proved to be lower than the final cost. Numerous flaws and omissions were discovered as the work proceeded, not so much in the structure as in the fittings required to make the building serviceable. Parker, the clerk of the stables, reported the problems to Dorset, who in February 1823 found so many objections that he asked for the plans to be reconsidered. This was not thought to be necessary, but there were serious difficulties about the water supply. Parker was not satisfied with his house and as a late addition Dorset demanded a clock turret. The final cost was £65,078 11s. 9d., but defects, including dry rot, disclosed themselves as soon as the building was in use, and in the 1840s expenditure on repairs and

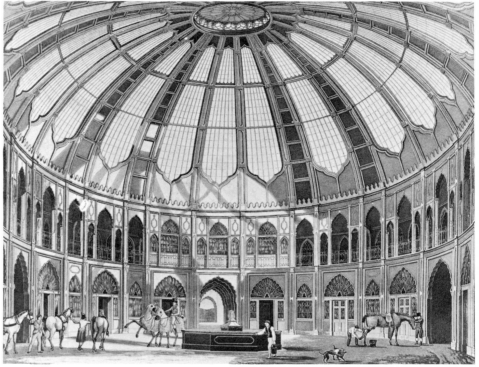

186. King George IV when Prince
of Wales riding on the promenade
at Brighton. The Steyne and Royal
Pavilion are in the background.

187. The royal stables at Brighton,
in the building known as the
'Dome', showing carriage horses
(left), saddle horses, and grooms.

renewals averaged £1500 a year. The former mews at Charing Cross was used briefly for the storing of records from Westminster Hall, but in 1835 it was pulled down.

Nash also designed for King George IV the royal stand at Ascot, constructed, at a cost of £5813, so that every occupant could watch the whole of the race. With the formation of the Jockey Club and the institution of the Stud Book, racing had been put on a firmer basis, just as cricket had benefited by the recognition of the MCC as the arbiter of the game. By 1800 the five classic races of the English Turf had all been established, as well as the Goodwood meeting. The first Derby in 1786 was won by Sir Charles Bunbury, and it is said that he previously tossed with the Earl of Derby to decide whose name should be given to the race. Would it have become the supreme event of the racing world if the fall of a coin had decreed that it should be called the Bunbury? When Thomas Creevey went to Epsom in 1824, he thought

188 (opposite). Façade of the Green Mews, designed by William Kent in 1732.

189 (above). Stables at the Royal Mews, Charing Cross, just before the move to Pimlico in 1820.

that 'the scene altogether *in and out* is the most extraordinary England can produce. . . . You would have supposed on looking around you that both Houses of Parliament were there.' Other sorts were there too. Feeling a hand brush his pocket, Creevey was relieved to find that his watch and four sovereigns were safe, but Lord Sefton, standing beside him, discovered that 'his purse was gone with 15 sovereigns in it, and the pocket turned inside out.'

A few days later Creevey found the scene at Ascot just as glittering. 'There is certainly nothing more perfect in England than this drive through Eton and Windsor Park, concluding with the course at Ascot, and the promenade upon it between the races.' Next year he recorded that 'your old acquaintance Prinney' was there, 'looking quite as well, and nearly as merry, as we have seen him in his best days'. The Prince Regent drove up the course in a coach-and-four with the Duke of Wellington at his side, followed by a phaeton and other carriages, 'and I should think 20 servants in scarlet on horseback, and as all his horses are of the greatest beauty, the whole thing looked very splendid.' Another of Creevey's anecdotes shows the high repute of English racing at this time. At Newmarket in 1829 he met one of the Russian delegates come to discuss the boundaries of newly-independent Greece.

He never was in England till about 3 months ago, and speaks English so well as to be quite up to all the expressions that belong to hunting, racing or anything else. . . . This diplomat seems to make the most of his time. He was living at Melton when I was there, hunting whenever he could find hounds, riding as hard as any one, and giving any prices for horses. . . . He went . . . thro' our stable on Monday, and being attended by Edwards, our trainer, the Russian observed to him, 'I had a horse out of your stable that win me a great race at Petersburgh, *Sharper*,' whom Edwards remembered very well. 'I run (continued the Russ:) two English horses, *Sharper* and *Mina*, against two Cossacks on Tartar horses.' 'And over what distance?' said I; '43 miles,' said he, and they did it, or *Sharper* did it, in 2 hours 53 minutes.'

Among his other services to the nation King George IV perhaps deserves some credit for the foundation of the London Zoo. For centuries – it goes back to the collection of strange beasts assembled by Henry I on his manor at Woodstock – the Crown had possessed a menagerie. By the end of the twelfth century it had been moved to the Tower of London, with a lion-keeper in charge, and the Master of the Horse had a distant responsibility for it. It had been stocked over the years less by deliberate purchase than by casual and sometimes embarrassing gifts from foreign princes or game-hunting Englishmen abroad. But by 1815 it had declined to 'one

lion, two lionesses, one panther, one hyena, one tigress, one jackal, one mountain cow and one large bear', whose total food bill was only a guinea a month. Seven years later only the bear was still alive, having been joined by 'an elephant and one or two birds'. But an enthusiastic keeper, Alfred Cops, had some encouragement from the King in rapidly acquiring a high-quality collection. This coincided with the foundation in 1826 of the Zoological Society to promote the study of animal life. Two years later the society was given the facility of using Regent's Park for the opening of a zoo, and a royal charter was granted in 1829. Cops's happy family was by now large enough to prevent necessary structural repairs at the Tower, and in 1834 the animals were moved to Regent's Park and the ancient royal menagerie ceased to exist.

A significant change had occurred meanwhile in the office of the Master of the Horse. During the reign of King George III there had been occasions when, arguably, a Master had departed with a change of ministry. In the endless groupings and shuffles of eighteenth-century politics the holder of a post with so much influence might be expected to use that influence on behalf of the ministry in office, and no one had firmer ideas about that than King George III himself. Even when the King was 'in opposition', as he often was, he recognised that the Master

190. *'Company going to and returning from His Majesty's Drawing Room at Buckingham Palace', in 1822. Carriages in the foreground are, from left, state landau, state chariot, state landau, state coach, state chariot and state landau.*

191. Entrance to the Royal Mews, Buckingham Palace. The Crown Equerry's house is to the left, his office to the right.

should be acceptable to his party colleagues. The politicians, on the other hand, acknowledged that this was a royal and personal appointment that must, if the King insisted, stand outside the political arena. An honest and forthright Master like Montrose could restore a decent perspective, but it was an increasingly unsatisfactory compromise and it was wearing thin.

The man who broke it was Charles Sackville, Duke of Dorset, who had succeeded Montrose on King George's accession and had done his best to see that the new mews building should be serviceable to the department. He was one of the Sackvilles of Knole, and he was a descendant of Lionel, the first Duke, who had been Master to George II in 1755. The Sackvilles, like the Dukes of Richmond, illustrate the close relationship often to be found between horsemanship and cricket. Members of the great hunting and racing families enjoyed their cricket in the summer months, and if they did not play themselves, they were generous with facilities for their servants and tenantry. Good cricketers also found employment as grooms and huntsmen. The second Duke of Dorset and his brother Lord John Sackville both played for Kent, and if Kent was the pre-eminent county in the early days, they helped to make it so. It was Lord John who issued the challenge for the famous match on the Artillery ground in 1744 when Kent played 'England' with its powerful Slindon nucleus. He went in first, with a player named on the score-card simply as Long Robin, and although he made only 5 and 3, he had his share in Kent's victory by one wicket in a low-scoring match. The great Newland was breaking loose in the second innings when 'illustrious Sackville' caught him. The game was commemorated in a ballad by James Love, *né* Dance, whose father designed the Mansion House. The poet senses the heartbeat of every anxious cricketer as he records the 'cautious pleasure' with which his Lordship observed the

192. Sculpture by William Theed on the pediment of Sir William Chambers' riding school at the Royal Mews. It shows Hercules taming the horses of Diomedes.

ball descending from Newland's lofted stroke, but

> Swift as the falcon darting on its prey,
> He springs elastic on the verdant way

and makes the catch one-handed while flat on his face. Kent had to make 58 to win, and with their last pair together and three still needed, John Waymark, one of Richmond's players, 'as sure a swain to catch as e'er was known', missed a crucial chance.

The fifth Duke of Dorset, however, was not a cricketer, and on his death in 1843, this was written of him by the dandy Thomas Raikes, a friend of Beau Brummell:

> This week died the Duke of Dorset, aged 76. He was never married, and the title is now extinct. He was a favourite of, and Master of the Horse to, George IV. He was a great patron of the turf in his youth, when Lord Sackville introduced the fashion of gentlemen jockeys. In those days, he, and his brother Germain, and Delme Radcliffe, were the best race-riders at Newmarket. They established Bilbury races, which were all ridden by gentlemen, to which they have succeeded Goodwood and Heaton Park. He was a little, smart-looking man, and a great favourite of the ladies.

So far the Master's appointment had not been explicitly subject to ministerial fluctuations, whatever may have been said occasionally behind the scenes, but in 1827 Dorset resigned because he would not work with the new Prime Minister, George Canning, a big-mouthed opportunist whose genuflections to principle embarrassed even his friends. King George was distressed at the loss of 'my dear little Sack', but Dorset had his own clear view of the changing nature of the appointment and he resigned it again in the 1830s rather than serve with a ministry

that contained Lord John Russell. Creevey said in one of his letters: 'The Duke, you know, *struck* as Master of the Horse, avowing to the King his decided hostility to Canning, and accordingly was one of the majority with Wellington.' This new conception of the office was to last for a hundred years, and by then the Master had lost all his administrative responsibilities. Meanwhile the Duke of Leeds acquiesced in the new arrangement and was Master from 1827 to 1830, when a Whig ministry came into office.

King George had only one legitimate child, the Princess Charlotte, who was married to Leopold of Saxe-Coburg, later to become the first King of the Belgians. Her death in 1817, after bearing a still-born child, left the throne without a successor after her father. Although King George III had had fifteen children, the family were threatened with extinction. Of the seven surviving princes only three were married, and they were childless. The four bachelors were victims of King George III's Royal Marriage Act, which was intended to preserve his children and other relatives from unsuitable unions. It failed because they simply omitted the ceremony. However, the four were given to understand that England had need of them, although they were elderly gentlemen now and had done the state some service in fields of endeavour other than that in which they were being called upon to engage.

The Duke of Sussex still considered himself bound by his marriage vows to Lady Augusta Murray although the marriage had been declared invalid under his father's statute. But the other three accepted the challenge. William of Clarence had spent years of domesticity at Bushey Park with the actress Dorothy Jordan, who had somehow managed to continue a successful stage career while bearing him ten little FitzClarences. But Dorothy was now dead and William married Adelaide of Saxe-Meiningen; Edward of Kent chose the widowed Princess of Leiningen, whom he

193. The Prince Regent driving to Ascot in a crane-necked phaeton with a 'lady of quality'.

194 (left). George Osborne, 6th Duke of Leeds, Master from 1827 to 1830.

195 (right). Charles Sackville Germain, 5th Duke of Dorset, described in 'Raikes's Journal' as a smart looking man and a favourite with the ladies.

had already been courting; Adolphus of Cambridge married Augusta of Hesse-Cassel; and an expectant England placed its bets.

Clarence had two little girls who died in infancy, and still-born twins. As the eldest surviving son he came to the throne (1830–7), but Kent became the father of Princess Victoria. A sailor all his active life, King William was not greatly interested in landed pursuits, but he maintained the stud at Hampton Court and his racing colours were seen at Goodwood and Epsom. His reign produced a further reorganisation of the Civil List. The Crown's expenditure was criticised by the agitator Richard Carlile at his trial on various charges of incitement to violence. He meant no personal disrespect to the King, he said, but he objected to the presence in the government of such officers as the Masters of the Horse and the Buckhounds; and he referred to an editorial in *The Times* which had described the Royal Household as 'a set of lords by way of menial servants' and 'domestics of a limited monarch at so many thousands each per annum for wearing out their lives in irksome yawning attendance on a King who feels oppressed by their contiguity to his person.'

Neither Carlile nor *The Times* influenced the reorganisation which followed belatedly but logically upon previous changes. In 1831 all salaries of ministers, judges and ambassadors, together with various other public charges, were taken out of the Civil List, which was then fixed at £510,000. On the accession of Queen Victoria further expenses were taken into the public sphere and a Civil List of £385,000 was voted solely for Household expenses. One consequence of this was a decision to break up the royal stud at Hampton Court. The Jockey Club protested, understandably, because of the effects on the racing breed; and so, unreasonably in view of their attitude to Household expenditure, did the House of Commons.

Long to Reign Over Us

On the morning that Queen Victoria (1837–1901) came to the throne as a girl of eighteen, she gave audience to her Prime Minister, Lord Melbourne; William Howley, Archbishop of Canterbury; Lord John Russell, 'the widow's mite', ubiquitous and ever-busy; and her Master of the Horse, William Charles Keppel, Earl of Albemarle.

Albemarle had been Master during most of the previous reign, and between 1830 and 1841 he lived in one of the department's houses at Hampton Court. To Queen Victoria's coronation in June 1838 he brought the experience that he had gained when helping to arrange King William IV's. The Queen having no consort, he rode with her in her carriage, accompanied by the Duchess of Sutherland, her Mistress of the Robes. 'The whole of this procession', said the *London Gazette*, 'was under the direction of the Master of the Horse, the Earl of Albemarle, G.C.H., and was formed in St James's Park at nine o'clock, and moved from the Palace at ten o'clock precisely . . .' and in due course came to the Abbey. The traditional coronation banquet was not held, but the occasion had a splendour denied to King William IV, who had been crowned at a cost of a mere £50,000. Later, on a damp and gusty February afternoon in 1840, Albemarle rode in the carriage immediately preceding the Queen when she was married to Prince Albert of Saxe-Coburg-Gotha. This was another lavish event, but in spite of the large parliamentary grants that fell eventually on the tax-payer, the public enjoyed such entertainments very cheaply. The richly dressed participants were mostly paying their own expenses.

Albemarle was a capable and compassionate Master who directed his department efficiently and cared about the men who worked in it. (He was a tactful man too. In the previous reign he and the Duke of Wellington had the awkward duty of persuading Mrs Fitzherbert to destroy King George IV's letters to her.) With the Civil List under consideration, Albemarle was required to review the personnel and expenditure of his establishment (RA Letter Book G/177–83), and in three columns he compared the position at the beginning and end of King William's reign, 1830 and 1837, with his estimates for the immediate future.

His special concern was with 'compensations, superannuations and pensions'. In earlier centuries pensions or *ex gratia* payments to sick or retired servants had been made at discretion, and often there was no money to do this decently. While it was agreed that such payments ought to be made, it was thought that they should not increase the total cost of the department, and Albemarle felt some difficulty about introducing what we should now call a contributory pension. He realised that a pension fund could only be established by deductions from current wages, but he thought it would be unfair to impose this suddenly on men who had held their posts for some time, and improper for them to have to 'sign receipts for sums larger than those they actually receive'. Some superannuation allowances had been included in

196. Queen Victoria riding
with Lord Melbourne (on her left)
at Windsor in 1840.

the department's budget since 1830, but Albemarle said that it should not also have to bear the cost, estimated at £1024, of redundancies 'caused by removal to make room for persons appointed by the Queen's command'.

To some extent the cost of pensions and compensations would be offset by a reduction in his own salary from £3350 to £2500, to come into force in the new reign. Albemarle's statement showed that between 1830 and 1837 stable salaries had fallen from £19,947 to £19,788; an addition of £100 for the second clerk of the stables, bringing him to £400, had been compensated by various small reductions in the wages of some coachmen, grooms and 'established helpers'. With further reductions in these categories, and his own substantial reduction, he anticipated a wage-bill in the new reign of £18,151. The cost of the buckhounds establishment had risen from £2525 to £2610 by the appointment of an additional 'groom to the hunters'. On the other hand, the policy of providing pensions and compensation, now costing much more than in 1830, would bring the total expenditure on salaries, including the buckhounds department, to £28,418. The post of second gentleman rider, at £150, was with the accession of a Queen held by a 'lady rider', at the same salary.

The Master's total establishment numbered 126, including nine for the buckhounds department, plus an unspecified number of 'weekly helpers', or casual labour, estimated to cost £2485 a year. The senior officer under the Master was the chief equerry and clerk marshal, who was paid £1000; and there were four equerries at £750 each, one equerry of the Crown stables at £445, four pages of honour at £230. The officer who acted as secretary to the Master and clerk of the stables was paid £700.

If there had been no procession at the Queen's coronation, Albemarle's work would have been considerably reduced, but through his secretary, R. W. Spearman, he had to invite the co-operation of other departments whose services were required. The Lord Chamberlain was asked to 'give directions for the Queen's barge-master and watermen, and to take the proper steps for the attendance of the Yeomen of the Guard' (RA Letter Book G/198), and a similar letter was sent to the buckhounds department for the attendance of the huntsman, whippers-in and riding foresters; to the Board of Green Cloth for the knight marshal and marshalmen; and to the Commander-in-Chief for the principal army officers, their deputies and adjutants. Albemarle estimated a total expenditure of £9800 'for articles required on account of her Majesty's coronation none of which would be required for any ordinary State Procession': £2050 for state and other liveries; £5060 for 'new dress carriages, new hammer cloths'; £2190 for 'new harness, dressings, pad cloths, &c &c'; £300 for saddlery, horse furniture, &c &c; sundries £200 (RA Letter Book G/208).

Amid all this pageantry Albemarle did not lose sight of humbler concerns, and a month after the coronation he is writing to the Treasury about the servants made destitute by the break-up of the Hampton Court stud:

> They would have no resources but the Poor House had I not taken upon myself to relieve their pressing necessities by advancing small sums of money to them in weekly payments. Two of them are incapable of work and one of them nearly blind. I have stated their ages, length of service, employment and wages, and I beg leave most earnestly to impress upon your Lordships the propriety of making some provision for these poor men and their families, and not allowing them to be thrown on the world, several of them incapable of work even if they could procure it, in a state of utter and hopeless destitution. (RA Letter Book G/188)

There is some mystery about this dispersal of the stud. Some of the paddocks at Hampton Court continued to be in use because in a letter in 1840, asking for some alterations to the stables there, the clerk, R. W. Spearman, mentions that 'the veterinary surgeon is obliged by his duties in attendance on the stud to be continually at Hampton Court' (RA Letter Book G/283). On the other hand, in 1837 when naming the twelve men who have lost their jobs because of the break-up of the stud, Albemarle refers to them as 'Servants of the late stud, Hampton Court Park'. Three of them had worked there for half a century or more, but three others for too short a time to qualify for pensions (RA Letter Book G/189). It is quite clear, therefore, that there were twelve men whose services were no longer required, but a search in the Royal Archives has failed to reveal why this decision was taken or what happened to the horses. If the horses were sent to London or Windsor, some at least of the men would in all probability have gone with them. Closing the stud may have been one of the economies implemented by the Master at the beginning of the new reign, but a likelier explanation is that there were no longer many horses to be looked after – the creams were notoriously difficult to breed. An account of the department from July 1830 to December 1836 shows that the stud bills, which had risen to £994 in 1832, had by the end of 1836 declined to £546 (RA Letter Book G/159).

On the other hand the attempt to breed was not abandoned. In 1840 a gentleman breeding creams in Penrith offered the Master a pair of them because he had heard that the Mews was in need of them, and in declining the offer Spearman said that the particular pair might not match existing stock and, further, that there was no immediate need of them as the Master had 'recently procured a supply from Germany' (RA MH/25.2.1840 and Letter Book G/271). Unfortunately, details of this purchase have not survived, but it must have been quite satisfactory, as letters in 1839 and again in 1842 show Spearman lending creams to the Army 'on the usual conditions', namely that they be taken care of, returned on request and not sold or disposed of without the Master's permission (RA Letter Books H/90 and G/328).

197. The 8th Duke and Duchess of Beaufort at Badminton, by Sir Francis Grant, 'presented by the gentlemen and farmers of the Beaufort Hunt and other friends' in 1864. The Duke was an accomplished horseman and a keen member of the Coaching Club. It was during his lifetime that the game of Badminton was invented and the famous Badminton Sporting Library initiated.

198 (overleaf). Queen Victoria arriving at St Paul's for the Diamond Jubilee Service, 21 June 1897, when the British Empire was at the zenith of its splendour. The Master of the Horse and the Master of the Buckhounds rode close behind the Queen's carriage. In the foreground is a deputation of officers from the Indian Imperial Service.

Breeding at Hampton Court was apparently resumed in 1850. A note dated March 1876 from Sir Thomas Biddulph, Keeper of the Privy Purse, refers to the expenses of the Bushey stud for the 24 years up to 1874. There is also a letter which refers to one of the pensioners of the stud and states that 'she was pensioned soon after the stud was formed in 1850' (RA Z201/39 and PP Vic. 11173/1894). One explanation seems to have been the acquisition of adjoining paddocks at Bushey Park, owing to the death the previous year of Queen Adelaide, the widow of King William IV. For many years William, when Duke of Clarence, lived at Bushey and the property later became the dower-house for his Queen. In August 1850, George Lewis, Spearman's successor as clerk, tells the Commissioner for Woods and Forests that 'as many of her Majesty's horses will shortly be moved from hence', it would be a convenient opportunity for the redecoration of the Pimlico stables. These horses may perhaps have been some of the creams going to the reopened stud at Hampton Court. Later Lewis also asks for drainage and other improvements at Bushey 'in consequence of the disease which has prevailed among the bloodstock there', and this should be carried out 'before the foals belonging to her Majesty's breeding establishment are weaned'. The correspondence indicates that quite extensive work was undertaken (RA Letter Book H/157 and 200).

The Master, considerably less sympathetic than he had been over his staff at the stud, wrote a sharp letter to the Countess of Burlington, principal Lady of the Bedchamber, and her satellite ladies on the difficulties his department had experienced in conveying them to 'drawing-rooms' at St James's Palace when they had not told him of their intention to attend (RA Letter Book G/240). Because of 'the inconvenience and mistakes that have arisen' he has been instructed by the Queen to 'require notice in writing from all the ladies *not in waiting*, to be sent to me at this office . . . at least one clear day before of their intention to attend any of the drawing-rooms, and only those ladies sending such notices will be sent for.'

Albemarle had his perquisites as well as his problems, writing to the Commissioner of Woods and Forests (RA Letter Book G/223) to say that in his office of ranger at Hampton Court he had 'always exercised the power of having venison from the park whenever he required it' so long as the stock, at present 500 head of deer, was maintained at an acceptable level. But the problems seem to have been endless, and it was still necessary to cover a good deal of paper whenever a horse was being sent from abroad. The consul at Tripoli sent a Barb for the Queen's stable, due to arrive at Plymouth with an Arab groom in charge of it, and the Master requested that it be sent on the first available steamboat to be met at Thames wharf (RA Letter Book G/251). After that there arose some difficulty in getting the attendant Arab, Hadji Mahomed, home again, 'on account of his ignorance of any language but his own' (RA Letter Book G/255). So far it had only been possible to arrange his passage as far as Gibraltar, and the Admiralty were requested to have him conveyed from there to Malta, where a representative of the consul would take charge of him.

On the Queen's marriage in 1840, the Master was required to make the necessary arrangements for Prince Albert's own personal stables. Another issue that came before Albemarle was the adjudication of a racing dispute – normally a matter for the Jockey Club, but the Master was the arbiter when one of the Sovereign's Plates was involved. In 1838 an owner called Ferguson, whose horse Harkaway had had three wins at the Curragh that year, complained to Albemarle that he had been deprived of a further win by an alteration in the time of the running of one of the Queen's Plates. Albemarle was firm that regulations which, on the recommendation of the stewards, had been approved by his office 'must not be altered', but as there

199. Cover picture from a souvenir issue of the 'Illustrated London News', showing the Golden Jubilee procession of 1887. The figure in the foreground is the Duke of Portland, Master of the Horse, who on this occasion preceded the Sovereign's carriage, followed by the Royal Princes.

200. King Edward VII, when Prince of Wales, and the Earl of Cork and Orrery, out with the royal buckhounds.

201. William Keppel, 4th Earl of Albemarle: 'a capable and compassionate Master who directed his department efficiently and cared about the men who worked in it.'

appeared to have been some hardship, he therefore suggested to the Jockey Club that there might be a case for declaring void 'Mr. Ferguson's bet respecting his horse winning a certain number of Plates, which by an after act he is precluded from the possibility of doing'. The Master's regulation of the Plates appeared annually in the Racing Calendar between 1739 and 1887, stating the distances, weights and conditions. Revised articles issued by the Duke of Norfolk as Master in 1847 show them to have been run at Newmarket, Ascot, Chester, Goodwood, York, Doncaster and 25 other courses. Several of the Masters were, incidentally, racehorse owners and members of the Jockey Club, and the Marquis of Ailesbury was also a rider, but their authority in racing was confined to the Sovereign's Plates. In 1887, however, the Plates were discontinued, the Duke of Portland then informing the stewards that 'the sum usually granted by her Majesty for the Queen's Plates will be otherwise applied until further notice.' The stewards expressed their regret at this, and said that they would 'endeavour to supply the loss by instituting races in somewhat similar conditions'.

For a few months in 1835 Albemarle was replaced by the Duke of Dorset during a brief swing of the political pendulum, and with the final defeat of the Whigs in 1841 he went out of office altogether. After the so-called 'bedchamber crisis' the Crown was forced into further compromises over senior Household appointments. By 1839 the Whigs' majority in the Commons had fallen so low that Melbourne thought it necessary to resign, and when Peel was asked to form a ministry, he was naturally unwilling that the ladies of the bedchamber, in constant personal attendance on the Queen, should all be the wives of Whig politicians. In later years Victoria admitted that she had been young and inexperienced and 'wouldn't have acted so again'. She had been emotionally dependent on Melbourne's gentleness and suave knowledge of the world, and she 'cried dreadfully' at the thought of losing him. Although she learned better later, she found Peel cold, unfeeling and disagreeable. So she clung to her ladies. She consented to having the Tory Lord Liverpool as Steward, but she would not have a clutch of Tory women in her bedchamber. Peel would 'deprive me next of my dressers and my housemaids; they wished to treat me like a girl, but I will show them that I am Queen of England.' Peel intended nothing of the kind. He wished only to replace one or two of the senior ladies, or those whose husbands were active political opponents. But with clumsy gallantry he allowed the impulsive girl to have her way and he refused office. He could afford to wait, since it was inevitable that the Whig government would soon expire in a surfeit of reforming zeal and the insolvency that always accompanies it. Meanwhile Melbourne agreed to carry on. 'What a blessed and unexpected escape!' the Queen said; adding of Peel, '*he* began it, not me.'

She could not ignore Melbourne's electoral defeat in 1841, nor even say that Peel began it, but by this time she had Prince Albert to guide her. The Prince Consort had a remarkable understanding of the country to which destiny, so often generous to nineteenth-century German princes, had now brought him. He realised that the Crown must stand above party and accept the personal inconveniences that might follow. Nor was it desirable, even on an immediate consideration, that the Queen's Household appointments should continue to be made at the whim of her German governess, the Baroness Lehzen. Queen Victoria came to like Peel, and she regretted his departure when it was his turn to resign (in 1846). So in 1841 they were able to make an amicable compromise. Peel, who had behaved admirably throughout, 'made many protestations of his sorrow, at what must give pain to the Queen (as she said to him it did)' in the loss of Lord Melbourne's enlightened presence. He hoped she would not object to Lord Jersey as Master of the Horse, and 'she said she would not, as she believed he understood it perfectly.' Peel allowed her to propose the name of the new Lord Chamberlain, although this office, along with the Lord Steward's and the Master's, now became contingent upon ministerial fluctuations. Melbourne had 'always been very particular to name no one who might be disagreeable to her in the Household, and Sir R. Peel said he felt this.' Victoria had to surrender only two of her ladies, together with the three senior officers and such of her equerries, lords of the chamber and grooms-in-waiting as held seats in parliament. Until 1866 the post of chief equerry and clerk marshal also changed with the ministry.

Future clashes on this issue were avoided because under Prince Albert's restraining hand Queen Victoria was careful to avoid the appointment of extremists of either party. On the Prince Consort's first coming to England, the members of his private household were chosen for him by the Queen, and his annual income was reduced from a proposed £50,000 to £30,000 on the motion of Colonel Charles Sibthorp, member for Lincoln, who was one of the great Victorian eccentrics. (Later he objected to the Great Exhibition because it would be a means of bringing a lot of undesirable foreigners into the country.) But Prince Albert presently made the Household appointments one of his special concerns, and in 1852 he wrote:

> As to the formation of the Household, the Queen made two conditions, viz. that the persons to compose her Court should not be on the verge of bankruptcy, and that their moral character should bear investigation. On the Queen's succession Lord Melbourne had been very careless in his appointments, and great harm had resulted to the Court therefrom. Since her marriage I had insisted upon a closer line being drawn, and though Lord Melbourne had declared 'that that damned morality would undo us all', we had found great advantage in it and were determined to adhere to it.

Away from pensions and politics, the reign opened with an equestrian event of great splendour, the Eglinton Tournament staged in 1839 by the thirteenth Earl of Eglinton at his castle in Ayrshire. Inspired by the romanticism of Scott's Waverley novels, it attempted to reproduce the circumstances of the mediaeval joust. The scene was described by the aged Disraeli in his *Endymion* (1880):

> Day after day the other guests arrived; the rivals in the tourney were among the earliest, for they had to make themselves acquainted with the land which was to be the scene of their exploits. There came the knights of the Griffin, and the Dragon, and the Black Lion and the Golden Lion, and the Dolphin and the Stag's Head, and they were always scrupulously addressed by their chivalric names, instead of by the Tommys and Jeremys. . . . Other guests gradually appeared, who were to sustain other characters in the great pageant. There was the Judge of Peace, and the Knight Marshal of the Lists, and the Jester . . . and the King of the Tournament.

Disraeli says that 'all contiguous Britain' intended to be present, brought by the new railroads and by steamers chartered at every port within a hundred miles, and although the lists, surrounded by vast and lofty galleries, could not accommodate them all, everyone was able to watch the procession from the castle. In the procession

> came a long line of men-at-arms and musicians and trumpeters and banner-bearers of the Lords of the Tournament, and heralds in tabards, and pursuivants, and then the Herald of the Tournament by himself. . . . Then came the Knight Marshal on a caparisoned steed, himself in suit of gilt armour, and in a richly embroidered surcoat. A band of halberdiers preceded the King of the Tournament, also on a steed richly caparisoned, and himself clad in robes of velvet and ermine, and wearing a golden crown. Then on a barded Arab herself dressed in cloth of gold, parti-coloured with violet and crimson, came amidst tremendous cheering the Queen of Beauty herself. Twelve attendants bore aloft a silken canopy . . .
>
> The other knights followed in order, all attended by their esquires and their grooms. Each knight was greatly applauded, and it was really a grand sight to see them on their barded chargers and in their panoply; some in suits of engraved Milanese armour, some in German suits of fluted polished steel, some in steel armour engraved and inlaid with gold.

Of the jousting itself Disraeli's account does not say very much, except that it 'was very successful; though some were necessarily discomfited, almost everyone contrived to obtain some distinction.' Ultimately the Black Knight and the Knight of the White Rose strove for the supreme prize, 'a golden helm to be placed upon the victor's brow by the Queen of Beauty'.

202. Henry Howard, 13th Duke of Norfolk, who held the unique distinction of being both Earl Marshal and Master of the Horse.

Queen Victoria was, so far as her husband and her advisers would allow it, a courageous and enterprising horsewoman. In 1834 she had made her first visit to Ascot, where she never failed to admire the brilliant scene, and on winning a bet with King William IV she found herself the possessor of a mare called Taglioni. Before her accession she was encouraged to ride forth on public appearances, to make herself known to the people over whom she would one day reign, and she continued to ride when she became Queen until her mother and her private entourage discouraged it. It might have an adverse effect on child-bearing, and everyone was anxious to avoid a recurrence of the farce that had occurred on the death of Princess Charlotte in 1817. Besides, she liked a horse to be spirited, and she took undue risks. Her horse Monarch 'went *beautifully*', but the bay Duchess was 'rather too quiet' and she wanted her mounts to give her 'something to do'. With Melbourne she went on stately rides which almost took the place of formal council meetings, and he felt it to be a blunder in public relations when, except during informal canters round the park, she was no longer seen publicly on horseback but went instead by carriage. Privately she practised horsemanship at the Royal Mews, instructed by her equerries, and was composed and competent. She recorded that she was merely 'astonished and amused' when on one of her excursions her horse swerved and nearly threw her, and she enjoyed Melbourne's dismay at the incident. Prince Albert rode as conscientiously and efficiently as he did everything else, although he came to prefer shooting, and he put his children on ponies almost as soon as they could walk. But the Queen was pregnant for much of her married life, and she therefore rode less and less. At Balmoral she was conveyed to the shooting-parties which Prince Albert so much loved, but she never cared much for hunting, and although she attended Ascot and other meetings, this was rather as a social outing, with foreign potentates attending her, than through any great enthusiasm for the sport.

The organisation of the Mews Department took a decisive turn with the creation in 1854 of the Crown Equerry as its administrative officer. Something of the kind had become inevitable now that the Master of the Horse, and even for a time the clerk marshal, were dependent upon ministerial fluctuation. There could be no satisfactory continuity when, for instance, the three short-lived Conservative ministries under the Earl of Derby briefly installed their own Master, or when the Earl of Cork and Orrery served each time for a few months in the last two ministries of Gladstone.

The new appointment was discussed in a rambling letter from the second Duke of Wellington, Master from 1853 to 1858, to Colonel Sir Charles Phipps, a former equerry who was now Keeper of the Privy Purse. Wellington seems to have lacked his father's austere sense of duty, and probably he was not a very zealous Master because in 1856 he wanted to resign but the Queen would not allow it. At the same time 'Viscount Palmerston mentioned to the Duke the observations which have been made upon the slackness of his attendance in the House of Lords, and he promised to attend better in the future' (RA R.20/42). His letter to Phipps (RA F.38/19) admits that the equestrian establishment had run down. There were only 29 horses in London, and he had never seen 'a more abominable set'. He feared that 'my own purchases don't promise much better than that which the old ones are become: it is however one satisfaction that I have always resisted *Royal* price', meaning that he had refused to pay prices inflated just because the horses were intended for the Queen. He does not propose to make any more purchases until after a forthcoming visit from Napoleon III of France, but then he will start disposing of the cripples.

203. George Child-Villiers, 5th Earl of Jersey. Peel hoped that the Queen would not object to him as Master of the Horse, and 'she said she would not, as she believed he understood it perfectly'.

Query are we to sell them for the little they will fetch? destroy them? or give them away? My notion is to try them on some of the Royal farms, they will draw carts beautifully, giving them away is liable to abuse.

In reply to this part of the letter Phipps agrees that 'some of the old steady horses must be kept in reserve' (RA F.38/20) until some confidence might be felt in the newer arrivals. On a suggestion by Wellington that 'since the London school is *hors de combat*', horses might be trained at a school in Knightsbridge, Phipps does not ask who is to blame for the difficulties of the London school, but he says that the training of royal horses at Knightsbridge would interfere with 'too many interests'. In a classic bureaucratic pronouncement he states that 'in a Royal Household you must not only try to do what is best, but to keep as quiet as possible.'

The appointment of the Crown Equerry followed the death of the Master's previous secretary, George Lewis, and the man chosen was a retired soldier, Major J. R. Groves. Wellington first wonders how he should be addressed:

> Groves is in truth Mr John Groves, in as much as he has left the Army, but he is commonly called Major Groves from his militia rank. Shall we call him Major, Captain or Esq? Major looks biggest for a Crown Equerry, and would please him best, and it is his habitual designation.

The salary was to be raised from £700 to £800, but the new officer would have to do more for the money. Wellington proposes to send him on journeys to buy horses, since it had proved unprofitable to make all the purchases from London dealers, and his out-of-pocket expenses will be paid by the Master himself unless the Queen thinks 'that the acquisition of better horses from cheaper markets justifies his sending in a bill'. Phipps is also asked to advise upon Groves's professional relationship with the equerries and such matters of protocol as the proper place for him to take his meals when he is not at the Mews.

In his reply Phipps deals with the various points that the Master has raised. First, he is pleased to know that Groves wants to change the old practice of receiving allowances in kind for coal, candles and domestic expenses, and he is to be paid £45 a year in lieu. Secondly, the Prince Consort has approved of his occasionally being sent into the country to buy horses, this having been one of the secretary's duties, and he should claim through the Master for his expenses: 'it would be quite out of the question that you should be saddled personally with the slightest expense upon this account.' Thirdly, 'it will add to his position and influence if he is always called *Major* Groves.'

Phipps then comes to the delicate problem of the Crown Equerry's precise status, since 'upon this being accurately and decisively determined, all future quiet to the Establishment and happiness to himself depend.' Obviously there was some difficulty about this, particularly in his relationship with the equerries who were in personal attendance on the Queen. These tended to be young men of title and a higher social position than a retired officer of the Essex Rifles who in effect would be only a civil servant.

> Major Groves then is to be termed 'Crown Equerry, Secretary to the Master of the Horse, and Superintendent of the Royal Stables.' The first title is given him to point out that the office is held by *a Gentleman*, the other two point out the duties of his office. He must receive the orders of the Equerries. . . . They are the modes by which the orders for the Queen and the Royal Household are communicated to the Stables, and they go through *him*, in order that he may be cognizant of everything that goes on in the Department. In short he must not be above doing *anything* that has been hitherto done by the Secretary to the Master of the Horse.

204 (left). Arthur Wellesley, 2nd Duke of Wellington, 'who seems to have lacked his father's austere sense of duty.' He wanted to resign as Master, but the Queen would not allow it.

205 (right). George Brudenell-Bruce, 2nd Marquess of Ailesbury. He was given a typical Gladstone directive to take 'the best possible security for the steady application of the best rules' to the management of the Master of the Horse's department.

He will have no entrée to the interior of the Palace; his duties and his position are entirely distinct, and belong exclusively to the Stables Department. I need not say that he will have a right to expect to be treated as an Officer and a Gentleman, and as a member of her Majesty's Household, by every person of all ranks belonging to it, but to give any idea of his having *any* position *in* the Palace, or in the Equerries' room, would only do harm to himself as well as to the Establishment. The quieter he keeps, and the more he confines himself to the discharge of his own duties, the happier and the more comfortable he will be. (RA F.38/20).

Any hopes that Groves may have had of assignments at Osborne or Windsor are quashed by Phipps's view that they will not be necessary. The headquarters of the department are in London, and that is where the Crown Equerry belongs. The second clerk of the stables is permanently resident at Windsor, and if Groves decides, as he legitimately may, to visit Windsor 'to see that all was going on satisfactorily there', he must find his own lodging and claim two guineas a week for it. On the whole, the situation of Major Groves seems to have been unenviable: officer and gentleman and menial all at once, placed firmly below the salt. Groves died in 1859 and was succeeded by Colonel Sir George Ashley Maude, who from the springboard of a better social position was able to raise the status of the post towards that of equality with other heads of departments in the Household, a status which it eventually reached and still enjoys. But Groves was unlucky in his Master. A Montrose or an Albemarle would have been more positive and negotiated a less equivocal situation for a man who, as well as being Crown Equerry, was still the Master's secretary.

The next step was to try to bring the Mews into line with the other Household departments. The departments of the Steward and the Chamberlain had already passed into the control of permanent officials – thus regularising a practice that had been growing for generations – and their titular heads were now seldom resident at Court. With a ministerial change in 1866, Colonel Sir Thomas Biddulph, Master of the Household, conveyed to Lord Derby, the incoming Prime Minister, the Queen's intentions for the stables. Biddulph's office had become the channel for her communications to the departments of the Steward and the Chamberlain, and she wished it to be recognised that the Crown Equerry should have this function in the Mews:

> The Crown Equerry will receive from the Queen such orders as her Majesty may be pleased to give, and will from time to time notify them to the Master of the Horse. Her Majesty trusts that the adoption of this system, which has been found beneficial to the service in the other Departments, may be the means of saving much trouble to the great officer holding the appointment of Master of the Horse, and at the same time increase the efficiency of that Department of the Household. (RA C.32/90)

Biddulph warned the Queen that 'it is perhaps unfortunate that the new Master of the Horse should be, as he hears, the Duke of Beaufort, who held the office before, on the old system, as with a new first officer altogether, the change would have been less felt.' The Queen's private secretary, General Charles Grey, was directed to tell Lord Derby that in the Master's department it was important to impose 'unity of system and management', and the Queen wished Beaufort to understand that the proposed change had been long in contemplation and in no way reflected upon his own importance. The Duke, who had already been Master under Derby in 1858–9, was unimpressed by these assurances and he refused the office: for reasons which Derby found so cogent that he would not trouble the Queen by enlarging on them.

> He is forced to confess that he fears he shall find the same difficulty in any other attempt which he may make to fill the office satisfactorily: and the Duke of Beaufort, by his superior judgment in every thing relating to carriages and horses, is so pre-eminently qualified for the discharge of the actual duties of the office that he would be a real loss to your Majesty's service for which it would be very difficult to compensate. Lord Derby is convinced of the inconvenience of enforcing, in the Master of the Horse's department, regulations which may be very beneficially applied in the case of the Lord Steward and the Lord Chamberlain. (RA A.35/1)

Then he comes to the crux: while Beaufort or any other Master would no doubt be 'only too happy to avail himself of the judgment and experience of the Crown Equerry', the Queen will appreciate the force of the Duke's argument that 'the authority and the responsibility should go together'. In other words, Maude is felt to have been overreaching himself, and Beaufort will not stand for it. He has temporarily withdrawn his resignation pending the Queen's further pleasure, and Derby is respectfully confident that she will not insist upon a policy 'which he is satisfied will not prove advantageous to your Majesty's service'.

With no Prince Albert now to stiffen her resolve – which almost certainly he would have done: he liked tidy bureaucratic arrangements – the Queen gave way. Grey concedes that while 'unity of direction conduces both to efficiency and economy', he admits the force of Beaufort's argument. 'The appearance of horses and carriages is very freely criticised, and the Master of the Horse is supposed to be responsible.' In the circumstances he agrees that the proposed changes shall be deferred, and next day he tells Derby that the Queen has agreed. But

> at the same time it is so desirable that there should not be frequent changes of system, consequent upon changes of government, and that a little more latitude should be allowed to the Crown Equerry, who is always on the spot, to act without the necessity of perpetual reference to the Master of the Horse (tho' he would, of course, report to him everything he does), that the Queen would ask the Duke of Beaufort himself to consider and prepare a system of management which, after having been approved by H.M., may be permanently established, and be binding on future Masters of the Horse.

A change might also, H.M. thinks, be advantageously made in the system of appointing footmen. As their duties are entirely in the house, it seems strange that they should be appointed by the Master of the Horse, and so much of the comfort of the establishment depends upon their selection that the Queen would be glad to have more direct control over it. (RA C.32/100)

So footmen, who originally accompanied carriages on foot or perched on stands attached to the coachwork, have become domesticated indoor servants.

The correspondence ends with a brief note from Beaufort accepting the post and thanking the Queen for her kindly consideration. He promises to be ready to 'facilitate the carrying out of any arrangements I feel to be beneficial to the service over which I am called upon to preside'. An immediate outcome of these discussions was that the clerk marshal ceased to vacate with the ministry, which was of some help to administrative continuity but not in the long run an important alteration since the post of chief equerry, which contained one part of the marshal's duties, was to be abolished in 1874, and that of the marshal himself in 1888. This followed naturally upon the rising status of the Crown Equerry, who in 1868 achieved what he had been seeking two years earlier. The Derby ministry, in which Disraeli was leader of the Commons, then fell, and Gladstone reappointed the Marquess of Ailesbury, who had already been Master between 1859 and 1866. Among his many other commitments at the time, Gladstone had been reflecting

206. Colonel Sir George Maude, who was Crown Equerry for thirty-five years. Though the Mastership was subject to political dictates, he maintained the continuity of the department and established the status of his office.

upon the organisation of the department, and in a circumlocutory way he said that if the Queen had 'seen reason to desire a more highly braced administration of the Department', this object might be achieved if he were authorised 'to inform Lord Ailesbury that your Majesty thought there was something to be desired, and that your Majesty wished the Master of the Horse to give his mind to the subject generally with reference to taking the best possible security for the steady application of the best rules to the management'. Who could refuse a directive as lucid as this?

Colonel Maude was Crown Equerry from 1859 until 1894, and he was knighted in 1887. His father being the son of a peer as well as a beneficed clergyman, he was a man of some wealth and social standing, and he had the further advantage of coming to the Mews with a reputation for gallantry in the Crimean War. At Balaclava his horse was shot under him and he lost the sight of an eye. (On his arrival at the Mews, however, he was reminded by Phipps that his new post was a civilian one and when on duty he should wear a civilian uniform just as the second Duke of Wellington had done when he was Master.) Maude was a fine horseman, and he later had great success as an owner, his horses winning the Derby, the St Leger and the Oaks.

Groves had been both Crown Equerry and Mews Superintendent, but on the appointment of Maude the two offices were divided. The new Superintendent, W. Norton, was another old soldier who also had been decorated in the Crimea and furthermore was a Knight of the French Legion of Honour. With Norton's loyal and unobtrusive help Maude established the authority of his office, and once the Crown Equerry had been recognised as the Queen's channel of communication with the department, he put himself on an equal footing with other officers of the Household. He could be forthright and uncompromising in defence of the rights of his domain, as indeed he needed to be when his work brought him into contact with so many other departments, offices and services. There were the police and the railway companies to be kept informed of transport arrangements, the Office of Works, the Office of Woods and Forests and the Surveyor-General to be consulted about the upkeep and repair of the numerous properties that the Mews administered, and the other departments of the Household to be considered in the endless battles about protocol.

Maude's defence of the Master of the Horse's precedence in ceremonial processions was to be consulted and quoted when it was challenged in the two following reigns, and he would never allow the Master or himself to be imposed upon. In 1888 he discussed with Sir Henry Ponsonby, the Queen's Private Secretary, the claim of members of the Household to be provided with Mews transport when dispatched on official business. It was obviously a long-standing grievance because Maude states that 'the Master of the Horse has refused such application over and over again' (RA C.71/127). Except the Master himself *ex officio*, no member of the Mews department had the use of a royal carriage for any purpose, and likewise the Mews did not provide transport for members of the Chamberlain's or Steward's departments, except in formal processions. It was up to them to make their own way. 'You ask where we would draw the line,' Maude writes in conclusion. 'Our line has always been a very simple one, and if that is departed from we at once get into difficulties.'

Then the Lord Chamberlain had a try (RA C.71/128). 'The funerals are now coming fast and furious,' he jocularly announced, and he thought there should be regulations for the conveyance of the Queen's representatives, as it was unfair to expect them to pay for the hire of carriages. To go in carriages provided by the

Master would be cheaper for them, and 'more worthy of her Majesty's representatives'. But Maude would not budge. His reply (RA C.71/130) said that he intended to stand by his contention that only the Master was allowed the use of royal carriages for any duty. This was a hard-and-fast rule observed by the department for many years. He was reluctant, too, to bend the regulations in favour of visiting royalty. After their official reception, which was arranged by the Mews, these people had a way of expecting transport to be available throughout their stay, and if the Queen wished it, this was provided. But Maude wants to know (RA F.46/16) why a carriage should be provided for the Queen of the Sandwich Islands when she was not an invited guest of the Palace. He might be able to 'rig up something suitable', but 'I should have thought the Foreign Office might have taken charge of her altogether.' Even a Guards regiment might have to be kept in its place. When the Colonel of the Scots Guards at Windsor sought permission for his officers to pass through the stables when on duty, Maude objected that this was 'an entirely new proposal' (RA Letter Book K/467). The Queen herself often used this route when driving or visiting the stables and 'it might interfere with her Majesty's privacy if the officer on guard and his escort were allowed to pass that way.'

In much of his correspondence Maude sometimes begins, 'The Master of the Horse directs me to say . . .', which indicates some measure of consultation, at least when the Master was in town; and often, of course, he is simply conveying the wishes of the Queen. But it is evident that he had fully informed himself of the rules and precedents governing his department; and when challenged on these, he was so often proved to be right that his pronouncements acquired an awesome authority. But sometimes he went too far, and in 1881 the Master, and eventually the Prime Minister himself, were brought into one of the disputes he had initiated in his energetic defence of his rights. The Duke of Westminster, Master from 1880 to 1885, appealed to the Queen to adjudicate a contention with the Office of Works (RA C.68/118). Ponsonby reminded her that with her approval he had given permission for the poor 'to pick up broken wood in Hampton Court Park', doing this in the belief that 'the Office of Works and the Master of the Horse were in harmony'. For this reason the Master had not been specifically informed, and 'Colonel Maude refusing to take orders from the Office of Works, refused to open the gates till he had received the Queen's orders direct.'

On learning that the Queen had in fact approved, Maude had forthwith opened the gates, so that the poor 'have not suffered'. But the Queen must still adjudicate on the protocol: a revealing indication of the Sovereign's continuing involvement in Household matters even when the departments were becoming institutional. Maude and his opposite number in the Office of Works, one Mitford, had obviously been contesting one of those in-tray and out-tray battles that never fail to bring the civil service to a wartime alert. Ponsonby tells the Queen of the rival dispositions:

> The First Commissioner [of Works] would not allow Colonel Maude's claim to control over the Park and complains of being treated with discourtesy. (Colonel Maude's first letter was a little stiff certainly, and so was Mr Mitford's.)
> The First Commissioner bases his claim to control of the Park by the Act of 1872. The Master of the Horse claims in virtue of the agreement with Lord Duncannon, which has never been changed, and denies that the Act of Parliament can affect the Queen's rights.
> The First Commissioner says that the Queen's rights are intact – but that he takes the Queen's pleasure and that he has a right as a Minister to ask the Queen for orders direct and not through the Master of the Horse. (RA C.68/118)

Ponsonby tactfully dismisses a suggestion that the royal Duke of Cambridge should be asked for an opinion as a person likely to know about such things, and 'as it is a

207. Hugh Lupus Grosvenor, 1st Duke of Westminster, Master from 1880 to 1885.

208. *Orlando Bridgeman, 3rd Earl of Bradford, who was Master twice, from 1874 to 1880 and 1885 to 1886.*

question of considerable importance', none other than Gladstone, then Prime Minister, should pronounce upon it.

Gladstone's reply is not in the Royal Archives, but evidently – upon a matter of such 'considerable importance' – he applied his powerful mind to the task of saying nothing. His non-conclusions are summarised by Ponsonby:

> He thinks that looking at the past they have both been a little in the wrong. And that looking at the future it should be decided what are the distinct powers of each.
>
> As he understands that neither party wishes to part company from the other, he suggests that the Duke of Westminster and Mr Lefevre, or their representatives, should meet and draw up some proposal conjointly to be presented to your Majesty as to what separate function each should exercise in the Park and who should take your Majesty's pleasure. (RA Add. A.12/690)

In forty years of entrenched widowhood – her silent reprimand to God – Queen Victoria cared little for pomps and ceremonies, and her ministers had difficulty in making her appear in public even for the duties that the Sovereign traditionally performed. The ministers were embarrassed, too, by her dependence on the rugged masculinity of John Brown, once Prince Albert's gillie at Balmoral and then her own. She brought him to Windsor as her personal servant and showed much forbearance in excusing him his duties when through addiction to the bottle he was manifestly unfit to perform them. The 'delightful rides' she took with Brown, in vehicles of many sorts and shapes, came near to relieving the Master and the equerries of their duty of personal attendance. But her vigilance in Household matters was unrelaxed.

Writing from Balmoral on the familiar black-bordered paper, she told Sir Thomas Biddulph in 1872 that she wished to set down formally her views

> respecting the sons of gentlemen, and people connected with the nobility, being allowed to have places in the Lord Chamberlain's, the Lord Steward's and the Master of the Horse's offices. The Queen will not absolutely forbid this, but it must be *clearly* understood that it is *not* to be to the *exclusion* of those who are the *sons* of faithful old servants of the Sovereign, who have most creditably given their children education to rise to higher posts. And this admixture would be a very good and wholesome thing. That division of classes is the *one thing* which is most dangerous and reprehensible, never

intended by the law of nature, and which the Queen is always labouring to *alter*. Look at the late Sir George Pollock and his brother [respectively a distinguished soldier and administrator in India, and a judge], their father was a saddler. The present Archbishop of York's father was a butcher, and so on. Lord Lyndhurst's father was a poor painter. (RA C.63/88)

Lyndhurst was three times Lord Chancellor, but it is questionable whether his father, John Singleton Copley, should have been described as 'poor'. He was born in Boston, Massachusetts, and when he came to England during the American revolution, he left behind substantial property which his legal-minded son later went out to recover. But the Queen had made her point, that the Household should not close itself to the career open to talent, and she told Biddulph that he 'may make any use of this letter he chooses'.

Maude and the Master had proof of this concern for Household appointments when in 1875 the Earl of Bradford, Master during Disraeli's ministry from 1874 to 1880, offered the position of veterinary surgeon to a London man, Henry Allnutt. It was to be on the usual terms, the officer receiving no salary but being required to send in his bills for work performed; and the Master reserved the right to call in other consultants (RA Z.195/139–41). But the Queen had other ideas, and a few days later 'Colonel Maude feels certain that the Master of the Horse will regret very much having made the appointment without taking your Majesty's pleasure thereon, and it would not have been done had there been any salary attached.' The Queen would have preferred Henry Simpson of Windsor, who in soliciting the post had taken the somewhat unprofessional step of presenting his credentials to John Brown. These were impressive. He named princes and noble persons who would speak for him, and he pointed out that he had attended the Prince of Wales's establishment at Cumberland Lodge and the Queen's own hounds at Windsor. Maude presently assured the Queen that the Master was full of apologies and would do whatever she wanted as he had no prejudice in favour of either candidate. Maude also had practical suggestions of his own. The wise course would be to allow the commission to Allnutt to stand for the moment, and it could always be revoked later. In effect he could be called to the London Mews while Simpson still attended at Windsor.

But such misunderstandings were infrequent, and Maude's correspondence with

209. Queen Victoria leaving Windsor Castle for a drive in her donkey-carriage (which is still kept at the Royal Mews). With her are Princess Beatrice and John Brown's successor, Francis Clark.

210. William John, 7th Baron Monson, Viscount Oxenbridge. Like Sir Henry Jerningham, an earlier Master, he was Captain of the Yeoman of the Guard.

the Queen shows on both sides a wealth of graciousness, humanity and warmth of feeling. He discusses with her the routes she might find convenient on her journeys, advises her gently on the horses it would be profitable to buy, tells her that Count Munster has brought her 'a daxhund dog' she might like to possess (RA Z.195/132), hopes that certain coachmen and footmen are giving her acceptable service.

The travel arrangements were sometimes elaborate, and the organisation for the Court's stay at Balmoral in 1887 were typical of what had to be done every year. The Mews Superintendent requests the Lords Commissioners of the Admiralty to provide a steamer to carry '19 servants, 24 horses, 1 donkey, 9 carriages, 2 tricycles and 1 perambulator' to Aberdeen (RA Letter Book K/448). Instructions have also to be sent to the manager of the North Scottish Railway; to Campbell's of Aberdeen to meet the personnel; and to Smart's of Aberdeen to convey the baggage.

Maude and the Queen had an immense concern for the Mews servants, and he had always to tell her of any who were ill or in domestic difficulties. A coachman with whom she was well pleased is indeed 'a very good man himself but has a bad extravagant wife and is always in debt in consequence' (RA Z.196/84); a clerk at the Mews took a train to Paddington and has not been seen since, having with him £25 entrusted to him for the payment of wages, and Maude feels for the wife and children who have been left penniless (RA Z.196/160); on the death of an old servant he has already written to the daughters, 'who are very respectable girls', and he thinks it will be possible to give them some money from the Queen's Bounty (RA Z.195/66); in a similar case the widow will receive a pension of £40 and a coal allowance, and he hopes the Queen will agree to her remaining in her house (RA Z.196/13). In 1877 there was a serious accident when Lord Bradford and his wife had been dining out, and it happened to the carriage in which Lady Bradford was returning alone (RA Z.196/54). The Queen sent a telegram from Balmoral wanting to know the circumstances, and Maude replied that it was difficult to know what had happened as the coachman was 'not in a state to render an explanation'. It appeared that at Stanhope Gate the near horse had kicked over the traces and the carriage had lurched into some iron railings. The coachman fell sideways between the forewheels, and it was feared that he had fractured his skull. 'There is hope of recovery but he will always be a damaged man.' The horse, too, had been injured and should recover, and it was almost as an afterthought that Maude added that Lady Bradford had nothing worse than bruises.

Maude, then, would do almost anything to help his people. In 1888 he wrote to tell a newly-bereaved widow that of course she might stay on in her house at Hampton Court (RA Letter Book K/466). More than that, he offered her the post of mews-keeper, 'as it will simplify matters about your house and will prevent your having to pay rates and taxes'. Her son would be able to deal with any correspondence attaching to the post, and for her further comfort the department would pay her £40 'for the man who does the sweeping, cleaning, etc.'.

He could be firm with the servants too. In 1888 it had come to his notice that the keeper of the Home Park at Hampton Court had been admitting strangers into the park to shoot (RA Letter Book K/474). 'I am directed by His Grace [the Master of the Horse] to inform you that this is quite irregular and you have no business to allow anyone to shoot without his permission.' The keeper was required to acknowledge this instruction, and he received a very sharp letter six days later when he had not done so. It was a different matter when soon afterwards this same man was in financial trouble and the bailiffs wanted to get into his house, which was royal property (RA Letter Book L/3). Maude queried the lawfulness of this. It had been established that no one had the right to enter the Mews at Windsor without

211 (above). Nasir ud-Din, Shah of Persia, and Prince Leopold during the State Visit of 1873.

212. The Shah brought several horses with him, which were stabled at the Royal Mews. One of them had a blue tail and 'caused some excitement in London at the time.'

authority, and he assumed that the same applied at Hampton Court. The bailiffs secured a magistrate's warrant, claiming that they only wanted to distrain on the keeper's furniture, which was his and not the Crown's, but Maude kept up the fight until told by the Office of Works (RA Letter Book L/4) that a similar issue over a house at Hampton Court Palace had been decided in favour of the plaintiff after a long battle in the House of Lords. 'I think therefore you had better at once remove your embargo on the distraint.' Maude's deeply personal concern for his servants was reciprocated by his Sovereign towards himself. Once Maude's son was very ill, and the Queen insisted on being kept informed; and when the young man was to see

213. Two Masters of the Horse, the Duke of Beaufort (driving his own drag) and the Duke of Portland, with King Edward VII when Prince of Wales, at a meet of the Coaching Club in Hyde Park.

214. Feeding the royal buckhounds, from a drawing in the 'Illustrated London News', 1879.

a specialist, she required his report to be telegraphed to her at Balmoral immediately (RA Z.195/181).

These illustrations of Maude's curious mixture of combativeness and clemency may suggest that he sometimes carried both these qualities to extremes. One example will have to suffice of the practical shrewdness that he brought to everyday business when his over-generous emotions were not involved. During the 1890s the Household treasury was querying the mounting cost of the buckhounds, and it was suggested that the previous Master of the Hounds, Lord Coventry, was to blame. Maude would not allow this. Coventry had been scrupulous in his accounts and had never overdrawn by more than £200 (RA C.21/93). The explanation was, however, that Coventry did not ride to his hounds, whereas the present Master, Lord Ribblesdale, 'rides hard: and a hard-riding Master makes hard-riding men, in which case the horses wear out sooner.' But Masters come and go, and an immediate emergency should not justify a permanent increase in the buckhounds allowance at the expense of the funds of the Master of the Horse. 'We went through all this in Hardwicke's time. He was the most extravagant Master I remember.' (Lord Hardwicke, according to Ribblesdale, had maintained his office in a state of 'debonair magnificence'.) It had been agreed then that £4000 was an adequate allowance for the buckhounds, and Maude saw no reason to alter it in the present circumstances.

Maude died at the Mews in May 1894, and the Queen, then at Balmoral, wrote in her Journal: 'Was much grieved on coming here to hear that good old Sir George Maude, who had been very *unwell* for some time, but was thought to be recovering, had died suddenly to-day of heart failure . . . He was a kind good man' (RA Queen Victoria's Journal, May 1894). It was reported to her (RA C.75/145–51) that the funeral had taken place 'in a pretty park at Coolhurst, Sussex', in the little church of St John's where his wife had earlier been buried. Servants from the Mews and the studs were present, together with a distinguished array of Household officers and English and foreign royalty. The Earl of Cork, Master of the Horse, laid a wreath for the Queen.

Sir George Maude made the Royal Mews the highly efficient and organised department that it is today, and if at times he was peremptory and belligerent, his defence of its status probably did more than anything else to enable it to survive a difficult future in which it would be assailed not merely by growing demands for economy but by the decline of the horse as a means of transport. He has an important place in the historical development of his office. The Crown Equerry is the heir of Ellis of Rochester, and Ellis by now has come a long way.

Forty years after Maude's death the Mews received a photograph of him and a curious little memento from a gentleman living in Kent who had often visited the stables as a boy. As a great friend of his father, Maude had frequently stayed with the family in Yorkshire and had used the occasion to look for Cleveland bays suitable for purchase. The correspondent remembers being at the Mews during the visit in 1873 of the Shah of Persia, Nasir ud-Din, and his mother had taken a number of photographs of the Shah's horses, one of which 'had a blue tail which caused some excitement in London at the time'.

At her Golden Jubilee in 1887 the Queen refused to travel in a closed coach and she drove through the streets in an open landau built by Barker of Chandos Street and first used at the laying of the foundation-stone of St Thomas's Hospital in 1866. At the jubilee it was drawn by eight cream horses and attended by an escort of Indian cavalry, and in the evening the Queen dined in the company of more than fifty royal personages. Ten years later the theme of the Diamond Jubilee was Britain's imperial splendour, and instead of the crowned heads of Europe the Queen met the premiers of her far-flung dominions. The nation's pride in her on those tumultuous occasions turned at her funeral into a bewildered sense of loss, for not many of her subjects had ever been ruled by anybody else.

She died at Osborne on 22 January 1901 (and was measured for her coffin by her grandson the Kaiser William II) and it was not until 4 February that she was finally laid in the mausoleum at Frogmore. These were anxious days for the Master of the Horse, the Duke of Portland, and the Crown Equerry, Sir Henry Ewart, because it was a long time since the Royal Mews, working with the office of the Earl Marshal, had arranged a royal funeral; and as King William IV had not been as prestigious as Queen Victoria, the precedents were not of much help.

It is impossible to think of everything, and the Crown Equerry had much on his mind during the days while the body was still at Osborne. There being no telephones for the prompt organisation of business, everything had to be done by telegram, and Ewart in London was bombarded with queries and instructions from the equerries and secretaries at Osborne and elsewhere.

> It is now decided that all equerries walk so you will not be able to have Brocklehurst for procession. Will you please see that Waller and John Clerk are warned.

> King says Duke of Grafton must have offer to walk in London, also Bigge. The latter may be unable to walk. The Duke of Grafton is to be asked to St. George's Chapel or if he wishes it to walk in procession from station at Windsor.

> The two carriages with ladies must go with pairs, thus you will have four-horse carriages.

> Captain Ponsonby decided that men and horses gun team to put up Cavalry Barracks, please inform commanding artillery Aldershot.

> Kindly say whether any arrangements for conveying pages of honour from London to St George's Chapel on Saturday.

> King thinks special trains for crowned heads only.

> The body of her late Majesty will be disembarked at Clarence Yard Gosport. Kindly arrange accordingly. Reply.

> Cloth armlets will be worn on drab great coats, crape on state liveries.

215. *Queen Victoria's funeral cortège on its way up St James's Street. The coffin was drawn by the used eight cream horses at the Diamond Jubilee; this time their manes were plaited with purple strands.*

Liveries will be as usual scarlet with crape on arm, but when epaulettes are worn there will be one thickness of crape on them. Cloth bands and not crape on hats, and no crape on cockades. Black gloves will be worn.

The King requires horses to be provided for nine Russian officers and four non-commissioned officers and men to ride in London funeral procession, please confirm.

Please suspend all further work regarding saloons for coffin until you hear from Knollys.

The gun carriage must arrive on Wednesday as Thursday will not give sufficient time. Can you arrange this and also that detachment arrives at same time.

I am requested to ask what instructions the Duke of Argyll has received for procession in London. [The Duke in fact had supplied his own instructions: he would wait at Windsor, 'and horse can be given to another Argyll.']

King thinks it would be dangerous to make exceptions as regards procession in any particular cases. If leave were given to one country other countries would put in a similar claim.

The King wishes me to make it clear that after luncheon Saturday special leaving at 3.15 will take away all who are not to be received. Special for royal family and missions to be in readiness and go when ordered, probably about 5.

Prince Albert's saddlery will not arrive in time, can you provide some for him and Duke Gunter Schleswig-Holstein.

German Emperor will be attended horseback by General von Scholl, rest of suite will walk. Scholl rides twenty stone, please confirm.

Count Gleichen has been commanded to attend here tomorrow as equerry so Colonel Waller will not be required.

Please inform the King of the Belgians, the King of the Hellenes and the King of Portugal about the suggestion that they should ride on Saturday and report their Majesties' intentions here.

Hope some gentlemen are told off to entertain Royalties and guests at Paddington. King says Keppel and Greville will help. How many trains are ordered?

Please have the kindness to secure rooms for me and my valet for the 30th. inst close to Royal Mews. Many thanks. (From Count von Wedel, Master of the Horse to the German Emperor.)

Am ordered from Osborne to inform you I am as Gold Stick to-morrow to drive. Will you kindly allow me place in one of carriages and tell me where I should join it. (From Viscount Wolseley.)

The King says that Lord Lawrence is to drive in procession with Duchess of Buccleuch and Lord Churchill with the Queen's two ladies and Lord Colville. Please inform Earl Marshal.

King says you can arrange with Wolseley to drive on Saturday. Communicate with him.

Seeing that these and similar communications all required information and instructions to be relayed to other people, and that visiting potentates had to be told of their place in the procession, it is surprising that the Mews officers did not collapse under the responsibility.

The Adjutant-General's department supplied forty horses from the riding establishment at Woolwich, stabled and foraged at the Royal Mews, and six officers to assist the royal princes and forty-two visiting princes into the saddle, and eight bays were provided by the Royal Horse Artillery at Aldershot to draw the gun-carriage at Osborne and Windsor. The only hitches occurred at Windsor, where one of the RHA horses, restive after a long wait in the cold, snapped its traces. A naval guard was then ordered to pull the carriage, using the horses' harness and the communication-cord from the train. Lieutenant Hickey, the Mews Superintendent at Windsor, also reported that the connecting-bar on the gun-carriage had broken, and drag ropes had had to be used on the downward incline. 'In my humble opinion I consider the brake a most flimsy construction, and should have been thoroughly tested beforehand.'

According to its well-disciplined habit the Mews made a record of the proceedings, and before King Edward VII died, arrangements for his funeral had already been drafted on the basis of this experience. It was noted, for instance, that the Master of the Horse and the Crown Equerry had both ridden, although at King Edward's funeral they did not, the Master (the Earl of Granard) travelling in the royal carriage and Ewart in his own. It is hard to imagine what experience dictated the memorandum 'No doctor to walk except in trousers.'

The Queen had left certain instructions in her will. There must be no undertakers; no grave funereal music, just Chopin and Beethoven and the Highland coronachs she had heard from Mr Brown; 'no black trappings of any sort or kind.' So the pall on the coffin was white and gold and the streets were hung with purple trimmed with white. On Friday 1 February the royal yacht *Alberta* took the coffin to the mainland, silently watched by warships of the greatest navy the world has ever seen. On Saturday morning people knelt in the winter fields as the special train went by, its windows blind; and so through the streets from Victoria to Paddington, the gun-carriage drawn by eight cream horses; and on to Windsor, where eighty-one guns saluted her, one for each year of her life, a short service at St George's and then to Frogmore, where Albert waited.

CHAPTER TWENTY Horse and Car

Two events in 1901 were symbolic of a changing world; the royal buckhounds were abolished and King Edward VII bought a Daimler. This car is still kept at Sandringham in working order, and is regularly insured, but its possession led at first to some ridicule when on a journey to Norfolk the car developed tyre trouble at Finchley and had to call at a bicycle-shop for repairs. The change to motor transport was gradual but inexorable, and soon after King Edward's accession a mart in the Harrow Road was disposing of carriage-horses at £150 a head. Until shortly after the First World War the horse still provided most of the motive power for cabs, dust-carts, fire-engines, trade vehicles and the like, and it still pulled gun-carriages in war. But conditions on the Western Front were uncongenial to the great cavalry regiments, which presently began to mechanise themselves with the advent of armoured cars and tanks. In civilian life a generation of coachmen translated themselves into chauffeurs; the cobbled streets built for horse traffic were replaced by smoother surfaces for the car and the electric tram; and the pomps of Rotten Row, where horses had been treated like mannequins, began to disappear as society ladies occupied themselves with the new problem of looking elegant on arrival after travelling heavily wrapped in an open vehicle.

The dispersal of the buckhounds had a discouraging effect on the hunting scene, but the King was a little too bulky now to sit a horse with any athletic intention and he was more interested in racing. There was a social consequence, too, as the Master of the Buckhounds supervised the rigid protocol observed in the Royal Enclosure at Ascot. Lord Ribblesdale, who was Master in the 1890s, has recorded the prodigious scale of his duties. In his book *The Queen's Hounds* (1897) he wrote:

> On the Gold Cup day there were sent from the Ascot offices in 1896, 12,753 telegrams 46,000 words of Press matter; and in 1897, 10,500 telegrams and 45,000 words; the diminution in the latter case was due to the fact that betting on the lawn of the Grand Stand was this year prohibited. For the Grand Stand luncheons alone, exclusive of the more solid viands, there were cooked – 1800 fowls, 1200 pigeons, 1700 lbs of salmon, 1500 lobsters and 500 quails.

King Edward gave the Londoners a piece of pageantry by reviving the state opening of parliament, which had been virtually discontinued by Queen Victoria since Prince Albert's death. But when he undertook a modest reconstruction of the Household, the first for some fifty years, one of the economies effected was the breaking-up of the buckhound pack. The salaries of officers with seats in parliament were reduced immediately, and cuts were ordered in certain other posts as soon as a vacancy should occur.

The King was nearly sixty when his mother died, older at his accession than any of his predecessors except King William IV, a third son who had not expected to

216. *Familiarising horses with the motor-car at Marlborough House in 1904.*

inherit and had not studied the business. King Edward, too, had been largely kept ignorant of the operations of government, while at the same time criticised for his scandals and dissipations. But once he was freed from his mother's watchfulness, in later years somnambulatory but still dauntingly prestigious, he developed considerable astuteness over a wide range of affairs. His association with foreign financiers was held to be vulgar, but the advice they gave him on his investments saved the taxpayer an appreciable amount of money. On a relatively modest Civil List King Edward managed to fulfil his heavy responsibilities.

He even made a profit on his racing, which in his sedentary years replaced shooting and yachting as his favourite sport. He submitted with affectionate resignation to his mother's 'Jobation' on the dangers of addiction. The Queen was wise in her warnings and reproofs because the Prince was a natural gambler and any money he lost would not necessarily have been his own. It was a specious defence that he made when after a card-playing scandal the Archbishop of Canterbury was commanded to warn him that his ways were dangerous:

> Horse-racing may produce gambling or it may not, but I have always looked upon it as a manly sport which is popular with Englishmen of all classes, and there is no reason why it should be looked upon as a gambling transaction. Alas, those who gamble will gamble at anything.

287

He knew enough 'Englishmen of all classes' ruined or disgraced by gambling on horses for this to have been sanctimonious nonsense. However, his own betting was moderate (apparently never more than £600 on one race) by the standard of the obsessional gamblers with whom he associated.

It was as owner, not as punter, that King Edward made his money. But he had little luck at first, and before he became the 'Teddy Boy' beloved of thousands of racegoers he had been booed on the course when it was alleged that his horses had received unfairly low handicaps. The turning-point was the purchase of the mare Perdita II, most of whose colts were sired by the Duke of Portland's St Simon. In 1896 King Edward won the Derby with their colt Persimmon, who beat Leopold Rothschild's St Frusquin 'by sticking out his tongue' as they passed the post neck-and-neck. The King's *annus mirabilis* was 1900, when Ambush II won the Grand National, and Diamond Jubilee, a brother of Persimmon, won the Two Thousand Guineas, the Newmarket Stakes, the Derby, The Eclipse Stakes and the St Leger. In 1909 the King won the Derby again with Minoru.

The introduction of the motor-car found the Royal Mews readily adaptable to changing fashions. The royal cars were kept and serviced there, and needed the attention of mechanics instead of farriers and grooms, and the Crown Equerry had to arrange journeys by car as well as by train and horse-drawn carriage. Some of the stables were converted into garages, but it was still unthinkable to use anything but the horse for foreign receptions and ceremonial occasions, and for this reason the equestrian establishment could not be substantially reduced.

The Masters of the Horse in this reign were the Duke of Portland (1895–1905), who had already done an earlier stint between 1886 and 1902; the Earl of Sefton (1905–07); and the Earl of Granard, an Irish peer, who was to continue until 1915. Other circumstances might change but not the venerable argument about precedence. In March 1907 the Home Office addressed a letter to Lord Knollys, the King's Secretary (RA W.65/58):

> ... We need just the further instructions as to whether His Majesty wishes the Master of the Horse to come immediately before the Treasurer of the Household or immediately after the Lord Chamberlain. You will see that it is possible that the latter, viz. to place him immediately after the Lord Chamberlain, would require an Act of Parliament, but the former, to place him immediately before the Treasurer of the Household, would not.

King Edward authorised the following reply:

> When the King goes in State to any function, the Master of the Horse is the only official who goes in the carriage with him. He is also head of one of the three Household Departments. It is evident therefore that he ranks as one of the Great Officers, and the King considers he should have precedence accordingly.
>
> His Majesty therefore wishes him to be placed in Class B, immediately next to, and after, the Lord Chamberlain. The procedure by which this is arrived at must of course be left to the proper authorities to decide.

One of the 'proper authorities' was the Duke of Norfolk, as Earl Marshal, and on 6 May 1907 he received an explicit direction (registered in the College of Arms by warrant of the Earl Marshal). The King, believing that 'the precedence assigned to the Master of the Horse should be further regulated and defined', states that 'in the exercise of our royal prerogative we do hereby declare our royal will and pleasure' that the Master shall be placed immediately after the Lord Chamberlain.

A matter affecting the Master's duties arose during King George V's serious illness in 1928–9: was he to attend Trooping the Colour when the sovereign himself could not be present? It was recalled that when King Edward, then Prince of Wales,

"Persimmon" 1900. phot? by Blaxentile

217. *King Edward VII on a favourite chestnut cob.*

218. *Photograph of Persimmon, King Edward VII's most successful racehorse, taken by Queen Alexandra in 1900. This horse won the Coventry and Richmond Stakes, Derby, St Leger, Jockey Club Stakes, Ascot Gold Cup and Eclipse Stakes.*

took the salute for Queen Victoria from 1895 onwards, the Master and the equerries did not attend: another indication of the very personal nature of the office. From his convalescence in Bognor the King said that the Queen would not attend and that his great-uncle, H.R.H. the Duke of Connaught, would take the salute as senior Colonel of the Brigade of Guards and senior Field-Marshal, not as representative of the Crown. In those circumstances he did not think that the Master and the equerries and certain other Household officials should be present.

This was soon followed by another round in the precedence dispute. Following a further challenge to the Master's status an appeal was made to Garter King of Arms (RA.GV, 0/1390). The King's Secretary, Lord Stamfordham, prepared a memorandum based on earlier discussions of precedence in the Household. One went back to Albemarle's time:

> When Lord Albemarle claimed a right to a place in the carriage with the Queen, the matter was referred to the [first] Duke of Wellington who, in a characteristic letter, decided that the Master of the Horse had no right to any place except by the Queen's will.

Characteristic or not, this was not wholly accurate and it did not take the matter much further. Stamfordham found a more helpful direction when Maude, in 1882, as Crown Equerry, recorded an instruction given by the Queen 'in consequence of Lord Sydney, the Lord Steward, having claimed precedence of the Master of the Horse in the carriage procession of 4 Dec, contrary to all previous custom'. She accordingly directed that, as by law established, the Chamberlain and the Steward have precedence on normal occasions,

> but that in all carriage processions the Master of the Horse shall take his seat as heretofore in the next carriage to her Majesty's or those of the Royal Family, and before any other person except the members of the Royal Family.

But in 1933, only three years later, the Earl of Shaftesbury, the Lord Chamberlain, writes informally to Lord Granard, who was Master again from 1924 to 1936:

> Year by year a mistake occurs in your office in the printing of the order of the seating in the carriage procession as regards the Master of the Horse and the Lord Steward. It is a comparatively trifling matter and I have always let it pass because I thought it would not occur again. You must know that the office of Lord Steward takes precedence of the

219. The 6th Earl of Sefton (on right), Master of the Horse from 1905 to 1907.

office of Master of the Horse and I feel bound to draw your attention to it and get the matter rectified because if left too long it is apt to become an established custom. You will be able to put it right in a few minutes.

Granard was not having that. In reply he quoted the ruling given by the Queen in 1882, 'and therefore you will see that you are mistaken in thinking that an error was made in the carriage list issued by this office'. Shaftesbury offered his 'humble apologies for thinking that a mistake could have been made in your office' but 'to my way of thinking, which perhaps is not as clear as it should be, it is not quite so "clearly laid down" for I suppose it might be a debatable point as to how far the Sovereign's ruling upon a point established by law is binding on all successive Sovereigns.' The debate continues. The issue has been raised again since then, and probably it always will be until parliament legislates.

Away from matters of State, the Royal Mews during King Edward's time was much taken up with its newest responsibility, the motor-car. The King was as interested in horse-power as he was in horses, and throughout his reign his enthusiastic patronage was a great incentive to the motor trade: a fact clearly shown in the Mews files. Whenever motor-cars are the subject of correspondence there always seems to be urgent prodding from the King, who kept his eye on the directives issuing from the Crown Equerry (Major-General Sir Henry Ewart, holder of the office from 1894 to 1910).

During the nine years of the reign the royal favour was divided between Daimler and Mercedes, each endeavouring to offer the best that the new technology could produce. In February 1906 Ewart wrote to a London representative of Mercedes about the new 45 to 50 h.p. car ordered for the King:

> I note that the price is £1,850, including delivery in London, accessories, lamps, and body, the amount to be paid after deducting the allowance of £700 for the small 20 to 24 h.p. car, being £1,150. Regarding your proposal to deliver a new car each year when your factory is established in England I would say that such a course is quite impracticable, and no such contract can be entered into, for the purchase of new cars will depend entirely on the wishes of His Majesty The King and when it becomes expedient to have new ones, due consideration will be given to the subject, and enquiries prosecuted in the ordinary way. (RA Letter Book O/678)

In 1907 the Daimler Motor Company sent a representative to discuss with Ewart the purchase of their latest 35–55 h.p. model in part-exchange for the royal Mercedes. They would also supply a new 28 h.p. shooting-brake, and they 'would venture to suggest' that the King would be interested in the forthcoming 1908 model of the Daimler, 'which will embrace several improvements'. In 1909 Hooper & Co., coachbuilders, of St James's Street, tendered to supply a new 'limousine-landaulette body' which would incorporate such extras as the royal crest, headlights with generator, paraffin side-lamps, horns, a speedometer and two clocks. Next year the Wolseley Tool and Motor Car Co. apologise for being unable to supply Queen Alexandra's new car before the date originally agreed, but in the meantime they will repair her present car free of charge.

There was the important matter of chauffeurs, and for these the King relied upon the Metropolitan Police. In a letter to the Commissioner asking for a fourth officer to be seconded to the Mews, Ewart pointed out that 'the three men we have got give His Majesty every satisfaction and I do not like bringing in a civilian stranger who might upset them' (RA Letter Book P/50). The drivers had to be fully conversant with each new motor-car, and on 7 April 1905 [Police Constable] Hems was sent to the Daimler works at Coventry for a course of instruction. Two weeks later he had

220. Drawing from the 'Illustrated London News' showing the training of horses in the riding school at the Royal Mews for the Coronation of King Edward VII in 1902.

to hurry back to London to acquaint himself with the new Mercedes (RA Letter Book o/83).

The Crown Equerry also had to put his mind to such essential items as fire extinguishers, and in March 1906 he is writing to a firm in Peckham:

> With reference to the orders placed with the Minimax Co. for the supply of fire extinguishers, I note that articles bearing this name are of foreign make. I would say that this extinguisher was ordered in a hurry in consequence of one of His Majesty's cars catching fire. When the present machines are worn out, English makers shall receive consideration. (RA Letter Book o/697)

Eccentrics had to be dealt with too. In 1906 a gentleman claiming to be 'Major commanding the London district of Motor Volunteers' wrote from Clapham to offer his own car, with himself at the wheel, if the King should wish to drive to Marienbad during his continental visits. When King Edward went by train to Marienbad in 1907, the bill from the railway company was £79 6s. This was for the hire of a special train to take him and his suite, including a dog that was the subject of an extra charge, to and from the coast, and the sum of £10 5s. 9d. paid to the Belgian state railways to haul the train from the French frontier to Eschen. The King had a car on this journey, too, a 40 h.p. Mercedes coloured 'purple lake'. It went from Antwerp by road after crossing from Harwich, and the Superintendent of the Mews, Captain John Nicholas, had to apply to the Foreign Office for passports for Charles William Stamper, 'His Majesty's motor Engineer', and Harry Payne, the chauffeur.

Reg. No. 582850.

221. *Radiator mascot from one of King Edward's later Daimlers.*

222. *The first royal Daimler (1901) at the Mews. It is still kept at Sandringham, insured and in working order.*

The comparatively short journeys to Sandringham were sometimes made by road, but the Court's annual exodus to Balmoral required preparations that began months beforehand. The schedule for 1907 provided for 22 horses, 4 vehicles and 17 servants to be dispatched from Windsor and 3 cars and the King's 3 shooting ponies from London, the King's own car being accompanied by his motor engineer, two chauffeurs and a 'washer'. In addition, 12 horses were to be hired from Campbell's of Aberdeen. Next year King Edward went first to Cowes Regatta, and seven servants, six horses, three carriages and a car were detailed to attend him. In instructing Campbell's to supply for the Balmoral journey the same number of horses as in 1907, Ewart told them that Lady Knollys, wife of the King's Private Secretary, 'wishes to have three fresh ones this time, which must be bays with black points, good-looking upstanding horses and thoroughly reliable, with perfect manners'. But Lady Knollys apparently did not know quite what she did want, as a perplexed coachman at Windsor writes to say that she 'thinks it would be best if we had three fresh ones, they were getting a bit the worse for wear, but of course it was her wish to have the same three, she hopes that they will be quiet and reliable'. Ewart had to write again to tell Campbell's that 'Lady Knollys is not very well and is frightfully nervous of motor cars, so that I must ask you to guarantee that the three horses you purpose sending will take no notice of motor cars'. Although the horses proved satisfactory, Lady Knollys was still being a nuisance two years later. First Campbell's were told that it had been decided not to hire any horses in 1910 – King Edward had died in May – but a subsequent telegram ordered three for Sir Arthur Bigge (Lord Stamfordham) and 'three for Lady Knollys must be excellent and thoroughly reliable kindly repeat this in your reply'. In the end the party was larger than usual: 25 stable servants, 32 horses, four carriages and six cars. By 1912 the total had risen to 34 men and 45 horses, and the Mews had to ensure that there was sufficient stabling and accommodation available at Balmoral, 'and in addition beds have frequently to be provided for valets of guests, etc.'.

A surviving summary of the carriages, liveries and escorts for distinguished foreign visitors between 1913 and 1933 gives an interesting summary of the varying kinds of arrangements which had to be made for different occasions. In 1913, for example, the French President was received with the 1902 state landau, with the horses in state harness and the coachmen in state livery. President Wilson in 1918 had five semi-state postilion landaus, with the men in scarlet coats. In 1920 the Emir Feisal of Iraq travelled in a clarence with one twin coach as his escort, whereas thirteen years later, as a King, he was accorded full state honours.

But no matter whether visits from foreign dignitaries were official or private, such occasions required careful planning at the Royal Mews, and so did the dispatch or reception of animals presented as gifts. The case of Gay Corinthian, to be described later, was in a class of its own, but there was nothing but trouble when Abdul Hamid II, Sultan of Turkey, decided that only a trained English horse would invest him with the right ceremonial magnificence. The request was made in 1908 through the British Embassy at Constantinople, and the Sultan's specifications were exacting. Price was no consideration, but the horse must be a chestnut gelding, 'free from vice' and 'having been ridden by a soldier and well broken in'. Both hind feet and one of the fore feet must be white, with a white spot on the forehead, 'but tail should be long'; a horse with three white stockings was believed in Turkey to be lucky. A secretary at the Embassy added later that the Sultan had further insisted upon having a Field-Marshal's gala saddle and bridle to fit the horse, 'although I have not myself any illusions as to his ever honouring that pigskin by sitting on it . . . but it is a fairly harmless fancy in which he can I presume be humoured'. King Edward decided to send the horse as a gift, and left it to Ewart to find one that fulfilled the detailed requirements. The long tail was as big a problem as any, as the best English horses did not wear them.

Ewart consulted the officers of the Chestnut Troop at Aldershot and put an advertisement in the *Field*:

WANTED, a thoroughly broken CHARGER, CHESTNUT GELDING, of English breed, (not a race horse) not above six years, height 16 to 16.2 hands, both hind feet and one (either) of the fore feet to be white, with a white spot on the forehead, and a long tail; one that does not shy and rear at crowds, gunfire, etc.; mouth not to be hard, and back rather hollow and easy; must be a good jumper and have a good trot and canter. A good price will be given for a suitable animal.
APPLY to Mr. G. Williams, 10, Wilton Road, Pimlico, S.W.

A firm of saddle-makers were asked to estimate for a saddle and set of harness based on a Field-Marshal's model but having the Star and Crescent in place of British emblems. The Foreign Office subsequently intervened to explain the doctrinal reasons why the saddle must not be made of pigskin.

Surprisingly soon, Ewart is telling the Foreign Office that he has 'succeeded in this difficult undertaking' and has found a long-tailed chestnut with the required markings and habits of mind, but his letter does not at this stage disclose the vendor or the price. He asks instead if he is 'right in assuming that, considering the political motive of the gift, the Foreign Office will refund the cost of the horse, harness, the expenses incurred by the Master of the Horse, etc., and that the money will not be expected to be forthcoming from the King's Civil List'. Telegrams meanwhile were sent to twelve people who had replied to the advertisement in the *Field*, telling them that Mr Williams of Pimlico was now 'suited'.

The horse, which is not named in the correspondence, was by Cherry Ripe out of Black and Blue, which makes an odd mix for a chestnut. After insurance and veterinary clearance Captain Nicholas arranged 'an approximate itinerary' that

*223. Captain John Nicholas,
Superintendent at the Royal Mews
in King Edward VII's time.*

would take the animal from Charing Cross to Marseilles, via Folkestone and Boulogne, and he allowed an extra three days for stabling at any of these points in case the spring weather should cause delays. The horse was to leave Marseilles on 28 April 1909 and go by steamer to Constantinople.

But it was too late. The horse never got further than Marseilles, and on 5 May Ewart is sending the Foreign Office an account of the expenses incurred by the groom 'on the journey to Marseilles and back with the horse intended for the ex-Sultan of Turkey'. Abdul Hamid had been deposed by a revolution of the Young Turks (a body containing veteran revolutionaries trained to manipulate the emotions of the immature) and the British government now had an unwanted and long-tailed charger on their hands. Ewart does not seem to have been very well rewarded for all the trouble this abortive deal had caused to himself and his staff. In May he acknowledges receipt from the Foreign Office of £100 'in part payment of chestnut horse purchased from Messrs M. & W. Milton on the 18th January 1909, for £350'. Messrs Milton were well-known dealers with extensive premises in Park Lane and it reflects well upon their organisation and efficiency that they had so swiftly produced a gelding of the required specification, tail and all. Probably they lost nothing on the deal, but the King obviously did, being £350 out of pocket on the purchase price of the horse and having incurred further expense on the saddle and equipment and on the arrangements for the journey. The last note comes from Balmoral more than a year later, when the new King's Secretary writes from Balmoral to the Superintendent at the Mews to enquire about the horse's fate: 'This horse was stopped in the Mediterranean somewhere and was ordered to be sent home to England. His Majesty would like to know what eventually became of it'. It had in fact been returned to the Royal Mews.

There was a smoother passage when in 1909 Letsie Moshesh, Paramount Chief of the Basuto, desired to present a pony to the King with the prayer that 'he may preserve me and the small land I am living on', as Ewart was able to report its safe arrival at the Mews, but even this simple matter required much correspondence and organisation. Attention to detail appears again in a note to the steward of Rufford Abbey, Ollerton, to arrange for the accommodation of the engineer and four 'motor servants' accompanying a visit of King Edward. It established the necessary priorities by explaining that 'the engineer, Mr Stamper, is an upper servant'. In September 1910, when the Court was still in official mourning for King Edward, the Department arranged the Duke of Connaught's visit to South Africa, and 'black gloves and crape bands have been sent in case it is desired to have mourning worn, and mackintoshes to meet the contingency of any possible inclement weather'. King George V's visit to India for the Durbar of 1911 required the purchase of special light-weight equipment for the coachmen and grooms accompanying him, and in yet another of its duties the Department had to arrange for 'the removal of the remains of the late Duke of Fife from Portsmouth to the Wolsey Chapel, Windsor Castle, on Saturday, 24 February 1912'. The Duke was the husband of the Princess Louise, eldest daughter of King Edward VII, and a gun-carriage and bearers were ordered to meet the coffin at Windsor while a special train was chartered to carry the King and his suite from Victoria.

Only a highly-organised and flexible department could have coped with a regimen in which routine work might at any moment be interrupted by the special duties that lay within its responsibility. Discipline was strict. There was a rigid classification between employees of the first class: the senior coachmen and grooms who had qualified after long service; a second class of 'established helpers' who were assured of regular employment, subject to good behaviour; and a third and

224. *The funeral of King Edward VII, with two grooms leading the riderless charger, a duty that in former days was carried out by the Master of the Horse.*

fourth class of 'weekly helpers'. Promotion from the fourth to the third class went by seniority and from the third to the second by 'seniority and selection'. An advertisement in about 1910 for 'young able-bodied men as stable helpers and drivers' at the Royal Mews required them to be 'square in shoulders, and very smart in appearance, and thin in leg'. They must know the town well and would have to give proof of their efficiency before being engaged. The wage was a guinea a week, but this was supplemented by clothing for all duties, full board and accommodation, free periodicals in the reading-room, billiards, and a coffee bar with provisions 'nearly at cost price'. A life pension was guaranteed in old age, and in the event of accident or ill-health a pension after ten years' service. After twelve to fifteen years a rise of £10 a year was given 'to well-conducted servants as vacancies occur; after which the next advancement is to become a warranted servant, of which there are 23, wages from £70 to £100 per annum, with quarters, fuel, light and furniture'. At the top was the state coachman at £175 to £200, with six other coachmen at £100 to £150, all having four furnished rooms, fuel and light. Promotion to coachman was from the 23 established helpers 'as vacancies occur'.

Standing orders were so long and specific that a new recruit of limited education could have absorbed them only by patient practice and the help and encouragement of men already familiar with the routine. With that help they were less formidable than they must have seemed at first, but they imposed a very high standard of service based on unremitting care of the horses and attention to a smart public appearance. Men lacking these essential qualifications soon revealed themselves, but for the right sort of man the Royal Mews offered an unequalled pride of service attested by the many employees who found there a lifetime of fulfilment.

If standards were high for the humblest servants, they were even more exacting for the professional staff. When in 1912 there was a vacancy for the honorary post of veterinary surgeon to King George V, Frederick Hobday was already well known to the Household. He had treated cattle at the Home Farm at Windsor and operated on both a retriever and a carriage horse belonging to the King. His operation for the relief of 'roaring' in horses had proved so successful that animals so treated were described as 'hobdayed'. On the private network the King was known to approve of the appointment of this eminent man as consultant to the Mews, but the thing had to be done properly. The King required the Master of the Horse to make 'a regular submission', the usual enquiries were ordered and Hobday had to tender a formal application. Here again we can see the Crown's personal involvement in matters affecting the stables.

The King was involved again in a curious and short-lived appointment in June 1914 of 'Mr E. L. Herman as Director of the King and the Queen's Continental Journeys' at a salary paid quarterly by the Master of the Horse. Mr Herman was to receive an allowance of £1 a day when travelling abroad, and when not required by their Majesties he might undertake other employment. He was to keep accurate account of expenses, and it was made clear that this was a second-class appointment: on the royal yacht or royal trains 'he will board with the servants', and when attending any of the royal palaces 'he will board outside at his own expense (excepting that coffee will be provided for his breakfast in the Palace)'; and he will receive an advance 'on account of small disbursements', of which he must keep a regular summary.

It is apparent from the correspondence that the Mews was by this time on much better terms with other departments than in Colonel Maude's day, and probably Maude's abrasiveness had been valuable in establishing the authority and prestige of the Master of the Horse as an officer who was not to be trifled with. But the Mews could still be forceful with anyone who tried to take advantage of it, and it was made clear to tradesmen and others in need of a lesson that this was an office acting in the name of the King, and no liberties were to be taken with it.

In 1907 Francis Coutts, carriage hirer of Ballater, ventured to express his disappointment at not having received any orders during the visit to Balmoral that summer. 'The same thing has happened more than once since I received your letter of 24 June 1898, a copy of which I enclose herewith.' Sir Henry Ewart thereupon took the trouble to have a list prepared of the use made of Mr Coutts's conveyances during 1907, and he said in reply that 'more work has been entrusted to your care than to any other firm. . . . In the circumstances of the case I fail to see any ground of justification for your disappointment, for it is impracticable to divide every little requirement among several firms in a stereotyped manner, and it will save much trouble and inconvenience if in future you give a question more consideration than you have done in this case before writing.'

Even Campbell's of Aberdeen came under rebuke in 1909, and Lady Knollys was at the bottom of it. The firm proposed to send for her use the same three bays as in the previous year, but this would not do. Captain Nicholas stated that 'the coachman wants the darkest of the three changed, because it is fidgety when being put to and also when waiting at the door. He mentioned this defect to your foreman when the horses were returned last year. Please make quite sure that the new horse you will send is thoroughly reliable, in order that there may be no unsatisfactory comments.' Campbell's replied in some surprise that, so far from complaining, the coachman had assured them that he had 'never had *three* (3) more satisfactory horses', but they would of course send a replacement as requested. Next, however, they reported that one of the tried and approved horses had broken a knee in an accident, and so they suggested that they supply instead three chestnuts, all 'with beautiful manners and extremely steady in all harness and go with style and action. . . . Nothing equal to them in this district and if they don't suit it will be impossible to do so.' They did not suit Lady Knollys, and Nicholas had to send this telegram to

225. King George V and Queen Mary riding up Fleet Street on the second of their Coronation processions in 1911. The carriage, drawn by creams, is the 1902 State Landau specially built for King Edward VII.

Aberdeen: 'Lady Knollys very keen on having bay horses – sure chestnuts won't suit – this lady is still unwell and most nervous – would suggest taking two or three good steady and reliable horses for the king's use – you have plenty of time to secure others by end of September to take their places.' When the firm further protested that the chestnuts were absolutely reliable, the correspondence was closed on this firm dismissive note: 'The chestnuts will not do, for the colour is not a royal one.'

Messrs Milton of Park Lane, dealers with whom the Mews did frequent business, were similarly not allowed to relax their standards. Ewart writes in 1907: 'I have weighed the two fore shoes which were taken off the horse that I purchased from you this morning, and the actual weight is 6 lbs 2 oz, which is monstrous. Please note that in future I will not look at any horses you may bring for my inspection unless they are properly shod.' Two years later Mr George Williams, a professional consultant, reported to Ewart that a new horse supplied by Milton's was a 'whistler'. The firm were reluctant to accept this:

> Of course this horse being a young horse was naturally excited, but I can assure you it is perfectly sound, and if you will take it I am quite willing to stand by it for 6 months and if he shows any signs of being a whistler I will take it back and refund the whole of the amount paid for it. I have every confidence in this horse.

When Ewart replied that he had made it a rule always to accept Mr Williams's judgment and proposed to abide by it now, Milton's requested a further trial: 'we suggest that you should allow Mr Williams to gallop him again for his wind in a few days' time – say this day week.' But Ewart would not budge: 'With reference to the defective horse, we have often had horses re-examined in the past, but always with the same result – we have never had one passed at a second examination. It was therefore considered advisable to make a rule in regard to the matter, and I regret that I cannot depart from it in this instance.'

226. Royal footman, riding grooms, state postilions and Indian orderlies in Dean's Yard, Westminster, on Coronation Day 1911.

Messrs Offord & Sons, coachbuilders of Portman Square, were in trouble for a different sort of offence. In 1912 a friend ('It is no business of mine, but I thought you would like to know') informed the Crown Equerry that at Lord's cricket ground he had noticed 'one of the Royal Carriages let out as a "stand" to a private individual with the usual placard bearing the hirer's name, and the name of the coach builder, Messrs Offord'. The Crown Equerry asked for 'an explanation of this proceeding' and received an apologetic reply, Offord's claiming that they had themselves been obliged to hire carriages to send to Lord's 'and amongst these were some with the Royal Arms on them that we presume were used last year for the Coronation. We had most of these painted over but one seems to have been forgotten. . . . We are exceedingly sorry.' Within the ranks, too, the proprieties had always to be observed. In 1913 the GPO in London returned to the Mews a telegram 'sent as on the service of the Master of the Horse, as there appears to be some doubt whether it should not be regarded as a communication of a personal or private character. If it is clear that the message should not have been sent at the public expense it may perhaps be thought right to request the sender to affix stamps of the proper value.' This communication is endorsed, 'Fault was duly acknowledged and the guilty personage paid up.'

But matters of rebuke and contention are remarkably infrequent in the daily transactions of the Mews, and the customary attitude is of approachability, kindness and courtesy. The Crown Equerry was accessible always to schemes for improved safety and efficiency. Electric light, with its facility for more consistent heating, was installed as early as 1911, and any inventor or manufacturer with a new device to recommend was invited to come and explain it. Similarly, in any complaint from a private person against the Mews and its servants the Crown Equerry would accept responsibility rather than play the heavy-handed bully and force the complainant into a civil action. In fact anyone who approached the Department on any matter was assured of a courteous hearing and, nearly always, a favourable reply.

Thus in 1909 the Japanese Ambassador requested permission for his government to copy Britain's royal carriages and liveries, and King Edward VII agreed to this provided that the colour and the arms were different. But Ewart added a personal note that if the Ambassador wished 'to send anybody to see our liveries or anything else connected with this department, we shall be very happy to show him anything he wishes to see'. Likewise, among many such requests Ewart went to some trouble in 1908 to provide material for an article on 'The Donkey on Duty' that a correspondent was writing for the *British Workman*, 'having regard to our late Queen's fondness for this animal and the use she made of it'. The correspondent submitted nine questions, not to mention a tenth for 'any additional particulars not covered by the above', which he based on the assumption that Queen Victoria had only one donkey whereas she had several, and he received answers to them all.

Ewart would fight for his men too, even if they were foreigners. Christian Troger, born at Seussen in 1884, was a footman accompanying Queen Alexandra in Ireland when in 1908 the German Embassy requested his release from the Royal Mews to perform his statutory military service at home. Ewart attempted to have him excused as being in the service of the British sovereign, but without success. A letter signed 'Stumm, chargé d'affaires' stated that any 'interposition from the part of this Embassy would be of no avail. The law does not allow any exceptions' and unless Troger reports to the military authority forthwith, 'he will expose himself to the punishments provided by the law'. Ewart had reluctantly to convey this uncompromising message to the royal party in Ireland, but this sort of concern for employees promoted the solidarity of the staff. So in a different way did the annual

227. Decoration from the letter heading of M. & W. Milton, 'Dealers in Horses, and Job Masters' of 6 Park Lane, who supplied horses to the Royal Mews at the beginning of the 20th century.

consignment of pheasants which the Duke of Portland sent from Welbeck Abbey. 'I am very pleased the men liked them,' the Duke wrote when acknowledging Ewart's letter of thanks in 1908. 'I like them to think I have not forgotten them and the pleasant association of nearly twenty years.'

In 1910 Ewart was succeeded as Crown Equerry by Captain the Honourable Sir Charles Wentworth Fitzwilliam, son of Earl Fitzwilliam, who had earlier been in charge of the stables in King Edward's establishment as Prince of Wales. On 15 June 1911 a perambulator was damaged by a royal carriage in Windsor Park, and only a fortnight later Fitzwilliam had the owner's acknowledgment of a new one, costing £2 12s. 6d., 'in compensation for my loss'. The promptness of the settlement, with no arguments about contributory liability, is even more impressive than the willingness to pay. Responsibility was accepted again a few days later when a royal coachman reported in London that 'a single-horse brougham came out of a side turning, pulled up as if to let me pass, gave me the tip to come on, then pulled across in front of me. I stopped as soon as possible, but my pole grazed his back panel. The footman can state that it was entirely his fault.' Generous consideration was naturally given to the petition of a postman at Brighouse, Yorks, who was bringing up seven dependent children on a wage of 24s. a week and a small army pension. His daughter Edith had been injured in the Long Walk at Windsor 'by one of His Majesty's horses and who Her Majesty was kind enough to forward a splendid bunch of flowers and enquire into her condition'. The father asked for Edith's fare to Yorkshire, her original return ticket having by now been forfeited, and the return fare for her mother to escort her. The total claim of £3 2s. od. was duly paid by the Mews.

Fitzwilliam went to the defence of Prince, a retired servant aged seventy-nine, who had been head groom to King Edward VII and had been employed by the Department for forty-seven years. In 1912 someone discovered that Prince occupied premises at Cumberland Lodge, Windsor, and claimed that as he was no longer in active service it should be treated as a grace-and-favour residence and so occupied 'on the terms on which such residences are usually held involving the payment by him of rates and taxes, the insurance of the premises and their proper maintenance as regards internal repair'. Fitzwilliam pointed out that Prince had lived there since 1874, a matter of thirty-eight years, and 'still has the care of a few old ponies belonging to Queen Alexandra'. He was sure that the King would wish him to 'be allowed to remain in possession to the end of his days free from the further liabilities in prospect'.

In addition to the execution of his routine duties the Crown Equerry never knew what odd requests each day's post might bring. The Science Museum at South Kensington sought permission to make photographs for public sale of 'the early velocipede – a primitive form of the bicycle known as the bone-shaker – lent to it in 1901 by King Edward; and just a week before the declaration of war he had an application from the Hereford City Liberal Association for leave to conduct an excursion party through the Royal Mews. The president of the association was a future Master of the Horse, Lord Chesterfield. In granting permission Granard added a note insisting that the chairman give an undertaking 'that no damage will be done by persons in sympathy with the Suffrage movement'.

The Great War brought inevitable changes to the Royal Mews. King George V, a man of immense probity, curtailed his hunting and shooting and brought economies into the Household. The equerries, most of them army officers, departed on active or administrative service, horses were withdrawn for military purposes, and although the senior men were mostly too old to serve, the younger members of

228. *Indian officers on leave from the Western Front in 1915, visiting the Royal Mews.*

the staff went off to fight. Four of them were to lose their lives at the front. Enough horses had to be kept at the Mews for such ceremonial activities as were still retained to preserve the functions of monarchy, and of course the studs had to be maintained as fully as possible. But fodder and materials were expensive and hard to come by, and as the war lengthened Fitzwilliam found himself in charge of a much reduced establishment, with a new Master at its head, Edward Scudamore-Stanhope, 10th Earl of Chesterfield, formerly Steward of the Household. The Superintendent, in succession to Captain Nicholas, was now Captain Andrew Benbow.

The wounded and foreign soldiers on leave found great pleasure in visiting the Mews and inspecting its historic treasures. Twelve Australian officers were granted free permits in 1915, Indian cavalry officers went round after attending small investitures ('Captain Benbow might take them round and they should particularly be shown "Delhi" and the other chargers'), and many parties of British wounded arrived after being given tea at Buckingham Palace. Although the Mews was not a catering establishment, J. Lyons & Co of Cadby Hall set out their charge for tea for 750 soldiers and 100 ladies: one shilling a head, including 16 waiters and four tea-makers and the hire of all china, plate and flowers. They would be obliged if Fitzwilliam would 'permit our using the laundry for staff purposes'. Other guests included the band of the Garde Républicaine, who were taken to the Mews after watching the Changing of the Guard.

Even in those sombre days the Mews still displayed its traditional thoughtfulness towards the humblest of people in the most trivial circumstances. In 1917 the King and Queen gave a tea and entertainment for soldiers and sailors at the riding-school at the Mews, and the Crown Equerry sent out the invitations. Horace Elsom, a stoker of the Naval Brigade, had his card signed by 'the Princess Mary, Princess Victoria and the Duchess of Teck, Lily Marchioness of Lincolnshire and others', and he sent it on to a frame-maker who lost it, and Mr Elsom was so upset that he threatened to sue. In despair the photographer appealed through his solicitor to Fitzwilliam. Fitzwilliam found a duplicate card and got his wife to ask the royal ladies to write their signatures again. Even little matters like this take time and trouble, and the photographer's solicitor recognised it when he begged 'to convey to Lady Fitzwilliam my high appreciation of her most kind courtesy in relieving a very difficult situation which in default of so generous a solution would undoubtedly have been productive of very considerable pecuniary loss to a small trader who could have ill afforded it'.

CHAPTER TWENTY-ONE The Last of the Cream

After the war, prices did not fall to their former level and all the great establishments were obliged to some extent to reduce their ambitions and their expenditure. Economies in the Royal Household fell upon all the departments, and the Mews was affected more than the others by the declining importance of horse transport. The upkeep of the pre-war equestrian establishment could not be justified on practical grounds, quite apart from the expense. Under the impact of a second and costlier war it might have been extinguished altogether, except that the carriages might have been preserved *in situ*, as a museum of patriotic pride and gracious memories, because its transport duties could have been entirely mechanised. It survived because the mounted horse and the horse-drawn carriage, superbly trained and caparisoned, are matchless in the historical pageantry that still stirs the imagination of the British people.

Large issues are reflected in small items, and in 1919 Sir Charles Fitzwilliam, the Crown Equerry, regretted to the officer in charge of the paddocks at Hampton Court that the Department could not afford to mechanise the chaff-cutter 'as the expenses have to be kept down as low as possible'. The same letter required a weekly statement of the amount of old and new hay in stock and also wanted to know how many potatoes were left. The supply of hay direct from Hampton Court was already proving a useful economy as this was cheaper than buying it from the London dealers, but the stud groom, George Gale, was feeling put upon. Supervision from London had never neglected *minutiae* – much else was going on in the world when an instruction was sent from the Mews to Hampton Court that the cream colt Belgravia was 'to be given a tablespoonful of Parrish's Food per day' – but the rise in costs was daunting. Between 1915 and 1920 the price of forage had trebled, so that the weekly cost of keeping a horse was now 35*s*. instead of 12–13*s*. The cost of harness and bridles and repairs to carriages had gone up too, and the Department had to do its best with contracting resources. This put heavy pressure on the staff, and George Gale, at least, thought that enough was enough. In February 1920 he wrote thus to the Superintendent:

> Re Hay I have 3 ricks of 19 and 3 parts one nearly done and in the one you are useing there will be enough to last till March 31st at your present rate of consumption this is of 1918 and the 3 part rick is the bad [one] in the Bull Paddock. I am sure it would be economical to keep this latter for chaff alone and let us start one of the 19 yr ricks as the horses waste half of this.
> May I put another man on until Francis gets back?
> Re your order as to getting the Creams used to being tied up how long can you give me to get this job completed for as you know I am very busy getting the remainder of the manure on to the 35 acres, loading and delivering hay to London, Stallions to get fit and nearly all the chain harrowing to do and a man short and the grass already growing like hemp all this causes me no end of anxiety so please give me all the time you can.

I should advise parting with Carlota for one, she has slipped foal twice is very shelly and delicate, very subject to Red Worm and I am afraid will never carry another foal through even if she conceives, also Cholderton Pearl *if* she is not in foal owing to badly cankered feet I hope she is in foal but I am not by any means sure.

Reading is 3 days overdue but still shows no signs of any milk this is a strange turn and quite a new experience they say one can always live and learn and this is more applicable to horses than any other thing, she is to all appearance in a perfectly (—) state of health and her foal is alive.

You have not replied to my enquiry as to a Rick Cover and time is getting on Sir.

He was allowed to hire a temporary replacement for the absent Francis, but that was all the joy he did get. Captain Benbow, the Superintendent, allowed him two months to get 'the creams used to being tied up', and meanwhile he was to furnish full particulars of the rick-cover he had asked for, and he was reminded that he had not yet reported any action upon instructions to dispose of a certain heifer.

Things were not what they used to be, and even more strenuous economies lay ahead. In 1920–1 the Crown Equerry was required to make a comprehensive review of horses, carriages, staff, wages, overheads and equipment, on the understanding that the old peacetime establishment would never be restored. In 1914 there had been 153 horses and a staff of 312, which included 157 weekly helpers. Although in 1920 expenditure on purchases and repair was cut to a minimum, there was a deficit

229. The cream stallion 'Pistachio'. This is one of many photographs taken at the Royal Mews by Mrs Albert Broom, whose altercation with the Crown Equerry is described on page 322. She may have been Britain's first woman 'press' photographer.

of £25,130 1s. 6d., this being partly due to a war bonus paid to employees. The saving effected by obtaining hay for the London horses direct from Hampton Court was estimated to total £2000 in the following year; another saving, begun in a small way during the war, was to allow the servants money compensation in lieu of articles of livery still fit for use, and by 1921 this would amount to £2283. But a reduction in the number of horses, and thus in carriages and in the men to look after them, was the only means of significant retrenchment. The officers of the Mews fought hard all the way and won some of their points. Because of this, and because of the allowances made for natural wastage as both men and horses came to the end of their active life, exact figures are impossible to determine. But Cumberland Lodge at Windsor was given up, the number of horses fell below 100, and servants were dispensed with. One clerk went as soon as the economy programme was launched in 1920, and Fitzwilliam said that it would be impossible to make any further reductions in the small administrative staff of three men – an accountant, a store-keeper and a clerk – since there was now only one in each class. But in July 1922 an order signed by the deputy treasurer to the King announced that twenty-two servants would have to be retired from 31 October.

It was done as handsomely as possible. By the King's own command 'a specially generous pension scale has been drawn up in view of the enforced nature of these retirements, and in the case of men who are ineligible for pension owing to not having done ten years' service, a gratuity of one month's pay will be given for each completed year of service.' All twenty-two received sums in excess of the pensions they would have earned if they had completed their service, and any who in the meantime found other employment received their full pay and allowances until the end of October.

One of the sad economies felt to be necessary was the sale and dispersal of the royal cream horses. It will be remembered that the creams were introduced by the Hanoverian kings from their stud at Herrenhausen. Importation continued regularly for the maintenance of the breed – for instance, as many as 34 horses were brought over between 1765 and 1792 – until it was interrupted in 1803 by Napoleon's seizure of Hanover and its incorporation into his confected Kingdom of Westphalia. King George III was so angry when the little French vulgarian was drawn by eight Hanoverian creams at his coronation that he decreed that only blacks should be used on English state occasions until Hanover recovered its independence. At about the same time the breeding of creams began at the royal

230 (left). One of the state stables at the Royal Mews, designed by Nash in 1824.

231. Two creams, 'Czar' and 'Adalbert', in the other state stable. When the cream horses were dispersed in the 1920s the stable was converted into a state carriage house.

stud in England. Although cross-breeding with native or Holland stock sometimes had successful results, the pure cream breed proved difficult to maintain in English conditions, and for a few years after 1837 the stud was broken up. In 1859 Queen Victoria imported a mare and stallion from Hanover – Platen, Hanover's Master of the Horse, requesting 'a large donkey stallion' as part of the deal. Two creams were acquired from Schaumburg-Lippe in 1893 and three from the Grand Duke of Saxe-Weimar, who was not himself a breeder, in 1901. When the Schaumburg-Lippe stud was sold in 1897, Herrenhausen and Hampton Court were the only two remaining.

In 1887 Maude wrote to General von Rauch, Oberstallmeister at Hanover (RA Letter Book K/429), to say that the Queen was 'anxious that this unique breed should be maintained, and as it is nearly thirty years since any fresh blood has been imported from Hanover, the horses here are very much inbred and we require a fresh cross of blood.' He proposed an exchange of two English mares or fillies for one Hanoverian stallion, and he wrote again (K/430–1) to urge an immediate arrangement as 'this race of horses is becoming deteriorated' and it would be unfortunate to waste even a year. But it appears that the Hanoverian stud was experiencing the same problems, and it was agreed that the two studs should exchange a mare and a stallion in the hope of refreshing both (RA Letter Book K/47). Mr George Williams, a veterinary surgeon who advised the Mews for many years, was sent out to inspect the Hanoverian offerings and he reported that the stallion Oswald was 14 years old, had never covered and was rather small (RA Letter Book K/465). Maude later said, however, that Williams had apparently been misinformed about the age and activities of Oswald, and in 1888 he was brought over in the company of the mare Bona, the exchange being completed by the dispatch of an English mare and stallion. A temporary improvement must have been effected because when the Schaumburg-Lippe stud at Buckeburg was sold in 1897 an offer to buy some of the stock was declined (RA Letter Book L/242).

Initially it was not so much economy as the difficulty of keeping up the breed that promoted an enquiry after the First World War. Experience had shown that it was necessary to introduce fresh blood, and this had been impossible during the war, when also the standards of fodder and supervision had deteriorated. As early as April 1919 Fitzwilliam asked the Hon. Cecil Parker to join a committee, along with Mr E. H. Leach of Newmarket and Mr Williams, to 'enquire into the circumstances of the cream-coloured horses, which are, from thin breeding or other causes, liable before long to die out'. Parker suggested co-opting at some stage Lord Middleton, 'who knows more about breeding than anyone does'. Great interest was also shown by another expert breeder, Mr G. Tyrwhitt Drake, of Cobtree Manor, Maidstone. Drake had creams of his own, but the largest was only 12½ hands, whereas 16 hands was the average for the horses that drew the state coaches. This underlined the problem at Hampton Court: not just to maintain the breed but to produce a steady supply of horses sturdy enough for their purpose. Drake gave the Mews some interesting examples of his experiments with cross-breeding, although his successes had been erratic and unpredictable.

He was a real enthusiast, and as soon as he heard rumours that the royal stud might be breaking up, he sought permission to buy some of the horses. He was allocated three, and as he was able to buy a further three at auction, they should be 'the nucleus of what I have always wished for, namely a stud of cream horses, providing of course I have any luck at all'. He hoped that his stock might be useful to the King later if he should ever decide to resume breeding. But it seems that his horses were never large enough, or they persisted in being the wrong colour. In 1936 he offered

232. The 10th Earl of Chesterfield (on left) with his wife and Captain Stapleton-Brotherton, at Epsom Races in 1931.

to present King Edward VIII with a four-year-old pure cream mare, 'about 15.2, good light bone. Active with nice action. Entirely suitable as a lightweight charger, excepting that she has rather a prominent forehead and Roman nose, as the Hanoverian creams had.' Drake hoped that 'for purely ceremonial purposes and for old times' sake' his proposed gift might be acceptable, but the Crown Equerry replied that 'his Majesty has told me he does not wish to ride a charger less than 16 hands and is particularly anxious not to have a mare.' Drake regretted that he had no suitable geldings or young stallions, adding, 'I find these cream horses awfully difficult to breed and have not had a foal out of the four mares for two years.'

A small incident that seems to reveal a slip-up in the Department's usually impeccable administration involves Drake and the unlucky Gale. In July 1920 the Superintendent acknowledges a cheque for £85 for the purchase of a half-bred cream mare, Bloomsbury, and her foal, by Lord John Sanger & Sons, Ltd, whose 'Circus and Hippodrome' had their headquarters at Horley. Benbow instructs Gale – along with reference to other matters requiring his attention – to put the horses on a train and inform Sanger's groom of their likely time of arrival. But it appears that Bloomsbury and her foal were already bespoken. In August Benbow writes:

> Gale,
> On the 3rd July Sir Charles Fitzwilliam visited Hampton Court, on which occasion he directed me in your presence to communicate with Mr. G. Tyrwhitt Drake regarding the disposal of the dun mare "BLOOMSBURY" and colt foal. Accordingly I wrote to Mr. Drake, who arranged with Sir Charles Fitzwilliam to see the mare and foal with the view to making an offer for them. Sir Charles went away for a few days after this, and during his absence wrote to me saying that Mr. Sanger had offered £85 for the mare and foal, and directing me to have them delivered to him: this, as you know, was done, and the deal was completed by the payment of the sum in question. When Sir Charles Fitzwilliam and I were talking over the disposal of this mare and foal you heard and understood that he intended Mr. Drake to have the first refusal, and I am at a loss to understand how it came about that Mr. Sanger approached Sir Charles in his absence from London and purchased the mare and foal without my knowledge. You will easily understand that there has been trouble over this deal, and I ask you to let me know if you communicated with Mr. John Sanger telling him that this mare and foal were for disposal. Mr. Tyrwhitt Drake is very much annoyed at having been offered the purchase of the mare and foal at his own price and eventually being told that it had been otherwise disposed of.

While the long correspondence with Drake was in progress the three-man Board of Enquiry met and were guardedly hopeful that the breed could be preserved. 'We were unanimously hopeful that, with the present prospects (there now being three young mares in foal), it was more than probable that sufficient animals would be obtained to perpetuate the breed. We felt that it was an experiment, but one that was well worth trying.' Selective cross-breeding might be fruitful, as it had already produced two animals true to type, and the committee also took encouragement from Drake's experiments at Maidstone. Among their practical proposals the committee suggested that in future seasons the stallions should be allowed to run in the paddock with barren or maiden mares, as this had recently been successful with three mares, and that the stallions themselves would gain more vitality from this exercise than if they were kept all the time in boxes.

As a result of a later visit to the stud in the company of Lord Middleton, Parker added that in the cause of vitality 'light work such as chain-harrowing or rolling would not come amiss.' The mares, after being served, should be taken away from other horses and kept isolated until no longer in season. The paddocks themselves, with about 90 horses on 70 acres, had been in use for some 200 years 'and

233. *The 8th Earl of Granard, who served twice as Master : from 1907 to 1915 and 1924 to 1936.*

234. *Trooping the Colour ceremony in Hyde Park, two years after the Great War. With King George V are the Duke of Connaught, Prince Albert (later King George VI), Prince Henry, and Prince Arthur of Connaught. In the picture can also be seen Queen Mary, the Princess Royal, and Mr Winston Churchill.*

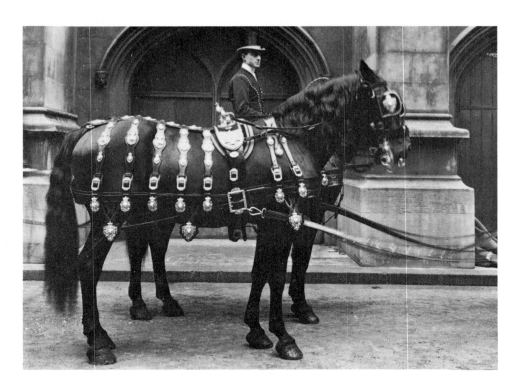

235. *A state black carriage-horse. The creams and blacks of Hanover were replaced respectively by the greys and bays.*

236. *'Vanguard', a state bay which at 18 hands was in its time the biggest horse at the Royal Mews.*

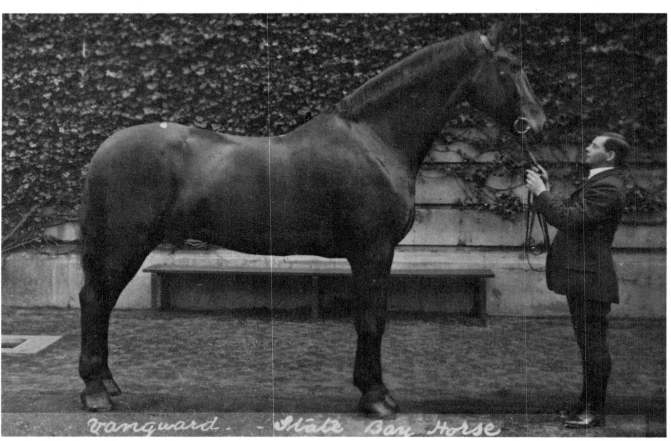

Vanguard. State Bay Horse

consequently must be more or less horse-sick'. Some parts were bare and covered with droppings, and nothing would foul land so quickly as that. It was recommended, therefore, that the paddocks should have a complete rest from horses for at least a year, being fed meanwhile by sheep or bullocks. A final criticism was of the stalls, which should be laid with non-porous bricks impervious to wet; and they 'should be periodically washed down with some disinfectant and the walls, ceilings and floors regularly lime-washed'. Poor Gale!

But ultimately the economic factor was decisive. The cost of maintaining the stud, with the wages of six helpers, was £2500 a year, and against the uncertain hope of successful breeding it was too much. So on state occasions the creams were replaced by the bays and this part of the stud was broken up. One died and two were destroyed; two were retained at Hampton Court for work on the farm; seven were assigned to cavalry regiments as drum horses with the band, which at least was an honourable and traditional form of retirement; two were sold to golf clubs, which was not; ten went to auction at Coombe Farm; two were sold to the King of Spain and the rest to private owners like Drake and Lord John Sanger, the circus impresario.

The discarding of the creams and other reductions in the strength put a heavy strain on the stock that survived, and the Crown Equerry had to turn down an appeal for help from the Duke of Atholl, Lord High Commissioner for Scotland. As the King's representative the Commissioner had to maintain 'royal state' on certain occasions, and it was cripplingly expensive to provide an establishment of horses, carriages, liveries (some of which had to be specially hired), and servants for this limited use. Acting on a suggestion from the King's Secretary, he enquired what temporary help the Mews might be able to offer. There could be none. Fitzwilliam replied that the Secretary had forgotten that orders had been given 'to reduce everything at the Mews to the lowest. . . . If carriages, horses and servants were sent to Edinburgh, and his Majesty by chance should require any state ceremony, it would be very difficult to arrange it under the reduced conditions.'

In 1924 Fitzwilliam was succeeded as Crown Equerry by Colonel Arthur Erskine, R.A., who had been equerry-in-ordinary since the war. Knighted in 1931, he was to hold the office for seventeen years, after which he served as extra equerry to King George VI and to Queen Elizabeth II. He found that the tide of economy, so far from receding, was continuing to encroach upon his department. As soon as he took office he had to reply to a memorandum from the King's treasurer enquiring about the horse establishment. He reported that during the previous two and a half years 29 carriage horses had been disposed of, and in that period only four had been purchased and four transferred from Hampton Court. That left a total of 58, and Erskine pointed out that their average age was too high to give security for the future. There were 33 horses, or 60 per cent, over the age of 13, and 15 of them were unsound and could not be relied upon for work in 1925. Ideally there should not be more than 20 per cent of that age. He would like to have 40 per cent aged between 12 and 9, and another 40 per cent eight and younger, instead of the present 27 per cent and 13 per cent. He planned to dispose of the 15 unsound older horses and buy 14 of eight years and younger, at a total cost of £2100.

He did not think it possible to reduce the present establishment of 19 hacks. Eight of these were required for special purposes, leaving only 11 for general use assuming that all were fit. Standards of riding had evidently declined even among equerries and members of the Royal Family, because 'when the difficulty of mounting so very many different types of "horseman", some good and mostly bad, is added, the establishment of 19 is by no means excessive.'

237. *The 5th Marquess of Bath, Master from 1922 to 1924, photographed at the Bath and West Show.*

238. *Colonel Sir Arthur Erskine, Crown Equerry (on right), at a rehearsal for the wedding of the Duke of Kent and Princess Marina in 1934.*

Next year (1925) Erskine recommended that the breeding of Cleveland bays at Hampton Court should be given up because it was no longer producing the required results. Latterly only one suitable horse per year had come from the stud, and even these were cross-bred. As one stallion and at least ten mares had been maintained to produce this result, the stud was not justifying its existence. With the recent reduction in the establishment, it was essential that every horse at the Mews should be able to take his place in the drawing of heavy state coaches: which meant that he 'should be of considerable substance and 17 hands in height'. Even in Yorkshire, the home of the Cleveland bay, horses of the required size were rare, 'and it seems unreasonable to expect Hampton Court to produce what even Yorkshire cannot produce.' Most of the big horses at present in the stables had come from numerous sources, British and foreign, with no one breed predominating. They were 'exceptional' big horses of various breeds. Erskine therefore suggested that it was unsound to expect to breed a consistent supply of pure-bred horses of a particular type when in fact the need was for horses of abnormal size and strength. It would be more economical to buy.

Although he recognised that as an example to encourage the breeding of horses in England, the King might wish to continue to breed even at a financial loss, Erskine concluded that it was his duty to recommend the closure of the Cleveland bay stud and the acquisition of carriage horses 'by purchase alone'. Hampton Court should continue, however, to rear the stud-bred hacks, as these were normal horses which were easy to sell in the event of a surplus. The Department's annual requirement of hacks was quite small, so that there would be no need to breed on a large scale or to keep as many mares as at present.

Erskine's advice was not immediately accepted, but a letter in 1932 to the Vicar of Hampton Wick tells its own story:

> You are probably aware that owing to necessary economies which have had to be made by this Department, His Majesty has reluctantly had to give up more than half of the Royal Paddocks at Hampton Court, and the number of those employed on the estate has been very considerably reduced.
>
> In these circumstances, the continuation of the annual grant to your Parish of £45 per annum has been under consideration and I very much regret to inform you that owing to the fact that there are now only 5 men employed on the estate, the annual grant will in future be at the rate of £20 per annum.
>
> I need not say that it is only after very careful consideration that this decision has been arrived at.

In the recession of the 1930s – during which King George V set an example to the country by giving up a sizeable portion of his Civil List – even an economy as small as this was not to be neglected. The Mews had been asked to save a further £3000 a year, but in a letter to the Treasurer of the Household Erskine opposed a suggestion that the Department should no longer be given a definite allowance. Latterly it had had an allocation of £55,750 a year, and Erskine had been saving about £3500 of this 'for the use of other departments'. He had been able to do this because he had a definite budget to work on, and after each quarterly summary of the accounts he knew where he stood. 'Also this definite basis on which to work inculcated the necessary pride and stimulus to the department to try and produce a regular surplus.' As the new financial emergency would oblige him to achieve a further surplus of £3000, he asked for an allocation of £49,250.

At Hampton Court the King gave a large portion of the Royal Paddocks as a playground for the children of the neighbourhood and for use as public allotments, and with this contraction of the stud some shrewd dealing was necessary in the

239. *The Riding School at the Royal Mews, about 1920. From the window at the far end, Queen Victoria used to watch her children learning to ride.*

purchase of new horses. When Erskine consulted Mr Gerald Manley, F.S.A.A., he was advised that he would have to go to the Continent as so few harness horses were now being bred at home. Manley mentioned three dealers in Holland with whom the Crown Equerry was already in contact, but he had to confess that his own method might appear haphazard and costly. 'I buy when a nice animal comes along and then run it along with a view to it turning out what is required. I have arrived at the conclusion that we shall all have to do this if we are to get horses of substance, quality, action and courage.'

Even so, the process could not be hurried, because in Manley's experience 'a big horse worked before six years old tends to go all to pieces.' It was bound to be hazardous too: 'You are doubtless aware that a great drawback to big horses is their wind. One may buy them perfectly sound but if they happen to get a chill or anything goes wrong, they are apt to turn "roarers" and thus all one's trouble and expense is to no purpose, as they are then only fit for slow work on the land.'

With this discouraging counsel, and the reduction in the funds available for purchase, Erskine had to look more discerningly at the horses offered to him by the dealers in Holland. He was seldom able to afford the greys so temptingly suggested to him, although the stock at Windsor was gradually running down. One grey that he bought from Holland in 1933, a gelding 16.2 hands, had to be rejected after veterinary examination on arrival. Erskine was quite firm in his determination not to buy it, or to pay its passage back to Holland, despite the dealer's assertion that its troubles were temporary and trifling. Hacks and chargers from the army helped to keep the establishment at reasonable strength, but Erskine always asked to be allowed to try them first: 'owing to the fact that I have to mount people who are most indifferent riders, it is essential that any horse bought should really be of a quiet temperament.' In a note to the remount depot at Melton Mowbray he again mentions the problem of finding placid and sturdy mounts for the equerries, 'who are mostly on the heavy side and some of them by no means good horsemen'.

If maintaining the supply of horses in the face of financial pressure was the Crown Equerry's most anxious problem in these post-war years, the daily routine of the Department was still varied and unrelenting. A decade later the adventures of Gay Corinthian show in lighter relief, but it is unlikely that anyone at the Mews would have thought so at the time.

CHAPTER TWENTY-TWO Gay Corinthian

The story of Gay Corinthian is informative on the work of the Royal Mews and it is a little cliff-hanger in its own right.

Early in 1928 King Amanullah of Afghanistan made a state visit to Europe in which he was received by the governments of Britain, Italy, France and the USSR. Behind the diplomatic courtesies and the lavish entertainment some shrewd calculation was going on, and it was assumed that Amanullah would extend strategic and commercial privileges to the country that did most to help him in the programme of westernisation that he had planned on his return. It was announced that King George V proposed to present him with a horse: perhaps out of personal esteem for his erstwhile guest or perhaps because his ministers advised him that it would be a politic thing to do.

The horse selected was a four-year-old chestnut colt, Gay Corinthian, by Captivation out of Lady Nought, and the Master of the Horse's Department acquired it through Mr J. Aitken, of Black Bear Lane, Newmarket – 'the only Aitken in Newmarket', he said in a letter to Colonel Erskine, the Crown Equerry. It fell to the Colonel to arrange the horse's conveyance to Amanullah's capital at Kabul, and he began his negotiations in the spring of 1928, having been advised that climatically mid-October was the best time for the horse to arrive at Peshawar, just to the east of the Khyber Pass, to complete his journey by road. The military attaché at Kabul was willing to be responsible for organising this final stage, and Erskine was anxious to reduce the total costs by getting the horse on a troopship going to Karachi or Bombay. 'I expect it would be possible to find some "horsey" officer travelling on the same transport who would be only too glad to look after the horse on its sea journey.'

The Director of Movements and Quartering at the War Office was at once co-operative, but where government departments are concerned a certain duplication of effort is held to be necessary, and Erskine had to discover which Foreign Office official was 'in charge of Afghanistan affairs in London' and get in touch with him. By this means it was arranged that Gay Corinthian should travel on a troopship leaving Southampton on 9 October, due at Karachi on 30 October. This was the *City of Marseilles*, taking the 10th Hussars to Egypt and the 15/19th Hussars on from Egypt to Karachi. The horse would then travel to Peshawar by rail, and for this part of the journey Erskine had to request the staff of the Commander-in-Chief in India to make the necessary arrangements, the expenses to be met by King George.

Major Featherstonhaugh, who was currently looking after the horse at Windsor, was told of the intended programme, and after finding an officer to look after him during the sea journey as far as Egypt, Erskine approached the colonel commanding the 15/19th Hussars for someone to take over between Egypt and Karachi, adding that 'I am sure His Majesty would like to give him some small

240. King George V riding
'Arabian Night', one of his
favourite chargers, in Rotten Row.

present in acknowledgment of all the trouble taken.' The next difficulty was raised by the War Office, who said that the horse-boxes in Southampton were small and cramped 'and animals carried in them need constant exercise.' Deck space being limited on a transport ship, it was proposed, and agreed, that a loose-box be constructed at a cost of about £25 to the Royal Mews. A more serious blow was a War Office decision taken at the end of July to change the destination of the *City of Marseilles* to Bombay. Alternative transport was offered on a ship leaving in mid-September, but Erskine, confronted with the problem when on holiday in Scotland, decided to adhere to the original arrangement, as September was a very hot month in the Red Sea and the horse would be 'less likely to come to harm, even with a longer rail journey the other end', if he were landed at Bombay. Officers in India, Egypt and Kabul had then to be told of the change in programme, and also the insurance company that was covering the journey. For an additional £2 the cover was extended until 14 November.

The time was now coming to prepare for the horse's embarkation. The War Office directed the necessary stores to be put on board, 'one officer's chest, one field veterinary chest, 5 lbs Epsom Salts and 8 oz Potassii nitres', together with forage. The horse was required to be at Southampton by 11 a.m. on 9 October in readiness for departure at 3, and Captain Benbow, Superintendent at the Mews, asked the Southern Railway when, in that case, he should leave Newmarket. The operating superintendent at Waterloo undertook to deliver him at Southampton at 5.30 a.m. if he left Newmarket at 6.21 the previous evening. In agreeing to this proposal Erskine asked that the horse-box be 'thoroughly disinfected and cleaned' for the journey. Erskine received at the same time particulars of the very efficient instructions issued by the Director of Remounts in India for the journey from Bombay to Peshawar. There would be short halts at Ahmednagar and Babugarh, and the horse would be rested for a few days if there were any doubts about his fitness. The Indian Railway Board had offered to conduct this transportation without charge. It was also satisfactory that Lieutenant Nigel Courage, of the 15/19th Hussars, would be able to look after the horse for the whole journey as far as Bombay as he was at present at home on leave and would be returning by the same ship.

It was Gay Corinthian himself who introduced the next complication. He had not been behaving well during the idle months at Windsor, and Erskine confessed to Courage that he had been in training until he was purchased but 'when put out of work he started to abuse himself and began to go to bits'. He had been returned to Newmarket, and 'I understand he has stopped his tricks, but I thought I had better tell you in case he tries his games again on the journey.' Erskine ended this letter by asking Courage to give 'a handsome tip' to any men who might help to look after the horse during the voyage, and to claim for reimbursement of this and of any expenses he might himself incur. When the *City of Marseilles* was at sea, Erskine took the trouble to convey the King's appreciation of the arrangements made by the Commander-in-Chief's office at Simla for the horse's transportation in India. 'If he is pulled down by the sea journey, the excellent arrangements you have made for his recuperation if necessary at certain points on his journey to Peshawar should give him every chance of arriving safely.' On 6 November Erskine is acknowledging a message from the War Office that the ship has arrived at Bombay and the horse is on his way. This 'is very good news, and I am sure His Majesty will be very pleased about it when I tell him.' From Courage, too, came a report that Gay Corinthian 'behaved very well on the boat and gave no trouble'. Unfortunately Courage had not received the Crown Equerry's letter in time to reward Sergeant Doughty, late of the 14/20th Hussars, and 'a recruit from the regement' (sic) for their willing and expert assistance. Erskine at once sent £5 to be shared between the two men; and on learning that, contrary to the original intention, Courage had not taken over his duties until the ship reached Bombay, he enquired of the 10th Hussars which of their officers had been in charge during the voyage. He was Lieutenant David Dawnay.

The scene darkened with a letter written from Delhi on 22 November to say that, in the view of the British Legation at Kabul, 'if the horse could not reach Kabul by the 20th November, it should not be sent there until April next at the earliest owing to climatic conditions being unfavourable. It has, therefore, been decided to keep the animal in India until the spring, and the Foreign and Political Department have arranged to defray the expenses.' Erskine did not receive this letter until 10 December, by which time he had cabled for information, but he replied at once to say that he agreed with the decision and 'it is needless to say that if His Majesty's health had permitted me to speak to him on the subject, the King would concur.' This refers to King George's serious illness at the end of 1928, from which it was thought for a while that he would not recover. But just before he was taken ill the King asked for cuff-links to be sent to Courage and Dawnay as personal gifts in

recognition of their help with Gay Corinthian; and Erskine promptly arranged for their dispatch in the War Office 'bag'.

So the next communication is something of a shock. Written from the office of the Privy Purse on 15 January 1929, it begins: 'As King Amanullah has now abdicated, the question arises as to what is to become of the thoroughbred stallion which His Majesty gave King Amanullah in April last.' It was the familiar story of the oriental despot intoxicated with western ideas going too far and too fast. Amanullah had launched a programme of public works that a primitive country could not afford, and his trendy reforms – which included the introduction of the bowler hat – weakened the traditional hold of the Moslem priesthood and outraged convention by seeking to emancipate the female population. He was deposed by the bandit Bacca-i Saqaw acting in the clerical and feminine interest.

Vexed with a delicate problem, the Foreign Office, who apparently had paid the cost of the horse in the first place, resolved that as he had been a personal gift, he should be regarded as the ex-king's personal property, and should be kept in India 'until its rightful owner is able to claim it'.

It is quite possible, moreover, that we may still hear more of ex-King Amanullah and if so it would be injudicious to dispose of his horse now. . . . A decision not to deliver the gift after all would be interpreted (the Indian Press being what it is) as a sign that we were definitely against Amanullah and be cited as a further proof that we had started the rebellion.

241. King George V with 'Anzac' at the presentation of new standards to the Life Guards in 1927. Framed enlargements of this photograph and the one on page 313 were presented, with an inscribed scroll, by the staff of the Master of the Horse's Department to the King on the occasion of his Silver Jubilee in 1935.

242. King Amanullah and Queen Souriya of Afghanistan. Unfortunately, no photograph could be found of 'Gay Corinthian'.

243 (left). Photograph from 'The Field' in 1919 of the black Arabian thoroughbred stallion 'Soueidan', presented to King George V by King Hussein of the Hedjaz. A 7-year-old, 15 hands, it took its brood-name by Bedouin tradition from its dam, Saada.

244. 'Red Knight' and 'Beaucaire', Cleveland bays owned by King George V, which won 1st and 2nd prizes at the Richmond Royal Horse Show in 1928.

Erskine endorsed this assessment, and Gay Corinthian remained at the Hapur remount depot near Delhi at the expense of the Indian government. Amanullah was briefly heard of again when he unsuccessfully attempted a counter-revolution later in the year, and he lived another thirty years without recovering his throne. When the horse had originally been detained at Delhi in the autumn, Erskine had prudently extended the insurance cover until midnight on 30 April, and only a week before its expiry he told the company that he did not intend to renew it. Presumably he thought that this would in future be the concern of the officials in India.

On 27 May he received another laconic note from the office of the Privy Purse: 'The Foreign Office have reported that they have received information from India that the King's horse died from biliary fever.' Communications were not rapid, especially when they had to pass from one department to another, and Erskine's concern now was to discover on what date the horse died. Tantalisingly, the Foreign Office so far could only deduce 'from the context' that he died on 29 or 30 April or 1 May, but a cable in the name of the Viceroy in person said that 30 April was the date and a veterinary certificate would follow to confirm it. So Erskine was able to close the file by reporting these facts to the London and Lancashire Insurance Co, of Chancery Lane, and asking 'whether I have to fill up any form to claim the insurance amount of £400'.

Doubtless he had to fill in several, but he had been doing it for months. For several government departments and army headquarters, both at home and abroad, the amount of work involved by the episode of Gay Corinthian is astonishing. The Royal Mews, at the hub of it all, had to carry most of the burden, and the Crown Equerry and his staff wrote literally dozens of letters to ensure that the business should run smoothly. Two things stand out: the patient attention to detail which did not flag when various setbacks caused the plans to be altered; and, once again, the unfailing courtesy and thoughtfulness of the Department, which never omitted to acknowledge the help given by other people and even remembered to transmit a reward to Sergeant Doughty and his unnamed recruit. It may be that for a relatively simple matter the paperwork and the protocol were excessive, but on the part of the Royal Mews this was a model of efficient administration.

Although no other episode had quite the same concentrated drama, various incidents large and small punctuated the routine of looking after horses, providing transport and organising Ascot processions and birthday parades. The Department was immediately involved in the General Strike of May 1926 because Hyde Park was closed to the public and application had to be made to the London County Council for the horses to be allowed to exercise in Battersea Park instead. The staff of the Mews volunteered as special constables, ten Oxford undergraduates were given beds and meals, and the Commissioner of Police used the Mews as the headquarters of a special troop of mounted constabulary. During the strike the King and Queen three times came personally to the Mews, and the King afterwards expressed his thanks for the loyal and cheerful service given in the crisis by members of the Household departments.

Gifts of horses and carriages were now rarer than they had been in more opulent times, but the people of South Australia presented a bay gelding called Erskine and in a characteristic gesture the King made a personal gift to the groom who had escorted him from Adelaide. Splendid gifts of an Arab thoroughbred from Sheikh Ahmed ibn Jabir of Kuwait and two from King Hussein of the Hedjaz were accompanied by detailed pedigrees and an account of what these signified: namely that all pure-bred Arabs were descended from seven very beautiful animals selected for breeding in the time of the Prophet, and although there had been many offshoots, only the stock of these seven families were regarded as genuine thoroughbreds. In their traditional way the Arab tribes were concerned only to preserve the purity of their stock, and they would not try to improve it by introducing new blood. The pure breed descended in the female line, and in pedigrees the mare was given pre-eminence. Animals named after their sires were not called horses but 'sons of horses', meaning that they were got by a pure-bred sire out of an inferior mare. For this reason the horses now given to the King took their brood names from the dam.

An historic carriage was given to Queen Mary by Lord Albemarle, himself the descendant of an earlier Master. This was a semi-state road landau built in 1830 by Adams & Hooper of the Haymarket on the instructions of the Duchess of Kent, mother of Queen Victoria. It was used by the Duke of Cambridge at the coronation of King William IV. But although the Mews was always anxious to replenish stock by any means, even gift horses had to be looked in the mouth. There was an interesting case of this in 1933 when Lady Sybil Grant, daughter of the late Earl of Rosebery, wrote from The Durdans at Epsom to offer a horse that had drawn her father's carriage in the years before his death. It was impracticable to keep horses at the Mews unless they were serviceable, and Erskine replied that 'owing to recent economies, I now have to try and buy one type of horse, namely one which will do for both state carriage work and, if necessary, for outrider work, which means buying horses about 16.2 hands.' He went with the superintendent to Epsom and found that this horse was only 16 hands, and although powerful would not fit into any of the teams. But the matter was happily settled when Erskine found out that the King would be pleased to have him for work in the gardens at Sandringham.

King George V's deep personal interest in horses is evident in his generosity to societies and private owners who were trying to preserve the great native breeds. He gave two challenge cups for Cleveland bays, he bought Fell ponies whenever they could be afforded, and when, in the financial crisis of the 1930s, the government's subsidy to the Fell Pony Society was withdrawn, his gift of money was the means of saving a valuable pony stallion called Black Lingdropper. The King regularly entered his bays at the Richmond Royal Horse Show, of which he was a patron, and in 1928 his two Yorkshire coach horses, Red Knight and Beaucaire, both won prizes. It was not only in horse-breeding that the King was eager to help and encourage his people. In 1930 Messrs Stratton-Instone, who supplied the royal Daimlers, wrote to say that in the current depression in the motor industry nothing could do more to stimulate interest and reduce unemployment than for the King to let it be known that he proposed to order new cars before the motor show in October. Thereupon five new cars were ordered.

Building on the example laid down by the Earl of Huntingdon in 1760, the Mews kept records of the arrangements made for big public events, and for future reference made a note of anything that went wrong. To the spectator of these events everything must have appeared to be going without a hitch, but the organisers watched with a more critical eye, and the great increase in London traffic was apt to create difficulties that could not have been foreseen. Erskine made some acid comments after the arrival of Prince and Princess Takamatsu of Japan in 1930:

> The Police did not keep Eccleston Bridge clear of traffic as on previous similar occasions. This is absolutely essential if the carriage procession is a large one.
>
> The Carriages came down Hudson's Lane to the Station too soon. Unless special instructions are given, the processional carriages should not leave Eccleston Bridge till the Royal Special actually arrives.
>
> Coachman Baker, driving the Master of the Horse's carriage, arrived at Victoria Station by the wrong entrance from Eccleston Bridge. This must not be allowed as it is apt to block traffic.
>
> In spite of the Crown Equerry writing personally to the Comptroller to Prince George saying that a Standard should be flown on Prince George's car, this was not done.

When the Prince of Wales returned from a Commonwealth tour in 1925, spectators in the forecourt of the Palace were not kept back from the roadway and some were nearly knocked down; provision for reversing the carriages at Victoria station was inadequate; and the route afterwards taken to the Palace could be improved upon. One year even the ceremony of Trooping the Colour left much to be desired:

None of the Princes or Staff saluted when 'God save the King' was played after the Ensign had taken over the Colour from the Regimental Sergeant Major. *This should be rectified next year.*

It would be better another year if it was explained to the Princes and Colonels of Regiments that they should turn into the Forecourt on return to the Palace through the South Gate after passing His Majesty, and not through the Centre Gate. This will make it easier for them to form up behind the King.

On return to the Palace, the Crown Equerry's Horseholder should be ready to take the Crown Equerry's horse in the Forecourt and not in the Quadrangle.

On the King going into the Quadrangle after the Household Cavalry had marched past, the Royal Salute was given by the Bugler at the Palace at the same time as the 'God save the King' was played by the band, which the King did not like.

Try and get the Bugler dispensed with altogether next year.

Make sure that the Brigade Major understands that the King goes his own pace down the Mall and that the Brigade Major must keep his proper distance from the King and not expect the King to keep his distance from the Brigade Major.

Even the last great solemnity of the reign, the King's funeral in 1936, was marred, in Erskine's never very euphoric view, by some court ladies who underestimated the traffic and dislocated the schedule by failing to reach the Palace

245. *The staff of the Master of the Horse's Department photographed at the Royal Mews in 1935 by Mrs Broom (who must have been forgiven for her earlier misdemeanour). The Master, Lord Granard, and the Crown Equerry, Sir Arthur Erskine, are seated fourth and fifth from right in the front row.*

on time. 'It would have been better to have ordered motors instead of carriages and still better to have advised the ladies to have slept the night previously south of the processional route.'

In numerous ways the Department was always alert to investigate new methods, whether mechanical inventions or veterinary techniques, that might be more economical or efficient. It might be a urine test to discover whether a newly-purchased mare was in foal or a delicate operation on a horse suffering from an undiagnosed malady; or a safety signalling device for motor cars marketed by a firm in Louth; or the 'Centaur Groom', an electric cleaner devised in Reading for scouring horses' coats and removing dead hairs and dirt grease that escaped the manual 'strapping' performed by the grooms. Many were rejected after experiment, but tests and demonstrations were never refused by a forward-looking Department intent upon perfecting its service.

In a sense this was an aspect of the patience and courtesy shown to anyone who came to the Mews with a request or a grievance, however trivial. Perhaps it was easy enough to display this in the ample days before 1914 when time and labour were accessible commodities, and some examples have been noted in an earlier chapter. But it continued in the more stringent days after the war, and it went far beyond the standard civilities owed by any organisation which is in the public eye. It is easy enough to find measured and courteous terms for declining a request and thereafter burying it; and quite another matter to treat any application irrespective of its apparent merits, seek expert opinion, write, when necessary, to a secretary at the Palace to ascertain the wishes of the Sovereign, and hold the attitude of wanting to say yes rather than no. After appropriate enquiry the Crown Equerry was nearly always authorised to say yes. This was still, as it had been before 1914, such a conspicuous quality of the Master of the Horse's Department that it is worth illustrating with some random examples.

Several go back to the immediate post-war years. Gerald du Maurier writes from Wyndham's Theatre to thank the Crown Equerry for the loan of a horse for the children at the theatrical orphanage; three carriages, with horses, liveries and coachmen, were lent for a 'parade of historic coaches' staged at the Olympia horse show; when the Treasury refused any longer to authorise payment for ladies-in-waiting travelling on duty to and from Windsor, the Crown Equerry softened the blow by laying on transport for their luggage; the Samuelson Film Company, making a film of Queen Victoria's coronation, were sufficiently interested in authentic detail to enquire whether the Duke of Wellington and his old enemy Marshal Soult were mounted or rode in carriages, and Fitzwilliam discovered that Soult went by carriage, but he was unable to find any record for Wellington – although 'probably he rode on horseback as a member of the Military Staff'; Morris, Russell & Co. were allowed to photograph the motor-car mascot which they had presented to the King many years before as a coronation gift; within a couple of years of each other Charles Glasgow of Paisley and H. H. Smith of London constructed models of the state coaches in the Mews, and were given every facility and encouragement by the Crown Equerry, who showed photographs to the King; enormous trouble was taken to establish the provenance of a 1910 Daimler acquired by the Los Angeles Museum, and by finding the chassis number in his files, Erskine was able to verify that it was a car that had been used by the King between 1911 and 1924; on condition that the fact should not be advertised, Erskine obtained the Queen's consent for a new royal car built by Hooper & Co. of St James's to be displayed at the motor show of 1935; when an American polo team came over to play a series of matches in England, arrangements were made for them to keep their fifty ponies in the stables at Hampton Court and to exercise in Bushey Park. Mostly these are trivial matters, but a busy and understaffed Department gave them consideration far beyond the call of duty. When in 1935 the Marquess of Linlithgow went to be Viceroy of India, he approached Erskine because he would need cars of abnormal height for his public duties and he had heard that his predecessor, Lord Willingdon, had bought two Daimlers from the Mews which would otherwise have gone to the dealers in part-exchange. Erskine replied that two of the royal Daimlers were in the course of being replaced and he offered to arrange for Linlithgow to inspect them; adding that even the smaller of the two might be suitable for his requirements 'as you can certainly wear a top hat inside it'.

Characteristic, too, was the correspondence with Sir Reginald Tuck of the famous firm of Raphael Tuck & Sons, Ltd, who in 1932 sought and were granted permission to make a set of coloured postcards of the Mews. This meant a lot of additional work for the staff, who had to prepare the carriages, put on their own liveries, and stand patiently while the photographer arranged things to his liking; and for the Crown Equerry also, as the captions printed on the cards had to be historically correct. (A set of the postcards, 49 in number, would if it were still obtainable, give a miniature history of the Royal Mews.) Tuck presented a complete album to the King, and Erskine wrote to say that he 'went through all the photographs one by one with me and he asked me to tell you that he thought the postcards quite wonderful and that they would form an unique record of the carriages, horses and harness in use during his reign.'

The innate humanity and courtesy of the men who ran this Department went naturally with a high sense of personal duty to the Sovereign and continuing responsibility to the public. It was not the flatulent urbanity of men who did not care. Wrong inferences should not be drawn from the Department's policy of accepting responsibility rather than involving servants of the Crown in litigation and public dispute. (As an example of this: in 1932 there was a collision between a royal brougham and a taxi, and a firm of coachbuilders sent an account for 30s. for bringing home the damaged carriage and an estimate of £90 15s. 0d. for mending it.

The Crown Equerry's only public comment on this was a letter, on the morning after the accident, to the Superintendent of Gerald Road police station asking him to 'thank Police Constable 291 "B" Sears for his able assistance in stopping the horse. I am sorry to hear that he was slightly hurt and I only trust it was really nothing much. It is mainly due to this Police Constable that the accident was not more serious, and I would be glad if you would kindly convey to him personally my appreciation of his valuable services.') However, the Department could still be polite but firm when circumstances demanded it.

Among four disparate examples, Erskine took his complaint straight to the King's Secretary when in 1930 a horse kept in the Palace Gardens was injured in his loose-box. As well as authorising medical treatment, Erskine went to see where the accident had happened, and he reported that this loose-box 'is a place in which no horse ought to be kept. I expect it was originally a potting shed and was converted into a horse box in the dark ages.' The shed was gloomy and ill-sited, and it was served by an ancient drain that was partially blocked. 'While on the subject, I should also add that I happened to see the hay which is issued out by the Office of Works to the garden horse. It is disgraceful! It isn't really hay at all but merely some sort of herbage which is musty and rank and not fit for consumption.' Erskine offered to keep the horse at the Mews until proper accommodation should be provided, although he was under no obligation to do this. 'I am at present', he added, 'feeding the horse on Royal Mews hay.'

He was willing to do battle with local authorities as well as with other departments. In 1932 he asked the surveyor of the Westminster City Council to warn motorists to relax their speed when rounding the corner leading from Lower Grosvenor Place into Buckingham Palace Road. This caused danger to themselves and to carriages leaving or entering the Mews, as cars did not give themselves time to pull up before they reached the gates. He therefore suggested a SLOW sign in steel block letters in the roadway before the corner. On 27 February the city surveyor replied that the proposal would be laid before the appropriate committee 'in due course'. This meant six weeks, after which the town clerk reported that the committee, obliged by economy to reduce expenditure, thought that it would be sufficient to instruct the constable on duty 'at or near the position' to deal with any case of excessive speed. That was fine, Erskine replied, when there was a constable on duty at the Mews gates, but the committee appeared to have missed the point which 'I explained verbally to their representative who came to see me about it. . . . The danger occurs when there is no Constable on duty.' Vehicles started entering and leaving the Mews at 6 a.m., and sometimes the last carriage did not come in until midnight. At present the police provided a man for special duty for eight hours a day, and it seemed unreasonable to ask for a longer period 'when a simple permanent device at the corner would solve the problem.' 'In due course' the council surrendered to this logic.

The Department's duty to give advice on the issue of royal warrants re-introduces the firm of Campbell's of Bon Accord, Aberdeen, who will be remembered as catering for the delicate requirements of Lady Knollys when she visited Balmoral. Great care was taken by all the Household departments in the issue of these warrants, which in a sense gave valuable 'consumer protection' by guaranteeing the quality of the goods or services provided. They were granted to individuals rather than to firms, and a renewed application had to be made whenever a change of management occurred, especially when a private firm converted itself into a public company; and they were liable to be withdrawn when the Household had ceased to use the product for a period of years. In 1930 Mr John

Graham, who had been managing director of Campbell's in the exigent days of Lady Knollys, reported that he had left the firm owing to illness but on recovering his health had started his own company, the Graham Motor Cab Co. He accordingly asked for Campbell's warrant to be transferred to himself; adding that Campbell's were still displaying the royal coat-of-arms even though he understood that their warrant had become void on his own resignation as managing director and that an application for its renewal had been refused.

The Lord Chamberlain's office advised that the Royal Warrant Holders Association be asked to deal with Campbell's alleged misuse of the royal arms, while the Crown Equerry told Graham that the granting of his application was 'out of the question, as there is a very strict rule laid down that no Royal Warrants can be granted to any new Company. All new Companies have to do satisfactory work for his Majesty for at least three years before an application can be considered.' Graham was reluctant to accept this. He pointed out first that although the royal arms had been removed from their premises, Campbell's were still displaying them on their vehicles. 'The chairman is a lawyer and thinks himself clever. I hope you will deal firmly with them. Please don't say I wrote you.' Then he went on to press his own claim to a warrant, basing it on a recital of his wartime services in the equestrian cause. Aberdeen, he added, now had no warrant-holder, and as a former president of the Royal Tradesmen's Association he thought he should have the first claim. Erskine terminated the correspondence by firmly telling him that 'it is impossible to hold out any prospect of your request being granted, owing to the fact that your new firm does not fulfil the conditions under which a Royal Warrant is granted.'

Finally, in the same eventful year, there was the forceful episode of the cardseller. It began with a complaint from a lady who alleged that she had been insulted by a woman selling postcards at the Royal Mews. The complainant, who said that she was herself an exservicewoman, ' the first English army sister under fire in France', understood from the staff and other visitors that such behaviour was habitual, and she thought it outrageous that visitors, who were 'the King's guests', should be abused in this way. The complaint was taken very seriously and the *vendeuse,* a Mrs Broom living in Fulham (whom we now know to have been a versatile photographer of some importance), had to explain herself to the Queen's Private Secretary. She stated that 'the incident complained of' started when a lady visitor wanted a more recent postcard of their Majesties than any that was on sale.

> I explained I only sold photographs I had had the honour of taking myself, but she could possibly obtain them from some firm outside the Royal Mews. The lady insisted that she intended to obtain one on the premises and became difficult to understand. So out of keeping with the dignity of their Majesties' Household were her criticisms and manner that, at last, rightly or wrongly I told the lad assisting not to serve the lady. She then said she would write to the Queen and see that I lost my position.
>
> During the, at least, twenty five years I have been permitted in the Royal Mews I have not experienced a similar situation and can only plead that my act was not one of anger, but of righteous indignation, and had no thought in any way of incurring their Majesties' displeasure.

Erskine regretted having to inform her that he had no choice but to withdraw her permit to take or sell photographs on behalf of the Royal Mews. 'I quite realise that the lady who made the complaint may be of an excitable nature, but the heated wrangle which took place shows clearly that his Majesty's best interests will not be served by allowing you to continue to hold the special privilege you have hitherto enjoyed.'

But the blow was softened by a characteristic piece of thoughtfulness. Erskine

246. *Ascot landau driven by postilion riders wearing Royal Ascot livery, at the Royal Mews, Windsor.*

247. *Clarence and early motor-cars at the Royal Mews.*

offered to buy the lady's existing stock of postcards and also any plates of photographs 'that relate to the Royal Mews and are of modern interest'. He was obliged to refuse, however, the lady's request to be allowed to see the letter of complaint as it was a confidential communication and 'I went as far as I could in reading you the substance of it'. He wished her to know that it was not on the unsupported complaint of this letter that he had come to his decision. The conflicting versions offered by the two principals make it impossible to decide where the blame really lay, but it is a fair assumption that the Crown Equerry was largely influenced by the feeling that, whatever the rights and wrongs of the matter, unseemly outbreaks of this kind could not be tolerated on premises of the Crown.

It was the Crown Equerry, and no longer the Master of the Horse, who – after consultation where necessary with the Sovereign or other Household offices – now made the decisions affecting the administration of the Department. This came about when in the 1920s the Master's office was re-defined and he ceased to have executive authority over the stables establishment. While he retained his ancient and honourable duty of personal attendance upon the Sovereign on state occasions, his former administrative functions passed to the Royal Mews as the transport office of the Royal Household.

One advantage of this was that the office could cease to be a political appointment. In King Edward VII's reign the Earl of Sefton had replaced the Duke of Portland in the usual way when the Liberals came into power in 1905–6, and this continued to be the system until 1924. Lord Sefton was succeeded after two years by the Earl of Granard, who held the post until the fall of Asquith's government in 1915. Until the end of the Coalition in 1922 the Master was the tenth Earl of Chesterfield, and his Conservative successor, the fifth Marquis of Bath, resigned when the Socialists took office in 1924. It was at this point that the pattern was broken, almost a hundred years after the Duke of Dorset had resigned because he would find it impossible to work with Canning. The Socialists agreed to the re-appointment of Lord Granard, who was Master through all subsequent political changes until the death of King George V in 1936. So long as he is willing to sit in the Lords as a cross-bencher and does not vote against the government, the Master is no longer affected by the rise and fall of ministries.

CHAPTER TWENTY-THREE

The Beaufort Era

Edward VIII, the ten-month King, intended to change many things. Although forty-one years of age, he still thought of himself as a man of a new progressive generation dedicated to social justice and pragmatic reforms. He disliked the stuffiness of some of his ministers, he had been resentful of his father's stern rectitude, and if he had had any understanding of the magnificent professionalism his mother had brought to her sovereign role, he would not have forfeited his throne in the way he did.

The King's youthful intrepidity in the hunting field had alarmed his advisers, but although he always enjoyed his sport, for his official duties he preferred cars and aeroplanes to horses, and he seemed to be impatient of ceremonial. From the pomps of palace life he liked to slip away to 'Fort Belvedere' at Sunningdale, in the environs of Windsor Great Park; there was a romantic escapist unreality even in the name of this unfortified retreat.

On 4 July 1936, in succession to Lord Granard, King Edward appointed as his Master of the Horse Henry Hugh Arthur Fitzroy, tenth Duke of Beaufort. The 'Keeper' of the royal stables first came to be known as the 'Master' during the lifetime of John of Gaunt and, with the strange continuity that persists through the ramifications of English history, it is a direct descendant who is Master at the present day. Six hundred years since the office was formally created, its essential concept lives on in the Duke of Beaufort: kinsman, personal friend and servant of the Sovereign, courtier, knight of the shires, soldier, horseman and huntsman. One of his forebears, the fourth Earl of Worcester, was Master to Queen Elizabeth I and James I; his grandfather, the eighth duke, twice held the office in Queen Victoria's reign; and his wife is a grand-daughter of the Duke of Westminster who was Master from 1880 to 1885.

Although, unlike his grandfather, the Duke does not consider himself to be a racing man, he has achieved renown as a huntsman, having been Master of the Beaufort pack for over fifty seasons. There have been hounds at Badminton since the house was built in the time of Charles II, and until 1760, when fox-hunting was introduced, they chased the red deer. The fox-hound pedigrees read back as far as 1770.

The Duke has also maintained the interest in cricket that has been shown by many of the great landed families. There was a time when the hiring of a groom would be influenced by the man's usefulness as a cricketer, and this might well have applied at Badminton, where until the post-war years the stables staff fielded their own team. A life-time supporter and one-time President of Gloucestershire County Cricket Club, the Duke still takes a great interest in the Club's progress. In coronation year he was President of the MCC.

The equestrian world regards Badminton as the home of the three-day event: a

248. The Duke of Beaufort,
Master of the Horse, saluting Her
Majesty the Queen as she arrives at
Westminster Abbey for her
Coronation, 1953.

sport which in the past two decades has brought more international honours to this
country than any other. The Duke first became aware of this all-round test of
horsemanship during the 1948 Olympic Games, at Aldershot, and felt that it was a
sport at which the British should excel. He invited the British Horse Society to run
an Event on his estate in 1949, and from small beginnings it has become one of the
great occasions of the year.

The presence of the Queen and other members of the Royal Family – and in
recent years the success of Princess Anne as a competitor – has heartened everyone
who cares about the equestrian tradition in Britain. Here the wheel turns full circle.
In the introduction to this book it was mentioned that the office of Master of the
Horse 'has usually been most solid and secure and successful when the incumbent
and the Sovereign have shared a personal interest in horses and have been able to
ride them.' No Queen in history has been a keener supporter of equitation or a more
accomplished horsewoman than Queen Elizabeth II, and none has given more

grace and dignity to the splendours of State. No Master has provided such steadfast support over so many years.

Within a few weeks of his appointment the Duke showed his knowledgeable eye for a horse when at a show he saw the potentialities of Cherry Grove, a chestnut charger in the service of the Chief Constable of Salford. On his recommendation the Crown Equerry (Sir Arthur Erskine) bought Cherry Grove for the King's own use. Here was a foretaste of the services he has given during his long tenure of the office. Although for the past half-century the daily running of the Master of the Horse's Department has been in the hands of the Crown Equerry, the Duke's expert knowledge and his personal interest in the men, the horses and the carriages has helped to preserve its historical identity during a period of rapid change.

King Edward VIII decided to close the Mews at Windsor and to transfer the staff and horses to London, but Trooping the Colour and Royal Ascot took place as usual in the only summer of his reign, and on a humbler level the Crown Equerry had the satisfaction of negotiating a safer access to the Royal Mews in London. Slow-moving carriage traffic was increasingly put at hazard by the motor-car, and in order to get something done he had to involve himself in correspondence with two successive Ministers of Transport, Hore-Belisha and Burgin. To Hore-Belisha he wrote: 'Everything outside my door that could be knocked down by a car has now been demolished by a car from time to time, lamp-post, pillar-box twice, and the railings three times, and a child pinned between a car and the actual stone pillar of the doorway, quite apart from constant skids on to the pavement.' A fatal accident seemed to be inevitable unless the camber were corrected and some more significant improvement effected than a white line in the middle of the road. It took more than two years before Burgin was able to report that the Westminster City Council, who had been steadily professing their lack of money, had succumbed to ministerial pressure and agreed to install traffic-lights to slow the cars.

The great event of 1937 was the coronation of King George VI, at which the Duke of Beaufort, as Master of the Horse, rode at the right of the royal carriage, behind the field officer of the escort but in front of 'Gold Stick'. Gold Stick-in-Waiting was a relatively new office, instituted in the reign of King William IV as a means of communication between the Monarch and the Army Council. It was held in monthly rotation by the colonels of the three regiments of household cavalry, and on ceremonial occasions the present incumbent carried a gold rod. But there were links with the much older office of the captaincy of the King's Gentlemen-at-Arms, and it was on this basis that Gold Stick had unsuccessfully but persistently claimed precedence over the Master.

In the autumn a state visit by the King of the Belgians again required a carriage procession, but the Crown Equerry also had his less exacting tasks, such as giving permission for boys to assemble at the Royal Mews before going on one of the camps which King George VI had fostered and personally attended when Duke of York. From Herbert Wilcox came a request for permission to borrow a suitable carriage for the scene of the Diamond Jubilee in the film 'Victoria the Great', in which Anna Neagle played the Queen, and he was granted the use of a postilion semi-state landau on condition that he would be responsible for its transportation to and from Denham Studios.

The organisation of state ceremonial continued to have its problems, and Sir Arthur Erskine noted several defects in the arrangements for the visit of the President of the French Republic, M. Lebrun, in March 1939. The troubles began on the special train which took the visitors from Dover to Victoria. The President and his wife and four ministers were to change their clothes during the journey, and

249 (top) Illustration from a scroll in the Print Room at Windsor Castle showing part of the coronation procession in 1937. The Master (no. 22) rode behind the Standard and before the Royal Dukes.

250. Their Majesties King George VI and Queen Elizabeth in procession at Royal Ascot in 1948. The Duke of Beaufort is opposite the King.

251 (overleaf). Badminton House in the 1740s, by Canaletto. The painting was commissioned by the 4th Duke of Beaufort.

State Coach conveying Their Majesties King George VI. & Queen Elizabeth

special labels were issued for the luggage required for this purpose. Unfortunately the entire French suite made use of these 'Wanted on Train' labels, with the result that the corridors were congested with their baggage. At Victoria 'the cavalry escort arrived 7 minutes late at the station in spite of written orders that they should arrive 20 minutes before the Special Train was due to arrive', and the Crown Equerry had sharp words with the adjutant of the Life Guards about this. Full of apologies, the adjutant could not understand the delay, since the escort had set out in good time: 'The only reason I can think of is that Colonel Thorp's horse is an exceptionally slow walker.' Next the Guard of Honour left the station immediately after the royal cars, thus obstructing the departure of the Prime Minister, the Foreign Secretary and other statesmen. The ministers' cars were further delayed because the luggage wagons set out too soon and blocked a narrow thoroughfare.

In the procession from Victoria Station the Master of the Horse rode in the third carriage, immediately behind the President and the Royal Family, accompanying M. Georges Bonnet, the French Foreign Minister, and two of the visiting wives, Madame la Générale Braconnier and Madame Loze. As the Royal Family were not present in a subsequent procession to the Guildhall, the Master represented the King and travelled in the leading coach with the President and Madame Lebrun. The Master's particular association with the Sovereign in such events was demonstrated again at Trooping the Colour, which proved to be the last before the outbreak of World War 2. In the King's absence the parade was taken by the Duke of Gloucester, and for that reason the Master, together with Gold Stick and certain other officers, did not attend.

Although Sir Arthur Erskine made his usual punctilious notes to prevent the recurrence of the hitches that – for the few people aware of them – had marred the French visit, it was to be several years before London again saw a state occasion on the grand scale, and by that time he had retired.

With the outbreak of war, Major G. Hopkins, the Superintendent at the Royal Mews, left immediately to rejoin his regiment, and all the younger men at the Mews soon followed him. The Crown Equerry and the horses moved to Windsor, and the Department was reduced to a skeleton staff just sufficient for its continuing transport duties.

For security reasons, there is little record of the wartime years. The whereabouts and journeys of the Royal Family had to be a closely guarded secret. But there was plenty to be done. Although the King and Queen stayed at Windsor during the worst of the bombing, they remained in London throughout most of the war and shared the sufferings of their people. They personally had a narrow escape when in 1940 six bombs were dropped on the Palace during a daylight raid. This incident led to a reappraisal of safety measures, and in the Mews two Daimler cars were reinforced with protective armour.

Care was also taken for the safety of the valuable and historic carriages kept at the Royal Mews, and it is surprising that it was not until the autumn of 1941 that any of them was moved out of London. With the co-operation of the Ministry of Works, plans were then made to transfer the gold state coach to the Earl of Rosebery's property at Mentmore in Buckinghamshire. As it was 13 feet high, alterations had to be made to the coach-house that was to accommodate it, and the route had to be carefully chosen to avoid low bridges. Because of the Cipriani paintings on the coach, it was imperative that the accommodation should be absolutely free from damp, and here it was fortunate that staff of the National Portrait Gallery were at Mentmore looking after paintings that were being stored there. They took the coach under their charge throughout its stay, maintaining a day-and-night guard.

252. Preparations at the Royal Mews on the morning of the Silver Wedding celebrations of Her Majesty the Queen and His Royal Highness Prince Philip.

253. Postilions in State Livery, June 1953. From left to right: J. Parkes, E. Long, A. Preece and A. Weddell.

The state liveries and harness were taken from London to Windsor, and after further investigation – the riding-school at Mentmore was not large enough – it was decided to move six of the other carriages to Ascot. These travelled, under police escort, on consecutive days, for if they went in convoy a bomb from a marauding raider might cause catastrophic damage. Sir Arthur Erskine being the man he was, letters of thanks were sent to the police authorities, the removal men (with a tip), the Ministry of Works, Lord Rosebery's agent at Mentmore and everyone else concerned in the operation. There remained the question of paying for it, including the structural alterations made at Mentmore, and the Treasurer of the Household was of the opinion that this was not the responsibility of the Privy Purse. 'What he feels on the subject is that the cost of protecting state property from enemy damage is not one which it was ever contemplated that the Civil List should have to bear.' If the Ministry of Works would not accept it, an application should be made to the Treasury.

Sir Arthur's successor as Crown Equerry was Colonel (later Sir) Dermot McMorrough Kavanagh, an Irishman from County Carlow whose ancestors had been Kings of Leinster at the time of Henry II's invasion. An official visit by the Regent of Iraq in 1943 involved a little of the pomp of earlier days, and the Crown Equerry had to supply cars and chauffeurs, and also to transport some of the guests to the official reception at the Palace.

Not long afterwards, Colonel Kavanagh was preparing for peace, and his first concern was to get the coaches back to London. At the end of May 1945 the Mentmore operation took place in reverse. The gold state coach returned unharmed, and the Director of the National Portrait Gallery was sincerely thanked for the assistance given by his staff, all ex-servicemen, who had tended it over the years, keeping it aired and dry and always at a suitable temperature.

The post-war period began with an interesting innovation in the Royal Mews, when the Crown Equerry decided that it would be appropriate to have a woman on his staff. Thus in 1946 arrived Miss Winifred Bateson, a former Section Officer in the WAAF. She was to be Chief Clerk for twenty years: the only woman to have held an administrative post in the Department. Her arrival more or less coincided with the return of the carriages, harness and liveries from Ascot and Windsor to London – and the Royal Mews was ready once again to bring colour and pageantry to an exhausted nation.

It is important to remember how much this meant after the long khaki-clad years with the shortages and the black-outs, and how much it meant especially to Londoners lately condemned to a troglodyte existence in the Underground stations. With great professional discipline the Mews was able in a very short time, quite literally, to 'get the show on the road'. The historic ceremonies of Trooping the Colour and the State Opening of Parliament were at once revived, and in 1946 Royal Ascot almost recovered its traditional splendour, since for some strange bureaucratic reason headgear had never been subject to clothing coupons. The occasion found the Master in his traditional place, riding in the leading carriage with the King and Queen and Viscount Lascelles.

On their visit to South Africa early in 1947 Their Majesties went in procession from the Palace to Waterloo Station, and later in the year London was *en fête* again with the marriage of Princess Elizabeth to Prince Philip of Greece. No duty imposed on the Crown Equerry can ever be surprising, and Colonel Kavanagh had to apply to the Ministry of Fuel and Power for petrol coupons for the Princess's use on her honeymoon. By this time a Socialist government had imposed bread-rationing on a country that had avoided it under the threat of Hitler, and the hotel

254 (left). Stables at Badminton, familiar to competitors at the Three-Day Event.

255. Mounted policeman at the Royal Mews with his horse Usher, ridden by the Master at Trooping the Colour in 1974.

256 (overleaf). Coronation procession, 1953, showing the Gold State Coach escorted by Yeomen of the Guard and carriage footmen. The Master of the Horse is directly behind the Standard. The coach was drawn by eight grey geldings, five of which (including the two in the picture) were presented to King George VI by Queen Wilhelmina of the Netherlands.

where the royal chauffeur stayed in nearby Romsey demanded nine bread units, seven 'points' and a tea coupon.

During the war, beset with the difficulties of feeding and replacement the royal stables had inevitably run down, and native breeding of large carriage horses had virtually ceased. As we know, the Mews required animals of a minimum height of 16.2 hands, and as well as being of strong bone and straight action they needed to be long behind the saddle as they had to carry so much harness. Even Yorkshire could no longer supply bays of sufficient strength, and the Crown Equerry had to look to Holland and his native Ireland. He was fortunate in the generosity of Queen Wilhelmina of the Netherlands, who in 1946 presented to King George VI five grey geldings in acknowledgement of Britain's hospitality when her country had been overrun by the Germans.

Colonel Kavanagh was remarkably successful in the purchases which restored the Royal Mews to its pre-war strength. Of the twenty-four state horses used in the coronation procession of Queen Elizabeth II in 1953, only three had been at the Mews before the war. The five greys presented by Queen Wilhelmina were among the eight which drew the coronation coach; one of the others was a pre-war purchase from Holland, and the other two had recently been acquired from Ireland. Each of the sets of red Morocco harness worn by these horses weighed a hundredweight, and four of them had also to carry postilions and heavy saddles. Kavanagh had been lucky enough to buy four pure-bred Cleveland bays, but the rest of the bays came from Holland. The state coach itself had not been used since the Opening of Parliament in 1939, and much restoration work was necessary after its long rustication in Buckinghamshire. It had new rubber tyres and interior cushions, the panels were touched up and the whole surface was re-gilded. It was

also, for the first time, illuminated with fluorescent lighting operated from batteries. Over the years many members of the public had written to complain that in the closed carriages the occupants were invisible. Other preliminary work included the cleaning of the coachmen's whips, new gilt for some of the bits, the overhaul of twenty-nine horse-collars and the provision of monograms for the furniture of the horse to be ridden by the Master.

The surveyor to the City of Westminster Council prudently suggested that it might be advisable to remove some of the surface dressing from the wood-paved streets, since if the day of the coronation were to be very hot, the dressing might inconvenience the horses. The Crown Equerry agreed that this would be a wise precaution, especially on gradients. He was particularly thinking of the state coach when the brake had to be used: on hot tar from the road surface it might slip. The day, unhappily, was not hot at all, but very cold and wet. At the Royal Mews it began early with the harnessing of the horses. The bosses, made of gold plate on copper, were so heavy that it took two men to put them on a horse, and then the saddlers had to stitch them securely to hold them in place. Then as early as 5.30 one of the chauffeurs had to drive a car to the trade door of the Palace to collect the Queen's page and footman, who would be going to the Abbey with refreshments to be taken by the Royal Family during the long and tiring day.

Like his predecessors on similar occasions, the Crown Equerry had been a key figure in the planning of the coronation. It was a year of strenuous and unflagging effort and, according to a member of his staff, may have contributed to the heart attack from which he died in 1958. On his retirement in 1956 he was succeeded by Brigadier Walter Sale, of the Household Cavalry, whose six-year tenure of office (until 1961) coincided with a quiet period in state ceremony.

The present Crown Equerry is Lieutenant-Colonel Sir John Miller, formerly of the Welsh Guards, a horseman of repute who was in the British Three-Day Event team in the 1948 Olympic Games and who today is a leading whip in the Combined Driving team. In his fifteen years he has done much to revive and sustain public interest in the work of the Royal Mews. He is responsible to the Sovereign for all transport except aircraft and ship, and to the Master of the Horse for keeping him in touch with the affairs of the Department and giving him notice of carriage processions in which he will take part. He has a staff of about thirty, all of whom are ex-servicemen: not because the Mews wants to be run on military lines but for the simple reason that only a soldier knows enough about ceremonial procedure, its terminology and its disciplines, to be able to take a leading part in a procession. Whereas in Queen Victoria's time the number of horses at the Mews in London and Windsor had risen to nearly 200, today there are only about 30 carriage horses on active duty, supplemented by a 'float' of younger animals under training – they cannot be fully used until they are four years old – and some older ones kept for routine work. Under the head coachman there is a coachman in charge of each of the three 'sets' of horses, a set numbering eight or ten; with the grooms, the ratio is roughly one man to each pair of horses. These men also have the care of more than 80 carriages and horse-drawn vehicles. Under the head chauffeur there is also a fleet of motor-cars.

The small administrative staff is headed by the Superintendent, who is responsible to the Crown Equerry for the day-to-day running of the Royal Mews. The Comptroller of Stores is the successor to the avenor who in mediaeval times, before he gradually took over some administrative duties, had to provision the horses. Finally, the Chief Clerk and his two assistants are, among other duties, the Department's channel of communication with the outside world.

257. *Royal Brougham on messenger duty at Buckingham Palace.*

258. *Her Majesty the Queen, Prince Philip, the Prince of Wales and Princess Anne setting off from Buckingham Palace in the 1902 State Postilion Landau for the Silver Wedding procession in 1972.*

The big public occasions, such as coronations, royal weddings and funerals, Trooping the Colour, Royal Ascot, the State Opening of Parliament, the Garter ceremony, reception of foreign Heads of State, may fairly be described as 'the tip of the iceberg' in the sense of being the events that people see and know about. Sir Arthur Erskine's retrospective self-searching and recriminations have shown the standard of perfection aimed at, and the organisation and hard work required to achieve it. As an annual routine the Royal Mews staff move to Windsor in April for the official Easter Visit, and in summer to the royal residence at the Palace of Holyroodhouse in Edinburgh. There is also an increasing involvement with the Lord Mayor's Show. Although this is not specifically a royal occasion, it reflects the ancient bond between the Crown and the City of London, and all the Department's carriage horses and all the men loyally take part.

For ceremonial events, 1969 was an especially memorable year, with the first state visit to Windsor for fifty years, the first investiture of a Prince of Wales since 1911, and a Sovereign's first personal presence at the General Assembly of the Church of Scotland since the sixteenth century. For this last event the Royal Mews staff were in Edinburgh for three weeks, with carriage processions nearly every day. The Scots were delighted by the ancient pomp that once again dignified their capital city, and they wondered why over the years they had seen so little of it. In 1975 they responded with equal enthusiasm to the ceremonies in honour of King Carl Gustaf of Sweden.

The background to these public events is a hard, unremitting routine. Every day the outdoor staff exercise the horses very early in the morning while the streets are still reasonably clear of traffic, in the company of office cleaners, milkmen, post office vans, and the Household Cavalry. Rehearsals for the larger ceremonies may start in summer as early as 4.30 a.m. Training of the horses is a continuing responsibility, with the young ones being taught the necessary skills and even the more experienced being kept familiar – by military marches, loud-speakers and simulated cheering, bangs and crowd noises – with the conditions they meet on their public appearances. The Department also has various regular duties. Twice daily a one-horse brougham goes from the Mews to the Palace to collect mail and messages for Downing Street and other departments. Again, every new ambassador coming to London has to be provided with a state carriage when he rides to the Palace to present his credentials. A particularly exacting occasion is the Garter ceremony at Windsor when the Mews staff – with the efficient help of the Automobile Association – are involved in an intricate traffic exercise. Scores of motor-cars carrying the Garter Knights and other dignitaries to and from the Castle have to be timed to the second, and the smallest error would disrupt the whole procession.

Though in most years there is a workable length of time between one ceremony and another, the demands of state can sometimes be perverse. There was an instance of this in November 1975 when, not long after the exertions of the Lord Mayor's Show, President Nyerere of Tanzania was received on an official visit. On the very next day was the State Opening of Parliament, and on a foul wet morning the coachmen wore mackintoshes over their livery as they prepared the carriages. The rain was unrelenting, and they came home wet and cold, the carriages and harness splashed with mud. It all had to be cleaned up at once, because on the following day the visitor and his retinue were out and about again on another ceremonial expedition.

In recent years public knowledge and understanding of the work of the Department have been stimulated by the policy of opening the Royal Mews to

259. Her Majesty the Queen and the Master of the Horse riding at Ascot with the Prince of Wales, the Countess of Lichfield and the Hon. Angus Ogilvy.

visitors on two afternoons a week. Through the year hundreds of people, including many foreign tourists, come to look at the carriages, the stables and the historic liveries and horse furniture, and this has proved a valuable form of contact with the general public.

The changes that the Duke of Beaufort has seen during his tenure as Master present in miniature the essential character of the office: its survival and its persisting identity through years of fluctuation. He has seen the sudden departure of the monarch who appointed him, the upheavals of war, and the coming of an era in which many traditional values have been brought into question. But as this last chapter closes, the Royal Mews is preparing for the Silver Jubilee of 1977, and nothing very much has changed in the stables since when on his own small scale Ellis of Rochester was coping with similar problems. It is true that the Master no longer has to carry the Sovereign's standard into battle or to arrange his pleasures in the hunting-field, and all the administrative duties of the office are no longer his responsibility. But at the Silver Jubilee the Master of the Horse will ride in procession close to the Sovereign, as possibly an unknown predecessor did when King Edgar was crowned at Bath almost exactly a thousand years ago. The heirs of the horse thegn, the marshal, the avenor and the clerk will once again be watching over the myriad details that lie behind the perfection of a royal progress.

Notes on the Masters

Sir John (de) BROCAS; M of H circa 1360

D. *circa* 1365. S. of Arnald de Brocas, originally from Gascony. 1314 King's Valettus in Edward II's Household; by 1330 Keeper of the Horse to Edward III; 1334 Chief Forester of Windsor and Chief of the Royal Studs; 1336 Warden of Nottingham Gaol and Constable of the Castle, town and park of Guildford. Served in the French wars: 1340 knighted at the battle of Sluys, and at Crécy (1346) led a force which he himself had raised. Settled at Basingstoke, having been granted lands in Hampshire and Berkshire. Two sons: Oliver, who predeceased him, and Bernard.

Sir Bernard (de) BROCAS; M of H circa 1371

B. 1330, d. 1395. S. of John Brocas. A friend of the Black Prince, he was a Household officer, ambassador, Constable of Aquitaine, Captain of Calais and Chamberlain to Anne of Bohemia (Queen of Richard II). Through his second wife he acquired the hereditary appointment of Master of the Buckhounds, at £50 a year, and the Manor of Little Weldon. 1353 granted the Manor of Beaurepaire, in Hampshire, where he settled, and was subsequently granted lands in Sussex and Kent; 1367–1395 Knight of the Shire for Southampton and Surrey, and Warden of the Parks in the Diocese of Winchester; 1376 Keeper of the King's Castle of Corfe and Warren of Purbeck. M. (1) Agnes Vavasour, (2) Mary, heir of Sir John de Roche. His son, also Bernard, was executed in 1400.

Sir Thomas de MURRIEUX (Morieux, Morers, Moreaux); M of H circa 1377

D. before 1388. S. of Sir Thomas Murrieux, High Sheriff of Suffolk. 1381 granted, for life, the custody of the Tower of London; 1382 Constable of the Tower and commissions of Oyer and Terminer in Suffolk and Bedford; 1383 granted lands in Billingsgate during the minority of an heir; 1383–5 Knight of the Chamber. Held the knight's fee of Le Brookhalle in Felsham and the manor of Thorpe Morieux in Suffolk. M. Blanche, natural dau. of John of Gaunt by Catherine Turneford; died without issue.

Sir Thomas de CLIFFORD, 6th Lord Clifford; M of H before 1388

B. 1365, d. 1391. Eldest s. of Roger de Clifford, 5th Baron, and Isabel de Berkeley. 1382–91 Knight of the Chamber; 1386 Governor of Carlisle and Warden of the Marches; Chief Forester of Inglewood; 1387 Keeper of the Forest beyond the River Trent; 1388 banished from Court by the baronial party; 1389 Lord of Westmorland; 1390/1 summoned to Parliament. M. Elizabeth, dau. of Thomas, Lord Roos; four children: John, who fought at Agincourt and married Elizabeth, dau. of Henry Percy (Hotspur); William, Lewis and Maud. Slain at Spruce in Germany whilst on a crusade against the infidels of Lithuania.

Sir John RUSSELL (Russel); M of H 1391

D. 1405. S. of Robert and Catherine Russell. Lord of the manor of Strensham in Worcestershire. 1378 summoned to Parliament as Knight of the Shire for Worcester; 1387 retained by the King to serve at Court; 1388 licensed to crenellate his mansions at Dormeston and Strensham; 1394 went to Ireland on the King's service; 1397 commission of Oyer and Terminer in Worcester; 1398 commission to inspect river banks and weirs in Worcester; 1398 discharged from having to serve overseas or within the realm. Died at Letheringham, Suffolk, but was buried at Strensham. M. Agnes; four children: John, William, Margaret, and Elizabeth.

Sir Richard REDMAN (Redmayne, Redeman); M of H 1399

D. 1426. S. of Sir Matthew, of Redman in Cumberland, Levens in Westmorland and Harewood in Yorkshire. 1388 granted all lands and tenements which the King held in Blencogo; 1390 appointed to survey and control repairs to the castle, gates and towers of Carlisle; 1390 retained for life to stay with the King. Within the next twenty-three years he was sheriff of Cumberland six times; 1392 jousted at Carlisle in the presence of Hotspur; 1399 went to Ireland on the King's business; 1400 treated for peace with the Scots; 1404 Commission of Array; 1405–21 Knight of the Shire for Yorkshire; 1415 helped to mobilize the army for Agincourt, and elected Speaker of the Commons; 1423–4 magistrate in the West Riding of Yorks. M. (1) Elizabeth, dau. of Lord Aldeburgh, (2) Elizabeth, dau. of Sir William Gascoigne; three children: Richard, Joan and Matthew.

HENRY IV/HENRY V

Robert (de) WATERTON; M of H 1399

D. 1426. 1392–3 accompanied Bolingbroke to Prussia on a crusade; 1399 as Chief Forester of Knaresborough raised 200 foresters for Bolingbroke at Ravenspur; 1400 Keeper of Pontefract Castle; 1401–2 sent on an embassy to the Dukes of Guelders and Bavaria to promote the marriage of a Bavarian prince to Henry's daughter Blanche; 1403 Constable of Tickill Castle, Squire of the Chamber and Steward of the Honour; 1405 Master of the Running Dogs, and subsequently taken hostage by the Earl of Northumberland; 1405 granted office of steward, master forester and bailiff of the Lordship of Hatfield; 1409 witnessed Henry IV's will; 1417 given custody of the Duke of Orleans. Received many grants of land and settled in Yorkshire. M. Cecily Fleming, heiress of Woodhall of Stanley, through whom he acquired the manor of Brotton in North Riding. His brother Hugh was Chamberlain and Keeper of the Wardrobe and his other brother John was Master of the Horse to Henry V.

HENRY V

John (de) WATERTON; M of H 1414

Brother of Robert Waterton. 1392–3 joined Henry Bolingbroke on the second expedition against the infidels of Lithuania; 1405 became the Earl of Northumberland's hostage in return for Robert Waterton's freedom; 1414 appointed Constable of Windsor Castle and Keeper of the Parks; Comptroller of Henry V's Household; 1415 Master of the Horse at Agincourt; 1417 commissioned to supervise the muster of the retinue of the Earl of Salisbury going to Harfleur. M. into the Clifford family, and lived at Methley Hall, Yorkshire.

Sir Henry NOON; M of H 1421

Probably s. of Henry and Thomasina (née Tyrell), of Shelfanger in Norfolk. Attended Henry V in the French wars where, in return for his gallantry, he was given the castle, lands and lordship of Condé in Normandy; 1420 acquired manor of Chipping Norton, Oxford; 1421 as King's Knight went to France in the King's service. Held the manor of Visedelou (Vis de Loup) in Shelfanger, Norfolk, where he increased his estate. M. Elizabeth; one son: Henry.

HENRY VI

Richard (de) Beauchamp, 13th Earl of WARWICK; M of H before 1429

B. 1382, d. 1439. Born at Salwarp, Worcs, s. of Thomas Beauchamp, 12th Earl of Warwick and Margaret, dau. of William Lord Ferrers; godson of Richard II; 1401 succeeded his father. 1403 retained to serve the King; 1408–10 visited Jerusalem and several European countries; 1413 Lord High Steward at Henry V's coronation; 1414 instrumental in supressing the Lollard rising; Captain of Calais; accompanied the English embassy to the Council of Constance; 1415 fought and wounded at Harfleur; 1428 charged with the care of educating Henry VI; 1430 arranged the truce with Scotland; 1437 Lieutenant of France and Normandy. M. (1) Elizabeth, dau. of Thomas Lord Berkley, (2) Isabella, widow of the Earl of Worcester.

Sir Walter BEAUCHAMP; M of H before 1429

Younger s. of John de Beauchamp of Powyk and Alcester, and uncle of John, Lord Beauchamp (later Master of the Horse). Studied law and was also a distinguished soldier under Henry IV and Henry V in the French wars. On his return from Agincourt elected Knight of the Shire for Wiltshire; 1416 elected Speaker of the Commons, but parliament was dissolved the same year; 1425 employed by his cousin Richard Beauchamp, Earl of Warwick, to argue his claim of precedence before the Commons. M. (1) Elizabeth, dau. of Sir Peter de la Mere, (2) Elizabeth, dau. of Sir John Roche.

Sir John STYWARD (Stiward, Stuard); M of H 1430

B. in Norfolk, d. circa 1447. Master of the Horse to Queen Katharine (wife of Henry V); Constable of Leeds Castle, Kent, where Eleanor, wife of Humphrey, Duke of Gloucester, was held during her trial for necromancy; 1428 Steward of the rents, issues and profits of Framesden, Suffolk; 1435 commissioned to take muster of Edmund, Count of Mortmain; 1439 Knight of the Body and Constable of Rochester Castle.

John, Lord BEAUCHAMP of POWYCK (Powick); M of H 1442

D. 1475. S. of William and Katherine Beauchamp of Powyck and Alcester. 1445 KG; 1447 granted 'in tail male' for his good service to Henry V and Henry VI title of Baron and Lord Beauchamp of Powyck; 1450 Lord Treasurer; 1457–60 Lord Steward. Purchased Beauchamp Court and Powyck Court, Worcester, and later acquired the whole manor of Alcester. M. Margaret; one son: Richard. John and Margaret Beauchamp were buried in the church of the Black Friars, Worcester, destroyed during the Reformation.

EDWARD IV

Sir Thomas de Burgh, Lord of GAINSBOROUGH; M of H 1465

D. 1495/6. S. of Thomas Burgh and Elizabeth d'Athol of Gainsborough. 1478 Commission of Enquiry into the lands, honours and rents possessed by the late George, Duke of Clarence; 1478 grant for life of the offices of Steward of Somerton Castle, lord- and manorship of Boston, Freston, Frampton, Donington etc.; 1478 commissioned to survey the King's manors of Wakefield, Conisborough and Hatfield, Yorks; 1477–83 MP for Lincoln and Notts; 1480 Steward and Master Forester of the manor and lordship of Epworth; 1483 KG; 1484 Steward of all lordships, manors and land in the Isle of Axholme, Lincs; 1487 summoned to Parliament as Lord Burgh of Gainsborough. M. Margaret, dau. of Thomas Lord Roos of Kendal; five children.

Sir John CHEYNE; M of H 1479

B. 1445, d. 1499. Younger s. of John Cheyne of Shirland, Isle of Sheppey, and Eleanor, dau. of Sir John Shottisbrooke. 1460s Esquire for the Body and Master of the Horse to Elizabeth (Woodville), Queen of Edward IV; 1471–81 MP for Wiltshire; 1474/5 left as a hostage in France; 1478 took part in a tournament during the marriage celebrations of Richard Duke of York and Lady Anne Mowbray; 1479 granted the presentation of the parish church of Myvote, diocese of St Asaph; 1483 grant to assess the subsidies of Wiltshire; 1485 KG and distinguished himself at the battle of Bosworth; 1487/8 Constable of Barnard's Castle; Privy Councillor. M. in 1479 Margaret, dau. of Sir John Chidiocke; died without issue.

RICHARD III

Sir Thomas TYRRELL (Tyrell, Tirel); M of H 1483

B. Gipping, Essex. Younger brother of James, later Master of the Horse. S. of William, and Margaret, dau. of Robert Dacy of Malden. Descendant of Walter Tirel, believed to have shot the arrow that killed King William II. 1478 Esquire for the Body; granted rent of the manor or lordship of Northweld, Essex; 1483 commission to assess subsidies and appoint collectors in Essex; 1484 Commission of Array in Essex; 1487 created Knight Banneret at the battle of Stoke; 1497 Knight Banneret at the Battle of Blackheath. Possibly m. twice (1) Elizabeth, (2) Margaret, dau. of Christopher Willoughby.

Sir James TYRRELL; M of H circa 1483

D. 1502. Brother of Thomas. 1471 knighted after the battle of Tewkesbury; 1477 MP for Cornwall; 1478 grant of the yearly rent of £20 from the issues of the King's manor or lordship of Ross-in-Holderness, Yorks; 1482 Knight Banneret; 1483 Commission of Array in Wales for the resistance of revels; 1483 commissioned to assess subsidies in ports; 1483 appointed to assess the King's lands in Cornwall; 1484 Steward of the Duchy of Cornwall, Chamberlain of the Exchequer, Lieutenant of the Castle of Guisnes; 1505 instrumental in the flight of de la Pole, Earl of Suffolk, and was beheaded having supposedly confessed to taking part in the murder of the princes in the Tower.

HENRY VII

Sir Thomas BRANDON; M of H circa 1485

D. 1509/10. S. of Sir William Brandon of Wangford, Suffolk, and Elizabeth, dau. of Sir Robert Wingfield; uncle of Charles Brandon, Duke of Suffolk. Henry VII's Buckler at the Battle of Stoke, Marshal of the Court of Common Pleas; 1497 knighted at the Battle of Blackheath; 1507 KG; 1509 Warden and Chief Justice of all the royal parks, forests, and chaces south of the Trent; 1509 Commission of Array, Justice of the Peace. Died, without issue, at Blackfriars, London.

HENRY VIII

Sir Thomas KNYVET (Knyvett, Chanivet); M of H 1510

D. 1512. Eldest s. of Edmund Knyvet of Buckenham Castle, Norfolk, and Eleanor Tyrrell. 1509 knighted by Henry VIII; Baron Knyvett of Escrick, Yorks; 1510 Esquire for the Body, King's Standard Bearer, Keeper of the New Park, Bailiff of the Lordship of Sutton Coldfield, and granted the lordship of Berkeley. In 1512 captained the *Regent*, largest ship in Henry's navy, and in a battle against the French at Brest his ship sank and he and the entire crew lost their lives. He left a widow, Muriel, and four children.

Charles Brandon, 1st Duke of SUFFOLK; M of H 1512

B. *circa* 1484, d. 1545. S. of Sir William Brandon and Elizabeth; nephew of Thomas Brandon. 1509–12 Esquire for the Body; 1509 Chamberlain of North Wales; 1510 Marshal of the King's Bench; 1512 Ranger of the New Forest; made a contract of marriage, never fulfilled, with his ward Elizabeth Grey, Baroness Lisle, and became Viscount Lisle; 1513 KG; Marshal of the King's Army in France; 1514 created Duke of Suffolk of the second creation; 1515 m., without the royal consent, Mary Tudor, widow of Louis XII and sister of Henry VIII; temporarily in disgrace but subsequently restored to Henry's favour and received many other offices. M. at least four times: (1) Anne Browne, (2) Margaret, the aunt of his first wife, (3) Mary Tudor and (4) Katherine, Baroness Willoughby de Eresby. Died at the Palace, Guildford, Surrey; buried in St George's Chapel, Windsor.

Sir Henry GUILDFORD; M of H 1515

B. 1489, d. 1532. 1511 served in a crusade against the Moors and was knighted by Ferdinand of Spain; 1513 King's Standard Bearer in the French campaign; 1520 accompanied Henry VIII to the Field of Cloth of Gold; 1522 Comptroller of the Household; 1526 KG; 1529 Knight of the Shire for Kent; signed articles against Cardinal Wolsey but remained his friend. M. in 1512, Margaret.

Sir Nicholas CAREW; M of H 1522

D. 1539. Heir of Sir Richard Carew of Beddington, Surrey. 1513 attended Henry VIII in France; knighted before 1517; Keeper of Greenwich Park; 1519 Sheriff of Surrey and Sussex; removed by the Privy Council from attendance on the King and sent to Calais as Lieutenant of Calais Castle; 1520 present at Field of Cloth of Gold; 1521 allowed to return to Court; 1527 envoy to France; 1529 MP for Surrey; 1529–30 sent as the King's envoy to the Emperor Charles V; 1531 entertained Henry at Beddington; 1532 envoy to France; 1536 KG; 1539 condemned and executed for his part in the Marquis of Exeter's alleged plot against the Crown. M. Elizabeth Bryan, dau. of Thomas Bryan, Vice-Chamberlain to Katharine of Aragon.

HENRY VIII/EDWARD VI

Sir Anthony BROWNE (Brown); M of H 1539

B. 1500, d. 1548. S. of Sir Anthony Browne and Lady Lucy Nevill; half-brother of the Earl of Southampton, from whom he inherited the Cowdray estates. 1523 knighted for bravery in Brittany; 1524 Esquire for the Body; 1528 and 1533 Ambassador to France; 1540 KG; 1544 at the siege of Boulogne; 1545 Justice in Eyre; named one of the guardians to Edward and Elizabeth in Henry VIII's will; 1546 Chief Justice of forests beyond the Trent. As a result of the dissolution of the monasteries received several grants of land, including Battle Abbey (1538), Southwark Priory and the Cistercian Abbey at Waverley. Died at Bayfleet and was buried at Battle. His son, Sir Anthony (later 1st Viscount Montagu), was a favourite of Queen Mary and was Master of the Horse to her consort, Philip of Spain.

EDWARD VI

Sir William Herbert, 1st Earl of PEMBROKE; M of H 1549

B. 1506, d. 1570. S. of Sir Richard Herbert and Margaret, dau. of Sir Matthew Cradock. Esquire of the Body to Henry VIII; 1546 Gentleman of the Privy Chamber; one of the executors of Henry VIII's will; 1548 KG; 1549 helped to quell the Cornish rising; 1550 President of the Council of Wales; 1551 created Lord Herbert of Cardiff and Earl of Pembroke; 1553 joined Northumberland in proclaiming Lady Jane Grey queen, but subsequently declared for Mary; 1556 Governor of Calais; under Queen Elizabeth supported Cecil and the Protestants; 1568 Lord Steward. M. Anne, dau. of Sir Thomas Parr and sister of Catherine; succeeded by his eldest son Henry.

John Dudley, 2nd Earl of WARWICK; M of H 1552

B. before 1528, d. 1554. Third but first surviving s. of John Duke of Northumberland and Jane, dau. of Sir Edward Guildford. 1547 Knighted at the coronation of Edward VI; 1550–2 Master of the Buckhounds; 1551 Captain of fifty men-at-arms; 1552 joint Lord-Lieutenant of Warwick with his father; 1553 licensed to retain one hundred men in livery. As one of the signatories to the letters patent in 1553, settling the crown on his sister-in-law Lady Jane Grey, he supported his father's proclamation of her as Queen; arrested with the Duke of Cambridge, committed to the Tower, found guilty of high treason and condemned to death. Released into the custody of his brother-in-law, Sir Henry Sidney. M. Anne Seymour, dau. of the Duke of Somerset. Died (thought to be through some disease he caught in the Tower) without issue, at Penshurst, Kent.

MARY I

Sir Edward Hastings, Lord HASTINGS of LOUGHBOROUGH; M of H 1553

B. circa 1520, d. 1573. Third s. of George Hastings, first Earl of Huntingdon. 1547–53 MP for Leicestershire; 1550–1 Sheriff of Warwickshire and Leicestershire; 1554–60 Warden of the Stannaries; 1555 KG; 1555–57 MP for Middlesex; 1557 Lord Chamberlain of Queen Mary's Household; Privy Councillor; opposed Mary's marriage to Philip of Spain; 1558 created peer; 1561 imprisoned for hearing Mass but released on taking the Oath of Supremacy. Died without legal heir at Stoke Poges.

Sir Henry JERNINGHAM (Jernegan); M of H 1557

D. 1571. 1526 Gentleman Pensioner; 1547 received the manor of Costessy, Norfolk; 1553 declared for Queen Mary and raised supporters in Norfolk; 3 August led the Yeomen of the Guard at the Queen's state entry into London; Knight of the Bath; Privy Councillor; Vice-Chamberlain; Captain of the Yeomen of the Guard (an appointment he resigned in 1557 on being made Master of the Horse); 1554 helped to rout the Wyatt rebellion; 1556 Chief Steward of the town and hundred of Tewkesbury, Glos, and Master of the Hunt there. His s. Henry m. Eleanor, dau. of Lord Dacre.

ELIZABETH I

Robert Dudley, 1st Earl of LEICESTER; M of H 1558

B. circa 1532, d. 1588. Fifth s. of Duke of Northumberland; brother of John, Earl of Warwick. 1553 MP for Norfolk; proclaimed his sister-in-law, Lady Jane Grey, Queen at King's Lynn; 1554 pardoned; 1559 KG, Privy Councillor and Lord Steward of the Household; 1562 High Steward of Cambridge University; 1564 created Baron Denbigh and Earl of Leicester; 1564 Chancellor of Oxford University; 1575 entertained the Queen at Kenilworth; 1585 commanded expedition to assist United Provinces against Spain; 1586 Governor of the United Provinces; 1587 recalled. M. (1) Amy Robsart, (2) Lady Sheffield, (3) Letice Knollys, Countess of Essex.

Robert Devereux, 2nd Earl of ESSEX; M of H 1588

B. 1566, d. 1601. Eldest s. of Walter Devereux, 1st Earl. Educated at Trinity College, Cambridge. 1586 Knight Banneret; 1588 KG; 1591 in command of a force sent to help Henry of Navarre; 1593 Privy Councillor; 1596 defeated the Spaniards in a sea battle off Cadiz; 1597 Earl Marshal and Master of the Ordnance; 1599 Lieutenant and Governor-General of Ireland; 1601 declared a traitor for his part in the plot to dismiss Elizabeth's councillors, and was executed. M. in 1590 Frances, widow of Sir Philip Sidney; was succeeded by his son Robert, Commander-in-Chief of the rebel army in 1642.

ELIZABETH I/JAMES I

Edward Somerset, 4th Earl of WORCESTER; M of H 1601

B. 1553, d. 1628. S. of William, 3rd Earl of Worcester, and Christian, dau. of Lord North. 1590 Ambassador to Scotland to congratulate James VI on his marriage; member of the Council in the Marches of Wales; 1597–8 deputy Master of the Horse in Essex's absence; 1601 Privy Councillor; joint Commissioner for the office of Earl Marshal on seven occasions; 1603 Earl Marshal at the coronation of James I; 1602–28 Lord-Lieutenant of Glamorgan and Monmouth; 1612-14 Commissioner of the Treasury; 1616-28 Lord Keeper of the Privy Seal; 1625 Lord Great Chamberlain at Charles I's coronation. M. Elizabeth, fourth dau. of Francis Hastings, 2nd Earl of Huntingdon. Buried at Raglan, Monmouthshire; succeeded by his second son Henry.

JAMES I/CHARLES I

George Villiers, 1st Duke of BUCKINGHAM; M of H 1616

B. 1592, d. 1628. Younger s. of Sir George Villiers. Introduced to James I in 1614 and rapidly became a favourite. 1614 appointed Cupbearer; 1615 Gentleman of the Bedchamber; 1616 KG and created Viscount Villiers; 1617 Earl of Buckingham; 1618 Marquis; obtained the dismissal of the Howard family from court; 1619 Lord High Admiral; 1623 created Duke of Buckingham. August 1628 assassinated by John Felton at Portsmouth. M. Lady Katherine Manners; succeeded by his s. George.

CHARLES I

James Hamilton, 1st Duke of HAMILTON; M of H 1628

B. 1606, d. 1649. S. of James, 2nd Marquis of Hamilton, and Ann, dau. of 7th Earl of Glencairn. 1628 Privy Councillor; 1630–4 commanded the British force under Gustavus Adolphus of Sweden; Charles I's adviser on Scottish affairs; intrigued with Charles I, also the Covenanters, and opposed Strafford and Montrose. 1641 allied with Argyll but in 1642 tried to prevent the Scots from supporting the English Parliament; 1643 refused to take the Covenant, joined the King at Oxford but was imprisoned in 1644; liberated by Fairfax in 1646 and attempted to mediate between Charles and Scots; 1648 led Scottish army into England; defeated at Preston. M. Margaret, dau. of the 1st Earl of Denbigh, when he was only fourteen and she was seven. Died without issue.

OLIVER CROMWELL

John CLAYPOLE; M of H 1653

B. *circa* 1625, d. 1688. S. of Sir John Claypole and Mary Angell of Northborough. By 1645 joined Parliamentary army; 1651 raised a troop of horse; 1654 led Cromwell's horse at his first inauguration ceremony; 1654 MP for Carmarthenshire; elected again but sat for Northampton in the Parliament; 1654 present at banquet given to Cromwell by Lord Mayor of London; sent to receive the Dutch ambassadors on their return to London; 1657 Lord of (Cromwell's) Bedchamber; Ranger of Whittlebury Forest in Northants; 1660 signed the Declaration of Allegiance to Charles II; 1678 arrested and sent to the Tower for plotting, but soon released. Died in penury. M. (1) Elizabeth, dau. of Oliver Cromwell, by whom he had four children, (2) Blanche by whom he had his only surviving child.

CHARLES II

Prince RUPERT of the Rhine; M of H 1653 (in exile)

B. Prague 1619, d. 1682. Third s. of Frederick V, Elector Pala-tine and King of Bohemia, and Elizabeth, sister of Charles I. First came to England 1636; appointed General of the Horse by Charles I; 1642 gained the first victory of the Civil War at Worcester; subsequently led Royalist troops in many battles; 1644 appointed General; 1645 urged Charles I to make peace; on the capitulation at Oxford was ordered to leave England; 1646 went to St Germain and was appointed Maréchal-de-Camp with command of English troops in French service. 1660 returned to England and became Privy Councillor and commissioner for government of Tangier; 1666 shared command with George Monck against Dutch; 1668 Constable of Windsor Castle; 1670 received charter for the Hudson Bay Company; 1672 Vice-Admiral; 1673 Admiral; 1673–79 First Lord of the Admiralty. He was also a scientist, a member of the Royal Society, and was responsible for the introduction of the mezzotint into England. Buried in Henry VII Chapel, Westminster Abbey.

George Monck (Monk), 1st Duke of ALBEMARLE; M of H 1660

B. 1608, d. 1670. Second s. of Sir Thomas and Elizabeth Monck of Potheridge, Devon. 1644 taken prisoner by Fairfax at Nantwich; imprisoned in the Tower; offered command in Ireland by the Parliamentarians on condition that he took the negative oath; 1647 became Adjutant-General and Governor of Ulster; 1650 formed an infantry regiment which later became the Coldstream Guards; 1651 Commander-in-Chief, Scotland; 1652 Admiral; fought three great naval battles in the Dutch wars; 1659 received Royalist overtures and supported the reinstatement of Charles II; 1660 KG; his regiment retained as the King's Guard; 1664 Lord of the Treasury; 1668 retired from public office. Died at the Cockpit in Whitehall, buried in Henry VII Chapel, Westminster Abbey. M. Anne Clarges, dau. of a farrier; succeeded by son Christopher.

George Villiers, 2nd Duke of BUCKINGHAM; M of H 1668

B. 1628, d. 1687. S. of George Villiers, 1st Duke. Educated at Trinity College, Cambridge; 1643 served under Prince Rupert; joined the Surrey insurgents and was routed at St Neots; 1648 fled to Holland; 1660 his estates, which had been forfeited under Cromwell, were restored to him; 1660-7 Gentleman of the Bedchamber; 1661–7 Lord Lieutenant of West Riding; 1662–7 Privy Councillor; 1668 seduced the Countess of Shrewsbury and killed her husband in a duel; 1674 dismissed from his offices and joined Shaftesbury's Country Party; 1677 imprisoned; 1683 restored to Court favour. M. in 1657 Mary, dau. of Sir Thomas Fairfax. Died of a chill (which he caught out hunting) in the house of one of his tenants, at Kirkby Moorside, and was buried in Westminster Abbey. He was a playwright, interested in chemistry, and an expert in architecture and landscaping.

James Scott, Duke of MONMOUTH; M of H 1674

B. 1649, d. 1685. Illegitimate s. of Charles II and Lucy Walters; also known by names of Fitzroy and Crofts. 1643 acknowledged by Charles II, made Baron Tyndale, Earl of Doncaster, Duke of Monmouth and KG; 1670 Privy Councillor; 1672–3 served against the Dutch and identified himself with the Protestant movement; 1679 dispersed Scottish insurgents at the battle of Brig but was replaced as commander of the troops by Duke of York; banished from England; retired to Holland but returned to England and was stripped of his offices; arrested at Taunton; released on bail. 1682 joined Russell, Essex and Sidney in plot to murder Charles II and Duke of York, but revealed the plot and was pardoned. Retired once more to Holland, but on death of Charles II was dismissed by William of Orange. June 1685 landed at Lyme Regis and was declared Head and Captain General of the Protestant Forces of England and the legitimate and legal heir to the Crown; 20 June proclaimed King at Taunton; 5 July defeated at Sedgemoor; executed at the Tower of London.

Charles Lennox, 1st Duke of RICHMOND and LENNOX; M of H 1681

B. 1672, d. 1723. Illegitimate s. of Charles II and Louise de Quérouaille (Kérouaille), Duchess of Portsmouth. 1675 created Baron of Settrington in York, Earl of March and Duke of Richmond in the English peerage and Baron Torbolton, Earl of Darnley and Duke of Lennox in the Scottish peerage. 1681 KG; Governor of Dumbarton Castle; 1693–1702 ADC in Flanders; 1714 Lord of the Bedchamber to George I; 1715 Privy Councillor; 1697 acquired Goodwood for use as a hunting lodge. M. 1692, Anne, dau. of Lord Brudenell; three children: Charles, Louise and Anne. Buried in Henry VII Chapel, Westminster Abbey.

JAMES II

George Legge, Baron DARTMOUTH; M of H 1685

B. 1648, d. 1691. Eldest s. of William Legge. Educated at Westminster and King's College, Cambridge. 1665–7 Lieutenant in the Dutch war; 1667 Captain; during the intervals of sea warfare, held appointments on land; 1668 Groom of the Bedchamber; 1670–83 Lieutenant-Governor of Portsmouth; 1672 Lieutenant-General of the Ordnance; 1673 Master of the Horse to the Duke of York; 1678 commanded troops in Flanders; 1682 Master-General of the Ordnance; created Baron Dartmouth; 1683 Master of Trinity House; 1683–4 engaged in the Tangier expedition; 1685 Governor of the Tower; 1688–9 Admiral and Commander-in-Chief of the Fleet; 1691 accused of conspiracy against the Crown and committed to the Tower, where he died of apoplexy.

WILLIAM III

Henry de Nassau, Count of AUVERQUERQUE (Overkirk); M of H 1689

B. 1641, d. 1708. Third s. of Louis, Count Nassau, and Elizabeth. 1670 accompanied William of Orange on a visit to Oxford; 1688 attended William on his journey to England as Captain of the Bodyguard and naturalised English by Act of Parliament; 1690 fought at the Battle of the Boyne and afterwards occupied Dublin with nine troops of horse;

1690–1 Major-General and served in the Flanders campaign; 1692–3 Deputy Stadholder; 1697 promoted to General in the English Army; Field-Marshal in the Dutch Army and comrade-in-arms of Marlborough. M. Isabella van Aersen, dau. of Cornelius, Lord of Sommelsdyck and Plaata; five sons and one daughter. Died at Lille and was buried in Auverquerque, Zealand; succeeded by second son who was raised to the peerage in 1698.

QUEEN ANNE/GEORGE I

Charles Seymour, 6th Duke of SOMERSET; M of H 1703, 1714

B. 1662, d. 1748. S. of Charles Seymour, 2nd Baron Seymour of Trowbridge; succeeded his brother Francis in 1678. Educated Trinity College, Cambridge. 1683 Gentleman of the Bedchamber; 1684 KG; 1685 Colonel of the Queen's Dragoons (3rd Hussars); 1687 stripped of his offices; 1688 took up arms for the Prince of Orange; 1689 Chancellor of Cambridge; 1689 *pro tempore* Speaker of the House of Lords; 1701 Joint-Regent; 1706 Commissioner for the Union with Scotland; 1708 supported Marlborough; 1711 lost his place in the Privy Council; 1716 retired from public office. M. Elizabeth Percy, dau. of Josceline, 11th and last Earl of Northumberland; thirteen children, of whom four survived.

GEORGE II

Richard Lumley, 2nd Earl of SCARBOROUGH; M of H 1727

B. *circa* 1688, d. 1740. Succeeded his father Richard, 1st Earl, in 1721. Educated at Eton and Cambridge. 1708–10 MP (Whig) for East Grinstead; 1710–15 MP for Arundel; 1710 Vice-Admiral of County Durham; 1711–12 Lieutenant-Colonel of the Horse; 1713 Lieutenant-Colonel of the Queen's Regiment of Horse; 1714 Colonel, 1st Troop of Horse Grenadier Guards; 1715 served against the Jacobites at the battle of Preston; 1722–40 Colonel, Coldstream Guards; 1735 Major-General; 1739 Lieutenant-General. Committed suicide, by shooting himself through the mouth with a pistol, at his house in Grosvenor Square. Unmarried.

Charles Lennox, 2nd Duke of RICHMOND and LENNOX; M of H 1735

B. 1701, d. 1750. S. of Charles, 1st Duke. 1722 Captain in the Royal Regiment of Horse Guards; 1722–3 MP for Chichester; succeeded to the dukedom; 1724 Fellow of the Royal Society; 1725 Knight of the Bath; 1726 KG; 1727 Lord of the Bedchamber; 1728 LLD Cambridge; succeeded to the dukedom of Aubigny in France on the death of his grandmother, Louise de Quérouaille; 1735 Privy Councillor; 1743 served in the war of the Austrian Succession at the Battle of Dettingen; 1745 Lieutenant-General under the command of the Duke of Cumberland; 1749 MD Cambridge. M. Sarah, dau. of the Earl of Cadogan; six children; succeeded by s. Charles; buried in Chichester Cathedral.

William Cavendish, 4th Duke of DEVONSHIRE; M of H 1751

B. 1720, d. 1764. Summoned to the House of Lords in his

father's barony of Cavendish in 1751 and succeeded to the dukedom four years later. 1741–51 MP for Derbyshire; 1755–6 Lord-Lieutenant of Ireland; 1756–7 First Lord of the Treasury and Prime Minister; 1757 Lord Chamberlain. M. Charlotte Elizabeth, Baroness Clifford, dau. of Richard, Earl of Cork; succeeded by s. William.

Lionel Cranfield Sackville, 1st Duke of DORSET; M of H 1755

B. 1688, d. 1765. S. of Charles Sackville, 6th Earl of Dorset and Mary, dau. of the 3rd Earl of Northampton. Educated at Westminster; 1706 succeeded to the earldom. 1708–13 Constable of Dover Castle and Lord of the Cinque Ports; envoy extraordinary to notify George I of Queen Anne's death; 1714 Groom of the Stole, First Lord of the Bedchamber, Privy Councillor and KG; 1720 created Duke of Dorset; 1727 bore the crown at George II's coronation; 1725–30 and 1737–45 Lord Steward of the Household; 1730–7 and 1750–5 Lord-Lieutenant of Ireland; 1745 Lord President of the Council; 1746–65 Lord-Lieutenant of Kent. M. Elizabeth, dau. of Lieutenant-General Walter Philip Colyear. D. at Knole; succeeded by s. Charles.

Granville Leveson-Gower, 1st Marquis of STAFFORD; M of H 1757

B. 1727, d. 1803. S. of John, 2nd Baron Gower. Educated at Westminster and Christ Church, Oxford. 1744 MP for Bishop's Castle; 1747 and 1749 MP for Westminster; 1749–51 Lord of the Admiralty; 1754 MP for Lichfield; 1754 called to the House of Lords; 1755–7 and 1785–94 Lord Privy Seal; 1760–3 Keeper of the Great Wardrobe; 1763–5 Lord Chamberlain; 1767–79 and 1783–4 President of the Council; 1784 Fellow of the Society of Arts; 1786 created Marquis of Stafford. M. (1) Elizabeth, dau. of Nicholas Fazakerly, (2) 1748 Lady Louisa Egerton, dau. of Scroope, 1st Duke of Bridgewater, (3) 1768 Lady Susannah Stewart dau. of Alexander 6th Earl of Galloway; succeeded by s. George Granville.

GEORGE III

Francis Hastings, 10th Earl of HUNTINGDON; M of H 1760

B. 1728, d. 1789. S. of Theophilus, 9th Earl; succeeded to the title in 1746. Educated at Westminster and Oxford. 1760 Privy Councillor; 1761 carried the Sword of State at George III's coronation; 1761–70 Groom of the Stole; 1762–5 Lord-Lieutenant of West Riding, Yorkshire. Died suddenly while sitting at a table in his nephew's house and was buried at Ashby-de-la-Zouch.

John Manners, 3rd Duke of RUTLAND; M of H 1761

B. 1696, d. 1779. S. of John, 2nd Duke, and Catherine Russell. 1721–79 Lord-Lieutenant of Leicestershire; 1727–36 Chancellor of the Duchy of Lancaster; 1755–61 Lord Steward of the Household; Privy Councillor; M. in 1717 the Hon. Bridget Sutton, dau. of Baron Lexington; succeeded by his grandson Charles.

Francis Seymour-Conway, 1st Marquis of HERTFORD; M of H 1766

B. 1718, d. 1794. S. of the Rt. Hon. Francis Seymour who was created Lord Conway, Baron Conway of Ragley, and of Charlotte Shorter; nephew of Sir Robert Walpole. 1732 Succeeded as Baron Conway; 1750 Viscount Beauchamp and Earl of Hertford; Lord-Lieutenant of Warwick; 1765–6 Lord-Lieutenant of Ireland; 1766–82 Lord Chamberlain; 1793 Earl of Yarmouth and Marquis of Hertford. M. in 1741 the Lady Isabella Fitzroy, youngest dau. of the 2nd Duke of Grafton; succeeded by his s. Francis (later Master of the Horse).

Peregrine Willoughby Bertie, 3rd Duke of ANCASTER and KESTEVAN; M of H 1766 (Dec)

B. 1714, d. 1778. S. of Peregrine, 2nd Duke. 1741–78 Privy Councillor and Lord-Lieutenant of Lincoln; 1745 raised a regiment for George II to fight the Young Pretender; 1755–65 Lord of the Bedchamber; 1755 Major-General; 1759 Lieutenant-General; 1760 officiated as Lord Chamberlain at George III's coronation; 1772 General. M. (1) 1735, Elizabeth Blundell, (2) 1750, Mary, dau. of Thomas Panton of Newmarket, Master of the King's Running Dogs. Died at Grimsthorpe of a bilious disorder; succeeded by his second son Robert.

Hugh (Smithson) Percy, Duke of NORTHUMBERLAND; M of H 1778

B. 1715, d. 1786. As Sir Hugh Smithson Bart., he married in 1740 Lady Elizabeth Percy, the sole heiress to the Percy estates. 1750 assumed the name of Percy in lieu of Smithson by Act of Parliament; 1766 created Earl Percy and Duke of Northumberland of the third creation. 1756 KG; 1762 Privy Councillor; 1763–5 Lord-Lieutenant of Ireland; 1784 was given the additional titles of Lord Lovaine, Baron of Alnwick, with remainder to his second son Algernon. Succeeded as Duke of Northumberland by s. Hugh.

George Brudenell Montagu, 1st Duke of MONTAGU; M of H 1780

B. 1712, d. 1790. S. of George Brudenell, 3rd Earl of Cardigan. Educated at Oxford. 1727 Page of Honour at the coronation of George II; 1749 on the death of his wife's father assumed the name of Montagu; 1742–52 Chief Justice in Eyre north of the Trent; 1749 Fellow of the Royal Society; 1752–90 Constable of Windsor Castle; 1752 KG; 1766 created Duke of Montagu; 1776 Privy Councillor; 1776–80 Governor to the Prince of Wales and Prince Frederick; 1784 FSA. M. in 1730 Mary, dau. of the Duke of Montagu and grand-daughter of John Churchill, Duke of Marlborough. Died without a male heir and the dukedom became extinct.

James Graham, 3rd Duke of MONTROSE; M of H 1790, 1807

B. 1755, d. 1836. S. of William, 2nd Duke, whom he succeeded in 1790. 1780 MP for Richmond; 1780–1836 Chancellor of Glasgow University; Lord-Lieutenant of Stirling and Dunbarton; Lord Justice General of Scotland;

1784–90 MP for Great Bedwin; Lord of the Treasury; 1789-91 Co-Paymaster General; 1789 Privy Councillor; 1804-6 President of the Board of Trade; 1812 KG; 1821-7 and 1828–30 Lord Chamberlain. M. (1) Jemima Elizabeth, dau. of John, 2nd Earl of Ashburnham, (2) Caroline Maria, dau. of George, 4th Duke of Manchester. Succeeded by s. James.

John Fane, 10th Earl of WESTMORLAND; M of H 1795

B. 1759, d. 1841. S. of John, 9th Earl; succeeded his father in 1774. Educated at Charterhouse and Emmanuel College, Cambridge. 1789 Privy Councillor; 1790-5 Lord-Lieutenant of Ireland, where he opposed catholic emancipation and was recalled by Pitt; 1793 KG; 1798–1827 Lord Privy Seal; Lord-Lieutenant of Northampton. M. (1) in 1782 Sarah Anne Child, dau. of Robert Child of Osterley Park, (2) Jane dau. of Richard Saunders. Succeeded by s. John.

Philip Stanhope, 5th Earl of CHESTERFIELD; M of H 1798

B. 1755, d. 1815. Only s. of Arthur Charles Stanhope; cousin and godson of the 4th Earl, whom he succeeded. 1784 Privy Councillor; 1784-7 nominal ambassador to Spain; 1789–90 Master of the Mint; 1790 joint Postmaster General; 1805 KG. M. (1) in 1777, Anne, dau. of the Reverend Robert Thistlethwayte, (2) in 1799, Henrietta, third dau. of the Marquis of Bath. Died without issue.

Francis Seymour, 2nd Marquis of HERTFORD; M of H 1804

B. 1743, d. 1822. S. of Francis, 1st Marquis, an earlier Master of the Horse. Educated at Eton and Christ Church, Oxford. 1761–8 MP for Lisburne (Irish House of Commons); 1765 Privy Councillor for Ireland; 1765–6 Chief Secretary to the Lord-Lieutenant of Ireland; 1766 Constable of Dublin Castle; 1766–8 MP for Lostwithiel; 1768–94 MP for Oxford; 1774–80 Lord of the Treasury; 1780 Cofferer of the Household and Privy Councillor. He was an advocate of the political union of Great Britain and Ireland with an independent Irish Parliament. 1793 took the title of Earl of Yarmouth; 1794 succeeded his father; 1793–4 Ambassador Extraordinary to Berlin and Vienna; 1807 KG; 1812–21 Lord Chamberlain of the Household; 1822 Vice-Admiral of Suffolk. M. (1) in 1768, the Hon. Alice Elizabeth Windsor, (2) the Hon. Isabella Ingram Shepherd; succeeded by s. Francis Charles.

Henry Herbert, 1st Earl of CARNARVON; M of H 1806

B. 1741, d. 1811. S. of Major-General the Hon. William Herbert, fifth s. of the Earl of Pembroke. 1780 created Baron Porchester of High Clere, Southampton; 1768–80 MP (Tory) for Wilton; 1793 Earl of Carnarvon; 1794 Colonel in the Army; 1806 Privy Councillor. M. Elizabeth Alicia Maria, dau. of Charles Wyndham, 1st Earl of Egremont, succeeded by s. Henry George.

GEORGE IV

Charles Sackville Germain, 5th Duke of DORSET; M of H 1821, 1835 (Jan)

B. 1767, d. 1843. S. of George, 1st Viscount Sackville of Drayton and grandson of the 1st Duke of Dorset. Educated at Westminster. 1776–1815 Receiver-General of Jamaica; 1785 succeeded his father as Viscount Sackville and Baron Bolebrooke; 1815 inherited the dukedom; 1821 bearer of the Sword of State at George IV's coronation; 1821 Privy Councillor; 1826 KG. Unmarried. Died in Harley Street; all his honours became extinct.

George William Frederick Osborne, 6th Duke of LEEDS; M of H 1827

B. 1775, d. 1838. S. of Francis Godolphin Osborne, 5th Duke. Succeeded to the title in 1799 and on the death of his mother in 1784 inherited the title of 10th Baron Conyers. 1827 KG and Privy Councillor; Lord-Lieutenant of the East Riding of Yorkshire and Governor of the Scilly Isles. M. in 1797, Charlotte, dau. of the Marquis Townshend; succeeded by his s. Francis Godolphin d'Arcy Osborne.

WILLIAM IV/VICTORIA

William Charles Keppel, 4th Earl of ALBEMARLE; M of H 1830, 1835 (April)

B. 1772, d. 1849. S. of George, 3rd Earl. Succeeded to the title in the year of his birth; 1806–7 Master of the Buckhounds; 1830 Privy Councillor; 1833 GCH (Civil); 1837 rode in carriage with Queen Victoria at her coronation. M. (1) in 1792, the Hon. Elizabeth Southwell, dau. of 17th Baron Clifford, who died in labour with her fifteenth child, (2) Charlotte Susannah, dau. of Sir Henry Hunloke; succeeded by his second s. Augustus Frederick.

VICTORIA

George Child-Villiers, 5th Earl of JERSEY; M of H 1841, 1852

B. 1773. d. 1859. S. of George Bussy Villiers, 4th Earl, whom he succeeded in 1805. Educated at Harrow and St John's College, Cambridge. Assumed the name of Child by Royal Licence in 1819, having married in 1804 the heiress of the banker Robert Child. Twice Lord Chamberlain to William IV. Succeeded by his s. George Augustus Frederick.

Henry Charles Howard, 13th Duke of NORFOLK; M of H 1846

B. 1791, d. 1856. S. of Bernard Edward, 12th Duke and Elizabeth Bellayse, dau. of Earl of Fauconberg. 1829–41 MP for Horsham; 1837–41 Treasurer of the Household; Privy Councillor; 1841 Captain of the Yeomen of the Guard; 1848 KG; 1853–4 Lord Steward of the Household; hereditary Earl Marshal; President of the Royal Botanic Society. M. Lady Charlotte Leveson-Gower, eldest dau. of George Granville, 1st Duke of Sutherland.

Arthur Richard Wellesley, 2nd Duke of WELLINGTON; M of H 1853

B. 1807, d. 1884. S. of the 1st Duke and Catherine Sarah Dorothea Pakenham. 1829-30 and 1831 MP for Aldborough; 1837-52 MP for Norwich; Lieutenant-General in the Army and Lord-Lieutenant of Middlesex. Succeeded his father in 1852 and took the title of 6th Earl of Mornington in 1863. Unmarried. Succeeded by his nephew Henry.

Henry Charles Fitzroy Somerset, 8th Duke of BEAUFORT; M of H 1858 and 1866

B. 1824, d. 1899. S. of Henry, 7th Duke, and his second wife Emily Francis, dau. of Culling Charles Smith. 1853 succeeded his father; 1842–56 MP for East Gloucestershire; KG, Privy Councillor and Lord-Lieutenant of Monmouthshire. M. in 1845, Lady Georgina Charlotte Curzon, eldest dau. of Earl Howe; succeeded by his eldest s. Henry Adelbert Wellington Fitzroy.

George Frederick William Brudenell-Bruce, 2nd MARQUESS of AILESBURY; M of H 1859, 1868

B. 1804, d. 1878. S. of Charles, 1st Marquess. 1839 summoned to the House of Lords in his father's barony of Bruce; 1868 succeeded to the title of Earl of Cardigan; Lord-Lieutenant of Wiltshire. M. in 1837, Lady Mary Caroline Herbert, dau. of the 11th Earl of Pembroke; succeeded by his brother Ernest Augustus Charles.

Orlando George Charles Bridgeman, 3rd Earl of BRADFORD; M of H 1874, 1885

B. 1819, d. 1898. S. of George Augustus Frederick Henry, 2nd Earl, and Georgina Elizabeth, dau. of Sir Thomas Moncrieffe. Lord-Lieutenant of Shropshire; 1842–65 MP for South Shropshire; 1852 and 1858–9 Vice-Chamberlain of Queen Victoria's Household; 1868 Lord Chamberlain; Privy Councillor. M. the Hon. Selina Louisa Forester, dau. of the 1st Baron Forester; succeeded by his s. George Cecil Orlando.

Hugh Lupus Grosvenor, 1st Duke of WESTMINSTER; M of H 1880

B. 1825, d. 1899. s. of the 2nd Marquis of Westminster, whom he succeeded in 1869, and Mary, dau. of the 1st Duke of Sutherland. Educated at Eton and Balliol, 1847–69 MP (Liberal) for Chester; 1860 Lieutenant-Colonel Queen's Westminster Rifle Volunteers; 1869 Lieutenant-Colonel Cheshire Yeomanry; became Hon. Colonel of both regiments; 1870 KG; 1874 Duke of Westminster; 1881 ADC to Queen Victoria; 1883 Lord-Lieutenant of Cheshire; 1884 High Steward of Westminster; 1888 Lord-Lieutenant of London; 1893 President of the Royal Agricultural Society. M. (1) Lady Constance Gertrude Leveson-Gower, dau. of the 2nd Duke of Sutherland, (2) the Hon. Katharine Caroline Cavendish CBE, dau. of Baron Chesham; succeeded by his grandson Hugh Richard Arthur Grosvenor.

Richard Edmund St. Lawrence Boyle, 9th Earl of CORK and ORRERY; M of H 1886, 1894

B. 1829, d. 1904. S. of Charles, Viscount Dungavon and Lady Katherine St. Lawrence; succeeded his grandfather in 1856. 1864 Lord-Lieutenant of Somerset; 1866, 1868, 1880–85 Master of the Buckhounds; Privy Councillor. M. in 1853, Lady Emily Charlotte de Burgh, dau. of the 1st Marquis of Clanricarde; succeeded by s. Charles Spencer Canning.

William John, 7th Baron Monson, Viscount OXENBRIDGE; M of H 1892

B. 1829, d. 1898. Created Viscount Oxenbridge in 1886. Privy Councillor; ADC to Queen Victoria; 1858–62 MP for Reigate; 1874 Treasurer of the Royal Household; 1880–8 Captain of the Yeomen of the Guard. M. in 1869, the Hon. Maria Adelaide Maude, dau. of Viscount Hawarden and widow of the 2nd Earl of Yarborough; died without issue and the viscounty became extinct.

VICTORIA/EDWARD VII

William John Arthur Charles James Cavendish-Bentinck, 6th Duke of PORTLAND; M of H 1886, 1895, 1901

B. 1857, d. 1943. S. of Lieutenant-General Arthur Cavendish-Bentinck; succeeded to the title of Portland through a kinsman. Honorary Colonel of the 4th and 5th Battalions of the Sherwood Foresters; Lord-Lieutenant of Notts; 1937–43 Chancellor of the Order of the Garter; 1933 Royal Victoria Chain. M. in 1889 Winifred Dallas-York DBE, dau. of Thomas York Dallas-York; succeeded by s. William Arthur Henry.

EDWARD VII

Osbert Cecil Molyneux, 6th Earl of SEFTON; M of H 1905

B. 1871, d. 1930. Second son of 4th Earl and Cecile Emily, dau. of the 1st Baron Hylton; succeeded his brother 1901. Lieutenant, 2nd Life Guards. M. 1898 Lady Helena May Bridgeman, dau. of 4th Earl of Bradford; one son.

EDWARD VII/GEORGE V

Bernard Arthur William Patrick Hastings Forbes, 8th Earl of GRANARD; M of H 1907, 1924

B. 1874, d. 1948. S. of George Arthur Hastings Forbes and the Hon. Francis Mary, dau. of Baron Petre. Lieutenant-Colonel of the 8th Battalion City of London Regiment; Lieutenant-Colonel in the Reserve of Officers (Scots Guards); Vice-Admiral of the Province of Connaught; Deputy Speaker of the House of Lords; 1905 Lord-in-Waiting to King Edward VII; 1906-9 Assistant Postmaster General; 1921 member of the Senate of South Ireland; 1922–34 member of the Senate of the Irish Free State; 1936–45 His Majesty's Comptroller at Ascot. M. in 1909 Beatrice Mills OBE, dau. of Ogden Mills; succeeded by s. Arthur Patrick Hastings.

GEORGE V

Edwyn Francis Scudamore-Stanhope, 10th Earl of CHESTERFIELD; M of H 1915

B. 1854, d. 1933. S. of the 9th Earl and Dorothea, dau. of Sir Adain Hay, 7th Bart. Educated at Eton and Brasenose, Oxford; Captain of the 4th Battalion Shropshire Light Infantry; retired 1887, the year in which he succeeded his father; 1892–4 Treasurer of the Queen's Household; 1894–5 Captain of the Corps of Gentlemen-at-Arms; 1910–15 Lord Steward of King Edward VII's Household; Grand Cross of the Order of Dannebrog and Order of the Red Eagle 1st

Class. M. Enid, 2nd dau. of Baron Nunburnholme; succeeded by his brother Henry.

Thomas Henry Thynne, 5th Marquess of BATH; M of H 1922

B. 1862, d. 1946. S. of John Alexander, 4th Marquess, and the Hon. Frances Isabella Catherine Vesey, dau. of the Viscount de Vesci. Lord-Lieutenant of Somerset; 1905 Under-Secretary of State for India; 1906–46 Chairman of Wiltshire County Council; 1895–6 MP for Frome Division of Somerset; Privy Councillor, KG, CB, TD. M. in 1890, Violet Caroline, dau. of Sir Charles Mordaunt; succeeded by s. Henry Frederick Thynne.

EDWARD VIII/GEORGE VI/ELIZABETH II

Henry Hugh Arthur Fitzroy Somerset, 10th Duke of BEAUFORT; M of H 1936

B. 1900. Only s. of 9th Duke, and Louise Emily, dau. of William H. Harford. 2nd title Marq. of Worcs. Educated Eton and Sandhurst; Capt. late RHG; Hon. Col. Royal Gloucs Hussars; 1925 High Steward of Bristol and of Gloucs, and of Tewkesbury from 1948; 1927 JP; 1928 D.L.; from 1931 Lord Lieut of Gloucs; 1945 Freeman City of Gloucs; Master of Beaufort Hunt; 1952–53 Pres. MCC; 1965 Chancellor of Bristol University; 1967–68 Pres. Hunters Improvement and National Light Horse Breeding Soc.; formerly Pres. British Olympic Assoc; Vice-Patron British Show Jumping Assoc; 1936 PC; 1937 KG; K St J; 1953 RVC; G.C. Order of Leopold (Belgium); GCO Leg. Hon. (France); GCO of Faithful Service (Roumania); GCO of Orange Nassau and GCO of House of Orange (Netherlands); GCO of St Olav (Norway); GCO of North Star (Sweden); GCO of Menelik II (Ethiopia); GCO of Christ (Portugal). M., in 1923, the Lady Mary Cambridge, elder dau. of the 1st Marq. of Cambridge. Heir: David Robert Somerset.

Summary

EDWARD III
c. 1360–1365 Sir John (de) Brocas
c. 1371–1377 Sir Bernard (de) Brocas
RICHARD II
c. 1377–1388 Sir Thomas de Murrieux
1388–1391 Sir Thomas de Clifford
1391–1398 Sir John Russell
1398–1399 Richard Redman
HENRY IV/V
1399–1414 Robert (de) Waterton
1414 John (de) Waterton
1421 Sir Henry Noon
HENRY VI
c. 1429 Richard (de) Beauchamp, Earl of Warwick
c. 1429–1430 Sir Walter Beauchamp
1430–1442 Sir John Styward
From 1442 John, Lord Beauchamp of Powyck
EDWARD IV
1465–1479 Sir Thomas de Burgh
1479–1483 Sir John Cheyne
RICHARD III
1483 Sir Thomas Tyrrell
c. 1483–1485 Sir James Tyrrell
HENRY VII
c. 1485–1510 Sir Thomas Brandon
HENRY VII
1510–1512 Sir Thomas Knyvet
1512–1515 Charles Brandon, Duke of Suffolk
1515–1522 Sir Henry Guildford
1522–1539 Sir Nicholas Carew
HENRY VIII/EDWARD VI
1539–1549 Sir Anthony Browne
1549–1552 William Herbert, Earl of Pembroke
1552–1553 John Dudley, Earl of Warwick
MARY I
1553–1557 Sir Edward Hastings, Lord Hastings
1557–1558 Sir Henry Jerningham
ELIZABETH I
1558–1588 Robert Dudley, Earl of Leicester
1588–1601 Robert Devereux, Earl of Essex
ELIZABETH I/JAMES I
1601–1616 Edward Somerset, Earl of Worcester
JAMES I/CHARLES I
1616–1628 George Villiers, Duke of Buckingham
1628–1649 James Hamilton, Duke of Hamilton
OLIVER CROMWELL

1653–1660 John Claypole
CHARLES II
1653 Prince Rupert of the Rhine
1660–1668 George Monck, Duke of Albemarle
1668–1674 George Villiers, Duke of Buckingham
1674–1681 James Scott, Duke of Monmouth
1681–1685 Charles Lennox, Duke of Richmond and Lennox
JAMES III
1685–1689 George Legge, Baron Dartmouth
WILLIAM III
1689–1702 Henry de Nassau, Count of Auverquerque
QUEEN ANNE/GEORGE I
1703–1712 ⎱ Charles Seymour, Duke of Somerset
1714–1715 ⎰
GEORGE II
1727–1734 Richard Lumley, Earl of Scarborough
1734–1751 Charles Lennox, Duke of Richmond and Lennox
1751–1755 William Cavendish, Duke of Devonshire
1755–1757 Lionel Cranfield, Duke of Dorset
1757–1760 Granville Leveson-Gower, Marquess of Stafford
GEORGE III
1760–1761 Francis Hastings, Earl of Huntingdon
1761–1766 John Manners, Duke of Rutland
1766 Francis Seymour-Conway, Marquess of Hertford
1766–1778 Peregrine Willoughby Bertie, Duke of Ancaster and Kestevan
1778–1780 Hugh Percy, Duke of Northumberland
1780–1790 George Montagu, Duke of Montagu
1790–1795 James Graham, Duke of Montrose
1795–1798 John Fane, Earl of Westmorland
1798–1804 Philip Stanhope, Earl of Chesterfield
1804–1806 Francis Seymour, Marquess of Hertford
1806–1807 Henry Herbert, Earl of Carnarvon
1807–1820 James Graham, Duke of Montrose
GEORGE IV
1821–1827 Charles Sackville Germain, Duke of Dorset

1827–1830 George Osborne, Duke of Leeds
WILLIAM IV
1830–1835 William Keppel, Earl of Albemarle
1835 Charles Sackville Germain, Duke of Dorset
WILLIAM IV/VICTORIA
1835–1841 William Keppel, Earl of Albemarle
1841–1846 George Child-Villiers, Earl of Jersey
1846–1852 Henry Howard, Duke of Norfolk
1852–1853 George Child-Villiers, Earl of Jersey
1853–1858 Arthur Wellesley, Duke of Wellington
1858–1859 Henry Fitzroy Somerset, Duke of Beaufort
1859–1866 George Brudenell-Bruce, Marquess of Ailesbury
1866–1868 Henry Fitzroy, Duke of Beaufort
1868–1874 George Brudenell-Bruce, Marquess of Ailesbury
1874–1880 Orlando Bridgeman, Earl of Bradford
1880–1885 Hugh Lupus Grosvenor, Duke of Westminster
1885–1886 Orlando Bridgeman, Earl of Bradford
1886 Richard Boyle, Earl of Cork and Orrery
1886–1892 William Cavendish-Bentinck, Duke of Portland
1892–1894 William Monson, Viscount Oxenbridge
1894–1895 Richard Boyle, Earl of Cork and Orrery
QUEEN VICTORIA/EDWARD VII
1895–1905 William Cavendish-Bentinck, Duke of Portland
1905–1907 Osbert Molyneux, Earl of Sefton
EDWARD VII/GEORGE V
1907–1915 Bernard Forbes, Earl of Granard
1915–1922 Edwyn Scudamore-Stanhope, Earl of Chesterfield
1922–1924 Thomas Thynne, Marquess of Bath
1924–1936 Bernard Forbes, Earl of Granard
EDWARD VIII/GEORGE VI/QUEEN ELIZABETH II
1936– Henry Fitzroy Somerset, Duke of Beaufort

Sources of Illustrations

Material from the British Library is reproduced by permission of the British Library Board; and from the British Museum by permission of the Trustees of the British Museum. The publishers also wish to record their thanks to the other museums, libraries, institutions, and private owners who have given their permission to reproduce illustrations.

1. (Half-title) By permission of the Duke of Beaufort. Photo: Peter Harding.
2. (Frontispiece) By gracious permission of Her Majesty the Queen. Photo: Rex Coleman (Baron).
3. By gracious permission of Her Majesty the Queen. Photo: Leslie Lane.
4. The National Museum of Antiquities of Scotland.
5. British Museum Dept. of Coins and Medals.
6. British Museum Dept. of Prehistoric and Romano-British Antiquities.
7, 8. British Library MS Harl. 603 f25.
9. British Library MS Cott. Claud. BIV f91v.
10. British Library MS Harl. 603 f22v.
11. Tenture de la Reine Mathilde. By permission of the Ville de Bayeux. Photo: Giraudon.
12, 13. British Library MS Harl. 603 ff23, 7v.
14, 15. British Museum Dept. of Mediaeval and Later Antiquities.
16. © Threshold Books Limited.
17. Aerofilms Limited.
18. Armouries Library, Tower of London. By permission of the Controller of Her Majesty's Stationery Office, Crown copyright.
19. © Threshold Books Limited.
20. British Library MS Roy. 15 EIV f287.
21. British Library MS Add. 12228 f78v.
22. British Library MS Roy. 10 EIV f254.
23. British Library MS Egerton 3028 f62.
24. © Threshold Books Limited.
25. British Library MS Cott. Claud DVI f12.
26. © Threshold Books Limited.
27, 28. British Library MS Roy. 10 EIV ff302, 237.
29. Patent Roll C66/75 Mem. 1. Public Record Office.
30, 31. British Library MS Roy. 10 EIV ff26v, 168.
32. British Library MS Add. 12228 f141v.
33. Cast in the Musée des Monuments Français, Paris, from an effigy in the Church of St. Denis. Photo: Giraudon.
34, 35. British Library MS Sloane 3983 ff5, 12.
36. British Library MS Add. 12228 f141v.
37. British Library MS Add. 42130 ff181v, 182.
38. British Library MS Egerton 3028 f8.
39. Aerofilms Limited.
40. Southern England Air Photos.
41. Monumental Effigies, C. A. Stothard, Plate 143.
42. British Library MS Harl. Charters 47 C 16.
43, 44, 45. British Library MS Harl. 4380 ff177, 117, 197b.
46. C. H. Wood (Bradford) Limited.
47. British Library MS Cott. Charters XII 45.
48. From the Parish Church of St. Philip and St. James, Strensham.
49. Photo: Fred H. Crossley, by courtesy of Canon Maurice H. Ridgeway FSA.
50. British Library Harl. Charter 112 C 30.
51. Photo: Fred H. Crossley, by courtesy of Canon Maurice Ridgeway.
52. Photo: Courtauld Institute. © Professor Lawrence Stone.
53. National Monuments Record. © Wakefield Express Service.
54. British Library MS Roy. 10 EIV f313b.
55. British Library MS Add. 12228 f150.
56. © Threshold Books.
57, 58, 59. Horda Angel-Cynan, J. Strutt. Photos: By courtesy of the Society of Antiquaries of London.
60. Bodleian E6.1. Art. Plate opp 111. By courtesy of the Bodleian Library, Oxford.
61. By permission of the College of Arms.
62. Monumental Effigies, C. A. Stothard.
63. British Library MS Harl. 4379 f99.
64. Lambeth Palace Library MS 6 f243. Reproduced by permission of the Archbishop of Canterbury and the Trustees of Lambeth Palace.
65, 66. College of Arms MS M.1. By permission of the College.
67. Mansell Collection.
68, 69. British Library MS Harl. 4431 ff153, 81.
70. By courtesy of the College of Arms.
71. British Library MS Cott. Vesp. FIII f8.
72. Vetusta Monumenta, C. A. Stothard. By courtesy of the Society of Antiquaries of London.
73. Threshold Books Limited.
74. Aerofilms Limited.
75. By courtesy of the College of Arms.
76. Eton MS 213 f10v. By permission of the Provost and Fellows of Eton. Photo: Courtauld Institute.
77. British Library MS Roy. 16 FIII f11.
78. Patent Rolls C66/471. By permission of the Public Record Office.
79. Glendower Studios, Gainsborough.
80. Monumental Effigies, C. A. Stothard.
81. British Library MS Roy. 14 EVI f125.
82. Royal Collection, Hampton Court. By gracious permission of Her Majesty the Queen.

83, 84, 85. By courtesy of the College of Arms. 83, 84 Photos: John Freeman.

86. By permission of the National Monuments Record. Photo: Crown copyright.

87. Tower of London. By permission of the Controller of Her Majesty's Stationery Office. Crown copyright.

88. St George's Chapel, Windsor. By permission of the Dean and Canons.

89. Tower of London. By permission of the Comptroller of Her Majesty's Stationery Office. Crown copyright.

90, 91. By courtesy of the College of Arms. Photos: John Freeman.

92. Musée Condé, Chantilly. Photo: Giraudon.

93. British Library MS Cott. Aug. 1 ii f76.

94. Musée Condé, Chantilly. Photo: Giraudon.

95. Royal Collection, Hampton Court. By gracious permission of Her Majesty the Queen.

96. Photo: John Freeman.

97. By permission of the Duke of Buccleuch. Photo: Royal Academy.

98. Country Life.

99. By permission of Hugh Paget Esq. Photo: A. C. Cooper.

100. © Threshold Books Limited.

101, 102, 103. From *Cowdray and Easebourne Priory*, W. St. John Hope. By courtesy of the Society of Antiquaries of London.

104. In Glasgow City Art Gallery. By permission of the Controller of Her Majesty's Stationery Office. Crown copyright.

105. By permission of the Earl of Pembroke. Photo: Sydney Newbery.

106. By permission of Leggatt Brothers. Photo: National Portrait Gallery, London.

107, 108. By permission of the Earl of Pembroke. Photos: H. H. Wills.

109. From the Brown Portfolio at the Society of Antiquaries of London.

110. From Leyton Parish Church.

111. British Library MS Harl. Charters 83 H 14 9232A.

112. 19th Century print. By permission of Warwickshire County Council. Photo: John Wright.

113. Bodleian E.6.1. Art Plate opp 249. By courtesy of the Bodleian Library, Oxford.

114. Mansell Collection.

115. British Museum Dept. of Prints and Drawings.

116. By courtesy of the College of Arms.

117. From the collection of the Duke of Beaufort. Photo: Peter Harding.

118. Fotomas Index.

119. British Library MS Harl. 1579 f151.

120. *Vetusta Monumenta*, C. A. Stothard. By permission of the Society of Antiquaries of London.

121. *History and Antiquities of Rutlandshire*, James Wright. By courtesy of the Bodleian Library, Oxford.

122. Fotomas Index.

123. British Museum Dept. of Prints and Drawings.

124. From *An Almain Armourer's Album*. Victoria and Albert Museum. Photo: Crown copyright.

125. British Library MS Add. 35324 f37.

126. From a Private Collection. Photo: Aberdeen Photographic Service.

127. From the collection of the Duke of Beaufort. Photo: Peter Harding.

128. Owner unknown. Photo: National Portrait Gallery, London.

129. By permission of the Duke of Hamilton. Photo: Scottish National Portrait Gallery.

130. Fotomas Index.

131. British Library MS Add. Charters 14975.

132. From a contemporary medallion.

133. From a document in the custody of the House of Lords Records Office. By permission of the Clerk of the Records.

134. By courtesy of J. G. Moore.

135. By courtesy of Oliver Warner Esquire.

136. Mansell Collection.

137. By permission of the Earl of Pembroke. Photo: H. H. Wills.

138. Fotomas Index.

139. Royal Collection, Hampton Court. By gracious permission of Her Majesty the Queen.

140. By permission of the National Portrait Gallery, London.

141. By permission of the Duke of Buccleuch. Photo: Tom Scott.

142. National Portrait Gallery, London.

143. From the collection of the Duke of Portland KG. Photo: John Freeman.

144. At Berkeley Castle. By permission of the Trustees of the late Lord Berkeley.

145. By permission of the Duke of St Albans. Photo: The National Army Museum.

146. Royal Collection, Kensington Palace. By gracious permission of Her Majesty the Queen.

147. Royal Collection, Hampton Court. By gracious permission of Her Majesty the Queen.

148. From Goodwood House, by courtesy of the Trustees.

149, 150. The National Portrait Gallery, London.

151. Mansell Collection.

152. By permission of the Historisches Museum am Hohen Ufer, Hannover.

153. At Clarence House. By gracious permission of Her Majesty Queen Elizabeth the Queen Mother.

154. Owner unknown. Photo: The National Portrait Gallery, London.

155. The National Portrait Gallery, London.

156. Fotomas Index.

157. Royal Library, Windsor. By gracious permission of Her Majesty the Queen.

158, 159. By permission of the Marylebone Cricket Club.

160. From Goodwood House, by courtesy of the Trustees.

161. At Hardwick Hall, a property of the National Trust. Photo: Courtauld Institute.

162. By permission of Lord Sackville. Photo: Courtauld Institute.

163. By permission of the Countess of Sutherland. Photo: David Sim.

164. By gracious permission of Her Majesty the Queen.

165. By permission of the Lady Aldington.

166. The Royal Library, Windsor. By gracious permission of Her Majesty the Queen.

167. Fotomas Index.

168. British Museum Dept. of Prints and Drawings.

169. The Royal Library, Windsor. By gracious permission of Her Majesty the Queen.

170. By permission of the Dowager Viscountess of Galway. Photo: Courtauld Institute.

171. By permission of the Marquess of Hertford. Photo: © English Life Publications.

172. From a Private Collection. Photo: Royal Academy.

173. © Threshold Books Limited.

174. By permission of the Middlesex Hospital. Photo: National Portrait Gallery, London.

175. By permission of the Duke of Buccleuch. Photo: Tom Scott.

176. From the collection of the Earl of Jersey.

177. By permission of the Marquess of Hertford. Photo: © English Life Publications.

178. Armouries Library, Tower of London. Photo: By permission of the Controller of Her Majesty's Stationery Office. Crown copyright.

179. By permission of the National Galleries of Scotland. Photo: Tom Scott.

180. By permission of the Earl of Carnarvon. Photo: National Portrait Gallery, London.

181. The Royal Library, Windsor. By gracious permission of Her Majesty the Queen.

182. From a Private Collection. Photo: Courtauld Institute.

183. By courtesy of the India Office Library and Records.

184. The Royal Library, Windsor. By gracious permission of Her Majesty the Queen.

185. Photo: John Freeman.

186. Radio Times Hulton Picture Library.

187. By permission of Brighton Borough Council.

188, 189, 190. Photos: John Freeman.

191, 192. Pictorial and Feature Services.

193. Mansell Collection.

194. National Portrait Gallery (Archives), London.

195. By courtesy of Lionel Stopford Sackville Esquire. Photo: A. C. Cooper.

196. The Royal Collection, Buckingham Palace. By gracious permission of Her Majesty the Queen. Photo: A. C. Cooper.

197. From the collection of the Duke of Beaufort. Photo: Peter Harding.

198. Royal Collection, Buckingham Palace. By gracious permission of Her Majesty the Queen.

199, 200. The Illustrated London News.

201. The National Portrait Gallery (Archives), London.

202. By permission of the Duke of Norfolk.

203. From the collection of the Earl of Jersey. Photo: Johnson & Johnson.

204. From the collection of the Duke of Wellington, Stratfield Saye House, Reading. Photo: Courtauld Institute.

205. The Royal Library, Windsor. By gracious permission of Her Majesty the Queen.

206. © Threshold Books Limited.

207. From a Private Collection. Photo: Photo Studios Ltd.

208. By permission of the Earl of Bradford. Photo: Courtauld Institute.

209. The Illustrated London News.

210, 211. The Royal Library, Windsor. By gracious permission of Her Majesty the Queen.

212. By gracious permission of Her Majesty the Queen.

213. By courtesy of Mrs W. G. Johnson.

214, 215, 216. The Illustrated London News.

217, 218. The Royal Library, Windsor. By gracious permission of Her Majesty the Queen. Photos: Elizabeth Johnston.

219. The Radio Times Hulton Picture Library.

220. The Illustrated London News.

221. Threshold Books Limited.

222. Photo: Sport and General.

223. Photo: Mrs Albert Broom. © E. G. Collings.

224. The Illustrated London News.

225. © Threshold Books Limited.

226. Photo: Mrs Albert Broom. © E. G. Collings.

227. © Threshold Books Limited.

228, 229, 230, 231. Photos: Mrs Albert Broom. © E. G. Collings.

232. The Radio Times Hulton Picture Library.

233. Photo: Mrs Albert Broom. © E. G. Collings.

234. The Illustrated London News.

235, 236. Photos: Mrs Albert Broom. © E. G. Collings.

237, 238. The Radio Times Hulton Picture Library.

239. Photo: Mrs Albert Broom. © E. G. Collings.

240, 241, 242. The Royal Library, Windsor. By gracious permission of Her Majesty the Queen. Photos: Elizabeth Johnston.

243. The Field.

244. Sport and General.

245, 246, 247. Photos: Mrs Albert Broom. © E. G. Collings.

248. By permission of the Duke of Beaufort.

249. The Royal Library, Windsor. By gracious permission of Her Majesty the Queen.

250. Sport and General.

251. From the collection of the Duke of Beaufort. Photo: Peter Harding.

252, 255, 258. By gracious permission of Her Majesty the Queen. Photos: Leslie Lane.

253. The Radio Times Hulton Picture Library.

254. © Threshold Books Limited.

256. Central Press.

257. Pictorial and Feature Services.

259. Richard Slade, Camera Press.

Illustrations on jacket: (*front*) by gracious permission of Her Majesty the Queen; (*back*) by permission of the College of Arms. Photo: John Freeman.

Index

Note: Index does not include Notes on the Masters.

Figures in italics refer to page numbers of captions to illustrations.